ASPEN

PUBLISHERS

IS Project Management Handbook

by George M. Doss and Michael Wallace

The *IS Project Management Handbook* is an invaluable resource that guides an information system (IS) manager through the project management process of designing, developing, and implementing any IS goal. This process includes scheduling and management techniques along with the essential tools for handling these techniques, such as Gantt chart schedules and reports. Written in a practical "how-to" style and organized for fast access to specific information, this book not only explains the project management process, but also takes you step by step through the implementation of IS goals. This "hands-on" approach is further executed by an enclosed CD-ROM containing templates for project management checklists and documents needed in the management process. In addition, the CD-ROM includes a series of presentations in Microsoft PowerPoint that give overviews of the chapters.

Highlights of the 2003 Edition

The 2003 Edition brings you up to date on the latest developments, including:

- New and updated real-world examples of positive and negative experiences in project management;
- Revised and improved project-tracking documents;
- All topics updated with the latest project management "best practices";
- Updated PowerPoint presentations for each chapter to help the project manager communicate critical points to upper management;
- Important concepts explained in an easy-to-follow format for the non-technical project manager.

4/03

For questions concerning this shipment, billing, or other customer service matters, call our Customer Service Department at 1-800-234-1660.

For toll-free ordering, please call 1-800-638-8437.

IS Project Management Handbook
2003 Edition

George M. Doss

2003 Edition prepared by
Michael Wallace

PUBLISHERS

1185 Avenue of the Americas, New York, NY 10036
www.aspenpublishers.com

This publication is designed to provide accurate and authoritative information in regard to the subject matter covered. It is sold with the understanding that the publisher is not engaged in rendering legal, accounting, or other professional services. If legal advice or other professional assistance is required, the services of a competent professional person should be sought.

—From a *Declaration of Principles* jointly adopted by
a Committee of the American Bar Association and
a Committee of Publishers and Associations

© 2003 Aspen Publishers, Inc.
A Wolters Kluwer Company
www.aspenpublishers.com

Permissions
Aspen Publishers
1185 Avenue of the Americas
New York, NY 10036

Printed in the United States of America

ISBN 0-7355-3565-5

0 1 2 3 4 5 6 7 8 9

About the Authors

Michael Wallace has more than 20 years of experience in the information systems field. After graduation from Lima Technical College, he began his career as a mainframe operator for Super Food Services, then moved to a programming position at Reynolds & Reynolds.

He became a consultant after graduating Magna Cum Laude from Wright State University (Dayton, Ohio) with a Bachelor of Science degree in Management Science. For eight years he was president of Q Consulting, a custom application development firm. Mr. Wallace has been an application developer, systems analyst, and technical and business consultant, and he recently assisted the State of Ohio in developing statewide IT policies.

Mr. Wallace is a Microsoft Certified Professional and a past vice president of the Columbus Computer Society, and he has served on the board of directors of various IT user organizations. He is presently a member of the Association of Internet Professionals and the Project Management Institute and recently graduated from the Executive MBA program at the Fisher College of Business at The Ohio State University.

After working as a practice manager and director for the last few years, Mr. Wallace is now the managing partner once again at Q Consulting, which now provides clients with guidance on IS strategy, disaster recovery planning, and policies and procedures. He has published several articles on business and technology topics and is the co-author of *IT Policies and Procedures: Tools and Techniques That Work,* published by Aspen Publishers.

Mr. Wallace can be reached by e-mail at *michaelw@consulting.biz*.

George Doss, a full-time writer in the area of networking and Internet technologies, has been involved with project management since 1964 with the introduction of the USAF base-level maintenance and supply computer system and with the introduction of the C5A airplane into the USAF inventory. Mr. Doss completed two other related books in this area: *CORBA Networking with Java* and *DCOM Networking with Visual J++*. Mr. Doss's diverse background in project management includes international experience for helicopter maintenance training. He has advised on systems methodology, project management, information systems planning, and an intranet training registration project. Mr. Doss has been the project manager and senior project manager for the development of global customer documentation suites. For a number of years he was involved in the enhancement of a large international corporation's project management system.

Summary of Contents

Contents

A complete table of contents for each chapter is included at the beginning of the chapter.

Section Two
Project Management Tools and Techniques

Section Three
Support Project Management Analysis

Introduction

The *IS Project Management Handbook* is a practical "hands-on" resource book that guides an information systems (IS) manager through the project management process of designing, developing, and implementing any IS goal. This process includes scheduling and management techniques along with the essential tools, such as Gantt chart schedules and reports, for handling these techniques.

This book covers the basic steps in IS project management: scope planning and defining, activity defining and sequencing, resource planning, time estimating, schedule developing, cost estimating, and budget developing. Quality control is considered throughout the process. Fundamental IS project management techniques and tools are covered: project modeling, Gantt charts and schedules, PERT/CPM techniques, risk analysis, and learning curve analysis. There are descriptions of the pros and cons of software packages that can be used at various points of the process.

The book further assists you by suggesting ways for you to:

- revitalize and optimize a legacy system;
- enhance profitability analysis;
- create a corporate team that supports IS needs and goals;
- develop opportunities;
- foster network scalability and interoperability; and
- improve service through customer involvement.

Written in a practical "how-to" style and organized for fast access to specific information, this book not only explains the project management process but also takes you step by step through the implementation of any IS goal. This "hands-on" approach is further enabled by an enclosed CD-ROM that contains templates for some basic project management checklists and documents, such as the Business Justification Plan and the Quality Control Plan, needed in the managing of the process. Many of these checklists and documents are also included in the appropriate chapters. In addition, the CD-

ROM contains a series of presentations in Microsoft PowerPoint that give overviews of the chapters.

AUDIENCE

This book is directed at IS managers who need knowledge about the IS project management process and how to apply it within their organizations to obtain competitive advantage in the marketplace. Information system CIOs, directors, and managers who are engaged in designing, developing, or upgrading an information system environment will find this book to be an invaluable "hands-on" aid in cost-justifying and implementing an IS solution in a defined, repeatable, and measurable fashion.

There is a dynamic technological environment for enhancing any information system. There is a need for a set of project management standards, tools, and techniques to help IS managers complete very small to very large projects. These projects go from the addition of hardware to the addition of a new application to a major redesign of a network from a client/server paradigm to an object-oriented paradigm.

Most of the new IS technologies require a team effort rather than an individual effort. In addition, the introduction of Internet technologies usually requires customer involvement and vendor assistance. Many IS administrators are becoming aware of a need for new management skills. The system administrator or IS technical manager usually does not have the time or the desire to read a number of books on generalized project management. This book addresses the critical need for a practical guide on how to plan, design, develop, implement, and control any IS project.

Learning how to use support tools and techniques is critical to the knowledge of the project management process. This handbook discusses not only specialized project management tools but also some commonly available tools such as Microsoft Excel and PowerPoint.

Finally, the bottom-line issue of the audience is money. These chapters show how a project can be managed to fit within a given budget. In addition, the importance of cost estimates for a reliable budget is discussed.

This book holds that the basis of good IS project management depends on how one answers the initial question, "Is this project viable?"

OUTLINE

The *IS Project Management Handbook* is a practical resource for the IS manager whose company is currently considering a project that changes any information system beyond a day-to-day operational procedure. This handbook will assist IS managers in addressing the concerns and challenges of project management by clearly describing the overall functions and interactions of each process component and supporting tools and techniques.

This complete "hands-on" guide assists IS managers in their knowledge of project management and how to incorporate this process into their company's operations. It takes the IS manager through a step-by-step process based on questions that one should ask and the consequences to various answers. It also shows how to use supporting tools and techniques to effectively implement the specifications of their IS projects.

The *IS Project Management Handbook* is organized into five sections: Section One introduces the key concepts behind the IS project management process; Section Two addresses a selected set of project management tools and techniques; Section Three discusses support management analysis; Section Four addresses people management for teams and customer involvement; and Section Five presents a set of scenarios for putting together the concepts, procedures, and techniques described in the rest of the book. The companion CD-ROM contains the required deliverable documentation templates (Microsoft Word) and sample presentations that can be used immediately by IS managers to "quick start" their own project management process.

CHAPTER SUMMARIES

Each of the 26 chapters discusses objectives for meeting the requirements of project management, as follows.

Section One: IS Project Management Process

Section One provides the basis for the "how-to" scenarios in Section Five by defining the important components of the IS project management process.

CHAPTER 1: WHAT IS IS PROJECT MANAGEMENT? In this chapter, you develop knowledge about project management basics and how to relate these basics to IS issues. There are overviews of the following topics, which are detailed in Chapters 2 through 10:

- scope planning and defining;
- activity planning and sequencing;
- resource planning;
- time estimating;
- schedule developing;
- cost estimating;
- budget developing;

- controlling quality; and
- managing risks and opportunities.

CHAPTER 2: SCOPE PLANNING AND DEFINING   In this chapter, you develop the skill to ask basic questions on planning a project scope and using selected tools and techniques that can enhance a project scope definition. Four examples of these questions are:

- What are the customer's measurable expectations, the deliverables?
- What are the expected milestones of those who funded the project?
- What are the primary activities that have to be done to meet the expected defined goals?
- What is the necessary time for quality validation?

CHAPTER 3: ACTIVITY PLANNING AND SEQUENCING   In this chapter, you develop the skills to ask basic questions on planning activities and to sequence them, and you learn how selected tools and techniques can enhance activity plan and sequence. (Activity scheduling is discussed in Chapter 6.) Four examples of the types of questions asked in this chapter are:

- What are the quality control points that ensure correct sequencing?
- What are the criteria for determining a correct activity sequence?
- What are the basic goals of the project?
- How can the scope plan be used in activity planning and sequencing?

CHAPTER 4: RESOURCE PLANNING   In this chapter, you develop the skill to ask basic questions about resources, learn to differentiate between headcount and skill-count, and become aware of selected tools and techniques that can enhance resource planning and definition. Four types of questions asked in this chapter are:

- Are the resources available?
- How are the resources to be acquired?
- When should the resources be acquired?
- From where should the resources be acquired?

CHAPTER 5: TIME ESTIMATING   In this chapter, you develop the skill to ask basic questions about time, learn to differentiate between time estimating and scheduling, and become aware of selected tools and techniques that can enhance time estimating. Types of questions asked and answered in this chapter include:

- Who determines the time estimates for the schedule?
- Who should have input into and be notified of the time estimates?
- Have time estimates been established for quality control?
- What is the duration of the project?

CHAPTER 6: SCHEDULE DEVELOPING In this chapter, you develop the skill to ask basic questions about scheduling, learn to differentiate between scheduling and time estimating, and become aware of selected tools and techniques that can enhance project schedules. Example questions in this chapter include:

- Have essential schedule approvers been identified?
- Are the projected milestones essential?
- How are budgetary procedures going to impact the schedule?
- Are there resources to meet the schedule?

CHAPTER 7: COST ESTIMATING In this chapter, you develop the skill to ask basic questions about cost estimating, learn to differentiate between a cost and a budget item, and become aware of selected tools and techniques that can enhance final cost estimations. This chapter discusses such questions as:

- Have cost estimates been done for quality control?
- How are cost estimates integrated into the budgetary process?
- Are the core cost estimates realistic?
- Who are the experts that assist in cost estimating?

CHAPTER 8: BUDGET DEVELOPING In this chapter, you develop the skill to ask basic questions about budgeting, learn to differentiate between budgeting and cost estimating, and become aware of selected tools and techniques that can improve project budgets. Four examples of the questions asked in this chapter are:

- What quality control costs go in the budget?
- Have internal and external costs been budgeted?
- How and to whom should the financial information be given?
- Have the results of risk management been considered for the budget?

CHAPTER 9: CONTROLLING QUALITY In this chapter, you develop the skill to ask basic questions about quality control, learn to establish quality control points, and become aware of selected tools and techniques that can enhance quality control. This chapter looks at such questions as:

- Who should handle quality control?
- What are the critical performance criteria for determining project success?
- Have quality control points been established for each major component and project milestone?
- How and to whom should the quality control information be given?

CHAPTER 10: MANAGING RISKS AND OPPORTUNITIES In this chapter, you develop the skill to ask basic questions about risk management, learn that risk and opportunity are different sides of the same coin, and become aware of selected tools and techniques that can enhance risk management activities. In this final chapter of the general project management process, some of the questions considered are the following:

- Who should handle risk management?
- What are the criteria for identifying a risk?
- What are the criteria for identifying an opportunity?
- What is an unacceptable risk level?
- When is an opportunity a risk?

Section Two: Project Management Tools and Techniques

This section describes selected tools and techniques for improved project management, and builds upon information discussed in Section One.

CHAPTER 11: PROJECT MODELING This chapter provides you with information on the concept of modeling and how it can be used to enhance IS project management, and it summarizes how to develop "what if" models using the following techniques:

- statistical;
- simulation; and
- extrapolation.

CHAPTER 12: GANTT CHARTS AND SCHEDULES In this chapter, you develop knowledge about the features and functions of Gantt charts. In addition, there is a discussion on how you can use Gantt charts to manage activities, time, resources, and costs. There is an example using Microsoft Excel to create a very basic Gantt chart.

CHAPTER 13: PERT/CPM TECHNIQUES In this chapter, you develop knowledge about the features and functions of PERT/CPM techniques. In addition, you are shown how you can use these techniques to manage IS project activities, time, resources, and costs.

CHAPTER 14: RISK ANALYSIS In this chapter, you first develop knowledge about the functions of risk analysis. Next, this chapter considers how you can use risk analysis to manage your project activities, time, resources, and costs and points out that risk analysis is a two-sided coin, with both risks and opportunities.

CHAPTER 15: LEARNING CURVE ANALYSIS In this chapter, you develop knowledge about the importance of learning curve analysis. In addition, examples are given on how you can use learning curve analysis to manage and control your IS project.

CHAPTER 16: DOCUMENTATION This chapter focuses on the criteria for project documents. Approximately twenty documents are discussed, including:

- market analysis report;
- business justification;
- commercial specification;
- organizational chart;
- project proposal;
- project specification;
- content agreement;
- schedule;
- design and development plan;
- initial budget requirements;
- initial funding requirements;
- quality plan;
- trial strategy;
- field introduction strategy;
- training strategy;
- communication plan;
- risk assessment; and
- third-party documents.

CHAPTER 17: MISCELLANEOUS SOFTWARE PACKAGES This chapter focuses on the use of Microsoft Excel, PowerPoint, and Word as tools for managing your IS project.

Section Three: Support Project Management Analysis

This section describes three important types of analysis: legacy software and hardware, profitability, and infrastructure. The information in these chapters builds on topics covered in Sections One and Two.

CHAPTER 18: LEGACY SOFTWARE AND HARDWARE In this chapter, you acquire knowledge of four types of legacy software and hardware: interconnections, service servers, access servers, and browsers. There are overviews for the following:

- Identifying key interconnectivity issues:
  - Bandwidth;
  - device configuration;
  - network configuration;
  - protocol implementation; and
  - traffic loads.
- Identifying the key issues for service servers:
  - chat;
  - directory;
  - e-mail;
  - news; and
  - search.
- Identifying the key issues for access servers:
  - firewalls;
  - gateways;
  - proxies; and
  - routers.
- Identifying the keys issues for browsers

CHAPTER 19: PROFITABILITY ANALYSIS In this chapter, you learn how profitability analysis might be applicable to managing your IS project. Examples show how to use profitability analysis at the project level.

CHAPTER 20: ANALYSIS FOR SCALABILITY, INTEROPERABILITY, AND PORTABILITY In this chapter, you identify three object-oriented goals (scalability, interoperability, and portability) for any new networking project and learn how these goals relate to other abstract components of your IS infrastructure.

Section Four: People Management

This section addresses two important people management concerns for any IS project: the IS team and the customer.

CHAPTER 21: TEAM MANAGEMENT In this chapter, an overview, you learn how to make a group into a team and how to use selected tools and techniques to enhance team management skills. In addition, you learn how to use return on investment (ROI) goals to enhance team management in selected situations:

- anti-computer sentiment;
- resistance to sharing data with others in the corporation;
- fear of change;
- preference for features or products not included in project proposal; and
- lack of trust.

CHAPTER 22: CUSTOMER INVOLVEMENT In this chapter, you learn how important it is to have customer involvement on a project management team and how to use selected tools and techniques to ensure their effective interaction.

Section Five: Putting It All Together

This section describes four scenarios using the information given in this text and walks you through the contents of the companion CD-ROM. The CD-ROM contains Microsoft Word templates for the documentation discussed in Chapter 16 and several PowerPoint presentation templates that can be used by a project manager.

CHAPTER 23: MANAGEMENT'S ROLE IN PROJECT MANAGEMENT The two major objectives of this chapter are:

1. Using the major ideas set forth in Section One, develop a manager's profile for project management for each of the three management levels.
2. Identify how the three managing levels should be involved in any project.

CHAPTER 24: PROJECT MANAGEMENT IN A MICROSOFT ENVIRONMENT In this chapter, you learn about project management for an environment that primarily uses Microsoft products. The two major objectives of this chapter are:

1. Learn issues that may be unique to a networking environment that uses Microsoft products because of default parameters.
2. Learn about installation and design issues that impact:
   - activities;
   - resources;
   - time; and
   - costs.

CHAPTER 25: PROJECT MANAGEMENT AND THE CLIENT/SERVER PARADIGM In this chapter, you learn how one may handle project management on a project using the client/server paradigm. The ideas in Sections One, Two, and Three are used to relate directly to the client/server paradigm.

CHAPTER 26: PROJECT MANAGEMENT AND THE CORBA PARADIGM In this chapter, you learn how to handle project management on a project using the object-oriented paradigm. The ideas in Sections One, Two, and Three are used to relate directly to the CORBA (object-oriented) paradigm.

Acknowledgments

First, I would like to thank my wife and best friend, Tami, for all of her support during my many projects. Second, thanks to Dr. George Jenkins, teacher, mentor, and friend for over 20 years, for getting me started as a writer. Third, a big thanks to Gina Spiezia, Managing Editor at Aspen Publishers, who was a pleasure to work with. Finally, thanks to Chuck Carlos and George Bleimes, my partners at Q Consulting, for their feedback and insights that greatly improved the final product.

Our heartfelt condolences to the family of George Doss, who sadly passed away before this edition was completed. Mr. Doss wrote in the Acknowledgments in the previous edition, "I am where I am today because I stand on the shoulder of giants." His contributions have added greatly to the field of IS project management and enable us to stand even higher as we attempt to live up to his legacy.

Michael Wallace
January 2003

Section One

IS Project Management Process

T his section lays the foundation for the "how-to" scenarios in Section Five by defining the key functions of the IS Project Management Process. The key functions discussed are:

- Scope Planning and Defining
- Activity Planning and Sequencing
- Resource Planning
- Time Estimating
- Schedule Developing
- Cost Estimating
- Budget Developing
- Controlling Quality
- Managing Risks and Opportunities

In addition, this section emphasizes the difference between being a project manager and just controlling a project. Controls should include project management techniques or actions taken from the analysis of the results obtained using project management software.

Project management has evolved into a profession with its own certification program. When a person successfully completes this program, one is qualified as a Project Management Professional (PMP). One needs to be proficient in nine areas:

1. Scope
2. Cost
3. Time
4. Human resources
5. Communications
6. Quality
7. Contract/procurement
8. Risk
9. Project integration

This book is just a broad view of these functions. These functions are known as the Project Management Body of Knowledge (PMBOK). This text narrows the discussion of these functions to those that pertain to an IS project manager. This means asking, "How many computers do I need for this IS project?" rather than asking, "How many tons of cement do I need for this construction project?" It also involves discussions about such things as scalability and network infrastructure (discussed in later sections).

Chapter 1

What Is IS Project Management?

§ 1.01   OVERVIEW

[A]   Objectives

At the end of this chapter, you will be able to:

- Name the seven basic elements of information system project management.

- Determine basic characteristics for the following: scope planning, scope defining, activity planning, activity sequencing, resource planning, time estimating, schedule developing, cost estimating, budget developing, quality controlling, and risks and opportunity managing.

- Distinguish the differences among three management levels: strategic, tactical, operational.

- Ask twenty questions related to the metaquestion, "Is this project viable?"

- Identify 100 sources for project management issues.

- List five advantages and two limitations of project management.

MANAGER'S TIP

A recent *ComputerWorld* article documented how most companies fail to learn from failed IS projects. Problems such as miscommunication, poorly defined goals, scope creep, and poor project management doom many projects. A study by Bruce Webster of PricewaterhouseCoopers of 120 lawsuits caused by failed IS projects showed that most disasters could have been avoided if best practices techniques in project management had been followed. A study by Effy Oz at the Pennsylvania State University in Great Valley of failed IS projects showed that the average abandoned project cost the firm an average of $4.2 million.

[B]   Seven Project Management Elements

What is information systems project management? Simply put, it is a documented parallel process—within a set schedule, within a defined budget, with available resources and skills—to achieve defined user expectations for a computing environment that has as its primary function the requirement to transmit data among human users.

Project management is a documented parallel process because you are not just managing one element, then the next; you are a juggler of people, events, money, tools, documentation, and training within the context of quality assurance and control, and risk management.

This definition will be expanded and clarified throughout the following chapters. For example, there are chapters on scheduling, budgeting, and resource managing. The phrase "human users" is used in this definition because it is possible to operate computing systems where human users are secondary to the system's function, such as high-level simulations in the petroleum industry or special effects in film production. Such projects tend to focus on software functionality rather than on human interaction with the information system; this is a case where the "medium is the message." This may not be a correct focus, but still is the one that is taken.

MANAGER'S TIP

While the ordering of these chapters does have a certain logic, they could have been reordered so, for example, Sections One and Two were reversed. One insightful person said of the proposed book that the author could claim that a manager should read the whole book before starting anything, including dinner. I do! This entire book should be read first, before becoming a reference book.

There are seven distinct elements to an IS project. Each of these elements is critical to the success of the project. These elements arc:

1. Managing levels
2. Project phases
3. Project activities
4. Tools
5. Analytical process
6. Environment
7. People

Element One: Managing Levels

One of the problems of project management is that many upper-level managers think they do not have to be involved in any project. However, this situation is far from reality; project management has three important managing levels:

- Strategic
- Tactical
- Operational

Each of these three managing levels is discussed in the first section of this book. There are specific types of actions that managers at each of these levels should do to ensure the successful fulfillment of the project goals. The following is an example of an action by each manager for a common goal:

- Strategic: Need to have customer input to identify product needs.
- Tactical: Develop a customer expectation checklist.
- Operational: Distribute and analyze a customer expectation checklist.

Element Two: Project Phases

Beyond these three managing levels there are six project phases. It is important to recognize that quality testing (monitoring) is a function of all phases. Quality testing also may be thought of as a separate project phase. This phase is what most people think of as the testing phase. Quality assurance and control extend across all project phases and should be considered separate from testing. The phases are the following:

- Planning
- Designing
- Developing
- Testing
- Implementing
- Verifying

Element Three: Project Activities

Besides managing levels and phases, there are activities that include all the managing levels and affect all of the phases. These activities include:

- Scheduling
- Budgeting
- Managing Resources
- Managing Risk/Opportunity
- Controlling Quality

Element Four: Tools

The fourth element is tools. A tool can be as simple as a pencil or as complex as project management software. Tools of project management include:

- Process historical data
- System infrastructure documents
- Project modeling
- Network optimization

- Gantt charts
- PERT/CPM techniques

While the last four are discussed because of their general nature and their potential to manage any project, it is recognized that one may not have the time to learn in depth these four tool types. However, one should be aware of their potential if one has the resources to use these tools.

Element Five: Analytical Process

The fifth element is the analytical process, which is actually ingrained in all components of the project management process. Over the years, certain areas or functions have been set apart for specific analysis processes. These include:

- Profitability
- Learning curve
- Scalability
- Interoperability
- Portability
- Risk
- Legacy (software and hardware)

Element Six: Environment

The sixth element is the environment. This can mean either a vendor or generic system paradigm. This book uses one vendor paradigm because of its significance to the Internet or intranets, Microsoft Corporation. The system paradigms are client/server and object-oriented. The Common Object Request Broker Architecture (CORBA) is discussed in this book as an implementation of object-oriented concepts.

MANAGER'S TIP

Microsoft has an object-oriented paradigm (DCOM, COM, or COM+, as the concept evolves); however, the use of Microsoft is the idea of one company having a "network solution" with a given product set. An essential question of a single vendor solution is, "Do the vendor's configuration values achieve the expected project goals?" In a multiple vendor solution this question is framed as, "How do I configure the various products to achieve the expected project goals?"

Element Seven: People

The seventh element is people. Although this is listed seventh, it is the most important element. People are discussed in this book as "the team" and "the customer." It takes both the project team and the customer to achieve success. On occasion, managing the relationship between the project team and the customer is referred to as conflict management; perhaps one should refer to it as opportunity management.

§ 1.02   PROJECT MANAGEMENT BASIC ACTIVITIES

[A]   Overview

There are at least eleven basic types of project management activities. These activities extend across the six project phases, that is:

1. Planning
2. Designing
3. Developing
4. Testing
5. Implementation
6. Verification

Some of the activities are more dominant in some phases than others; however, any project of any size is dynamic. While scope defining is obviously a part of the planning phase, one may have to return to it more than once.

Some of these eleven basic types of project management activities can be merged as one, such as scope planning and scope defining. In a large IS project, one should have as much of a detailed breakdown of activities as feasible. The following are the 11 activities that make up the project administrative process discussed in this section of the book:

1. Scope Planning
2. Scope Defining
3. Activity Planning
4. Activity Sequencing
5. Resource Planning
6. Time Estimating
7. Schedule Developing
8. Cost Estimating
9. Budget Developing

10. Quality Controlling

11. Managing Risks and Opportunities

There are two other activities that could be added to this list, documenting and training. They are foundational activities to any project. One of the ongoing discussions throughout this book is the design and development of document templates that assist in stating the goals, functionality, and results of each activity. Chapter 16 in Section Two is a consolidation of the ideas on documentation put forth in this section of the book. The level of training required is dependent on the decisions reached during the resource planning activity. Skill definition is important to the training requirements.

[B]   Scope Planning

One of the first actions you must take is to define the goals and performance expectations of your project, and get an agreement on them. Second, you must determine how individual software and hardware system components (protocols, firewalls, servers, e-mail, browsers, etc.) fit into the overall objectives. The scope plan is the strategic view of the constraints and assumptions of the project as developed by the project team. You should have, as a minimum, the following 13 types of data:

1. Basic team list
   - People with technical skills (programmers, DBAs, network, intranet, Internet)
   - Marketing people
   - People with project management skills
   - Representatives for the external users
2. Criteria for communications (training, documentation, status reporting)
3. Criteria for establishing timelines
4. Criteria for identifying skill requirements
5. Criteria for selecting resources
6. General budgetary requirements (Who is going to pay for the costs?). See the note on the following page.
7. General costing requirements (How much can you expect to spend?)
8. Historical and marketing data
9. Performance benchmarks
10. Risk benchmarks
11. Start and end dates of the project

12. User or customer expectations (users should be on the team)

13. Validation system benchmarks (success requirements)

The list is not by priority (rather, alphabetical by first word). The priority can change. Notice the uses of the words "criteria" and "benchmarks" in the above list.

MANAGER'S TIP

The action of negotiating who pays for the project is a time when the project manager, or IS administrator, wears the hat of business manager. This activity is business management first; it is project management second. The team should verify that there is sufficient funding for the project. Sufficient funding for any project should be secured prior to the project actually starting.

[C]   Scope Defining

You take the benchmarks and criteria listed in the section above and make the ideas concrete. It is the time to get a "firm" first commitment from all the parties involved. Notice it is *firm*, not *final*, commitment. Your project goals will evolve; scope definition is not complete on day one. This is a tactical view of the project. This is important so that users' expectations are not set in stone or concrete.

The scope definition should have as a minimum the following 12 types of data:

1. Basic definitions of responsibilities

2. An organization chart that shows links among people and their defined responsibilities

3. Clear definition of your responsibilities as IS project manager

4. Communication policy that includes:
   - Who sends information
   - What kind of information is sent
   - When information is sent
   - Who receives what types of information
   - What type of communication is used
   - Why that type of communication is used

5. Descriptions of the quality control and verification systems used in the planning, design, development, and implementation phases of the project goals

6. Firm start and end dates for basic usage

7. Essential milestone dates (some databases will be available day one, others on day x)

8. List of *realistic*, manageable project goals

9. List of resource estimates: human and material

10. Lists of cost estimates: human, materials, and time

11. Risk benchmarks, from a simple "nothing will be done with a minimal risk" to a complex statement on how to handle very dangerous risks

12. Threat (security) policy that illustrates how types of threats are handled

The framework of scope planning determines how detailed the scope definition will be.

[D]   Activity Planning

When you have the details, definitions, and descriptions of the actions for your project, you should clearly plan the activities required to complete basic integration into the system based on expected goals.

Your activities, when defined, give, as a minimum, the following 12 items:

1. Design, development, control, and implementation activities

2. Expected actions of support team members

3. Firm start and end actions

4. Flow chart of activities (think critical path)

5. How the quality control and assurance systems are to be implemented in all project phases

6. How to handle the established communications policy

7. How to implement a realistic security policy

8. IS project manager's administrative activities for this project

9. List of cost estimates associated with each function, application, or service

10. List of key milestones with their importance to the project's expected goals

11. List of realistic manageable activities

12. List of resource and skill estimates associated with each function, application, or service

[E]   Activity Sequencing

When you have sequenced your activities to implement your project goals, you should have a clear statement on the order of activities and their relationships to one another, including time, people, equipment, materials, and cost. The usual presentation is a flow chart. The following is a list of eight items you need at this point:

1. A flow chart or some other visual presentation that shows the activity sequence

2. Communication points sequenced so that all appropriate parties involved know the project status

3. Criteria for communicating the status of quality control

4. Criteria for being able to change the activity sequence if necessary

5. Critical path of activities (optional)

6. Procurement activities, identified within the sequence

7. Quality control and verification activities scheduled throughout

8. Resource input activities sequenced

MANAGER'S TIP

Activity sequence as used here means the complete list of activity sequences, including one for each operational area, quality, training, documentation, and project administration. All should be linked to the project goals.

[F]   Resource Planning

Resources come in many different formats—people, equipment, and materials. The important human resource is not headcount, but skills. Equipment categories that have to be considered are permanent or temporary, available or unavailable, and legacy or new. Software versions and compatibility of hardware must be considered.

There are other resource considerations, but they are outside this book's range. For example, do you have resources to train the network user to function at an expected defined level of expertise? (Select an e-mail application that is not user friendly and see what happens.)

Your resource definition should include as a minimum the following seven items:

1. Chart on how resources are linked to functions or services

2. Firm resource requirements and consequences of not having them

3. Policy on who determines resource requirements

4. Procedure for turning an unavailable resource into an opportunity

5. Resource change policy

6. Resource utilization policy

7. Resource requirements policy

[G] Time Estimating

Time management experts or software tools should be used to develop time estimates. This activity can use historical data for establishing benchmarks. Pessimism is better than optimism in doing time estimates. One should know the criteria used by either the experts or the tools for establishing the estimates. The primary cause of failure of projects is unrealistic time estimates.

The following are seven types of information you need when you finish your time estimates:

1. Criteria for associating cost and time estimates and potential changes

2. Criteria for establishing time measures

3. Criteria for formulating time estimates

4. Methodology for validating time estimates based on defined project goals

5. Procedure for associating time estimates with tasks and acquisitions

6. Quality control and validation time estimates (20 percent of your project is suggested)

7. Time estimates based on skill types and levels rather than on headcount involved

---

MANAGER'S TIP

The 20 percent for quality may seem high to you, but this does include time to minimize risk. This does not include time to resolve a major risk issue.

[H] Schedule Developing

Time management software tools can be used to develop schedules. This is where ordered activities and fixed times are combined. A schedule can be a simple calendar with activities inserted on milestone days, or an elaborate flowchart with dates placed on directional arrows. Two potential tools for establishing schedules are Gantt charts and PERT/CPM techniques.

Your schedule should include as a minimum the following nine items:

1. Scheduled communications points

2. Consistent and coherent timelines

3. Allocated time for risk management

4. Criteria for changing the schedule

5. Notification schedule for status on project changes

6. Quality control and verification schedule

7. Schedule based on the project scope definition

8. Timeline (calendar, flow chart)

9. Timeline for acquiring skills, equipment, and materials

MANAGER'S TIP

The schedule should be readable to all involved. An issue with project management software is that you can easily develop a schedule too complex to be read easily.

[I]   Cost Estimating

Cost management software tools should be used to develop cost estimates. This activity can use historical data for establishing benchmarks. It is better to be on the pessimistic side than the optimistic side in doing cost estimates.

Here are seven points on cost estimating:

1. Cost estimates based on skill types and levels rather than headcount

2. Criteria for associating cost to time estimates and potential changes

3. Criteria for establishing cost benchmarks

4. Criteria for formulating cost estimates

5. Methodology for validating cost estimates based on the expected project definition

6. Procedure for associating cost estimates with people, equipment, and materials

7. Quality control and validation cost estimates (10 to 20 percent of your project costs is suggested)

[J]   Budget Developing

Budgeting is taking cost estimates and entering them into a formal financial structure. A budget is to cost as a schedule is to time. At the end of budgeting, you should at least have the following six items:

1. A budget or budgets that are consistent to the project's scope definition

2. A separate budget line for risk management in your budget or an identified component of another manager's budget line

3. Links between your budget for this project and any supporting budgets

4. Procedure for handling outside resources payments

5. Procedure for making changes and updates to the budget reporting system as relevant to agreed-upon project changes

6. Separate budget lines for quality control and verification (optional)

MANAGER'S TIP

There should be one project budget, whether it is a part of the formal budget system or not.

[K]   Quality Controlling

Here are three questions you need to answer so the hidden monsters under the bed do not assault your expected project goals:

1. Do you have consistent quality standards?

2. Have you established a quality control system for the project?

3. Have you formulated verification activities?

Benchmarks or success criteria of the quality and performance of the project should be established at your earliest planning sessions. Benchmarks should not be established after the project is completed or at the halfway point.

What are the realistic expectations of your customer for the project? Get the expectations in writing and get the customer's agreement. You should be as specific as possible about expectations. This is the first project benchmark.

Quality is not just accuracy but a relationship to customer expectations. If a customer asked for three specific functions and you gave the customer seven functions that are similar to the ones specified, have you really attained quality?

[L]   Risk and Opportunity Managing

To establish a risk management process you need to ask yourself two core questions:

1. Do you have a list of assumptions and guidelines for handling potential threats and opportunities?

2. Are there identified fixed points in the project cycle for assessing risks?

When planning the project's scope you have to think in terms that a risk is a threat. However, you may be one of those unique people who can see a way to turn a risk into an opportunity. Perhaps you require six months to develop a product, and then someone invents a utility that can cut that time in half or less. Can this development affect the project? Of course it can!

MANAGER'S TIP

A risk is not necessarily a problem, but it can have an adverse or disastrous consequence on the project's outcome.

When you define the project scope, you should establish how to handle threats and opportunities. Unfortunately, in risk management most people think only of the threats to the project. What if someone comes up with an idea that a component of a hardware product or a software application can be omitted and the project can still achieve the customer's expectations? This is an opportunity!

There should be defined activities for handling threats. There should also be activities that handle opportunities if they arise. A simple activity rule would be: Until a threat (an opportunity) reaches a certain risk level (your definition), no action shall be taken.

Risk assessment is important to planning resources. You need to determine the minimum skill level requirements to perform the task(s) at hand. "Headcount requirement" is not the correct way to think. Perhaps for some activities a novice can do them, while for other activities an expert is needed. Possibly the lack of a skill can be turned into an opportunity.

The essential tasks should be ordered in your project so that you can evaluate potential threats and opportunities. A minimum recommendation is at least one risk review during each phase of the implementation of the project, preferably at every meeting. Quality assurance and control should always be on the outlook for potential performance risks.

You should set aside time for risk management during each key phase of your project. If you have no threats to the project in a given phase, you may have generated an opportunity.

You should have cost estimates for risk management in each project phase. If you have no threats to the project in a given phase, you have generated an opportunity for either moving funds to another phase or reducing the budget.

The schedule (activities plus time) should have at each key milestone an activity that assesses the project's status and determines if there are potential threats and opportunities. You need to know how the formulated schedule impacts the outcome of the project. Time analysis is a major component in risk management.

In your budget there should be funds factored in for risk management. The most logical line is the one to allocate money for contractors. Another line to consider is for quality control and verification. You may need additional funds if your product needs more testing than you estimated.

§ 1.03   THREE MANAGEMENT LEVELS

[A]   Overview

As mentioned earlier, there are three distinct management levels at which a project is controlled. These levels are:

- Strategic
- Tactical
- Operational

[B]   Strategic Level

Many upper-level managers think they do not have a part to play in any project except perhaps to be critical. However, this conception is far from the truth. These managers establish the strategic position of the project. A strategic manager needs to say more than "I want this enhancement to the information system." There should be measurable strategic goals from upper-level management. These goals are really how a tactical or operational manager is ultimately evaluated. The clearer these goals are, the more secure the tactical and operational managers will be in achieving successful project results.

What does it mean to be a strategic manager besides being labeled a part of upper-level management? The word *strategy* comes from the Greek word *stratégos*. This word means "general-of-the-army," thus the military connotation of the words *tactical* and *operational*. A strategic manager should be thought of as a Greek general, not a twentieth-century general who is more a bureaucrat than an active participant. A strategic goal may be as simple as "enhance the network to do a specific function within a specific time frame and within a specific budgetary amount." This statement with appropriate values is measurable. The tactical manager's first task is to negotiate the statement so it is realistic and manageable.

A strategic manager heads an area of the organization that includes the IS project as a part of that person's performance goals. This manager should have the budget authority and should be assisting the IS project tactical manager in resources, equipment, and materials.

[C]   Tactical Level

This leads to the definition of the tactical manager. This manager type is the one responsible for the overall flow of the project process so that the strategic goals are met. This manager is usually called the IS administrator, a business manager, or project manager.

A military definition of tactics is the handling of the field troops, while strategy is one of positioning the battlefield. The word *tactics* comes from the Greek word *taxis*. Tactics is the act of arranging or disposing of the troops for battle. Operations is where the shooting, the work, takes place.

  Alexander the Great managed at all three levels. This type of management is not possible in the current corporate environment, but is possible in a small startup company.

MANAGER'S TIP

Many new project managers mistakenly believe that merely because they are managers, they can automatically rally the support of all those assigned to them. Most seasoned managers readily subscribe to the adage that respect is earned and not bestowed by title (so hard to gain, so easy to lose). All too often, the respect of those being led is forfeited because of the lack of basic interpersonal or management skills.

[D] Operational Level

The operational managers are the people who handle the day-to-day operations or activities that have been defined in the project plan. Notice that managers are referred to in the plural sense here, because in a large project you may have many operational managers reporting to the tactical manager. These people may not be called managers but may be called project leads. The functions are the same no matter the label.

  So how does one move from the military ideas of historical figures such as Carl von Clauswitz and Alfred Thayer Mahan to the present-day corporate environment? The first global companies of the late nineteenth and the early twentieth centuries used the military model in their expansions. Of course, many of the ideas, concepts, techniques, and tools that make up what may be defined as IS project management have their origins in projects of the United States military. The foremost example is the development of the first nuclear-powered submarine, USS *Nautilus*, under the management of Admiral Hyman G. Rickover in the mid-1950s.

  War has always been a project with a few added enhancements such as logistics, even before Alexander the Great did his thing. We want to apply these ideas to the less bloody (one hopes) effort of IS project management. As each of the project activities is mentioned, the responsibilities of each of these manager types are discussed in terms of how they relate to that specific action.

§ 1.04 EVALUATING PROJECT VIABILITY

[A] Overview

One of the fundamental aspects of a project in the preproposal stage is the need for adequate research. Evaluating a project with a checklist and metaquestions helps to answer many of the issues that the successful project manager will integrate into the bigger picture with the help of upper management. But if management fails to properly evaluate the market and scope of the project, success may well be out of reach.

MANAGER'S TIP

Several years ago a large business-to-business (B2B) medical supplier decided to catch the Internet wave and launch a Web site that, in theory, would make it easier for the supplier's clients to make purchases. The project failed on several critical fronts.

First, the marketing department had neglected to ascertain the fact that, doctors, for example, seem to be too busy to use the Internet while at work and tend to make their purchases using existing Customer Relationship Management (CRM) programs. They have little interest in or time to learn how to use a new technology.

Secondly, the site build was outsourced to a Web company that promised short development time and complete software integration. But the project leaders (there were two in succession) should have first established that the Web builders could handle the project. The builders could not figure out how to get the shopping cart to work with the point-of-sale software and the site crashed on the day of the soft launch. Their last-ditch solution was to suggest a million-dollar middleware purchase, which the IT people at the medical supply company researched and discovered was unnecessary. Eventually, the site was rebuilt by in-house talent, and the launch was pushed back a year. The Web builders did quite well, because 75 percent of their fee had been paid up front.

What could or should have been done? The project manager, along with upper management, should have researched the pros and cons of in-house versus outsourced development, using a project viability evaluation form. In retrospect, the site could have been done just with in-house talent and with a longer development cycle.

[B]   Using a Project Viability Evaluation

A project viability evaluation is like a risk virus vaccine. Note that the following is an example of how you might prepare the evaluation form; its parameters will depend on your formulation, using 20 questions that clarify the particular customer's objective (see Exhibit 1-1: Sample Project Viability Checklist). If you cannot resolve your concerns in 20 questions, you need to review and revise your premises. In addition, a 20-question evaluation helps the customer clarify the problem and shows the customer that you have a formal project process. A positive result can be used to gain upper management's buy-in.

The two leading questions should look something like this:

- What funding exists for this project?
- What are the project's measurable objectives?

Exhibit 1-1: Sample Project Viability Checklist

Project Name:	Comments
1. Are potential materials and equipment available to achieve project results?	
2. Are potential resources available to achieve the project results?	
3. Are potential costs going to be too high to achieve project results?	
4. Are there appropriate project justifications to achieve project results?	
5. Are there appropriate skills available to achieve project results?	
6. Are there budgetary monies available to achieve the project results?	
7. Are there project tools available to ensure control to achieve project results?	
8. Do the project results meet the strategic goals of the company?	
9. Do the project results reflect efficiency and innovation?	
10. How may project results affect any product pricing?	
11. How may project results meet customer needs?	
12. How stable is the IS organization for achieving the project results?	
13. How stable is the technology required to achieve project results?	
14. How will the results impact the return on investment (ROI)?	
15. Is the deadline realistic to achieve project results?	
16. What are the events that can cause the project to fail?	
17. What are the events that can make the project successful?	
18. What are the possible impacts of the end results on the information system?	
19. What are the possible resistant concerns to project results?	
20. What is the level of formal authority of the IS project manager to achieve the project results?	

If the answer to the first question is negative or unknown, you might have a *conversation*, but not a negotiation, with the customer. If the customer does have a potential figure in mind, then that becomes the point of negotiation for the response to the second question.

Even when the answers are negative or unknown, however, you should continue the conversation through the other 18 questions. The answers to these questions may actually lead to a positive response.

This kind of project manager/customer dialogue can provide the project team with a realistic scenario for making their estimates. Also, the project team can use the responses as a foundation for essential project documents such as the Scope Plan, Activity Plan, Project Schedule, and Project Budget.

MANAGER'S TIP

I have seen only one project succeed when there was not a clear definition of funding. The corporation wanted to become International Organization for Standardization (ISO)-compliant for internal and external benefits. It was thought that using the ISO process would save money in product design, development, and testing. More importantly, it would generate new business.

[C]   Asking the Correct Questions

The broadest questions for developing any set of project evaluation questions are of course:

1. How?
2. Why?
3. When?
4. Where?
5. Who?
6. What?

These questions are called *metaquestions*, which means first-ordered questions. They are the broadest and simplest questions you can ask; of themselves, they are also the most ineffective. They are the first categorical steps toward clarification or refinement. How-type questions involve methodology (tasks and activities, as discussed in Chapter 3), skill prerequisites, and financial concerns (that is, cost estimates and budget, which are discussed in detail in Chapters 7 and 8). Why-type questions involve justifications such as cost-benefit analysis, customer expectations, benchmarks, standards, and especially measurable project goals. Questions on benchmarks and standards are important to the quality control assurance process and the risk management program discussed in Chapters 9 and 10. When-type questions involve time estimates and a schedule, which are discussed in more detail in Chapters 5 and 6. Where-type questions consider location definitions, and resource prerequisites. Who-type questions involve primarily skill types and level pre-requisites, and the responsible agents. What-type questions involve resources (skills, equipment, materials, and project duration); that is, production time plus wait time. Resource questions are discussed in Chapter 4.

The first step in using metaquestions is to narrow them down using cate-gorical statements that include the characteristics, functions, and goals of a project, such as a specific customer definition rather than global customer definition. The second step is classifying a potential project in terms of what is and what is not—the foundation of the forms for a project Scope Plan (Chapter 2). These statements are then turned into questions based on the "Big Six."

This process helps ensure as risk-free an environment as possible. Then, you finally ask the question "Is the project viable?" The response will be a clear "yes" or "no."

[D]   Developing the 20 Questions

On your first try do not expect to have 20 questions ready to determine a project's viability; this is only a suggested technique based on the old game that begins with the question, "Is it living or non-living?" The format estab-lishes two contrasting points and requires a "yes" or "no" answer. Perhaps, the first question you could ask is: "Are there measurable goals?" If the answer is "yes," then the second question you might ask is, "Are sufficient funds avail-able to complete the customer's measurable goals?"

The 20-question game is immediately over if the first question is "no." You should never go to upper management to discuss a project without mea-surable project goals; instead, you might discuss an opportunity with upper management if there are no measurable goals.

You can use the 20-question game in two situations. First, with no mea-surable goals, an opportunity can be discussed in terms of its future possibili-ties. Second, with measurable goals, you can determine if you have the capa-bilities (skills) and resources (especially time and funding) to successfully complete the project on schedule and on budget.

Before discussing a project's viability with upper management, you might brainstorm with some of your staff and those who would be involved in the project. Brainstorming is an excellent technique for generating ideas or suggestions that can be later ordered in a rational sequence. Do not get hung up on the order of the goals, unless one or more are critical to all the others. If this is the case, then you have the basis for using the critical path method at a later point—that is, when calculating activity and time esti-mates.

MANAGER'S TIP

Always keep a copy of the results of study of a project's viability in your documentation library, whether the process was implemented or not. It can provide valuable technical and business process information for future projects.

The following brief list of questions is not definitive, but it shows the kinds of questions you could ask when brainstorming:

- How complete is the list of measurable goals?
- Why should this project be done?
- How much funding is required to complete the critical goals and any other goals?
- What types of tasks and skills are required?
- When are the goals to be completed?
- When are management tools required?
- What are the required benchmarks and standards?
- Who has tactical responsibility for the project?
- What are the potential impacts on the system's infrastructure?
- How can potential risks be determined?

Below are 10 questions in the "yes-no" response format for the project viability process:

1. Are there measurable project goals?
2. Is there sufficient justification (cost-benefit analysis, customer relationship, or general market environment) to begin this project?
3. Is there sufficient funding?
4. Does the present staff have the skills to achieve the defined potential tasks?
5. Can the goals be achieved within the expected duration (time)?
6. Are the necessary management tools available, and are there appropriate skilled personnel available?
7. Have the implications for possible benchmarks and standards been considered?
8. Is there a written statement of tactical responsibility?
9. Are there any critical impacts on the system's infrastructure?
10. Have criteria of potential risks been established?

While some of the above questions might not be completely answered at a meeting on project viability, they should be able to be answered with a high degree of probability.

The following set of 20 project questions in the preproposal phase could be used to create a checklist that reflects a set of "yes-no" responses and to develop a local template. This process is a requirement for any discussion of project viability with upper management.

MANAGER'S TIP

Exhibit 1-2 is a checklist and instructions for creating and using project viability questions.

---

1. What are the measurable project goals? The active word is *measurable*. If you do not have measurable goals, you are building your project process on sand and you only need to wait for the first tide (risk) to wash you out to the depths of failure.

2. What potential materials and equipment are available? At this point you should have some sense of the requirements for the types of materials and equipment to be used for each goal.

3. What and where are available resources? You need to know what the resources are and where they are available. You might find resources outside the IS group or even outside the corporation in the case of a consultant. If some resources are not immediately available, you will need to determine if they are critical to the project's success.

4. How do possible project costs compare to project benefits? You should do at least a basic cost-benefit analysis so that you can present the results to upper management and justify or not justify the project's viability.

5. Why should this project be done? Without specific justification, how can you get approval to do the project? You may need more than the customer wants or has the funds to do. This scenario is potentially fraught with danger.

6. What and when are appropriate skills available? You need to have measurable and specific skill-level descriptions that include technical requirements.

7. How will the project's budget items be funded? Unfortunately, budget items for a given project are probably scattered over a number of different budgets. You need to create a project budget, even if it is outside of the formal financial structure, so that you can manage the entire process.

8. What and where are the required project management tools for achieving project results? Project management tools can be as simple as a set of index cards or as complex as a utility that can manage a project based on PERT (Performance Evaluation and Review Technique). Remember, the more complex a tool, the greater the learning curve. Garbage in is garbage out no matter how sophisticated the management tool. The problem is that the more complex the tool, the harder it is to identify the garbage.

Exhibit 1-2: Checklist for Project Viability Questions

Measurable goals	❑
Acceptable assumptions	❑
Acceptable constraints	❑
Identified deliverables	❑
Identified risks	❑
Identified opportunities	❑
Identified project impacts	❑
Identified stakeholders	❑
Established project process	❑
Adequate duration	❑
Criteria for time estimates	❑
Schedule requirements	❑
Acceptable deadlines	❑
Cost-benefit analysis	❑
ROI impacts	❑
Adequate available funding	❑
Customer	❑
IS	❑
Other	❑
Budget requirements	❑
Criteria cost estimates	❑
Project authority adequate	❑
System infrastructure effects	❑
Compatibility	❑
Interoperability	❑
Portability	❑
Scalability	❑
Technology stability	❑
Quality control	❑
Identified process	❑
External standards	❑
Internal standards	❑

Exhibit 1-2 (*Continued*)

External benchmarks	❑
Internal benchmarks	❑
Quality assurance	❑
Identified process	❑
External standards	❑
Internal standards	❑
External benchmarks	❑
Internal benchmarks	❑
Resources	❑
Equipment	❑
Internal	❑
External	❑
Materials	❑
Internal	❑
External	❑
Skills	❑
Internal	❑
External	❑
Contacts	❑
Internal	❑
External	❑
Project management tools	❑
Internal	❑
External	❑
Development tools	❑
Internal	❑
External	❑
Facilities	❑
Internal	❑
External	❑
Logistics requirements	❑
Training requirements	❑

Exhibit 1-2 (*Continued*)

Internal	❏
External	❏
Documentation requirements	❏
Internal	❏
External	❏
Communications requirements	❏
Internal	❏
External	❏

Instructions for Using a Viability Checklist

General Instructions

- This checklist is only a framework for you to create your own 20 questions.
- There are two required questions in any situation:
    1. Is there funding available for a potential project?
    2. Are there measurable goals for a potential project?
- Each of these items will require its own set of questions based on the metaquestions (How?, Why?, When?, Where?, Who?, and What?) that lead to a "yes," "no," or "not applicable." From these questions, the list should be narrowed to 20 for the meeting with the project initiator.
- Do not expect to have an acceptable set of questions on the first try.
- When presenting your questions it might be effective to have a slide for each. The potential customer should focus on each question rather than on the 20 as a whole. It is more important to have a visual presentation rather than you just asking each question.
- You might include some very brief talking points on each slide such as "Criteria for adequate funding."

Specific Instructions

Measurable goals: "Win the game" appears to be a measurable goal; however, does it mean the game must be won by more than one point? In the same manner, the goal of completing the project on time and on budget is not measurable. What must specifically be completed?

Acceptable assumptions: An assumption is a prediction that action or an event will be fulfilled. An example is "There will be potential risks, but they will all be overcome."

Acceptable constraints: A constraint is a limit, limitation, or parameter such as the duration or funds available for the project.

Identified deliverables: A deliverable is a measurable result, product, or service of the project.

Identified risks: A risk is an event that will bring failure to the project.

Identified opportunities: An opportunity is a situation that can shorten the project's duration or lessen funding requirements.

Identified project impacts: An impact can be either short-term or long-term. When a long-term risk is forgotten, such as when the maintenance time required for a piece of hardware in the field is ignored in the design of the project, the cost can reduce any profits from the project.

Exhibit 1-2 (*Continued*)

Identified stakeholders: A stakeholder is potentially anyone in the organization, members of an external funding group, users, and interested government regulators.

Established project process: When there is no established project process, there is no management. There is firefighting. Would you want to do business with someone who cannot tell you how they are going to achieve your measurable goals?

Adequate duration: Duration should be defined as to the amount of working days available for the project. An absolute duration includes such things as weekends. One might speak to a six-month duration; however, what is the actual production time?

Criteria for time estimates: If you do not have measurable and object criteria for time estimates, the project will fail.

Schedule requirements: A schedule needs to consider in a project's duration its production time and its wait time. It is an allocation of activities with deadlines or milestones.

Acceptable deadlines: Acceptable deadlines are realistic. They can also be defined within either a pessimistic or an optimistic scenario.

Cost-benefit analysis: An IS cost-benefit analysis is required before determining the viability of the project. Any questions should be formulated within the context of the results of the cost-benefit analysis.

ROI impacts: A Return on Investment is more than a financial saving. An ROI could also be an adequate security system that protects data and its loss to a cracker (thief), which could be difficult to quantify.

Adequate available funding: If there is no available funding, the project is only speculation.

Budget requirements: A project budget is a formal structure that is based on changing cost estimates. A project budget is not a corporate annual budget that is based on headcount and activities.

Criteria for cost estimates: If you do not have measurable and object criteria for cost estimates, the project will fail.

Project authority adequate: A written document that establishes the parameters of authority for the project manager must be completed prior to start of the project.

System infrastructure effects: The infrastructure is more than the visual components (hardware, software, and people). It includes the intangible tangibles: compatibility, interoperability, portability, and scalability.

Technology stability: Do you know of any potential technology that could impact the measurable goals of the project?

Quality control: Quality control is the definition component of a quality program. You need to know the potential impacts of internal and external objective and measurable standards (procedures) and benchmarks (performance level) on completing the project's goals.

Quality assurance: Quality assurance is the performance (the data-gathering) component of a quality program. You need to know the potential uses of internal and external objectives and measurable standards (procedures) and benchmarks (performance level) on completing the project's goals.

Resources: You need to have knowledge as to resource requirement types potentially required before determining the viability of the project. The knowledge should include internal and external equipment requirements, materials, skills, contacts, system and development tools, facility requirements, and finally training and documentation needs. Why do you need all this data up front? You need to be able to judge as adequately as possible your capabilities to do the customer's stated measurable goals.

Exhibit 1-2 (*Continued*)

Training requirements: Training requirements need to consider the availability of internal and external classes. Will the training include hands-on situations? What is the learning curve scenario? What are the potential funding requirements? When is the training requirement to determine the critical path?

Documentation requirements: Documentation requirements have to consider if all or some of the documents are written. What kind of funding is needed? What type of documentation is required (technical, customer, or training)?

Communications requirements: Communications requirements have to consider the methods for getting information to a person in an appropriate manner? Who gets what information must be defined. Do you give weekly reports to the customer using e-mail or do you give monthly presentations of project status? What are the benefits and consequences of using e-mail? Consider that e-mails can be forwarded to people outside of the project's environment and sometimes be interpreted on an emotional level.

Example Questions

Below are 10 questions in the "yes no" response format for the project viability process:

1. Are there measurable project goals?
2. Has sufficient justification (cost-benefit analysis, customer relationship, or general market environment) to do this project been given?
3. Is there sufficient funding?
4. Does the present staff have the skills to achieve the defined activities or tasks?
5. Can the goals be achieved in the expected duration (time)?
6. Are the necessary management tools available and are there appropriate skilled personnel available?
7. Have the implications for possible benchmarks and standards been considered?
8. Is there a written statement of tactical responsibility?
9. Are there critical impacts on the system's infrastructure?
10. Have criteria of potential risks been established?

While some of the above questions might not be answered absolutely at a meeting on project viability, they should be answered with a high degree of certainty. A "maybe" answer should be turned into a "yes" or "no" prior to a definite start of a project.

9. What benchmarks and standards have been identified in the quality control and assurance program for the deliverables? It is critical that you identify required standards and benchmarks to ensure the success of any project that requires quality management. Remember that a quality deliverable means customer satisfaction.

10. How do the project goals reflect efficiency and innovation? Because something may be a buzzword on your or the customer's tongue does not mean it is tasty. You do need to consider how the project's goals will impact the IS infrastructure and its efficiency and how any innovation or enhancement will ripple through the system.

11. What are the critical assumptions and constraints for managing the project's goals? There is only one rule at this point: You MUST define them.

12. Who should have written tactical authority for the project's management? If you are going to be a project manager, you must have written authority to do what is legally necessary to complete a project on schedule and on budget. This authorization should come from the upper management level. You cannot begin a project without this legitimization.

13. How do deliverables relate to the project goals? You need to have a list of deliverables associated with each goal; these could include training or special documentation. You might also consider the types of presentations that have to be delivered as each goal is developed and completed.

14. How stable is the technology required to achieve project results? You need a set of assumptions and constraints that relate to any technology to be used in the development of deliverables. Introducing a new technology during the project duration could create a devastating ripple effect.

15. How will the results impact the return on investment (ROI)? ROI as used here is more than a simple cost-benefit analysis. ROI impact might mean a significant improvement in your system scalability in a given area, so that your customer would be very satisfied.

16. How realistic are the deadlines to achieve project results? There is only one rule at this point: you MUST have realistic deadlines. You should not be expected to start a project the day after it is approved by your management and your customer because complex issues need to be resolved first.

17. What are the events that could cause the project to fail? You manage risks by considering them before they happen. This activity is a part of defining assumptions and constraints.

18. What are the events that can make the project successful? You must not ignore the positive. The project may be happening at the correct time and in the correct place.

19. What are the possible impacts of the end results on the information system? Because you are an IS manager, you must filter all data through the defined goals of your group.

20. What are the criteria for the various types of estimates? Remember, any estimate comes in three flavors—pessimistic, realistic, and optimistic, so you need to determine the basic project cost and time estimates in each of these three flavors. You will also need to describe your potential skill requirements in the same manner.

At the preproposal survey step, you are not looking for details or precise data except in a few areas, but you do need to establish clear parameters. As in football, you must first establish the playing area, the goal posts, the end field, and the yardage lines. If you are managing the creation of an XML-based application for defining a financial database for corporate budget items, you will need data that can be determined from:

- What are the budget items?
- What kind of database is it?

- When is the database to be accessed?
- Where is the database located?
- Why does the application for the database need to be XML-based?
- Who is to access the database?
- How is the database to be accessed?

Just by using the metaquestions, you can quickly establish the types of data you need in this critical area. Other critical areas include:

- Sources of funding
- Basic assumptions and constraints
- Potential impact, especially on the system's infrastructure
- Potential possibilities for risks and opportunities
- Technological requirements

The development of any checklist or form should begin by asking questions about the project. In such a case, you must consider the potential rather than the actual.

MANAGER'S TIP

The checklist and instructions in this chapter are examples only. Based on your situation, you will need to create your own set of questions. With examples you will be able to understand better how to create your own 20 questions.

---

§ 1.05   ABC's OF PROJECT MANAGEMENT ISSUES

Below is a list of one hundred–plus sources that can and usually do generate project management issues. The essential purpose of the scope plan, and ultimately the responsibility of the project manager, is to control the parameters or negative limits of these sources. Each letter is limited to a maximum of five sources because of the defined constraint of the page length for this book.

- A—acceptance criteria, activity definitions, aims, analysis, assumptions
- B—bargaining, benchmarks, benefits, best practices, budget
- C—champion, communications, constraints, control, cost
- D—data, decision making, deliverables, design, documentation
- E—effectiveness, efficiencies, environment, expectations, expediencies
- F—failure, feedback, financing, functionality, funding

- G—gates, geopolitics, goals, government, groupings
- H—hardware, hiring, historical data, human relations, human resources
- I—idealism, implementation, information, infrastructure, IS strategy
- J—job assessment, job description, job satisfaction, job rotation, just-in-time
- K—kicker, kickoff meeting, KISS principle, knowledge management, kowtowing
- L—lag-lead times, leadership, learning curve, legal concerns, life cycle
- M—marketing, media, methodology, milestones, mission
- N—needs assessment, negotiations, networking, noise, normal
- O—objectives, operational management, organization, obsolescence, ownership
- P—partnering, performing, phasing, planning, prototyping
- Q—qualification, quality, quantification, quantity, quota
- R—reengineering, resistance, rewards, risk management, roles
- S—schedule, skills, stakeholders, standards, strategy
- T—team building, technology, time management, total quality, training
- U—understaffing, unions, upgrading, user-friendly, user involvement
- V—validation, value management, variance, verification, version
- W—what if, work authorization, win-win agreement, work environment, workload
- X—X factors
- Y—you
- Z—Z factors

The X factors are the improbable technical factors, while the Z factors are the improbable emotional factors.

§ 1.06   SOME PROJECT MANAGEMENT ADVANTAGES AND LIMITATIONS

Using project management techniques allows you, the IS project manager, to guide and control a process with a clear focus to achieve a set of measurable goals to a successful conclusion. As with any technique, project management has its advantages and its limitations. The following are just some of the potential advantages:

- A clear picture of the task and the participants' responsibilities
- Early identification of performance errors
- Means of accountability
- Product integrity
- Team participation

From some people's view, there may be more limitations than advantages; however, here are only two limitations:

1. The project plan has to be kept simple, to limit misinterpretations.
2. Changes in the project may make administrative paperwork intolerable.

§ 1.07   USING ESSENTIAL TERMS

The following 50 terms are essential to a full discussion of any project, and they form the supports for the framework of this book. Beyond these terms, you must also consider local technical concepts, that is, software, hardware, and infrastructure.

MANAGER'S TIP

A networking system's infrastructure is defined not only by objects that you can see and touch, but also by such concepts as interoperability, portability, and scalability.

An **assumption** is a prediction that something will be true, either an action or an event that ensures project success.

Authority is the investment in managing and controlling a series of tasks such as a project. For example, the critical statement the strategic manager has to make is, "The project manager has the authority to make all decisions required to achieve a successful project."

A **benchmark** is a specific technical level of excellence.

A **checklist** is an organized list, possibly a standard of action, that usually has to be followed in sequence to accomplish a specified goal. However, a checklist can be as simple as a set of options for answering the question, "Have I considered the following items for this activity or task?"

A **consultant** is a person from outside the normal resource pool with experience in solving a specific project issue.

Control is the monitoring of progress and the checking for variances in the plan.

A **cost–benefit analysis** is the development of a ratio to determine if a project is financially viable.

A **critical activity** or task if not completed means project failure.

A **deliverable** is a clearly defined project result, product or service.

An **estimate** is a guess based on opinion, or a forecast based on experience. Cost, time, and resource estimates are the foundations for project planning.

Expectation is a stated project goal that can become a perceived undocumented result.

Goal characteristics have to be measurable, specific, and potentially possible.

Information system project management is a documented parallel process within a set schedule, and within a defined budget, with available resources and skills to achieve defined user expectations for a computing environment. The computing environment's primary function is to transmit data among users.

Innovation is a significant change or breakthrough.

Interoperability is to what degree the various network components work with one another successfully.

Management is the process of working with people, resources, equipment, and materials to achieve organizational goals.

Management team is a supervisory team that coordinates broad issues that affect the corporation.

The **market analysis report** documents and verifies market opportunities and justifies the features, services, and applications for the project goals.

A **model** is a theoretical environment with as much data as possible to reflect reality adequately for decision-making.

An **objective** is a set of measurable goals to achieve a defined target that, if not achieved, has critical results.

An **opportunity** is a situation that will positively affect the project in time, money, resources, or all three in a significant manner.

An **organization** is an entity created to achieve what the separate individuals could not accomplish.

Portability is a characteristic of software. It is the degree to which the software can be transferred from one environment to another.

Process is a systematic and sequential set of activities (tasks) to achieve a set of measurable goals.

A **program** is a type of recurring project, such as the annual budget, not to be confused with a set of programming codes.

A **project** is an organized set of tasks to reach a measurable outcome within a specified duration.

Project management has many aliases, including program management, product management, and construction management. In all cases, it is the managing, controlling, and integrating of tasks, resources, time, and costs to achieve defined measurable outcomes within a specified duration.

The **project manager** is the person with overall responsibility for managing and controlling the project tasks (defined and undefined) to achieve a measurable outcome within a specified schedule and budget.

A **project team** is an organization that is put together to achieve a specific set of measurable goals within a specific time and with limited resources, equipment, and materials.

Quality assurance is based on performance. It is the establishing of performance standards, then measuring and evaluating and measuring project performance against these standards. It is the component of quality management that considers project performance deviations.

MANAGER'S TIP

From the beginning of the project, the project manager should confirm that the Quality Assurance team enjoys good communications with all members of the project team that will be supplying QA with documentation. This process ensures accurate testing and improved functionality.

Quality control is the component of quality management that considers the system or development processes of a project. It is the tasks used to meet standards through the gathering of performance information, inspecting, monitoring, and testing.

A **resource** is anything that supports the project. This includes, in general terms, money, skills, materials, time, facilities, and equipment.

Resource planning is establishing support requirements for a project as to costs, availability, start date and end date (length of time for use plus duration), and technical specifications.

A **risk** is a performance error that can have a significant or disastrous impact on the success of a project or major activity. It is more than a problem; its effect can have an adverse or disastrous consequence on the project's outcome.

Scalability is to what degree a system can be enhanced without a major change in design.

The **schedule** is the duration of the project, including production time and wait time. It is also a production plan for the allocation of tasks with deadlines.

Scope is the amount of work and resources (skills, materials, and equipment) required for project completion.

Skill level is a factor used by a project manager in planning the project's budget, rather than using a headcount.

Specific goals are project goals that are measurable, unambiguous, and match exactly the customer's stated expectations.

The **sponsor** is the one who provides the resources and the working environment to make possible the achievement of project goals.

A **stakeholder** is any person or organization interested in the project. This includes the customer, your boss, you, the team, and interested government regulators.

A **standard** is usually an external, industry-accepted document for achieving quality for one or more of the project-defined expected goals.

A **Statement of Work (SOW)** is an integrated set of descriptions as to project tasks, goals, risks, and resources to complete a measurable outcome.

A **strategic manager** heads an area of a corporation that includes the IS project as a part of that person's performance goals.

A **system** is an interactive set of tasks or groups that forms a whole with dynamics that impact all the components.

The **tactical manager** is the one responsible for the overall flow of the project process so that the strategic goals are met.

The **Third-Party Market Agreement** provides the plans whereby the project or a part of the project is to be the responsibility of a third-party developer.

Adding Supportive Terms

Any other term used in Chapters 2 through 10 is supportive to the long list of essential terms. More than 250 terms are defined throughout this book and all are included in the glossary.

MANAGER'S TIP

Some of the definitions are duplicated in other chapters, but their contextual meaning may vary according to how you use the book—whether as a reference guide or as a textbook.

Exhibit 1-3: Project Proposal Checklist

Technical Section:	Yes	No	Comments
Executive Summary	❏	❏	
Requirements Analysis	❏	❏	
Solutions	❏	❏	
Alternate Solution	❏	❏	
Scope of Work	❏	❏	
Parameters	❏	❏	
Methodology	❏	❏	
Technical Solution	❏	❏	
Prototype/Demo	❏	❏	
Beta Test	❏	❏	
Installations	❏	❏	
Standards	❏	❏	
Benchmarks	❏	❏	
Maintenance	❏	❏	
Training	❏	❏	
Documentation	❏	❏	
Risk Analysis	❏	❏	
Appendix/Glossary	❏	❏	
Index	❏	❏	
Administrative Section:			
Executive Summary	❏	❏	
Commitment Statement	❏	❏	
Solution	❏	❏	
Statement of Work (SOW)	❏	❏	
Activities	❏	❏	
Deliverables	❏	❏	

Exhibit 1-3 (*Continued*)

Organization	❑	❑	
Task Responsibilities	❑	❑	
Project Management Process	❑	❑	
Tracking System	❑	❑	
Reporting System	❑	❑	
Quality Control	❑	❑	
Contractors/Consultants	❑	❑	
Personnel Qualifications	❑	❑	
Appendix	❑	❑	
Index	❑	❑	
Financial Section:			
Executive Summary	❑	❑	
Cost Model	❑	❑	
Contract	❑	❑	
Cost Summary	❑	❑	
Cost Estimate Basis	❑	❑	
Payment Structure	❑	❑	
Overhead Rates	❑	❑	
Facilities Rates	❑	❑	
Cost Schedule	❑	❑	
Additional Cost Criteria	❑	❑	
Appendix	❑	❑	
Index	❑	❑	

Exhibit 1-4: Project Planning Checklist

Project:		Date:		
Prepared by:		Yes	No	NA
Acceptable variances from performance have been identified.				
Activities are comprehended by the team.				
Activity responsibilities have been clearly defined.				
Adequate tools are in place to complete activities.				
Approval process is satisfactory.				
Approval at work has been given by responsible managers.				
Consultant parameters have been clearly stated.				
Contingency policy is in place rather than padding.				
Cost estimates are realistic.				
Critical path has been identified.				
Customer has given measured objectives.				
Customers are adequately involved in the project process.				
Deliverables have been clearly identified.				
Documentation program is adequate.				
Exit process exists.				
Facilities are adequate.				
Flexibility is possible in the project.				
Gantt chart is available as a working tool.				
Historical IS data has been used, when appropriate.				
Identification of appropriate standards and benchmarks has been made.				
Overtime is minimized.				
Performance objectives are clearly defined.				
Plan is comprehensive with no unknown omissions.				
Political issues have been identified and handled.				
Potential consequences have been analyzed and accepted.				
Potential risks have been identified with contingency solutions.				
Procedures are in place to handle resources availability.				
Procedures are in place to objectively handle cost estimates.				
Procedures are in place to objectively handle time estimates.				
Program for recognition is excellent.				

Exhibit 1-4 (*Continued*)

Project:		Date:		
Prepared by:		Yes	No	NA
Project communication program is adequate.				
Project goals enhance the corporate goals.				
Project Manager has adequate authority to make decisions.				
Project mission has been communicated to the full project team.				
Quality Control and Assurance program in place.				
Review process is satisfactory.				
Satisfactory reporting system is in place.				
Schedule is realistic.				
Team members are qualified.				
Team members' roles have been clearly described.				
There are no activities with lengthy durations.				
There is an adequate testing process.				
Time estimates are realistic.				
Training for project success is adequate.				
Written measured project objectives or goals are given.				

On the CD-ROM

On the CD-ROM are:

1. Exhibit 1-1 Sample Project Viability Checklist.doc

2. Exhibit 1-2 Checklist for Project Viability Questions.doc

3. Exhibit 1-3 Project Proposal Checklist.doc

4. Exhibit 1-4 Project Planning Checklist.doc

5. Chapter 1 Overview.ppt—Chapter Overview, What Is IS Project Management?

Chapter 2

Scope Planning and Defining

§ 2.01 OVERVIEW

[A] Objectives

At the end of this chapter, you will be able to:

- State a definition for scope planning.
- State a definition for scope defining.
- Identify five data types required for a scope plan (the parameters).
- Identify five data types required for scope definition (the procedures).

- Ask 20 basic questions on developing the scope of project, such as: What are basic quality control points? What are performance benchmarks? What are the drop-dead dates? What are the financial benchmarks? What historical data are available? What skill levels are available? What skill levels are needed?
- List eight potential scope plan and definition killers.
- Identify two essential support functions to manage the scope plan.
- Identify 17 documents that have their origin in or are related to the scope plan and definition.
- Evaluate four types of changes to the scope plan and definitions.
- Identify how the three managing levels are involved in scope planning and scope defining.

MANAGER'S TIP

In a recent television commercial, a small group of people huddles around an office computer screen. They watch intently as a colleague at the keyboard raises his hand and strikes the Enter key. Everyone stares at the screen with an air of intense anticipation. Onscreen a counter registers their first sale and the employees let out a collective sigh of relief. Then more sales register and the small crowd cheers. But within moments the counter spins wildly out of control as thousands of sales click on the screen. Silently, their expressions change from elation to panic as the small group realizes that the have just been buried alive by success.

   This wickedly funny commercial about scalability issues related to e-commerce is an excellent example of a disaster scenario that a competent project manager plans for from the first day of the job. And the scope plan is the tool to create to manage the type and the flow of data throughout the project, as well as to plan for the results of the project.

[B] Using Essential Terms

A number of terms are important to this discussion, but three are essential. They are defined as follows:

An **assumption** is a prediction that something will be true, either an action or an event that ensures project success, such as "there will be identified potential risks, but somehow they will be overcome."

A **constraint** is a parameter, limitation, or a boundary for the project plan such as the budget or the schedule.

The **scope plan** is the strategic view of the constraints and assumptions of the project as developed by the project team.

Adding Supportive Terms

Besides the three essential concepts given above, additional terms, concepts, and document definitions are important when planning and defining the project scope. Some of these terms are essential to discussions in later chapters. In some cases it is not the detail that is important, such as with the documents noted, but the parameters for developing these documents. Details or new data are actually added to many of the documents because of project milestones or even for unforeseen change. You may have to simply state in the scope plan that something has been considered and there is no further need for more details due to reasons that you specify. This action preserves for history your earliest justifications for the project's direction.

Several important project management organizations are also listed for your consideration. So many concepts and terms are given here because the scope plan is the framework or foundation for the whole project.

The additional terms are as follows:

An **activity** at the operational level (a task at the tactical level) is the effort required to achieve a measurable result that uses time and resources.

An **audit** is a formal study of the project as a whole, or a project's component, as to status (progress and results), costs, and procedures.

A **baseline plan** is the initial approved point from which any deviations will be determined using standards and benchmarks.

The **budget** is a plan where costs are organized into debits and credits (expenses and revenues). It is a formal plan that uses a chart of accounts to give structure to estimates for expenses and revenues.

The **Business Affiliate Plan** provides information when the project or a part of the project is to be the responsibility of a third-party developer.

The **Business Justification** is the general rationale for making the financial investment.

The **Commercial Specification** is an evolution of the Business Justification. It identifies the market need and gives adequate requirement and limitation data for the design and development group(s).

MANAGER'S TIP

Without appropriate market research, the project is probably destined to fail. One well-known Internet company failed to keep an eye on Net market trends and began an affiliate marketing project when affiliate marketing was already dead on the Net. The heavy investment required to get the project off the ground was part of the financial drain that brought the company to its knees.

Communication is oral or written transfer of data or information among individuals.

Communications is the process of getting the correct data to the correct person at the correct time in a cost-effective mode.

MANAGER'S TIP

Communications is one of the most fundamental issues that a project manager has to address. Some traditional communications tools are whiteboard diagrams and weekly update meetings, while other collaboration tools (software) can be provided on a company intranet to allow people to share documents and discuss issues. Whichever tools are used, they should be readily available to all project members as well as to any managers involved in the project.

A **confidence level** is the acceptance level of risk usually determined statistically by a percentage of time or cost.

The **Content Agreement** is the written "contract" between the development group and the marketing group as to the content and functions of the project.

Contingency is the rational preparation for change.

Corporate values are a common set of beliefs held by the corporate stakeholders about their business environment.

A **critical path** is when there is no available time for the slippage of the activity or task (no slack time).

A **cross-functional team** is the most common type of team for a corporate IS project and includes many technical and support groups with a multiple set of skills, ideas, goals, attitudes, and so forth.

The **Customer Documentation Strategy** provides how timely, high-quality project documentation becomes available. There really is a triad in quality: control and assurance, documentation, and training.

Dependency means that a task has to be completed before a succeeding task can be completed. For example, coding has to be completed before code testing can be completed.

The **Design and Development Plan** drives the project Integration Plan that captures all major design and development deliverables and milestones for management tracking and reporting.

MANAGER'S TIP

When there is a time crunch, the design phase is often the first part of the project to be squeezed out. This could spell disaster, because the design phase charts the blueprint for project deliverables. In the case of product deliverables, the design specs will help quality management test better and more wisely, as well as ensure consistent quality.

An **event** is a point in time such as the start or end of an activity or a task.

Feedback is an activity that should be held on a regular basis; it is where the status of the project being evaluated can be clearly stated based on measurable standards or benchmarks.

The **Field Introduction Requirements** document reflects the strategy and detailed plans to verify conformance to specification and functionality as defined in the Project Specification.

A **gate** is another term for milestone or a major project event.

Headcount is a factor used by business managers in planning an annual budget, but it should not be used by project managers.

The **Initial Budget Estimates** provides a view of the expected developmental costs. Estimates are usually based on the Preliminary Project Specification. This document is updated in the Project Cost Update.

The **Initial Funding Requirements** document is for monitoring and reporting project costs at each major phase of implementation. It should include comparisons to the original funding document used to establish financial targets and expected milestones and deliverables. This document can also be included in the Project Cost Update.

The **International Organization for Standardization (ISO)** is a consortium that sets standards in a variety of areas.

ISO 9000 is a quality system standard for any product, service, or process.

ISO 9001 is a quality system standard for design, production, and installation of a product or service.

ISO 9002 is a quality system model for quality assurance in production and installation.

ISO 9003 is a quality system model for quality assurance in final inspection and testing.

ISO 9004 is a set of quality management guidelines for any organization to use to develop and implement a quality system.

A **learning curve** is a graphical representation of repetitive tasks that, when done on a continuous basis, lead to a reduction in activity duration, resources, and costs.

A **management review** is a regularly scheduled performance review.

A **milestone** is a clearly defined date of start or of 100 percent completion.

A **node** is a network event that is achieved or is not achieved. A milestone is a node type.

An **operational manager** is a person who handles the day-to-day operations or activities for a specific functional group or area that has been defined in the project plan.

An **organizational chart** is normally a visual representation of who reports to whom. It shows the hierarchical and perhaps functional relationships among organizational groups. The Project Organization Chart must include the core project responsibilities of each team member.

Organizational culture is a common set of assumptions, principles, processes, and structures held or used by members of a corporation, company, or even a project team.

Performance is the measurable level of action to achieve a measurable project goal. It is the act or level of work demonstrated and judged based on identified skill level.

A **phase** is a project segment such as planning, designing, and developing.

PMI stands for the **Project Management Institute,** a professional organization that studies and promotes project management.

Program Evaluation and Review Technique (PERT) was developed for the United States Department of Defense in the late 1950s. Specifically, it was developed by the consulting firm of Booz, Allen, and Hamilton for the U.S. Navy's Polaris submarine project (Polaris Weapon System). It combines statistics and network diagrams.

The **Project Cost Updates** document updates initial project cost estimates at each major phase of implementation with comparison to the Initial Budget Estimate.

A **project's duration** is the total number of calendar days involved from start to end, including the project manager's activities in closing the project.

The **Project Proposal** is a formal response to the Commercial Specification that describes the requirements for a project.

A **project schedule** is the duration (work-time plus the wait-time) of the project cycle.

The **Project Specification** is a formal response to the Commercial Specification that specifies the requirements for a project.

The **Project Support Plan** ensures that the project is supportable in a market environment. This plan should include a process for customer support.

Quality management uses control and assurance to prevent risks and, if a risk occurs, to minimize it.

The **Quality Plan** defines the roles of quality control and assurance in all phases of the project process.

Responsibility is the obligation or accountability given through assignment to complete a specific activity or task.

Role is a skill set with a label that perhaps explains the reasons for the actions and behavior of the actor.

MANAGER'S TIP

At the fictional Internet company depicted in the commercial mentioned earlier, scalability was not adequately addressed. An Internet project scope plan would have to focus on key issues, such as load time or hosting.

Scope defining is extending the measurable goals to become general procedures with measurable constraints and viable assumptions.

Scope planning is defining the project goals and the performance expectations of the goals in measurable terms, and getting agreement on them.

A **task** is a cohesive work unit that is meaningful for tracking; that is a set of activities. Writing a line of code is not a task, but writing a module that handles a specific function is.

A **team** is a group with a common purpose and with skills that compliment one another.

The **Third-Party Market Agreement** provides the plans whereby the entire project or a part of the project is to be the responsibility of a third-party developer.

The **Third-Party Service Plan** defines how the project is to be serviced by a third-party developer.

A **trade-off** is an act of balancing project constraints.

The **Training Strategy** shows how training is to be designed, developed, implemented, and verified.

The **Trial (Beta) Strategy** identifies the software and hardware elements in the project that are a part of any trial. The "where," the "when," and the "whom" should be included in the strategy. This provides a clear identification of the testing requirements plus the extent of the resources and capabilities necessary to trial.

Variance is any deviation from the planned work, whether it is costs, time, or resources.

[C]   Scope Planning Definition

Scope planning is taking the *goals* of the customer and making them *measurable*. The accounting group says they want a firewall to protect their data.

Scope planning is the first action of the project team that also includes activity planning and sequencing, and developing time and cost estimates. All these activities are usually encompassed within the planning phase of the project. There may be only one meeting or the project may require more meetings than anyone desires. A goal of installing a new firewall would probably require far fewer meetings than the goal of installing a new accounting system, which would have rippling impacts across the company.

MANAGER'S TIP

Lifeboats on ships have two sets of numbers painted on them. One is the identification number; the other is the lifeboat capacity. Lifeboats are resources designed for the project of saving lives, but only for a given scope, or number of people. If too many people board the lifeboat, all can be lost. That's why sidearms are issued to the ship's officers when orders are given to abandon ship.

[D]   Scope Defining Definition

Scope defining is extending the measurable goals to become general procedures with measurable constraints and viable assumptions. The details of the procedures are developed during activity planning and sequencing. A scope definition for installing an accounting firewall would include a statement that the firewall should:

- Adhere to the procedures or standards outlined in the corporate security policy.
- Use security standards such as the Digital Encryption Standard (DES).
- Use a server interface from RSA Data Security.

In the above definition, we go from a local procedure to the use of a specific interface. All three actions could actually be used, or only one component. The essential point is that the scope definitions must be measurable. Either you did the specific action or you did not. Beyond this, there are at least two more measurable points that need to be added: cost and time constraints. The operational activities are to produce support data in the activity planning of the project process.

When the team concludes the scope definition, three conceptual items will be stated in measurable terms:

1. Intent
2. Problem
3. Justification

For example, a very simple straightforward scope definition could be:

The intent of the team is to install and configure a firewall from RSA at a specific cost within three months of the acceptance date of the initial project plan.

The measurable problem is that accounting has no formal security protection. The measurable justification is that there has been at least one unauthorized attempt per week to get into the accounting database.

MANAGER'S TIP

A constraint is a parameter, limitation, or boundary for the project plan. An assumption is a prediction that something will be true, either an action or an event that can ensure project success.

[E]   Data Types for Scope Planning

One of the first actions you must take is to establish the goals and performance expectations of your project. Second, you must determine how the individual components of your system (protocols, firewall, servers, e-mail, browsers, etc.) fit into the overall objectives. Actually, it is more than the system's components; it is the system's infrastructure that includes scalability and reliability. You should have as a minimum the following data:

- Benchmarks
  — Performance
  — Validation
  — Risk
  — Data
    * Historical
    * Marketing
- Time Parameters
  — Start Date
  — Milestones
  — End Date
- Selection Criteria
  — Skills
    * Type
    * Level
  — Time Lines
  — Resources

- * People (skills)
- * Equipment
- * Materials
- • Communications
  - — Reports
  - — Documentation
  - — Training
- • Team
  - — Customers
  - — Support
  - — Technical
  - — Management
  - — Marketing

The outline list is not by priority or importance. The priority is your decision.

[F]   Data Types for Scope Defining

The parallel activity to scope planning is scope defining. With scope defining you establish the procedures (constraints and assumptions) for managing the scope plan. Scheduling and budgeting come later in the project process because you must do activity timing and sequencing, resource defining, and cost estimating. Here is a basic outline of the minimum types of scope definition requirements needed in any project:

- • Methodology
  - — Resources
  - — Integration
  - — Communications
    - * Who
    - * When
    - * How
    - * Why
    - * Where
  - — Risk Analysis
  - — Support Services
- • Costing
  - — Direct
    - * Human
    - * Time

         * Equipment

         * Materials

      — Indirect

- Timing
- Responsibilities
  - Support
  - Management
  - Customers
  - Technical
- Quality Controlling
  - Design
  - Development
  - Implementation
  - Testing
  - Validation

To contrast scope planning and scope defining, here is a straightforward example: In the scope plan you state milestones, while in the scope definition you state how you will manage these milestones for success and potential failure.

[G]   Ten Example Questions for Scope Planning

In Chapter 1, we determined basic characteristics for eleven key project areas, including scope planning and defining; it is the nine other activities that use as a baseline the parameters and procedures of the scope plan and definitions. These activities can generate many questions that can be used to clarify or further refine the details of the project scope. Here are 10 examples of questions that refine the scope plan parameters of the project:

WHAT ARE THE CUSTOMER'S MEASURABLE EXPECTATIONS, THE DELIVERABLES? If this question is not answered with a high degree of precision, then your project is built on a sandy beach and it will float out to sea at the next high tide. The fundamental word in the question is *measurable*. There cannot be such a thing as an unspoken priority of the customer. Anything that is not measurable is at its best a dream; at its worst, chaos. This is not a goal: "The project will install a reliable e-mail application in a timely manner." There needs to be no discussion of "timely"; however, what does "reliable" mean? To have a measurable project goal, all specific functions and their benchmarks should be defined for the e-mail application. This includes such things as potential downtime or the number of e-mail messages the customer could retain on the server.

WHAT ARE THE EXPECTED MILESTONES OF THE FINANCIAL SPONSORS OF THE PROJECT?   In any activity sequence there are always the same two doors. The front door is the start date. The back door is the end date. The rest of the activities are a walk through the house. The importance of a scope plan is that you logically plan to see all the rooms in the shortest distance. You need to define the parameters where there are status reports to the funding sponsors to reassure them that expected milestones have been met.

WHAT ARE THE PRIMARY ACTIVITIES THAT HAVE TO BE DONE TO MEET THE EXPECTED DE-FINED GOALS?   This is at the tactical level of planning, so formulating the secondary activities is a responsibility of the operational managers. The scope plan is used as a part of the defining activity to identify:

- People in positions of responsibility
- Logical project phase (design, development, etc.)
- Time estimates
- Cost estimates
- Skills required
- Materials required
- Equipment required

These components usually are resolved as separate questions or as major project functions, and the tactical and operational managers then merge them into one coherent project plan.

WHAT RESOURCES ARE REQUIRED FOR SUCCESS?   This question has three important prongs. The first prong is identifying the people involved and determining their related skills. The second prong is the determination of the people and activities that require special equipment. The third prong is deciding what materials are required, from pencils to special software. The concern here is to determine the relationships of resources to project activities. A method for linking the activities is to identify them as:

- Critical
- Major, but not critical
- Minor

WHAT IS THE NECESSARY TIME FOR QUALITY VALIDATION?   Quality control activities need to be established throughout the schedule. There should be validation activities in the activity sequence. Never schedule all of the quality control for the end or last phase of the project. The fundamental activity is to validate that the measurable goals of the scope plan have been achieved. There has been more than one instance where a military contract has been revoked because of an audit that found failures in achieving nonmeasurable goals.

WHAT IS THE AMOUNT OF TIME ALLOCATED FOR COMMUNICATING PROGRESS? There should be a communications program (sequence). There may be one sequence for the coordinating committee and another for the product development group. There may be different sequences as the product evolves. There should be essential activities during the project to evaluate the success of the communications system. The tactical manager needs to keep the scope plan visible on a continuous basis to all the team members.

HAVE POTENTIAL THREATS AND OPPORTUNITIES BEEN IDENTIFIED FOR SCHEDULE CHANGES? There should be activities in the scope plan that evaluate potential threats and opportunities. You need to consider that a given configuration, such as for a server, may take longer than expected.

WHAT ACTIVITIES OR EXPECTED GOALS REQUIRE TRAINING? A scope plan should include training requirements that are consistent with the measurable goals. Training comes in two forms: internal training to enhance the skills of the team and product training for product users. Even what appears to be the simple installation of an e-mail program requires training. The end-user needs to be comfortable with the interface. Is there such an interface that is completely intuitive except to the developer? The customer needs to be made aware of the constraints of the program. Training could be just sending a short brochure on the use of the product. However, life is usually not that simple, so the training organization probably needs to be involved in a training program for any new product or information system enhancement. The end-users need to have an established "comfort zone."

WHAT ARE THE CRITERIA FOR DOCUMENTING THE PROJECT ACTIVITIES? As with training, there should be a consistent set of document requirements in the scope plan. Some people think the writing group does all documentation, but that is far from the truth. As mentioned earlier, there is a need for project documentation by the project team. There need to be criteria or standards for product design and development documentation. These types of documentation are the foundation for the customer documentation developed by the writing group. The planning activity that has to be done is establishing documentation requirements, and naming who is responsible for writing each document and perhaps even editing it.

WHAT ARE THE STANDARDS AND BENCHMARKS FOR QUALITY CONTROL? Beyond having a defined set of quality control procedures, these procedures should be supported by standards and benchmarks. As used here, a standard is usually an external industry-accepted document for achieving quality for one or more of the project-defined expected goals. Benchmarks are specific technical levels of excellence. These standards and benchmarks should be collected and placed in a location that is available to any team member.

[H] Ten Example Questions for Scope Defining

The sibling of scope planning is scope defining. This procedure involves refining the procedural requirements for the project process. There should be parallel procedures to manage all of the parameters established in the scope plan. There could be one procedure to manage one parameter, several procedures to manage one parameter, or one procedure to manage multiple parameters. Here are 10 examples of basic scope defining questions that use time, cost, and resource estimates:

HOW CAN THE SCOPE DEFINITION FOR IMPLEMENTING THE PROJECT BE USED IN DEVELOPING THE SCHEDULE? In developing the activity sequence, use the scope standards, descriptions, and definitions formulated during scope definition. The constraints and assumptions of the project should be a major factor in developing the sequence and then the schedule.

HAVE DELAYS BEEN CONSIDERED IN THE SCHEDULE? As a part of developing the scope definitions, the time should consider start–end time dependencies and lead–lag-time relationships. You should consider when setting up a schedule that you say the activity is completed from X day to Y day or from X period to Y period. Users need to be aware when their expectations might be fulfilled. The schedule is the duration of the project, production time, and wait time.

HOW DO COST ESTIMATES AFFECT THE SCHEDULE? Costs should be divided over all the phases (planning, designing, developing, controlling, verifying, and implementing) of the project. The assumption here is not that every phase gets an equal share, but each phase gets an equitable share. Never take from the quality control activities to improve another part of the schedule.

HOW DO RESOURCE ESTIMATES AFFECT THE SCHEDULE? You should have a procedure that ensures the resources are available when an activity is scheduled. There is at times the unspoken assumption that resources will be available when required and as ordered. God helps those who help themselves. It is important to define critical resources just as you would define a critical path of actions. A key component of a critical path is the flag that signals when resources must be available. Remember, resources can be skills, equipment, materials, time, or money.

ARE THERE ANY INTERNAL OR EXTERNAL PROCUREMENT POLICIES OR STANDARDS THAT AFFECT THE SCHEDULE? You need to be aware of all procurement policies and procedures that impact the project end date. A project may be stopped or heavily impacted because a policy or a corporate procurement procedure was not followed. An example of an external policy is any federal policy that affects a project goal.

HOW IS TRAINING TO BE ACCOMPLISHED? After the training requirements are planned, the training program has to be defined. A project constraint should be that courses must reflect the project goals. An invalid assumption is that a course will automatically reflect project goals without any project team interaction. It may be that a team member can learn the required skill with at-hand, online training or may have to go to a formal class. Group training requirements have to be defined as to specific learning objectives and training time. Skill training requirements, and any necessary user training, should be defined. A part of this definition should include who pays for this training, directly and indirectly. (Why is "indirectly" used? Because there is the reality that the customer gets "free" training by paying more for the product.)

MANAGER'S TIP

The act of negotiating who pays is not a part of the project process, but the business process. In this case, the IS project manager wears a business manager's hat.

HOW IS DOCUMENTATION TO BE ACCOMPLISHED? After the documentation requirements have been planned, a standard process is needed for writing the documentation. One word processing application of the same version must be used by all writers in all groups. This standardization is important so documentation can be easily exchanged. Cut-and-paste is a significant part of the technical writing world. Criteria should be established on such things as a document template that includes font type and size, location of page numbers, header types, and so on.

HAS AN ORGANIZATIONAL STRUCTURE WITH LINKED RESPONSIBILITIES BEEN DEVELOPED? An organizational chart is normally a visual representation of who reports to whom and shows hierarchical and perhaps functional relationships among organization groups. The project organizational chart needs to include the core project responsibilities of each team member. This does not mean all the responsibilities of each team member, only those associated with the project. This type of chart can establish redundancies, or in a more positive light, backups, in responsibilities.

HAS A COMPREHENSIVE QUALITY ASSURANCE AND CONTROL PROGRAM BEEN DEFINED WITH STANDARDS AND BENCHMARKS? The basis for defining the quality control process is through related standards and benchmarks. Quality control points need to be specified throughout the entire project process. Quality control acts as a reviewer of the scope plan and definition, to verify coherence. The quality control process should be defined separately from the testing and viewed more as the validating process. The function of this program is to monitor for performance errors.

HAS A TIMELY CUSTOMER REVIEW PROGRAM BEEN ESTABLISHED?   Customers or end-users should be a part of the project team. Customers should have an opportunity to review project progress during the design, development, implementation, testing, and validation phases. Usually customers are asked to be involved only in the testing phase, and perhaps at implementation. This is usually the time you actually get the unspoken expectations of the customer that should have been stated during the writing of the measurable project goals.

As you can see, as the team does scope defining, they are also involved in other project functions:

- Activity planning and sequencing
- Cost, time, and resource estimating
- Establishing quality control procedures
- Considering support efforts such as training and documentation

[I]   Eight Scope Plan and Definition Killers

A scope plan is the glue that holds together all of the other project activities. Beware: Many activities that can play the role of scope killer if you do not pay attention to them. The specific reasons for these activities are discussed in detail in the next eight chapters, including:

1. Defining measurable goals and objectives of your project
2. Defining the responsibilities of the people involved in the project
3. Establishing rational milestones
4. Establishing realistic cost and budgetary parameters
5. Determining skill levels versus headcount
6. Developing risk and opportunity management criteria
7. Determining the impact of the use of outside resources (procurement)
8. Having an involved quality assurance and control program that is enforced

All of these activities are probably done almost at a subconscious level by any good project manager. Just in case you are not working on the unconscious level today, below are conscious comments on two important support functions.

Exhibit 2-1: Scope Plan and Definition Questions Checklist

Project Name:	Comments
1. Are there any internal or external procurement policies or standards that affect the schedule?	
2. Has a timely customer review program been established?	
3. Has an organizational structure with linked responsibilities been developed?	
4. Have delays been considered in the schedule?	
5. Have potential threats and opportunities been identified for schedule changes?	
6. Have skill levels been defined?	
7. How can the scope definition for implementing the project be used in developing the schedule?	
8. How do cost estimates affect the schedule?	
9. How do resource estimates affect the schedule?	
10. How is documentation to be accomplished?	
11. How is training to be accomplished?	
12. What activities or expected goals require training?	
13. What are the criteria for documenting the project activities?	
14. What are the funders' expected milestones?	
15. What are the *measurable* customer's expectations, the deliverables?	
16. What are the primary activities required to meet the expected defined goals?	
17. What are the standards and benchmarks for quality control?	
18. What is the amount of time allocated for communicating progress?	
19. What is the necessary time for quality validation?	
20. What resources are required for success?	

[J]   Two Essential Support Functions

The best of us sometimes fail in two areas. This is an overview of these two areas (each function has its own chapter) as they are applicable to scope planning:

1. A quality assurance and control function that intertwines with all activities

2. A documenting function that states what you said you would do and what you have done

---

MANAGER'S TIP

All of the end documents become the final version of the scope plan, a living project document. The project's scope should evolve from the constraints and assumptions of the project's future to the results of the project's history.

Scope Planning and Quality Control Procedures

The following are three questions you need to answer so the dark things in the night do not attack your project.

1. Have the quality standards been made consistent?
2. Has a quality assurance and control system been established?
3. Have verification activities been formulated?

Benchmarks of the quality and performance of the system's infrastructure as related to the project should be established at your earliest planning sessions, not after the project is completed. What are the realistic expectations of your customer(s) based on the defined measurable goals? Get it in writing. You should be as specific as possible about expectations. Everyone will be happier when the project is completed. Use Exhibit 2-2: Goal Analysis Form to each goal of the customer to make sure the project adequately addresses each goal.

Benchmarks should be clearly formulated in the definition of the goals and objectives of the project. The use of external appropriate benchmarks or standards for project activities and for evaluation of the end goal would make your project more valid to the world. This can be significant to your customers and perhaps to yourself.

At the forefront of defining integrating activities should be quality control. Do you know of a project that was completed without a change? You must have activities that show how to handle change. You must establish benchmark actions at the beginning of the project for validating the project's end.

+--+
| **MANAGER'S TIP** |
+--+
| The above points are not negotiable. |
+--+

Exhibit 2-2: Goal Analysis Form

Goal Statement		
Strengths	Advantages	How to Maximize
Weaknesses	Disadvantages	How to Minimize

When you plan your resources, you have to look at all the resource types and in particular how the resources impact the quality of your information system. If a new skill requirement is identified halfway into the project cycle, has a process been defined that can handle this issue? What skills are required to adequately control and verify any project goal and the status of the project?

Across any activity sequence there must be quality control activities. Are there also validation activities in the activity sequence? Never say, "We will do all of the quality control at the end."

Doing time estimates for quality control can be tricky because time estimating can be at certain moments more of an art than a science. There are many time management software packages available to assist you. A specific amount of time should be allocated for quality control. You should set a benchmark of 20 percent of the estimated time for the project. This task should be done at the beginning of the planning phase.

A specific cost estimate should also be established for quality control. Again, you should set a benchmark of 10 to 20 percent of the estimated total cost for the project. This task should be among the first tasks of your integration planning.

Within any schedule the quality control and verification milestones should be clearly defined. The quality control time line may be defined as a separate time line; however, when and where quality control flows into the main project cycle must be stated.

It is recommended to have at least two lines in your budget for quality control. The lines are *controlling* and *assuring*. You may want to divide these two lines into salaries, equipment, and materials.

[K]   Scope Planning and Related Documentation

This is an abbreviated discussion of the document types that are applicable to scope planning. You need to be familiar with all possibilities so you are prepared to ask for the information and also be prepared to give information to others when you determine this is vital to the success of the process.

In a later chapter, there is a discussion of these documents in detail and the development of templates for them. Here is a list of potential documents that you may find useful because they have their origin in the scope plan or are inputs to it:

- Market Analysis Report
- Business Justification
- Commercial Specification
- Organizational Chart
- Project Proposal
- Project Specification
- Content Agreement
- Schedule
- Design and Development Plan
- Initial Budget Estimate
- Initial Funding Requirements
- Project Cost Update
- Quality Plan
- Trial Strategy

- Field Introduction Requirements
- Project Support Plan
- Customer Documentation Strategy
- Training Strategy
- Communication Plan
- Business Justification Update
- Risk Assessment
- Business Affiliate Plan
- Third-Party Documents

Market Analysis Report

This report documents and verifies market opportunities. The report is the justification for the features, services, and applications for the project goals. The report should include adequate descriptions of the input so the IS project manager has sufficient information to make design decisions. The report should also include revenue gains. The counter to this is a statement on revenue losses if this activity is not taken.

Business Justification

This document is the general rationale for making the financial investment. The Business Justification may include:

- Competition data
- Concept (as compared to definition)
- Distribution strategy
- Impact on products
- Market need
- Market window
- Required functions and characteristics
- Return on investment (ROI)

Commercial Specification

This specification is an evolution of the Business Justification and identifies the market need. The specification gives adequate requirement and limitation data for the design and development group(s). There should be design flexibility to achieve expectations. The Commercial Specification describes *in detail* what the project requirements are and for what targeted market.

Organizational Chart

There should be an organizational chart of the team, with a description of major project responsibilities. There must be a detailed statement of the IS project manager's responsibilities. All other responsibility statements should be linked to this description. The format of the chart should be at your discretion or in accordance with corporate policy.

Project Proposal

This proposal is a formal response to the Commercial Specification that describes the business requirements for a project.

Project Specification

This specification is also a formal response to the Commercial Specification that specifies the technical requirements for a project. There should be a section on possible noncompliance that describes deviations from the Commercial Specification.

Content Agreement

This agreement is the written "contract" between the development group and the marketing group as to the content and functions of the project. This should include the following:

- Hardware requirements (availability status)
- How end users use the project's functional results
- Software features and requirements
- Start and end dates for completion of the project

Schedule

The schedule can be as elaborate as required to implement your project. It should be useable. There could also be links to key players and groups and their responsibilities to the implementation of the project goals. The quality control milestones and the verification milestones should be included.

Design and Development Plan

This plan drives the project Integration Plan that captures all major design and development deliverables and milestones for management tracking and reporting.

Initial Budget Estimate

This document provides a view of the expected development costs. The estimate is usually based on the Preliminary Project Specification. The document gives estimates for direct labor as well as capital and expense requirements. This document is updated in the Project Cost Update.

Initial Funding Requirements

This document is for monitoring and reporting project costs at each major phase of implementation. There should be comparisons to the original funding document used to establish financial targets and expected milestones and deliverables. This document can also be included in the Project Cost Update.

Project Cost Update

This document updates initial project cost estimates at each major phase of implementation with comparison to the Initial Budget Estimate. The concern here is how the costs (actual expenditures) and revenues go into the budget (the financial plan). The costs are usually reported on a monthly basis.

Quality Plan

This plan defines the role of quality control in all phases of the project process. It also defines the deliverables, functions, and specific activities required of quality control to ensure the successful completion. Quality procedures that are specific to each project goal should also be identified in an appendix of this document. The Quality Plan should be updated before each major phase review to reflect changes.

Trial (Beta) Strategy

This strategy identifies the software and hardware elements in the project that are a part of any trial. It should include where, when, and by whom the trial will be conducted. This provides a clear identification of the testing requirements plus the extent of the resources and capabilities being tested. Remember that strategy is planning the position of the battle.

Field Introduction Requirements

This document reflects the strategy and detailed plans to verify conformance to specification and functionality as defined in the Project Specification. This document should be concerned with such events as how the customers become users of the project.

Project Support Plan

This plan ensures that the project is supportable in a market environment. This plan should include a process for customer support.

Customer Documentation Strategy

This strategic document provides how timely quality project documentation becomes available. There really is a triad in Quality: Control, Documentation, and Training.

Training Strategy

This document can have two components: internal requirements and customer requirements (external). The strategy should show how training is to be designed, developed, implemented, and verified. The emphasis of the strategy should be based on the customer's needs and expectations.

Communications Plan

The Communications Plan should have a global component as well as "local" communications processes. You may desire a local form so your developers can communicate to one another on status.

Business Justification Update

This document tracks the implementation of any project goals that have performance criteria to assure that they meet previous commitments and management expectations. The update may have a one or more years' view of:

- Revenues
- Maintenance Costs
- Investment
- Return on Investment (ROI)
- Customer Impact

Risk Assessment

It is important that any risk assessment consider both threats and opportunities. The risk assessment should be against established thresholds. An example of a threshold is that no action is taken until a certain number of errors are found within a given constraint.

Business Affiliate Plan

This plan provides information when the project or a part of the project is to be the responsibility of a third-party developer.

Third-Party Market Agreement

This agreement provides the plans where the project or a part of the project is to be the responsibility of a third-party developer.

Third-Party Service Plan

This plan provides how the project is to be serviced by a third-party developer. The question is, "Will the third party do customer service?"

[L] Changes in the Scope Plan and Definitions

Changes to the scope plan can come intentionally or unintentionally. An intentional change could be because of a technological breakthrough that causes a goal to be changed or because a standard is changed that requires a change to the scope plan. An unintentional change could be the team looking at the data that has to be protected and finding that the accounting group also uses data from the human resource group; the new firewall would also have to protect this data. Another example would be the accounting group and the procurement group both finding that their databases needed mutual security of the firewall.

These kinds of changes are corrupting and beguiling. They can destroy your cost and time estimates more quickly than a rapidly rising tide can destroy your sandcastle. These changes test the mettle of the project manager.

The changes are never benign unless they lessen cost and time estimates. Here are a few more examples that you, the project manager, need to look out for; they can come at any time and from any direction:

- The customer asks for a change and believes it is not really a change. For example, the customer wants the security level to be elevated from minimum to medium.

- The customer asks for a monthly status report on the security server or the need for a "small" functional change.

- The team wants to be helpful to the customer and do a little extra service, like creating a customized interface to the firewall so the accounting manager can do "something" with the firewall. This is the kind of thing that provides material for the Dilbert cartoons.

What can you do about these types of changes? You need to cut them off at the pass. You need to be proactive by

- Getting everyone at the kickoff meeting to sign off on the scope plan and definitions
- Keeping the scope plan actively present through an "info campaign"
- At each weekly review, discussing the status of the scope plan
- When an operational manager wants to make a technical change, ensuring that it does not change the scope plan intentionally or unintentionally
- Ensuring that quality control looks for scope changes

[M]   Determining Valid Data Types and Data

Frequently the phrase "scope creep" is used to express a problem of project management. Creep implies a very slow movement. Actually, the phrase might be better phrased as "scope earthquake." When there is a poorly defined scope plan without measurable objectives and without associated procedural standards and performance benchmarks there is a potential risk for disaster that is like an earthquake—hidden, sudden, destructive, and deadly.

Without a well-defined scope plan and its support documents such as the Business Justification, there is not an objective baseline for negotiations on customer expectations, valid cost and time estimates, and workable schedule and budget.

Exhibit 2-3: Data Type-Data Refinement for a Scope Plan is an example form of 20 survey questions, plus instructions that you must consider five additional variants for each question. The survey is used to get the assessable assumptions and constraints for defining valid estimates (cost, time, and resources) and parameters of the project. The form is based on the terms and procedures discussed in this chapter to get a set of data types and data used in the scope plan to stop "creep."

MANAGER'S TIP

WARNING: If you think you do not have time to use the form, recognize your house (that is, the project) is being built on sand with the tide coming in rapidly. Would you feel comfortable to travel to an unknown location by the shortest route without the use of a map? The scope plan is a map; you have to decide how precise the map needs to be so you are either a project manager or a project firefighter.

The scope plan sets the "mode" or "manner" for all of the other project documents. It is the standard and the benchmark for all of these documents.

Exhibit 2-3: Data Type/Data Refinement for a Scope Plan

1. What are the measurable customer's goals and deliverables?
2. How will the goals be funded and budgeted?
3. What are the critical activities for achieving the critical goals?
4. What resources are critical for success?
5. What are the criteria for defining pessimistic, realistic, and optimistic estimates?
6. Have potential threats and opportunities been identified for schedule changes?
7. What activities or expected goals require training?
8. What are the criteria for documenting the project activities?
9. How should the project's scope definition be used to develop the schedule?
10. Where have delays been factored into the schedule?
11. How do cost estimates affect the schedule?
12. How do resource estimates affect the schedule?
13. Are there any internal or external procurement policies or standards that affect the schedule?
14. How is training to be accomplished?
15. How is documentation to be accomplished?
16. Who is to create the organizational structure that links responsibilities activities and deliverables?
17. What are the standards and benchmarks for the quality assurance and control program?
18. What are performance criteria for the quality control assurance program?
19. What is the necessary time for quality validation?
20. Who should be involved in a customer review?

Instructions for the Scope Data Type/Data Refinement Form

Basic Terms

Five basic definitions are used for consistency of responses when forms are filled out:

The **scope plan** is the strategic view of the constraints and assumptions of the project as developed by the project team.

A **constraint** is a parameter, limitation, or a boundary for the project plan.

An **assumption** is a prediction that something will be true.

A **scope definition** is a measurable goal that becomes general procedures with measurable constraints and viable assumptions.

Scope planning is defining the goals and performance expectations of your project goals in measurable terms and getting an agreement on them.

Exhibit 2-3 (*Continued*)

Warnings

- The space given on the form is not to be considered a constraint as to length of response.

- Each response on the form should be completed and either read "See attachment XXX," or "No response is required."

- Each attachment needs a clear identifier so each can be associated correctly with the main form.

- Each response needs three estimate scenarios: pessimistic, realistic, and optimistic. The criteria for each scenario must also be given.

- Each question must be answered in the context of who, what, where, why, when, and how. For example, the last question on the form has five variants that need to be considered in the completed response:
  - How should you manage a customer review?
  - Why should there be a customer review?
  - When should you hold a customer review?
  - Where should you hold a customer review?
  - What are the assumptions and constraints for holding a customer review?

Specific Instructions

1. Goals and deliverables are data types. The actual customer goals and deliverables are data.

2. Is the funding in weekly, monthly, or quarterly increments?

3. The critical items define the critical path. A critical path is the minimum activities that can be achieved in the least time to do the defined measurable goals that are necessary to complete the project.

4. Critical resources are the minimal required resources as defined in a pessimistic scenario.

5. These criteria need to be based on objective sources (standards and performance benchmarks) and defined prior to writing estimates.

6. A threat is not necessarily a risk. A risk produces project failure. An opportunity can be used to reduce a project's duration or funding.

7. Training includes hands-on learning curves. The lack of defining the informal training may cause a bigger risk than the defined training events.

8. Documentation requirements because of project goals should be considered in the manner as the training requirements. A document on a software application or utility should not be written without input from the programmers.

9. The scope plan should include event durations, milestones, and so forth. These should be used to create a visual schedule.

10. Factored delays are contingencies, not padding.

11. A cost estimate may generate a budget item. When the funding is available does affect the schedule.

12. A resource estimate may generate a budget item. When the resource is available does affect the schedule.

13. Corporate procurement policies and procedures that potentially affect the scope of the project need to be explained.

14. Training may be internal, external, hands-on, formal, or informal. There might be online courses, classroom experiences, text, or seminars.

Exhibit 2-3 (*Continued*)

15. Documentation can be produced by a writing group, technical personnel, or purchased out-of-the-box.

16. The "who" of this question is not necessarily an individual; it can be a team.

17. There must be identified procedural standards and performance benchmarks for any quality program. The standards can be external (organizations or companies) and/or internal (corporate, IS, or project team developed).

18. Quality assurance's performance criteria should be based on objective criteria from the standards and benchmarks collected in response to question 17.

19. Validation should be defined at the beginning of the project, not as an afterthought.

20. The response may be more an emotional one than a rational one. Begin by defining what you mean by a customer review.

A Potential Scope Plan Structure

The following is a potential 10-part scope plan:

1. Scope definition
2. Project assumptions and constraints
3. Authority statement
4. Organizational structure with responsibility links
5. Baseline plan
6. Estimate criteria
7. Communication program
8. Risk management parameters
9. Training program
10. Documentation program

Support Documents Used with the Scope Plan

Business Affiliate Plan
Business Justification
Commercial Specification
Content Agreement
Customer Documentation Strategy
Design and Development Plan
Field Introduction Requirements
Initial Budget Estimates
Initial Funding Requirements
Market Analysis Report
Project Cost Updates
Project Proposal
Project Specification
Project Support Plan
Quality Plan
Statement of Work (SOW)
Third-Party Market Agreement
Third-Party Service Plan
Training Strategy
Trial (Beta) Strategy

§ 2.02 MANAGEMENT INVOLVEMENT

[A] Overview

At this point in the project process all management levels are directly involved. "Directly" here means that the strategic manager is present in person at least at one occasion of the scope planning and defining activities, namely the first meeting.

[B] Strategic Scope Planning and Defining

The strategic manager should attend the first meeting and state at a minimum the following:

- The project supports certain corporate goals.
- The tactical manager has full authority to manage this project to its conclusion.
- Here are the conclusions of the evaluation we conducted for starting the project (based on the 20 questions given in the previous chapter).

By doing this in military terminology, the strategic manager, the general, has established the position of the battlefield. In emotional terms it will establish:

- Positive feelings in the team players, the soldiers, as to the importance of the tasks
- That the project manager can make decisions without delays
- That the goals of the project have already been deemed to have corporate value

[C] Tactical Scope Planning and Defining

The tactical manager's primary responsibility is to ensure that there are measurable defined goals in the scope plan and definition.

- This task may seem impossible to do; do not rush. Would you like to drive over a bridge that was built without any design plans?
- You should not be pressured in planning; the results are guesses, not managing.
- You need to use historical data, but leave "we have done this before" attitude in a locked closet.
- The only silly question is the unasked question.
- You should focus on the customer's needs rather than on the technical needs.

- Recognize that everything has equal value.
- Remember the most important word in any project process: *client* or *customer.*

There is one guiding principle for the tactical manager over all others: Never seek understanding. How do you measure understanding? Understanding is a very vague concept. You need to seek written agreement and as tight a set of measurable scope definitions as possible. Understanding is similar to building your castle on sand.

You need to manage the scope plan and its definitions as a contract. In a contract you have to identify constraints, the baseline, the terms, valid considerations, schedule, budget, required reports, monitoring procedures (all the various control mechanisms), and the cost procedures (historical and financial).

[D]   Operational Scope Planning and Defining

The operational managers should assist the tactical manager in fulfilling that manager's primary responsibility by acquiring the support data to have realistic measurable goals.

- Recognize that creating the scope plan and definition is a team effort.
- Remember the purpose of the project: customer satisfaction.
- Remember, you are accountable for some part of the project process on a day-to-day basis and you need to set forth a realistic set of measurable responsibilities to the tactical manager and to the team.
- Identify how you and your team can be most efficient and effective in achieving the defined project goals for the scope plan and definition in a timely and cost-efficient manner.
- Do not let your specialized concern—whether it be technical, training, documenting, or marketing—override listening to what the customer has to say.

On the CD-ROM

On the CD-ROM are:

1. Exhibit 2-1 Scope Plan and Definition Questions Checklist.doc

2. Exhibit 2-2 Goal Analysis Form.doc

3. Exhibit 2-3 Data Type-Data Refinement for a Scope Plan.doc

4. Chapter 2 Overview.ppt—Chapter Overview, Scope Planning and Defining

---

Chapter 3

Activity Planning and Sequencing

§ 3.01 OVERVIEW

[A] Objectives

At the end of this chapter, you will be able to:

- State a definition for activity planning.
- State a definition for activity sequencing.
- Identify 10 data types required for an activity definition.

- State seven required categories of information for sequencing planned activities.

- Ask 20 basic questions on activity planning and sequencing such as: How do available resources impact the activity sequence? How should the scope plan be used in activity planning and sequencing? What are the criteria for a correct activity sequence? What are the quality control procedures that ensure correct sequencing? What are the required activities? What is the basic sequence of the project goals?

- Use 20 key words to assist in sorting activity sequences.

- Ask 10 questions to develop an activity plan of the introduction of Java into the information system.

- Identify how the three managing levels are involved in activity planning and sequencing.

MANAGER'S TIP

Consider the real-life case of a software startup company with limited resources, in which the head of development also functioned as the creative director. That meant that the company's first product would be the design of one person with almost unlimited authority and no one to answer to. When the first build of the technologically sophisticated product was complete, the potential clients who were interested in the application were very unhappy with the look and feel of the user interface.

Because there had been no design phase written into the development (activity) plans, there was never an adequate critique of the user interface, even at the internal level. This lack of planning lengthened development time because a new user interface—with more intuitive navigation and more commercial visual design—had to be designed.

In other words, the Activity Plan must include all aspects in the development of a project, including the design implementation phases, if applicable.

[B]   Using Essential Terms

While there are a number of terms important to this discussion, 11 terms are essential:

An **activity** at the operational level (a task at the tactical level) is the effort required to achieve a measurable result that uses time and resources.

An **event** is a point in time such as the start or end of an activity or task.

A **task** is a cohesive work unit that is meaningful for tracking a set of activities. Writing a line of code is not a task, but writing a module that handles a specific function is. A task is a set of activities.

A **deliverable** is a clearly defined project result, product, or service.

A **milestone** is a clearly defined date of start or date of 100 percent completion of a set of tasks.

A **gate** is another term for milestone or a major project event.

The **activity plan** is a set of definitions that includes the task constraints from the Scope Plan.

Activity planning is documenting a plan that establishes constraints and assumptions for any tasks taken during the project process.

Activity sequencing is the determination of a logical order of activities or tasks that are used in developing a realistic and achievable schedule.

A **constraint** is a parameter, limitation, or a boundary for the project plan such as the budget or the schedule.

An **assumption** is a prediction that something will be true, either a task or an event that ensures project success such as "there will be identified potential risks, but they will be overcome."

[C]   Activity Planning Definition

Activity planning is documenting a plan that establishes constraints and assumptions for any action taken during the project process. This is detailing the scheme. It is stating how a goal is to be accomplished. Any of the following is a specialized or support instance of activity planning:

- Activity sequencing
- Resource estimating
- Time estimating
- Cost estimating
- Risk defining

Some of the documents of activity planning are:

- Project Plan
- Schedule
- Budget
- Quality control project procedures
- Risk management controls

Activity planning is at the tactical level of project management. The activity doing is at the operational level within the constraints of the activity plan. Another definition of activity planning is the establishing of the project parameters. An associated basic definition of project management is ensuring that project operational actions adhere to the project parameters within the context of resources, time, and cost.

Information system (IS) project management focuses on the plans and actions required to achieve measurable and defined goals in a computer-based environment. Computer or IS jargon has to be merged with project management jargon. I know that I am doing IS project management when I see an activity plan statement that says something like the following:

"The goal of this project is to introduce a firewall from vendor 'X' in our system by 'D' date at 'C' cost and that its installation will be validated using quality control standard G1942." The key word of course is firewall.

[D]   Activity Sequencing Definition

Activity sequencing is the determination of a logical order of activities that are used in developing a realistic and achievable schedule. Developing a schedule is first a combination of time estimates and sequenced (ordered) activities. Second, the schedule includes start–end dependencies and lag–lead-time relationships.

For a small project, all you need is a pencil and sticky notes to establish a basic sequence. For example, you could write your activities on sticky notes and then stick them to the wall or on your desktop until a logical order and associations are made. This is an inexpensive and very effective method of sequencing.

The metaquestion is, "What is the best type of activity sequencing so that it communicates the quickest, cheapest, and most effective form of enterprise network integration?" One form of activity sequencing is the Critical Path Method (CPM). CPM in its simplest form is selecting the "must" activities, doing them in the shortest possible amount of time, and covering the shortest duration. One should also use project management software to assist in creating various scenarios.

[E]   Ten Data Types for Activity Defining

An activity plan is a set of definitions. A definition includes the activity's parameters or constraints from the scope plan. There should be measurable components to any activity definition. One would not say, "You should not spend too much on this activity," but one should state that the budget includes a specific amount of money for this project. You should have as a minimum the following 10 types of data for the activity definitions:

- Phases
  — Design
  — Development

- — Testing
- — Implementation
- — Validation
- Costs (all directed toward the budget)
  - — Functions
  - — Applications
  - — Services
- Sequence
  - — First
  - — Milestones
  - — Last
- Communications
- Procurement
- Team responsibility
- Support
- Management
- Technical
- Customer

A simple activity definition could include these ten items:

ACTIVITY:

TIME:

COST:

SKILLS:

EQUIPMENT:

MATERIALS:

PROJECT PHASE:

RISKS:

REQUIREMENT LEVEL:

OWNER:

[F]   General Activity Sequencing Information

At the end of doing activity sequencing, you should have a clear statement as to order of activities and their relationships to one another, including variables of time, people, equipment, materials, and cost. The usual presentation is a flow chart. Here is some of the information you should have as a result of this activity:

- Communications points (status reports)
- Critical path (optional management tool, but highly recommended at any time)
- Equipment acquisition points
- Quality control and verification activities
- Resource input activities sequenced with the operational activities
- Sequence based on the project phases, from design to implementation
- Visual sequence of the activities

[G] Ten Example Questions for Activity Planning

The 10 questions that follow should assist you in either formulating your activity plan or in identifying omissions in the plan. Remember, the activity plan is not the plan for operational activities but the constraints and assumptions for performing the operational activities.

DOES EACH ACTIVITY HAVE ASSOCIATED COST, TIME ESTIMATION, RESOURCE REQUIREMENTS, QUALITY CONTROL BENCHMARKS, DESIGNATED RESPONSIBLE ACTIVITY LEADER, AND POSSIBLE RISK FACTORS? For any activity definition to be complete, one needs to know that all the bases have been considered. An activity may include just a simple statement such as, "There are no known risks." This statement documents that you did consider the risk factors, whereas its omission leaves an open question.

HAVE CRITERIA FOR DEFINING A CRITICAL ACTIVITY BEEN CREATED? Before any activity is labeled critical, you should have created criteria for defining an activity critical. Why? You need an objective benchmark. Anyone may think his or her activity is the most important to the project. Criteria should be based on the defined expected outcomes. The opening question for establishing the criteria is, "What types of activities must be done to complete a goal within a timely manner?" Obviously the development of this set of criteria should be near the top of the agenda for activity planning.

HAVE CRITERIA FOR STRATEGIC, TACTICAL, AND OPERATIONAL ACTIVITIES BEEN CREATED? There are strategic activities beyond just the involvement of the strategic manager. Strategic reviews by the team are needed to look at the overall status of the project. At least one of this type of review needs to be at the end of each project phase. Operational activities are the support activities to the tactical activities and are the responsibility of the operational managers. Any important implications that are found in developing the operational activities should be brought to the table for the team to consider—or at least for the consideration of the tactical manager. The tactical manager's responsibility is the project process. It may be difficult for an IS project manager to review operational activities, as that person wears two hats, tactical and operational. The tactical hat has to always come first.

HOW DOES THE AVAILABILITY OF RESOURCES IMPACT THE ACTIVITY PLAN? An important resource to discuss is the skill levels required. Headcount is not a valid resource. The availability or unavailability of a resource may make an activity critical. In addition, special equipment that is not available within the company needs to be identified. The method for acquiring the equipment should be identified. If consultants are needed, then the implications of corporate procurement policies need to be added to the definition.

HOW SHOULD THE SCOPE PLAN BE USED IN ACTIVITY PLANNING? The scope plan, one of the earliest documents of the project process, should be used to write the project plan. All tactical activity plans need to be linked to the defined goals in this document. Any support documents such as documents of the IS infrastructure or historical data should be used in parallel to answering this question.

WHAT ARE THE CRITERIA FOR CREATING AN ACTIVITY PLAN? This is the first item on the activity planning agenda. These criteria are required to distinguish between tactical and operational activities. These criteria should be based on the defined customer needs, not on technical needs. If a technical requirement is found to have major risk implications, then the original goal needs to be negotiated with the customer. One should not use an alternative technical solution that may or may not achieve the goal.

WHAT ARE THE DOCUMENTATION PREREQUISITES FOR THE ACTIVITY? An activity that has to be defined is the parameters for documentation. There should be a document trace throughout a project. One learns the requirement for a documentation trace if your company goes for ISO 9000–9004 certification. It should be acknowledged that design documents may be used by the writing group to develop user documentation or the same documents may be used by the training group to develop one or more courses because of the project results.

WHAT ARE THE QUALITY CONTROL PROCEDURES THAT NEED TO BE IN THE ACTIVITY PLAN? There should be quality assurance and control procedures to cover all activities, not just the results of operational activities. The quality control team can be used as an objective benchmark for viewing project status as long as they do not get too involved in red tape. The procedures need to emphasize the objective of minimizing performance errors that may result in potential risks.

WHAT ARE THE CRITERIA FOR RISK MANAGEMENT THAT MAY IMPACT ACTIVITIES? These criteria are not necessarily based on sophisticated risk analysis but on the experiences of the team. If the team lacks in experience, perhaps it is advisable for an outside expert to give advice on these criteria. A risk is a performance error that can have a disastrous effect on the project's outcome.

WHAT ARE THE TRAINING REQUIREMENTS FOR THE ACTIVITY? There is training required to meet the goals of the project and there is training because of the achievement of the goals. The first type of training needs to focus on skills. One should know the amount of time required on an individual basis and group basis, and this amount needs to be factored into the cost estimates. The second type is user training. This comes in two flavors, company and customer. There needs to be a set of measurable training objectives developed during the project process and then implemented in a realistic manner.

[H] Ten Example Questions for Activity Sequencing

Do not confuse activity sequencing with scheduling. The schedule includes the activity and the amount of time that the activity requires to be completed in a logically defined timetable and includes start–end dependencies and the lag–lead-time relationships. You need to first decide the relationship of the product to the process status; that is, you design a product before you develop it.

In the next section is a set of key words that could be used to assist you in activity sequencing. The questions here help you identify any gaps in the sequences. Would you sequence a configuring activity before installing it? In a project with 5,000 activities, one might actually make this mistake without a distinctive notation.

HOW DO DOCUMENTATION REQUIREMENTS IMPACT THE PROJECT SEQUENCE? You need to document design, development, testing, and implementation activities. A short way of saying this is you should document all project strategic and tactical activities. You need to have documentation on operational activities that impact the end goals. The technical group may have its own requirements, but there should be specific documentation standards and templates for your project. All documents should have one ultimate focus, the customer's needs. If there is a user document, when does the writing group need this information and at what level? If there are changes in the operational method to achieve the project goals, how do they impact end documentation?

HOW DOES POTENTIAL TRAINING IMPACT THE PROJECT SEQUENCE? If you are lacking in certain skill levels, how does this impact any activity sequence? If the impact is significant, perhaps you need to procure outside consultants with the required skill levels. Do users have to be trained to use the results of the project? For example, if you are installing a new application, such as one for e-mail, do the users need to be trained? If so, what are the activities that require their training? Training may be as simple as sending out an informational bulletin with the details on using the basic functions. Do not forget to include information on how to use the help function.

HOW DO PROCUREMENT POLICIES IMPACT THE PROJECT SEQUENCE?   You need to identify any procurement policies or procedures that might affect any activities that involve the use of outside sources. These policies may require certain operational activities that ultimately impact one or more tactical activities. An example is that you might need three separate bids to use any outside consultant. A supplemental question is, "Are there any corporate policies that might impact your project activities?"

HOW DOES THE AVAILABILITY OF RESOURCES IMPACT THE PROJECT SEQUENCE?   Resources are skills, equipment, materials, time, and money. You need to sequence an activity to acquire the equipment. It is important to define critical resources in the same manner you would for a critical path of activities. On a very large project you might create a procedure for handling required resources at the tactical manager's level.

HOW DOES THE BUDGETARY CYCLE IMPACT THE PROJECT SEQUENCE?   Is the budgetary reporting cycle monthly or quarterly? How does the annual budget cycle affect the project? Before you get to the budget, you must make cost estimates. Costs should be planned over all the phases of the project (planning, designing, developing, controlling, implementing, and verifying). There is always the temptation to take from quality control to support another activity. This is a bad temptation.

HOW SHOULD THE SCOPE PLAN BE USED IN ACTIVITY SEQUENCING?   In developing the activity sequences you should use the standards, descriptions, and definitions formulated for the scope plan. The parameters and constraints stated in the scope plan should assist in determining the sequences of the project activities. Are some goals more important than others? If so, then the activity sequence directed toward those goals should also be given a higher priority.

SHOULD THE CRITICAL PATH METHOD (CPM) BE USED FOR SEQUENCING?   If you established criteria for what activities are critical, then you probably also want to use the Critical Path Method. A project management tool such as CPM does become useful for resolving a critical path quickly using various scenarios. In addition, the development of a critical path can be used as a benchmark for developing other activity sequences. There is no such thing as a single line sequence. You should have a set of linked activity sequences for the major planning areas and even sequences for each project goal.

WHAT ARE THE CRITERIA FOR IDENTIFYING THE SEQUENCE OF ACTIVITIES? The criteria depend on the size of the project. The criteria for sequencing are determined by such things as the number of goals, the use of a critical path, the number of planning areas, and the number of operational groups.

WHAT ARE THE QUALITY CONTROL PROCEDURES THAT ENSURE CORRECT SEQUENCING? Quality control considerations are universal to all activities. You need to establish quality control activities linked into all project sequences. There need to be validation points throughout the project.

WHAT ARE THE TYPES OF LINKS FOR DEVELOPING THE SEQUENCE? The obvious links are tactical ones to the operational areas, quality control, and links among the sequences that relate to training and documentation. Links are the solution to the multiple activity sequences. This is an instance where the use of a sophisticated project management software tool is of great value to the tactical manager.

[I]   Using Key Words for Sequencing

Automated project management software tools are available to aid in the sequencing of your project. The tools are also let you establish a schedule. Remember, a schedule is a set of sequenced activities with associated time, based on activities and their dependencies. The advantage of an application such as Microsoft's Project or IMSI's TurboProject is not the ease of input but the types of visual output and the ability to develop scenarios easily. The input needs to be reliable or the output will be garbage.

One can use sophisticated project management software; however, even with the best program, one needs to do some up-front thinking. Here is an example of a technique you can use with two easily available tools from Microsoft: Excel and Word. In either case, you enter key words in the first column and, if necessary, refining words in the next column. After you have entered all the activities, you simply do a sort on column A, column B, and so on. The following list was sorted using this method. You have a type of activity related to each key word, so that you know all the activities in a phase such as the design phase. With a sorted list it is easier to enter this data in a project management application. The following are 20 recommended key words:

- Analysis
- Assign

- Configure
- Design
- Development
- Document
- Draft
- Edit
- Final
- Implement
- Install
- Introduce
- Notify
- Preliminary
- Report
- Review
- Step N
- Test
- Train
- Validate

[J]   Creating a Task Identification Checklist

A major project document is the activity plan, which really is a task plan. A task is a group of activities. An activity is the smallest management unit for the day-to-day operational area. The activity plan, contrary to its title, should not be bogged down in the minutiae of operational activities, but unfortunately this does happen. Exhibit 3-1, Task Identification Checklist, is an example form of 14 questions, plus instructions on how to consider six additional variants for each question, which you really need to do.

You need to use a formal process of reviewing the tasks and their sequences to meet the project measurable goal. You build your cost, time, resource, and skill estimates with durable concrete rather than with adobe, which might come apart in a heavy rain.

A standard statement about project failure is that failure is probably caused by "bad" cost or time estimates. One worker in an interview said that he had worked on four projects and three of them failed. He stated the projects failed because of "poor" estimates.

If one identifies failure based on "poor" cost and time estimates, then one must also identify the reasons for the "poor" estimates. If you justify each of your project tasks, your involvement in the project will not be a reason for failure.

MANAGER'S TIP

A project can fail because a person in upper management might arbitrarily decide that it might make the manager look good to cut funding to the project, thus causing project failure. You may be angry at the decision, but at least you can look yourself in the mirror and know you were professional in handling your project responsibilities.

In the current economic climate, many projects are being terminated even in apparently healthy companies as a means of cutting costs. Other projects that are in full swing may suffer resource or budget cutbacks. In these circumstances, project managers must remain flexible, able to rethink scope, and, if necessary, oversee the redesign and retasking of a project.

[K]   Activity Plan Structure

The structure (the data types) of your activity plan should be based on criteria developed using questions such as those given above. These criteria should also be used to determine your data types and data requirements. Thus, the first step in developing any form or checklist is to identify common and related groups of criteria. You must use one form for each task scenario. There may be functional differences, but you may have more data types in common than you might think. The Statement of Work is, of course, dependent on the project type.

The two important sets of data types are all of the task assumptions and task constraints. These probably will flow out of the project assumptions and constraints that were fully defined in the project plan.

Another step in developing data is to consider all the tasks needed for a deliverable, and then all the activities required for a given task. Next, you need do an analysis of what data are required by milestone or gate. At this point of activity sequencing, you would need to include the start and end dates.

Besides using the essential definitions, you must look also at the supportive definitions. An activity uses resources—that is, money, time, skills, hardware, or software. As it does so, you need to have estimates. One way to define resources is to label them as critical, major, or minor; the most common way to define estimates is as pessimistic, realistic (which is most likely), or optimistic.

MANAGER'S TIP

In the Program Evaluation and Review Technique (PERT), an optimistic time estimate is an improvement only 1 time in 20, while a pessimistic time is the negative of this ratio. Before doing any estimates, you should decide the criteria for each of these three estimate types.

The activity plan becomes the foundation for the formal schedule. Data requirements are determined by the corporate and project environments. The following is an example of a structure or chapters for an activity plan, which in turns implies types of data required:

1. Project goals and deliverables
2. Project assumptions and constraints
3. Criteria for estimates
4. Critical tasks and their critical activities
5. Skills criteria
6. Contingency criteria
7. Finance
8. Communications
9. Procurement
10. Quality management and verification
11. Training
12. Documentation
13. Risk management tasks
14. Appendixes
    - Contingency Plan
    - Slippage Policy
    - Market Analysis Report
    - Initial Funding Requirements
    - Initial Budget Estimates
    - Quality Plan

Numbers 7 through 13 of this activity plan could have a separate section for each project phase such as design, development, testing, implementation, and verification.

The simplest form for any project activity is as follows:

Estimate	Optimistic	Realistic	Pessimistic
Cost			
Time			
Equipment			
Material			
Skill			

§ 3.02   EXAMPLE OF ACTIVITY PLANNING AND SEQUENCING: INTRODUCTION OF JAVA

[A]   Overview

The example of activity planning given here is a very brief process template for the introduction of Java into your information system. The questions are to establish a foundation for activity planning. The first step is to identify the key characteristics of the product, the goal. The second step is to ask refining questions using these characteristics to define the basic project activities.

Sun Microsystems' first white paper on Java, the language, outlined 10 major programming environmental characteristics. The eleventh characteristic is simple. The outcome of the project validates this characteristic as to whether the introduction of Java into your information system is simple. However, no project activity could or should be based on this characteristic.

The list here is an alphabetical listing of the 10 characteristics of Java:

1. Architecture-neutral
2. Distributed
3. Dynamic language
4. High-performance
5. Interpreted and compiled
6. Multithreaded
7. Object-oriented
8. Portable
9. Robust
10. Secure

After getting a clear definition of each of these characteristics, the team might begin to formulate activities against them. For example, the team could have an activity plan for the object-oriented characteristics that includes as a part of the definition that either CORBA (Common Object Request Broker Architecture) or DCOM (Distributed Component Object Model) will be used in the final implementation of Java. In reality, it is recognized this may be an improbable statement, but then there are many improbable project activities in reality.

[B]   Activity Planning Questions

Following are 10 questions associated with the 10 characteristics to begin the process of activity planning:

WHAT HAS TO BE CHANGED IN THE LEGACY INTRANET(S) THAT ASSIST IN AN ARCHITECTURAL-NEUTRAL ENVIRONMENT?   While Java should work on any platform, hardware or software, there are exceptions. The legacy hardware has to be verified that it meets the minimum capabilities to process Java applets, and more importantly, Java-developed applications. As to software, it should be noted that the two major browsers, Internet Explorer and Navigator, handle Java applets differently. So you have to develop a series of activities to verify how applicable Java is to your IS infrastructure. There should be activities to consider adding Java to all graphical user interfaces (GUIs) if there are differences in Java applet handling in the major browsers.

WHAT ARE THE BASIC GOALS FOR IMPLEMENTING A DISTRIBUTED NETWORK? One way to determine the Java design approach is to consider the computing environment's sophistication and complexity. The highest level of sophistication is the use of an enterprise-class application. The lowest level addresses only the interactivity of Web pages and applications. There should be activities that check all enterprise-class applications for compatibility with Java applets.

WHAT CAN BE ACHIEVED WITH JAVA'S DYNAMIC EXECUTION? Programming wise, Java permits the complete use of the capabilities of the object-oriented (OO) paradigm concepts. From a nonprogrammer's view, this means the real use of plug-and-play software modules. There should be activities to analyze the implications of the use of plug-and-play software on the information system.

WHAT IS REQUIRED TO CHANGE THE LEGACY SYSTEM TO ACHIEVE THE EXPECTED HIGH PERFORMANCE IN A JAVA ENVIRONMENT? Java as an interpretation of bytecode objects may be acceptable. However, Java permits a runtime translation of the bytecode into native machine code. This permits the implementation of Web applications into small programs that are fast. There need to be activities to compare Java requirements against legacy capabilities.

WHAT DO THE INTERPRETATIVE CHARACTERISTICS OF JAVA MEAN FOR THE DESIGN OF AN INFORMATION SYSTEM ENVIRONMENT? Java is compiled and interpreted. It is first complied into a platform-independent binary bytecode format. Second, Java is interpreted by a platform-specific Java runtime environment. This means when a Java runtime environment is installed on any computer, whether it is a PC or a Mac or something else, the compiled Java program runs on it. This has major implications for an environment that has multiple versions of the same applications. There should be activities to clarify the environmental implications for managing different versions of any application.

WHAT IS REQUIRED TO MAKE FULL USE OF THE CAPABILITIES OF MULTITHREADING? Multithreading permits a form of parallel executions. This means for the client a superior interactive response. The dark cloud in a clear sky is if the operating system does not support parallel threads. Then the capabilities cannot be achieved. A set of activities should be established to define the multithreading capabilities of the system. If there are no multithreading capabilities, then there need to be activities to study the impacts of this lack.

WHAT HAS TO BE IDENTIFIED IN THE SYSTEM INFRASTRUCTURE TO USE JAVA'S OBJECT ORIENTATION? The requirement is to identify *all* concrete and abstract components in the system infrastructure. The Java and object-oriented paradigms require a change of view that an object is only a receiver or a sender as in the client/server paradigm. For example, a client within the OO paradigm can be a receiver and a sender. The infrastructure components have to be decomposed into logical, intuitive, and distinct objects so the Java hierarchy of system objects can be realized. There need to be activities to study the implications of the OO paradigm on the system's infrastructure.

WHAT HAS TO BE IDENTIFIED IN THE SYSTEM TO ENSURE FULL JAVA PORTABILITY? Java uses the IEEE standards for data types. A requirement is to identify each computer's operating system and application as to how these standards are addressed. When Java portability is implemented, this action eliminates maintenance, redundant implementation, and testing. There need to be activities to validate the degree of portability possible for the system.

WHAT IS REQUIRED TO ACHIEVE ROBUSTNESS AND THUS A HIGHER LEVEL OF RELIABILITY? The client sees the end result of a robust application, reliability and stability. The programmer sees data checking at compile time rather than at runtime, better memory management, an elimination of normal corruption, and correct method invocations. There should be activities that define the degree of robustness possible on the system.

WHAT HAS TO BE DONE TO THE SYSTEM TO ENSURE FULL JAVA SECURITY FEATURES? Java security is linked with safety and trust. The key to Java and the other two features is a security policy that is enforced consistently and at the same time recognizes the balanced needs of both users and the system administration. There should be activities to study the impact on the system's security structure, and how the security policy has to be changed.

MANAGER'S TIP

This is a broad sweep template for thinking about an OO programming language for activity planning. It does display some of the constraints one must identify in any OO effort.

What may be the result of considering the questions and these activities? One should read closely any vendor's documentation and then develop a series of possible activities required to implement the product before even starting a project.

[C]   Activity Sequencing

You should have a clear view as to the requirements of the Java programming approach and its relationship to user expectations. A visual presentation could be a checklist of three columns: Java attributes, specific results, and priority level of the specific results according to user expectations. A set of side notes of cost, training, and the like should also be included. Here is some of the information you should have as a result of using this checklist:

- Activities overview for developing skill requirements for a defined level of Java implementation
- Areas that might require documenting
- Areas that might require training
- Cost estimates for achieving a defined level of Java implementation
- Determination as to the use of a Java requirement (full, partial, or none)
- List of equipment needed to achieve a defined level of Java implementation
- Java attributes and the requirements to achieve a defined level of use of the attributes
- Priority listing of Java implementation by attribute or characteristic (high, medium, or low)
- Resource statement to achieve a defined level of Java implementation
- Statement as to the place of quality control

§ 3.03   MANAGEMENT INVOLVEMENT

[A]   Overview

This is the time when the tactical manager, with the authority given by the strategic manager, comes to center stage. There are two keys to success here. First, the tactical manager, who is the IS project manager, should first recognize a basic principle of team management. The collection of people known as the team acts as an individual, although possibly in a dysfunctional manner. Second, the guiding light is that the customer's needs come before technical needs.

   Criteria for what is an activity, what is a critical activity, what are the project phases, and what is an operational area should be developed up front. You need objective benchmarks for the small things. There can be lengthy arguments over one activity, but not over a hundred activities. A person can usually identify more easily with the small than the large.

Besides the benchmarks there should be brought to the table outside standards that are applicable to the project. Outside does not necessarily mean outside of the company. Your project may be in a division of a large corporation and the local training and documentation groups may have to adhere to corporate standards for these areas.

[B] Strategic Activity Planning and Sequencing

Is there any need for strategic activity planning and sequencing? Of course there is; there should be strategic reviews. The strategic manager should chair these reviews so a degree of objectivity can be achieved. The presence of this manager changes the character of the project team. These reviews should be held at a minimum at the end of each phase including the planning phase.

[C] Tactical Activity Planning and Sequencing

The tactical manager has a number of actions at this point; however, if the following is not done the others will be less than secure. All team members need to attend all of the meetings on activity planning and sequencing. There can be no substitutes! As said earlier, the team at first may act like a dysfunctional person, and one member change can change the nature of the beast. This is the point where each operational manager becomes a stakeholder in the project. It is interesting in hockey to watch, as different lines are on the ice, their interactions and especially when a line is changed because of injury. Just like the character of a line of professional hockey players can change, so can a project team's character change. This is another short lesson in team management.

Here are 16 actions the IS administrator, or project manager, should accomplish during the activity planning and sequencing phase:

1. Be prepared to run the meetings.
2. Assign resource (skills, equipment, and materials) dependencies.
3. Construct a sequence of activities and their associated times, which becomes the basis for the schedule.
4. Define procurement requirements, that is, the need for outside resources.
5. Define project activity parameters and constraints based on the project goals.
6. Determine skill levels required for critical activities and groups of activities.

7. Develop cost estimates against an activity or a group of related activities.

8. Ensure the operational managers bring to the table support activity data.

9. Establish a project organization structure that includes links between an activity and a person.

10. Establish benchmarks for handing project administrative paperwork, training, and documentation.

11. Have a comprehensive quality control policy with specific activities and a defined sequence of activities that requires the involvement of this function through the project process.

12. Identify potential risks and opportunities.

13. Identify standards that may impact the project activities.

14. Link budget items with defined activities with customer needs.

15. Remember customer needs come before technical desires.

16. Write the activity plan using fully confirmed project activities.

[D]   Operational Activity Planning and Sequencing

Probably the operational managers need to acknowledge (more than the tactical manager does) that the customer comes first, and the technical considerations second. No operational area is more important than the defined goals of the project. No operational area is more important than another operational area. It takes the whole to achieve success. This is another guideline for team management. When a major sports team plays as individuals, that team usually loses.

Here are 10 actions that the operational managers should accomplish during the activity planning and sequencing:

1. Identify technical issues or risks that may impact the activity plan.

2. Come to meetings with support data for activities from their area.

3. Attend all the meetings; do not send an alternate.

4. Inform team of outcome of meeting in a positive manner.

5. Identify the implications of required skill levels.

6. Identify training and documentation requirements.

7. Identify standards and benchmarks that might impact project goals.

8. Establish cost estimates.

9. Prepare an operational sequence of activities.

10. Identify the impact of parameters and constraints of project goals on operational effort.

Exhibit 3-1: Task Identification Checklist

Organization:		Date:	
Source:			
Attachment ID:			

Estimate type: Critical ☐ Pessimistic ☐
     Optional ☐ Realistic ☐
     Standard ☐ Optimistic ☐

Item	Reference Document
1. Task measurable goals and deliverables	
2. Task assumptions and constraints	
3. Criteria for resource requirements	
4. Critical tasks and their critical activities	
5. Skills criteria	
6. Contingency criteria and requirements	
7. Funding requirements	
8. Communications requirements	
9. Procurement policy and procedural requirements	
10. Quality control and verification requirements	
11. Training requirements	
12. Documentation requirements	
13. Risk management concerns	
14. Miscellaneous Comments	

Instructions for Task Identification Checklist

Essential Terms

- An activity is an event with a start and finish date that uses resources such as designing a section of an application.
- A task is a collection of activities such as designing all the sections of an application.
- A deliverable is the designed application or product.
- A milestone or gate is the actual start and finish dates of the designing task for the application or product.
- The rational basis for how, why, when, where, who, and what is defined by assumptions and constraints. Thus, an assumption or a constraint can have up to six basic components.

Warnings

- Each reference document entry should read "See attachment XXX."
- Each attachment needs a clear identifier so each can be associated correctly with the main form.
- Each task needs three estimate scenarios: pessimistic, realistic, and optimistic. The criteria for each scenario must also be given.

Exhibit 3-1 (*Continued*)

- Each response must be answered in the context of who, what, where, why, when, and how. For example, the following are six variants that need to be considered in completing a potential response:

  1. Who is responsible for defining a critical task?
  2. How should a critical task be defined?
  3. Why should a given task be defined as critical?
  4. When should a given task be critical?
  5. Where should a critical path be done?
  6. What are the assumptions and constraints for a critical path?

General Instructions

- Use one form for each task.
- Identify tasks based on the statement of work.
- Each task needs a set of activity assumptions and constraints.
- The result of a task must be measurable.
- Consider tasks needed for a deliverable and then the activities required for a given task.
- You should identify objective criteria for task identification. The essential sources are standards and benchmarks. There needs to be consistency for the estimates.
- The checklist is an outline for when an example activity plan organization is given. Each "chapter" should be considered in developing task identification responses.
- Do an analysis of what data are required by milestone or gate.
- Include start and end dates.
- Identify each task's requirement for resources, that is, cost, time, skills, hardware, and software. This means you need estimates and their criteria.
- Define all estimates in three scenarios: pessimistic, realistic (most likely), and optimistic.

A simple format for essential data for a task is as follows:

Estimate	Optimistic	Realistic	Pessimistic
Cost			
Time			
Equipment			
Material			
Skill			

For the last three estimates, in the blanks enter the attachment ID.

Specific Instructions

1. The measurable goals of a task need to reflect the defined goals of the project found in the scope plan.
2. Use the scope plan to assist you in defining the assumptions and constraints for tasks. You cannot say "not applicable" for this requirement. All tasks have assumptions and constraints.
3. Define resources as critical, standard, or optional. A brief justification should be given for each task.

Exhibit 3-1 (*Continued*)

4. A critical task should be defined only when there is objective supporting evidence such as the need for a design phase for a new piece of hardware or software. Identify tasks that might be needed when a situation is worse than pessimistic. This means the critical path breaks down.

5. Skills criteria should determine the resource requirement, not headcount. For example, you might say for an optimistic scenario that a network security technician with more than five years' experience could do the task in one week. For a realistic scenario, a network security technician with two to four years' experience could do the task in less than one month. For a pessimistic scenario, a network security technician with less than one year of experience might do the task in three months.

6. There must be a change mechanism or requirement for each task sequence, which should be included in the contingency section of the response. Informal padding should not be done. State the range of your needs and the criteria for a range.

7. State when funding is required. Do say that all the funding must be up front. Funding requirements should be given in monthly increments.

8. Communicate requirements of how correct information is to get from you to other people in the correct amount of time. You might give verbal or written task updates to the project team once a month or after task X is completed. Or you could e-mail messages to keep your team informed.

9. The tasks that are required for resource availability need to be defined. Identify appropriate corporate procurement policy by task. Identify any special requirements the project manager has to administer.

10. Identify quality control procedures by task. Give applicable procedural standards and performance benchmarks.

11. Identify the criteria for defining the training requirements for tasks. Include data on both formal and informal training, especially hands-on experience requirements and learning curve impacts.

12. There need to be some activities for administrative documentation as well as documentation that might be used by the training and documentation groups.

13. Discuss potential risks and solution procedures. Risks particularly happen when a pessimistic scenario breaks down. Padded cost and time estimates are two of the three major reasons for project failure.

14. Criteria need to define the policy activities, the project administrative activities, and the work activities. An example of policy, an operational manager does not discuss privately with a customer about making changes. Any change needs to go through the project manager and be documented.

Task and Activity Sequence Assistance

1. The first step in sequencing is to use the Critical Path Method (CPM). All sequencing must resolve the critical activities and their shortest time line.

2. Do not confuse task or activity sequencing with scheduling. The schedule is a formal document that includes the tasks and the amount of time that the tasks require to be completed.

3. Identify the criteria for task and activity sequence.

4. Establish sequences based on defined deliverables.

5. Determine resource availability effects on sequences.

6. Consider the budgetary cycle impacts on sequences.

7. Consider documentation requirements and their impacts on sequences.

8. Consider training requirements and their impacts on sequences.

9. Determine the procurement policies that affect sequences.

10. Identify quality control procedures that might impact sequences.

11. Give the necessary links for the various sequences.

Exhibit 3-2: Activity Planning and Sequencing Questions Checklist

Project Name:	Comments
1. Does each activity have an associated cost, time estimation, resource requirements, quality control benchmarks, designated responsible activity leader, and possible risk factors?	
2. Have criteria for defining a critical activity been created?	
3. Have criteria for strategic, tactical, and operational activities been created?	
4. How do the availability of resources impact the activity plan?	
5. How should the scope plan be used in activity planning?	
6. What are the criteria for creating an activity plan?	
7. What are the documentation prerequisites for the activity?	
8. What are the quality control procedures that need to be in the activity plan?	
9. What are the criteria for risk management that may impact activities?	
10. What are the training requirements for the activity?	
11. How do documentation requirements impact the project sequence?	
12. How does potential training impact the project sequence?	
13. How do procurement policies impact the project sequence?	
14. How do the availability of resources impact the project sequence?	
15. How does the budgetary cycle impact the project sequence?	
16. How should the scope plan be used in activity sequencing?	
17. Should the CPM be used for sequencing?	
18. What are the criteria for identifying the sequence of activities?	
19. What are the quality control procedures that ensure correct sequencing?	
20. What are the types of links for developing the sequence?	

Exhibit 3-3: Change Order Request

Project:		Date:	
Requestor:		Required Date:	
Manager/Team Leader:			
Change:			
Justification:			
Schedule Impacts:			
Cost Impacts:			
Resource Impacts:			
Approval			
Agree/Disagree:		Date:	
Project Manager:			

Exhibit 3-4: Task Analysis Chart

Project:		Issued:		Sheet:		of	
Preparer:		Revised:					

Measured Objective:	
Performance Standard/Benchmark:	

Step	Time Estimate	Cost Estimate	Resources	Owner

Exhibit 3-5: Task Responsibility Chart

Project:		Issued:		Sheet:		of	
Preparer:		Revised:					

Description of Activities	Project Activity Owners (code)			

Code: P = Prime   S = Support   Blank = Not Applicable

On the CD-ROM

On the CD-ROM are:

1. Exhibit 3-1 Task Identification Checklist.doc
2. Exhibit 3-2 Activity Planning and Sequencing Questions Checklist.doc
3. Exhibit 3-3 Change Order Request.doc
4. Exhibit 3-4 Task Analysis Chart.doc
5. Exhibit 3-5 Task Responsibility Chart.doc
6. Chapter 3 Overview.ppt—Chapter Overview, Activity Planning and Sequencing

Chapter 4

Resource Planning

§ 4.01   OVERVIEW

[A]   Objectives

At the end of this chapter, you will be able to:

- State a definition for resource planning.
- List eight components for a resource definition.
- Identify six data types for a resource plan.
- Ask 10 basic questions about resource planning such as: What are the required resources (skills, equipment, and materials)? Why should the resources be required? Are the resources available? How are the resources to be acquired? When should the resources be acquired? Where should the resources be acquired?
- Differentiate between headcount and skill count.
- Relate resource planning to procurement activities.
- Explain the requirements for three procurement documents.
- List 11 attributes needed by the IS administrator to be a successful project manager.
- List eight abilities needed by the project team.
- State five criteria for selecting vendors and consultants.
- Explain solutions to three resource issue scenarios.
- Identify 10 differences between project planning and business planning that involve resources.
- Identify how the three managing levels are involved in resource planning.

MANAGER'S TIP

When it comes to selecting the people needed to complete a large-scale project, IS project managers often must decide whether to use outside resources such as consultants or just use in-house talent. In the late 1990s the city of San Diego was involved in a Y2K remediation project, which its IS subsidiary could not handle because of the project's size and complexity and a looming deadline. PricewaterhouseCoopers was brought in to hire off-shore manpower (Saytram in India), and oversee every aspect of the project. PricewaterhouseCoopers tracked the progress of the code remediation abroad and, as time grew short, suggested that the city's project managers communicate directly with the off-shore company to save time to meet the critical deadline. In this win-win situation, project managers from all points stayed in close contact in order to best manage extensive in-house and off-shore resources.

[B]   Using Essential Definitions

Any discussion in Section One also impacts this chapter; any discussion here must be filtered through these three fundamental concepts:

A **resource** is anything that supports the project. This includes, in general terms, money, skills, materials, time, facilities, and equipment.

Resource planning is establishing support requirements for a project as to costs, availability, start date and end date (length of time for use plus duration), and technical specifications.

An **estimate** is a guess based on opinion, or a forecast based on experience. Resource estimates are one foundation for project planning.

Adding Supportive Definitions

Besides the three essential concepts on resource planning given above, you must also consider at least the following definitions:

An **action plan** is the description of what is required to be completed and when it is to be completed.

The **activity plan** is a set of definitions for the efforts required to achieve measurable results. At the project level the efforts are tasks, while at the operational level they are activities and tasks.

The **Content Agreement** is the written "contract" between the development group and the marketing group as to the content and functions of the project.

A **contingency plan** is the preparation for a pessimistic scenario to become reality.

MANAGER'S TIP

A regional hospital in New England initiated two large-scale clinical system (software) implementation projects. In both projects, the budgets were guesstimates based on subjective criteria for risk. The greater the degree of uncertainty, the more likely would be later unforeseen costs. Because of their experience and knowledge, the in-house project team did an excellent job of identifying and preparing for contingencies, so the risk estimates in both projects later proved sound.

Criticality is a position on the team where the individual in this situation has specific skills, usually technical, that if not available to the project, puts the entire project at risk.

Effectiveness is the attained measure of quality to complete an activity, task, or event. It is also the skill required to define goals and to accomplish them.

Efficiency is the measurement of output based on amount of input. It is also the skill that can accomplish maximum output with a minimum of input.

Leveling is the technique used to smooth out peaks and valleys in the use of resources.

An **optimistic estimate** is an assumption that holds that everything will go as planned.

Padding is an informal action, such as adding time or cost to an estimate, that should not take place. Any such estimates should be formalized in a contingency plan.

A **pessimistic estimate** is an assumption that if something can go wrong, it will.

The **Project Support Plan** ensures that the project is supportable in a market environment. This plan should include a process for customer support.

A **realistic estimate** is an assumption that there will probably be a few difficulties, but with compromise, the difficulties will be overcome.

[C]   Resource Planning Definition

A resource is anything that supports the project. The obvious supports are skills, equipment, materials, time, and money. Resource planning is establishing support requirements for a project as to costs, availability, start date and end date (length of time in calendar days plus duration), and technical specifications. While it may be easy to get technical specifications for equipment and materials, the team should try to be as specific as possible about required human skills as well.

Resource planning is a parallel function in time to project planning, activity planning, and cost and time estimating. Resources should be linked to goals and their associated activities, and, in turn, to the cost and time estimates for the activities. Resource planning requires that operational managers make commitments to ensure the right resource is there at the right time and in the right location.

[D]   Resource Definition Components

Your resource definition that is concerned with skills, equipment, and materials should include as a minimum:

- Specific resource requirements
- Chart on how resources are linked to goals and activities
- Impact statement (if resource is unavailable)
- Policy on how to manage changes in resource requirements
- Policy on when resources are required
- Policy on who determines resource requirements
- Procedure for turning an unavailable resource into an opportunity
- Resource utilization policy

Specific resource requirements would be for equipment and materials, including their structural specifications. A skill resource should identify minimal performance expectations for success. When the skill has been defined at the novice level, this becomes a benchmark for evaluating the procuring of an expert. You then set an expectation for overachievement of the novice level. This practice becomes important if the schedule has to be shortened or modified.

[E]   Data Types for Resource Planning

A resource plan should have at least three sections: skills, equipment, and materials. All definitions should be measurable. You would not have a resource definition such as "a Java programmer is required." What are the measurable expectations from the programmer to achieve a specific project goal? You certainly need this information if you have to procure a programming consultant. Likewise, you would not say, "The project requires a firewall." You need to specify the security technical functions and benchmarks required just as a starting point to this resource description. Cost estimates should be given against these six data types:

- Resource type criteria
  — Skills
  — Equipment
  — Materials
- Resource description criteria
  — Who
  — When
  — Where
  — Why
  — How
- Links
  — People (skills)
  — Equipment
  — Materials
- Impacts
  — Having
  — Not having (risk management)
- Usage criteria
  — Who
  — When

- — Where
- — Why
- — How
- Change requirements
  - — Skills
  - — Equipment
  - — Materials

[F]   Ten Questions to Assist in Defining Resources

These 10 questions may help you focus on the decisions as to required skills and other resources you need to achieve effective project goals:

WHO DEFINES THE RESOURCE REQUIREMENTS? Are special teams required that consider skills, equipment, and materials? In the first round of planning resources, there might be these three teams or more establishing resource requirements; however, there needs to be a coordinating team that ensures consistency. Everyone should bring to the table his or her needs; someone else may have a solution. The tactical manager, or project manager, should be the approval point for all resource acquisitions that require project budgetary considerations.

HOW DO RESOURCES RELATE TO ONE ANOTHER?   One type of link is a given person with given skills who must have given equipment and materials for a specified and given amount of time. Why is this important? You may have to lease a special piece of equipment for a given period. Without such a written linkage, you, the project manager, might receive notification of the arrival of a piece of equipment and would not know immediately where the equipment goes.

HAVE THE PROJECT SCOPE DEFINITIONS BEEN USED TO PLAN RESOURCE ESTIMATES? The basis for defining the resources should be the defined project scope. One of the considerations should be *any* special requirement. The constraints formulated in the scope plan could also include what is *not* to be used. This is really a range or a specific constraint. For example, you might say that a firewall to be integrated into the IS network must be a packet filter type, not an application-link gateway type. This statement should automatically preclude discussions by certain interested vendors because you included the "not" specification. Remember, a product under consideration might have most of the required functions, but not the complete set. What are the implications of the missing functions?

WHAT ARE THE IMPACTS OF THE MILESTONES ON THE RESOURCE ESTIMATES? An important linkage to time is the availability of a required skill level. Perhaps an expert in a given area can do the activity in a third of the time needed by a novice. If the expert is not available, how does the time for training impact the project schedule? What are the expected and realistic experiences for any technician? One needs to consider ideas that maximize technical skills. For example, a programming skill in one language can be migrated to another language.

WHAT ARE THE EFFECTS OF THE COST PARAMETERS ON RESOURCE ESTIMATES? Is it better to pay $50 an hour to an expert or $10 an hour to a novice? The expert would have to be able to do the work in one-fifth of the time for the dollar amount just to be even. What is the impact of the results? Are the people involved on the project full-time or part-time? It can be surprising how many different categories resources can be divided into that can impact cost.

WHAT IS THE CONTROL SYSTEM TO MANAGE RESOURCES AND ANY CHANGES? If a new skill requirement is identified halfway into the project cycle, has a process been defined that can handle this issue? A further question is, why did it take halfway through the project for a new skill to be identified?

HAVE RESOURCES BEEN CLOSELY RELATED TO COST ESTIMATES? Have skill types and levels, rather than headcount, been defined? The broadest question is, "Have the resources (skills, equipment, and materials) been related to all the delimiters?" For example, you can ask, "Since I do not have a given skill, do I have a threat or an opportunity?" Perhaps not having a given skill gives you a new perspective on how to accomplish the project more easily. Remember, six heads do not necessarily equal the six skills required.

WHAT DOCUMENTS ARE REQUIRED TO CONTROL RESOURCES? It should be determined who is responsible for doing project resource management. It can be several people. To whom should resource status be communicated? The control system could be simply three documents, one each for skills, equipment, and materials. Updated documents could be attached in e-mails to concerned individuals. Remember to include version numbers and dates on the documents.

WHAT IS (ARE) THE RANGE(S) FOR HAVING AN INADEQUATE RESOURCE(S)? Determine what are the minimal skill-level requirements. Perhaps a novice can do some activities, while an expert is necessary for other activities. Remember, a lack of a skill can be turned into an opportunity. Perhaps there is another way to achieve the goal without the skill. Also, there may be a justification for a person to acquire the skill, which could benefit the company in other ways after project closure.

WHAT PROCUREMENT POLICIES HAVE TO BE FOLLOWED? Has it been determined what impact outside policies will have on the project? Remember, any large company (it can be true for small companies also) may have three different procedures for contracting outside people, for leasing equipment, and for buying materials. You need to define project activities that ensure that these policies are followed.

[G]   Refining Data by Asking Additional Questions

Because activities use resources, the data for the refinement of resources begins with the activity plan, as discussed in Chapter 3. The 10 questions that follow should assist you in identifying your resources or in identifying omissions in the resource plan. Remember: the resource plan is not only for identifying resources for operational and administrative activities; it also includes their utilization and availability constraints and assumptions.

The following 10 questions are used to answer the fundamental question of this step in the project management process: "What is the purpose of _____ and why do we need this resource?" These questions do not require responses that are specifically data (bits and bytes) oriented; they are purpose-oriented (hunks of data) so that they can assist you in identifying resource data types.

1. How can the scope plan be used to refine the resource plan?
2. How should measurable criteria for defining critical resources be created?
3. How should measurable criteria for estimating resources (emphasis on skills criteria) be defined?
4. How should measurable criteria for strategic, tactical, and operational resources be created to eliminate padding and create a source for contingencies?
5. What are measurable criteria for defining the training requirements (learning curve) for the use of resources?
6. What are the measurable criteria for writing the resource plan?
7. What are the measurable criteria for risk management that may impact resource acquisition?
8. What are the documentation prerequisites for defining and describing a resource?
9. What is the impact of the availability of resources (that is, having or not having them) on the project?
10. When should resource requirements be defined for the quality management procedures?

These questions as well as the 10 in the previous section, must be answered in the context of your defined optimistic, realistic, and pessimistic measured goals for the project. Additionally, many of these questions can be changed to ask "why." For example, question 9 above could be restated as "Why should we be concerned with the availability of resource X?" You might say, "There is no concern."

The resource plan should be developed in concert with the activity plan (see Chapter 3). Thus, many of your resource questions will be the same as or similar to the ones developed for the activity plan. Both are baseline project documents; the guiding rule is simply that the activity or task needs to be defined before its resources.

MANAGER'S TIP

WARNING: It is bad management to try to use an available resource to define activities for a project.

As discussed above, before you use the query process to determine resource data types and data, you must ask questions about structure of the Resource Plan and the management procedures for project resources. You need to test the water before you jump in.

[H]   Headcount versus Skill Count

Resource planning determines the required skills, not headcount, which ensure that all deliverables are within defined milestones. A common thought at this time is, we need six people for the project. What does that really mean? I (the author) think I have the skills of a particular type of writer but I do not consider myself a writer of plays. One cannot say one programmer is like any other programmer. This equivalence is not logical, only physical. Headcount is a nice concept for counting, but not for managing. One hockey line, five players, is not the same as another line, except for the number of players. The planning of skill types and skill levels is more important than "body" count. If you cannot find a given skill, can you substitute with another skill type? It is amazing how many times this question could be answered with a "yes."

Perhaps the biggest resource issue for you, as the project manager, is the need to recruit or allocate for skills rather than headcount. For business managers, headcount is a cardinal "bean counting" concept for establishing a budget. You can more easily define a salary for a head in a given organizational slot than try to determine salary by the head's skills. The assumption (and not a very good one) is that the ups-and-downs of the use of these skills should level out on an annual basis for any given individual; if not, a corporate reorganization is required. The consideration of skills versus headcount is important to project management because of the baseline goal of completing the project successfully on schedule and on budget.

[I]   Creating a Resource Plan Checklist

Exhibit 4-1: Resource Plan Checklist is a "parent" form for resource management. You as the project manager must establish the assumptions and con-

Exhibit 4-1: Resource Plan Checklist

Organization:	Date:

Resource Definition:

Resource Type:

Estimate type: Critical ❏   Pessimistic ❏
  Optional ❏   Realistic ❏
  Standard ❏   Optimistic ❏

Resource Description:

  Hardware ❏   Software ❏   Skill   ❏   Support ❏

  Consultant ❏   Available ❏   Not Available ❏

                                  Source:

Measurable Objectives:

Training required: ❏   If checked, describe:

Documentation required: ❏   If checked, describe:

Time estimates with measurable criteria:

Cost estimates with measurable criteria:

Dependencies:

Events:

Hardware:

Software:

Skills:

Support:

Consultant:

Training:

Learning curve:

Exhibit 4-1 (*Continued*)

Documentation:
Timing:
Standards:
Benchmarks:
Performance level:
Contingency:
Quality control:
Effectiveness:
Efficiency:
Variances:
Risk Analysis:
Special Issues:

Instructions for Resource Plan Checklist

General Instructions

- Cost and time estimates for resource should include the following five situations:
    1. Resource descriptions
    2. Links
    3. Impacts
    4. Usage criteria
    5. Change requirements
- You should identify not only resources for operational and administrative activities but also their utilization and availability constraints and assumptions.

Exhibit 4-1 *(Continued)*

- You should identify any resource based on required skill level rather than by a head-count. You need three skill resource definitions for pessimistic, realistic, and optimistic.

- When not included specifically in the checklist, the why, what, where, when, and how of any response need to be considered.

- You should give measurable criteria for critical resources.

- You should state measurable criteria for estimating resources.

- You need to list measurable criteria for strategic, tactical, and operational resources.

- You need to state measurable criteria for any training or documentation requirements for the use of resources.

- You should list the measurable criteria for any potential risk that may impact resource acquisition.

- You should give potential impacts of the availability of resources on the project's success.

- When required, you need to note quality control requirements.

- When there is no applicability to a given answer on the checklist, state: "There is no applicability."

- You should relate resources to cost, time, and activity estimates.

- You should relate the project scope definitions resource estimates.

- You should show any critical resource relationships.

- You should show any critical effects of the cost parameters on resource estimates.

- You should give the impacts of departmental milestones on the resource estimates.

- You should give a control system to manage resources and any changes.

- You should identify when possible procurement policies need to be followed.

- You should not use an available resource to define activities unless it is critical to project goals.

Resource Identification Process

Before filling out the checklist, you should do the following steps:

1. Make a list, as specific as possible, of required resources.
2. Identify mandatory resources.
3. Identify resources as belonging to a pessimistic, an optimistic, or a realistic scenario.
4. Identify resources that belong to a contingency plan (based on a pessimistic scenario).
5. Group resources by project phase—planning, designing, developing, testing, or implementing.
6. Order the resources by priority—you need to define what you mean by priority.
7. Group resources by users—can be by administrative unit or individual.
8. Group resources by impact—this means as mandatory or optional such as the resource has to be available before X activity or task.
9. Group resources by availability—full-time, part-time, have to buy, have to rent, and so forth.
10. List resources by training requirements.

WARNING

All criteria (standards, benchmarks, and goals) and skills should be measurable. You would not have a resource skill definition such as, "An XML programmer is required." What are the measurable deliverables from the programmer to achieve a specific project goal?

Exhibit 4-1 (*Continued*)

Specific Instructions

- Each resource requires three forms for each of these scenarios: pessimistic, realistic, and optimistic.

- Internal source includes responsible estimator, title, phone number, organization unit, e-mail address, and any other special personal identifiers

- External source should include all internal source data plus company address, and the name of the responsible company representative for the project.

- Date should be in the form of mm/dd/yy.

- Estimate type should include explanation of critical or optional in the last section of the form, special issues.

- Resource description should be included as an attachment with the form. A description should be written in the context of the key definitions given in the chapter. For example, a resource description for a piece hardware would include company name (part number), general use name, when required in the project, who is to use it, when and where is it to be used, what project goal is it for, present availability, procurement requirements, a permanent acquisition or a temporary lease, duration of use, and skill level requirements for use.

- Objectives should include the associated project goal. When appropriate, you should give related procedural standards and performance benchmarks, which justify the requirement of the resource.

- The training description should include availability, why required, what is the training to achieve, when and duration of the training, and where the training is to be given. The names of the students should also be given as an attachment.

- The documentation description must include availability, why required, what is the documentation to achieve when it is to be used, and who needs the documentation.

- Time estimates are one of the three major reasons for project failure. The description used is measurable and precise. Any estimate should take into consideration all these instructions.

- Cost estimates have the same impacts as time estimates.

- A dependency is a must requirement before a given project event (task) can be started or completed. For example, a person must acquire a certain level of knowledge before beginning the task (learning curve and training).

- The standard description should include name, organizational source, date, version number, where it can be located (may be a URL), pertinent paragraph numbers, and relevant quality control considerations.

- The benchmark description should be similar to the standard description.

- The performance description should be measurable and should include the source for the performance level.

- Contingency is not padding. A contingency is a factor based on pessimistic or optimistic measurable criteria.

- Quality control descriptions should include information that can be integrated into a quality control program.

- The risk analysis description should be based on the estimate type of the form: pessimistic, realistic, or optimistic.

- The special issue should include any special considerations to clarify any prior descriptions on the form.

straints for resource estimates. Resource estimates affect both cost and time estimates. A cost estimate may become invalid because of resource padding. A time estimate may become invalid because the resource's duration was estimated as too little or too much.

After this form is completed, specialized forms might be created to gather further data. However, an important instruction with this is, "Attach additional information."

The keys to the form are two necessary actions:

1. Three estimates are needed for each resource: pessimistic, realistic, and optimistic.

2. Each resource needs to be defined as critical, optional, or standard.

One of the most common mistakes in project management is only to have one estimate, whether it is cost, time, or resource. Each estimate must have a range, with the criteria for this range defined by the project before any resource definition. For example, in PERT a criterion was that an event would or would not happen once in 20 times.

In addition, by having three estimates, you minimize one of the most dangerous informal actions in any project, padding (unknown "protection"). Instead, you need to move to a management position of having a known contingency. An obvious example of padding is the situation in which a manager states that a task needs four people when in fact it needs two. An optimistic scenario might be one person, while a pessimistic might be four. Each scenario needs its own cost and time estimates.

When you have a set of forms that fulfill the second requirement, a sort can be done quickly to identify resources that have to be used in defining a critical path. A critical path is a document that gives the required activities (the critical resource list is a constraint) and the least amount of time (duration) to achieve a project goal.

In addition, when a resource is identified as critical, you need to know if it is available. A checkmark indicating the unavailability of a resource is a flag for a potential risk. By knowing this, you can develop actions to eliminate this bump in the road.

Because there is a trend to use software to handle resource management, this form should give the data type information required to do the necessary input. It would be best to discuss the form with the software developer and to determine any additional information that can be defined. Likewise, if the reviewed software does not assist significantly in manipulation, look at other software applications. Do not buy a vendor resource management application without extensive review.

When you use a management application, you will need, at a minimum, the following information to ensure an adequate resource database:

- Identify calendar data.
- Identify cost (when and specific amount) of resources.
- Identify criticality of each resource.
- Identify links between resources.
- Identify links to tasks and people.
- Identify locations of resources.
- Identify physical amounts of each resource.
- Identify resource scenarios: pessimistic, realistic, and optimistic.
- Identify types of resources (hardware, software, skills, or materials)
- Identify usage of each resource.

Exhibit 4-1: Resource Plan Checklist points directly and indirectly to these requirements.

§ 4.02   PROCUREMENT: GOING OUTSIDE FOR RESOURCES

[A]   Overview

You realize that you have to hire people with special skills outside of your organization; this is procurement. This can involve corporate policies or practices such as the following:

- "You must have three bids."
- "You must run an advertisement."
- "You must follow federal guidelines on gender, race, age, etc."

Even if you are a business of one, federal and state guidelines might be very important to you also.

Your company's procurement policy or policies may have a significant impact on your selection of resources (skills, equipment, or materials) for your project.

Has a contracting (outsourcing) system been established if required for skills, equipment, and materials?

If outside resources are required, then a system must be formulated to procure these resources. The best thing to do is formulate a system even if at the moment no outside sources are required. Here are some questions you need to answer to develop your procurement process:

- Are there required guidelines to be followed for outsourcing?
- What is the impact on the end date if these guidelines are followed?
- Have you considered all the appropriate guidelines, policies, and practices for procuring people and materials?

There are many types of policies that can impact the procuring of skills and materials. You may say your company is a small one and you do not have to worry about any procurement procedures. Do you know what is the number of people that can be in a company before federal guidelines take effect? When you have the need for outside resources, you should have activities to determine if there are procedures you must follow.

Sometimes when resource planning is done, a larger-than-expected team is needed to work on just acquiring resources. An example of a project that requires a large procurement team is the building of a new airplane. Remember, many large companies, and some small companies, have three different types of procedures for contracting outside people, for leasing equipment, and for buying materials. Have you defined activities that ensure that these procedures are followed?

In sequencing activities, you should always consider what tasks are needed to handle procurement. You need to be aware of all procurement policies and procedures that impact the end date. Your project goals may be hampered because a policy or a procedure was not followed.

Your cost and time estimates can be seriously impacted when there is a delay in acquiring any required skills, equipment, or materials. It is better to be pessimistic than optimistic on cost and time estimates in the area of procurement.

The schedule should have the flexibility to handle the procurement of outside resources (skills, equipment, and materials). There should be time in the schedule to work within the procedures required to manage any procurement.

One of the difficult budgetary issues is the paying of contractors. Where in the budget the expenditure appears is important, but also significant is *when* the expenditure has to be paid. If you have set up your budget to meet certain financial milestones, a late payment can have an impact on status reports.

As with people and skills, there is equipment and capital cost. If the equipment is acquired for the customer's ultimate ownership, there is no capital cost to the project involved. There is a budgetary transition and a possible profit item for "handling and shipping." When the IS organization purchases the equipment, there is a project capital cost. When there is amortization, the project cost is only for a time-usage basis; the rest is to the IS organization. In all instances, there should be a negotiation for the lowest possible cost.

[B]   Three Important Procurement Documents

Business Affiliate Plan

The Business Affiliate Plan provides information when a component or an application for the information system is to be developed by a third-party developer. The plan can consist of the following:

- Explanation for the need for a third-party developer
- Method used to qualify the third party
- The part the third party plays in the marketing program training requirements
- Documentation requirements
- Quality control system description

Third-Party Market Agreement

The Third-Party Market Agreement provides the plans when the IS application or component is to be marketed by a third-party developer. This agreement may include the following:

- Product Content
- Delivery Schedules
- Marketing Strategy
- Verification Strategy
- Documentation Strategy
- Training Strategy

Third-Party Service Plan

This document provides details on how the project component for the information system is to be serviced by a third-party developer. The question is, "Can the third party do customer service?" The plan may include details on:

- Customer training
- Customer documentation
- Diagnostic tools
- Support process

§ 4.03   PROJECT PROCESS SKILLS REQUIRED

[A]   Overview

Types of skills that most people forget to think about are the ones for the project manager, the project team, and consultants. Most of the time, the project manager and the project team members are involved because of the positions they hold in the company rather than the skills they have. All these people should know what is expected of them personally to achieve project success. More time is usually spent on establishing qualifications for a consultant; however, there is one type of consultant you get without getting to identify required skills, the one from the vendor. However, you should have a set of expectations for this type of consultant, too.

[B]   IS Administrator as Project Manager

Besides having the obvious abilities to walk on water and turn water into wine, what are the core qualifications of the IS administrator (project manager) for managing a project of any importance?

- Accepts customers as a part of the effort
- Is an organizer
- Is comfortable with details
- Is decisive
- Is not afraid of change
- Is technologically aware
- Can quarterback the team
- Can see how the parts fit into the whole
- Can seize the moment (the opportunity)
- Has proven ability to accomplish tasks
- Recognizes the difference between "smoke and mirrors" and the "real stuff"
- Thinks as a project manager, not as a business manager

The above list is usually used to select the project manager. For the IS administrator, as the project manager, it is a list of actions needed to be done to be a success. The last item on the list is one based on experience rather than education. You should always ask the obvious question because you may be surprised by the answer.

[C]   Being a Team Member

The secret of success for creating a team is finding the correct size and mixture. Do not attempt to do everything discussed in this book with three people. It is not headcount that is important, but skill interplay. The following are some mental criteria for being a successful team member:

- Accepts change
- Accepts customers as a part of the effort
- Can compromise
- Can work within an organization

- Is comfortable with details
- Is technologically comfortable but able to recognize that this is a business effort, not a place for hacking
- Can be a player on a team
- Has proven ability to accomplish what is required
- Is a specialist, not generalist

MANAGER'S TIP

The comfort zone for being technologically comfortable is in degrees. Therefore, on a team, besides information system personnel there should be representatives from human resources, marketing, training, documentation, and the customer base.

[D]   Selecting Consultants and Vendors

The first act of many project managers in a major project is to get consultants or bring in local IS support vendors. Before acquiring the consultants or vendors, establish the criteria for their selection. This is the type of information you should get from them before they grace your doors:

- Development, design, maintenance, and support levels available
- Rates
- References from where they have done similar work
- Resumes with emphasis on experience related to the project goals
- Knowledge of security solutions

MANAGER'S TIP

Feel free to ask a vendor to give you customized resumes on its consultants that reflect your project goal requirements.

Once they have passed this hurdle, you need to interview the consultants and vendors and state some issue that you think you are going to have and ask them for their ideas and suggestions. Do the same thing with all candidates, so you can evaluate their solutions and your comfort zone.

[E]   Resource Management Issue Scenarios

The following three scenarios represent some of the resource issues that may arise during the project, and possible solutions for each:

Scenario One:

Issue: You need a skilled resource for a given percent of time, but can only have the resource for half of the percent.

Solutions: First, you should consider an alternate resource. Second, consider revising the activity in increments. Third, if neither will work, put the issue forward to the strategic manager.

Scenario Two:

Issue: You know you need a specific resource (a skill) on a particular date for a particular amount of time.

Solutions: First, request for a person by name well in advance of the date. If there is resistance, then put forth your schedule and issue to the strategic manager.

Scenario Three:

Issue: You cannot get resources because other projects have slipped.

Solutions: First, you should see if alternate resources are available. Second, you should work with the other project manager to see if you can use the resource on a part-time basis. Third, you need to determine the impact of your current solution. Fourth, you should determine your drop-dead date if you cannot resolve this issue and inform the strategic manager.

[F]   Project Planning versus Business Planning

Project managers and business managers may work in the same company, but they have distinctly different requirements. The IS administrator who has to be both types of managers has a difficult row to hoe. Here are 10 differences between project planning and business planning involving resources:

1. Project planning requires a place for contingency planning, while business planning does not.
2. Project planning needs to plan for the maximum use of resources, while business planning tries to minimize the use of resources.
3. Project planning cannot plan easily for peak periods, while business planning can more easily recognize peak periods such as Christmas sales or end-of-quarter requirements.
4. Project planning needs skills, while business planning considers headcount.

5. Project planning does not necessarily have to consider long-term benefits, while business planning does.

6. Project planning usually requires highly skilled personnel, while business planning can smooth out the skill requirements.

7. Project planning usually has limited financial histories to use as an estimating tool, while business planning has at least last year's budget to use for planning.

8. Project planning cannot survive on underplanning, while business planning might.

9. Project planning is concerned with achieving goals, while business is concerned with profit.

10. Project planning relies on contract services more than business planning.

§ 4.04   MANAGEMENT INVOLVEMENT

[A]   Overview

All levels of managers may have to be involved in resource management at one time or another. The tactical and operational managers may consider the most difficult task of resource planning to be estimating the time required to get through the bureaucratic red tape of procurement. This red tape has developed over the years in large corporations because a few managers have abused their rights in acquiring resources. Perhaps project management was left in these managers' closets. Resources cost real money that shows up on someone's bottom line. The skill levels are the least definable and measurable of the three types of resources. The acquisition of skills may be the most valuable resource that comes out of resource planning if they are equated not only to the project goals but also to the corporate goals. Actually, the most difficult resource activity is properly scheduling resources.

[B]   Strategic Resource Planning

Is strategic planning needed for resource planning? The answer is yes. The strategic manager should review the resource requirements. It is usually corporate policy for the strategic manager to review capital spending. This is an instance where the strategic and tactical managers decide if there is going to be equipment amortization. This manager might be able to add justifications for the resources in the context of corporate goals. A resource might be required for a long-range effort rather than just for the short-range effort of the project. The strategic manager should support any procurement effort in a timely fashion.

[C] Tactical Resource Planning

The fundamental tactical actions of the project manager include the following:

- Assist the operational managers in preparing documentation for procuring resources.
- Assist the operational managers in identifying resource links.
- Consider customer needs in acquiring resources.
- Consider if there are alternatives.
- Develop a formula for the availability of people.
- Emphasize the need for skills rather than headcount.
- Ensure that there are budget allocations to support resource requirements.
- Ensure that criteria exist that establish resource needs.
- Identify skills first by labor classification such as programmer, then by name.
- Know why and how a resource is going to be utilized in the project.
- Resolve capital spending.
- Resolve issues of the availability of resources to meet the schedule.
- Validate the need for any resource through a detailed analysis.
- Work with operational managers to ensure a balancing of resources.
- Work with the strategic manager to identify available resources.
- Write the resource plan.

Most of the actions listed above may seem straightforward. However, one that is tricky because it happens at the operational level is the balancing of resources. For example, a program manager should work with any operational manager who has a programmer working one week on the project for four hours and the next week for 80 hours. This varied work schedule is not a balancing of resources.

Also, when an operational manager seeks to get equipment six weeks before it is needed in the project schedule, the project manager needs to ask why the early acquisition is necessary. This situation, too, does not involve a proper balancing of resources.

Another tricky action is the determination of employee work hours. Full time does not mean being available 100 percent of the time. Here is a brief example of what it may mean to be a full-time employee in a company (excluding overtime, which is a moving variable):

- There are 52 weeks in a year with 40 work hours per week. This means a total of 2,080 hours of work a year.
- An employee gets at least two weeks' vacation a year. We need to subtract 80 hours from the yearly total, so we now have 2,000 hours available.

- An employee may be sick five days a year, so another 40 hours is removed from the total, leaving 1,960 hours.

- The company has 10 holidays a year so there goes another 80 hours, leaving 1,880 work hours a year.

- An employee will probably be involved in miscellaneous activities such as attending meetings (consider 20 percent of the year for these activities). The total for these activities comes to 416 hours, so we now have 1,464 hours.

- Each employee gets five days of training a year, so we now have 1,424 hours of work a year for a full-time employee.

From one company to the next, these figures will vary. Just plug in your own values. The 20 percent figure for miscellaneous activities may seem high to you. The 80–20 rule was used in this case.

Three guiding principles for a project manager are never to make the following assumptions:

1. A skill will be available when needed and for the time required.

2. Equipment will be delivered on time as required.

3. Resource requirements will stay stable throughout the project.

The project manager needs to work within these three resource constraints:

1. Vendor resources will be available on a restricted basis.

2. Computer resources may be limited even for an IS project.

3. Skill resources are usually available on a part-time basis.

[D]   Operational Resource Planning

It is the responsibility of the operational managers to give to the IS administrator— the tactical manager—realistic requirements and detailed justifications for any resource needs. The scope plan should be used as the starting point. The customers' needs should be the core for the utilization of any resource, not technical justification.

Operational managers need to consider alternative solutions to resource requirements if they hope to achieve the project goals. Achievement is not less than the goal or more than the goal; it is the goal. There is a tendency in some programming groups to give more than required and not provide exactly the functions the customer requested. Resources should be utilized to meet defined, measurable goals.

Here are some of the actions required of an operational manager for managing the resource plan:

- Balance project resources.
- Be able to justify why and how a resource is going to be utilized.
- Consider customer needs in acquiring resources.
- Consider any alternatives.
- Develop a formula for the availability of people for your group.
- Emphasize the need for skills rather than headcount.
- Procure approved resources.
- Support the tactical manager with justifications for the resource plan.
- Work with the tactical manager to identify resource links.
- Work within the constraints and assumptions of the scope plan in identifying resource requirements.

Exhibit 4-2: Resource Plan Chart

Project:			Issued:	
Preparer:			Revised:	
Resources	**Contact**	**Number**	**When Required**	**Availability/Notes**
			Sheet:	of

Exhibit 4-3: Resource Planning Questions Checklist

Project Name:	Comments
1. Are there alternate types of resources for unavailable ones?	
2. Are there resources that require capital funding?	
3. Have resources been closely related to cost estimates?	
4. Have skill level resources been defined in measurable terms?	
5. Have the project scope definitions been used to plan resource estimates?	
6. How do resources relate to one another? (chart)	
7. What are the critical resources for the project?	
8. What are the effects of the cost parameters on resource estimates?	
9. What are the impacts of the milestones on the resource estimates?	
10. What are the impacts on the project because resources are unavailable?	
11. What are the specific resource requirements?	
12. What documents are required to control resources?	
13. What is (are) the range(s) for having an inadequate resource(s)?	
14. What is the control system to manage resources and any changes?	
15. What is the policy on changes in resource requirements?	
16. What is the policy on when resources are required?	
17. What is the resource allocation policy?	
18. What is the resource utilization policy?	
19. What procurement (contractors) policies have to be followed?	
20. Who defines the resource requirements?	

On the CD-ROM

On the CD-ROM are:

1. Exhibit 4-1 Resource Plan Checklist.doc

2. Exhibit 4-2 Resource Plan Chart.doc

3. Exhibit 4-3 Resource Planning Questions Checklist.doc

4. Chapter 4 Overview.ppt—Chapter Overview, Resource Planning

Chapter 5

Time Estimating

§ 5.01   OVERVIEW

[A]   Objective

At the end of this chapter, you will be able to:

- State a definition for time estimating.
- List seven impacts on the project because of time estimating.
- Recognize seven time estimating principles.
- Evaluate the use of time sheets for time estimating.

- Identify five data types for time estimating.

- Ask 10 basic questions about time estimates such as: Have time estimates been established for quality control? What are the financial impacts of the time estimates? What are the time increments to be used? What is the project's duration? Who determines the time estimates, which become the basis for the schedule? Who should have inputs into the time estimates? Who should be notified of the time estimates?

- Differentiate between time estimating and scheduling.

- Identify 10 types of information for time estimates, criteria, policies, or procedures.

- Answer two core questions on the time-estimating process.

- Identify five steps for determining time–cost trade-offs.

- Identify how the three managing levels are involved in time estimating.

MANAGER'S TIP

There are basically two ways to create and schedule time estimates on a project. One is to be given a deadline—originating with upper management, clients, or elsewhere—by which the project must be delivered. Real-time, end-goal planning is required with this type of scheduling. The other is to set estimates and produce a plan to which all invested parties agree. This type of planning is called open planning. Although open planning sounds ideal, it is far too easy to let timelines (and budgets) creep, unless you have the luxury of working in a blue-sky R&D department.

In reality, most project managers will work with time definitions of some sort, so time estimates must be calculated wisely. Bear in mind the project manager who saw that the system upgrade project that was being led would not be completed on time, so the testing phase was cut short. The operational manager noticed the shortcuts (risk) that were being taken, forced the weighing of two factors against each other: the risk of missing the deadline resulting in customer dissatisfaction versus the risk of bringing up a system that could have problems that adequate testing would have revealed. The decision to push the deadline back was eventually made by the management team that oversaw the project, not by the project manager acting alone.

[B]   Using Essential Terms

You need to recognize that any discussion on estimates—whether time, resource, or cost—is relevant to the discussion in this chapter. However, the following five concepts are essential to any discussion about time estimates:

An **assumption** is a prediction that something will be true, either an action or an event that ensures project success.

A **critical path** is the most vital series of interlocking activities in a project. The other activities arise from and depend upon the execution of these activities on the critical path. The length of time required to accomplish the entire project is directly related to the length of time required by activities on the critical path.

Duration is the total time involved for an activity or task, including production time and wait time.

An **estimate** is a guess based on opinion or a forecast based on experience. One of the foundations for project planning is time estimating.

Time estimating is concerned with the duration of an individual activity or groups of related activities (tasks).

Using Supportive Definitions

The following concepts are used to refine the discussion of time estimates:

A **critical activity** or task, if not completed, means project failure.

The **Critical Path Method (CPM)**, in its simplest form, is selecting the "must" activities or tasks and doing them in the shortest possible amount of time and within the shortest duration. It is characterized by the fact that a slip in an activity time along the critical path will cause an equal slip in the expected completion date of the end event. All the events along this path have zero slack.

The **end–start dependency** means that an activity or task must end before another can start.

An **event** is a point in time such as the start or end of an activity or task.

Lag time is the time between two activities or tasks because of their natures.

Lead time is the overlapping time of two activities or tasks.

A **learning curve** is a graphical representation of repetitive tasks that, when done on a continuous basis, lead to a reduction in activity duration, resources, and costs.

Logistics is the process of getting the correct resource to the correct location at the correct time.

A **management review** is a regularly scheduled performance review.

An **objective** is a set of measurable goals to achieve a defined target that, if not achieved, has critical results.

A **quality audit** is an independent evaluation or test of some component of the project by qualified personnel.

Risk analysis is a technique, tool, or method for assessing, either quantitatively or qualitatively (or both), the impacts of an identified risk or a potential risk identified through a scenario.

The **schedule** is the duration of the project, including production time and wait time. It is also a production plan for the allocation of tasks with deadlines.

Scheduling is the task that formalizes the time estimates within a calendar structure. It is an integration of sequencing tasks, resource planning, cost estimating, and time estimating.

Slack time is the difference between earliest and latest (start or finish) times for an activity, a task, or an event.

Slippage (time) is expected when you know about a schedule problem before the due date; it is unexpected when you learn about it after the fact, that is after the due date.

The **start–end dependency** means that an activity or task must begin before another can end.

The **start–start dependency** means that one activity or task must start before another.

[C]   Time-Estimating Definition

Time estimating is more than establishing the amount of time you will need for an activity or for a resource. Time estimates include the following:

- Hours to do the activity with a given skill level
- Resource availability (full or part time)
- Continuous or incremental effort
- Project phase
- Assumptions for establishing a time estimate
- Constraints on establishing a time estimate

Time estimating is a parallel event to activity sequencing, cost estimating, and resource estimating.

There should be a defined realistic time estimate to meet identified measurable goals and, as appropriate, any project activity or grouping of activities. People who are familiar with the activities should do the estimating. One might also consider consultants who do time estimates in the case of a very large project with a critical end date. It may be important even to get vendors to give installation and configuration time benchmarks for their products.

MANAGER'S TIP

Project management considers the maximum use of time, while business management usually considers the minimum use of time.

[D]   Impacts of Time Estimating on the Project

The first place a project fails is with time estimates. The usual failure is that the estimates are unrealistic. The failure is usually based on the project manager's view of time compared with the views of involved business managers and customers. A key to good estimates is to have a measurable definition of the skill types and levels available.

When a project manager puts forth the total time estimates, the response usually given by the customer or a business manager is, "It cannot possibly take that long!" You should respond with strong supporting justification.

The start and end dates of the project should not be formally agreed upon between the project manager and the customer in fixed terms until this process is completed. If the end date is absolute, the project goals should be redefined. Time management is a critical part of the project process. This is another area where the use of project management software can be of great value. Scenarios can be set up to study and analyze the impacts of time changes. A one-day change can ripple through the schedule either positively or negatively.

The time estimates can affect a number of items or events in the project process. Some of these are:

- Cost estimates
- Activity sequencing
- Schedule
- Project benchmarks
- Resource planning
- Budget cycle
- Risks

You can see from the above list the reason that time estimates may be the core reason for the failure of a project. Can time management be done if the data are faulty? Firefighters rather than managers are needed to deal with bad estimates. Time estimates and activity sequences are the core basis used to develop the schedule. Most project reports are based on the status of the schedule. A bad estimate can throw off the expected date when pieces of equipment or materials are required. If you are on a regular budget review cycle, bad estimates can impact the receiving of funds. Bad estimates significantly increase the potentials for risks.

All time estimates should have associated cost estimates. The time and cost estimates do not have to be detailed to everyone. However, those responsible for time and cost estimates and budgetary planning should be involved. You may ask, "Why should every time estimate have a cost estimate?" A set of activities may require more time than expected or inexplicably cost more than the total of the individual items.

One can see from this discussion that time estimating can be at certain moments more of an art than a science. As noted earlier, many time management software packages are available to assist in doing your project. Perhaps the trickiest time estimate is the one for quality control. How do you do a time estimate for a major development failure that was caught by quality control that requires a significant amount of time for further testing? Bear in mind that if you do have measurable goals, then you have the core measurements for quality control. The time allocation for quality control might be 20 percent of the estimated time for the project. This task should be at the beginning of the planning phase. With this type of allocation, quality control can be your "left hand" in managing the project, the right hand being your own authority as given to you by the strategic manager.

MANAGER'S TIP

One solution for a nasty bug is a contingency fund. It should be a separate budget item in the project budget.

An example of a time estimate that is omitted frequently is the amount of time it takes to communicate with people, such as in meetings. Do not forget the number and length of conferences. Eight people in a room for an hour is one workday! It should not be shown as one hour. What does this idea communicate? You should not have conferences unless something really has to be said. Do not set up meetings for every Tuesday morning. Just make a statement to keep Tuesday mornings available for a meeting when required.

MANAGER'S TIP

A time-controlling technique is to have a published agenda for any meeting and a meeting report template so that you can state the points of a meeting in an expected manner quickly.

[E] Seven Time-Estimating Principles

When you collect time estimates, follow some principles to put some science into the art of making time estimates. The following is a list of these principles that will help you improve this project function:

1. Get the person who is to do the activity to do the estimating.

2. If no one is knowledgeable about the activity within the group, ask an outside expert.

3. Base time estimates on the productivity of the average.

4. Do all the time estimates, then do a total view.

5. Revise time estimates from the smallest to the largest.

6. Do not factor in the possibilities of part-time availability, overtime, or the project end date in getting the original time estimates.

7. Review of the time estimates should be by knowledgeable and objective people.

When you get an estimate from the person who is responsible for the activity, you get not only an estimate but also a commitment. This action also adheres to the principle of "ask an expert."

One area of expertise is the technical support department of the vendor that has a product you need to achieve a project goal. People in tech support should have historical data as to the amount of time it took to install and configure their product into another system. If they do not have this type of data, then immediately look somewhere else for another solution.

By using average productivity, you at least tone down one of the areas of failure: optimism. This also sets a minimum expectation when a better-than-average worker is available. You would also expect any contractor to exceed significantly this type of time estimate.

By waiting until all time estimates are available, you have a level playing field. There is no pressure to make the final estimates lower. Also, a sense of fairness will exist throughout the group. You may also get a realistic view of the time estimates for individual operational activities. All estimates should be factored at the same time to achieve a balance of the parts.

It may seem easier to adjust the largest time estimates first. It is not. If, after the lower estimates are changed, there is no significant result, then you should challenge the higher estimates. Ask questions that can lead to further justifications for the estimates, or that lead to a lowering of the estimate.

You should not factor in the possibilities of part-time availability, over-time, or the project end date in getting the original time estimates because they should be factors for developing solutions or benchmarks after everyone has defined his or her estimates. These possibilities are really constraints of the scheduling activity.

Review of the time estimates should be by knowledgeable people who are not a part of establishing the original time estimates. This team should be looking for "padding." Using the 80–20 rule, one might expect padding to run toward 20 percent in the larger estimates. One needs to look at one's own experience in this area. This does not mean you should automatically take 20 percent off all the time estimates.

[F]   Time Sheets and Time Estimating

One of the difficulties in using historical data such as time sheets is that they are unreliable. Programmers tend to put down eight hours a day against a project when they may have only directly worked four hours, the other four being such things as doing e-mail, going to meetings, or surfing the Internet. There are usually no codes for these activities.

Reliable time sheets can be a very valuable source of data. I do time sheets when writing a book. I note on a calendar start and end times for each writing session against a chapter. Over several years, I have acquired a trustworthy benchmark for estimating how long it takes me to do an average page of text. Thus when I go to do a book of a given length I know about how many hours it should take me. I also have an idea of how many hours I spend on an average day writing, so with time per page and writing per day, I can set up a schedule. The legal duration of the project is established by the book contract. An estimated duration of the project is the estimated time to do the writing divided by the average number of hours worked per day.

The point is, if you, the IS project manager, can find a method for setting up a reliable process for identifying time usage, you will have some excellent data to support any project time estimates. I was able to set up such a process and was able to manage time utilization for 16 writing projects and give customers reliable time benchmarks. For such a process to be successful, programmers need to see an advantage in keeping reliable time sheets.

[G]   Five Data Types for Time Estimating

Five data types you need to set up project time estimates include the following:

1. Quality control
2. Validation
3. General criteria
    — Procurement requirements
    — Material availability
    — Skill requirements
    — Equipment availability
4. Finance
    — Cost estimates
    — Budgetary requirements
5. Goal definitions

[H]   Ten Helpful Questions on Time Estimating

The answers to the following questions should be based on your goals and objectives for your project and the activities to achieve them. Think in plus and minus terms, in terms of an optimistic date and a pessimistic date for an activity. The completion point could be a range of days rather than a day. You still need an absolute date at the end of the range, but at least it is the pessimistic date.

ARE THERE TIME ESTIMATES FOR COMMUNICATING?   Time estimates should be formulated to show when and how long it will take to communicate with people. Communication includes writing and e-mailing project reports and status. Do not forget the number and length of conferences, and remember that eight people in a room for one hour equals a workday, not one hour.

HOW DO CHANGES IN TIME ESTIMATES AFFECT PROJECT RESULTS?   You should have time allocated for risk management in each of the key phases of the project to evaluate time changes. If you have no threats to the project in a given phase, look for opportunities.

WHAT IS THE PROJECT'S DURATION?   A project's duration is the total number of calendar days involved from start to end. A project that begins on March 1 and ends on September 30 of the same year has a duration of 214 days. Take all the time estimates if given in duration and determine if there is an overestimate, in which case the end date cannot be achieved. This determination is done even if the customer has given an absolute fixed date. For example, suppose a customer has stated that the project must be ready because there is going to be a rollout that starts on a given date. A question one could ask is, "What has to be demonstrated at the rollout?"

WHAT ARE THE TIME INCREMENTS FOR THE TIME ESTIMATES?   You can simply have a time line in calendar days with an activity sequence flow chart. A project management software program can assist in developing time estimates. Remember, there are many ways to present time estimates. For instance, is your definition of a man-month the same as my definition?

WHAT IS THE FINANCIAL IMPACT OF EXPANDING OR SHORTENING A TIME ESTIMATE?   All time estimates should have associated cost. The costs do not have to be detailed out to everyone. However, those responsible for cost estimates and budgetary planning should be involved. You may ask, "Why should every time estimate have a cost estimate?" A set of activities may cost more separately than they appear to as a whole.

WHAT IS THE IMPACT OF THE QUALITY CONTROL AND ASSURANCE PROCESSES ON TIME ESTIMATES? Quality control should have a specific amount of time allocated. You could set a benchmark of 20 percent of the estimated time for the project. This task has to be a part of your original estimating.

WHAT ARE THE IMPACTS OF THE RESOURCES ON THE TIME ESTIMATES? "Can four people be used instead of two and do the work in half the time?" is an invalid question. The question should be concerned with skill types and levels. A better question would be, "Can one expert do the work of two novices in less than half the time?"

WHAT ARE THE IMPACTS OF FOLLOWING PROCUREMENT POLICIES ON TIME ESTIMATES? It is better to be pessimistic than optimistic on time estimates in the area of procurement. Your time estimates can be seriously impacted when there is a delay in acquiring any required skills, equipment, or materials.

WHO DETERMINES THE TIME ESTIMATES THAT ARE USED TO ESTABLISH THE SCHEDULE? This is the point where you need at least an objective committee to analyze the time estimates. People doing the analysis need to be knowledgeable and have some criteria or standards to establish the validity of the time estimates. They should not accept a comment such as, "Oh, I think this activity might take so many days." This is not an effective statement unless there is a reason or reasons behind it. A more comfortable statement is, "I estimate the action will take this much time for these reasons."

WHO SHOULD HAVE INPUTS INTO OR BE NOTIFIED OF THE TIME ESTIMATES? When a time estimate has been distributed and is changed, there should be a list of those to be notified. Why was the phrase "been distributed" used in the previous statement? It can happen that even during this process, where supposedly estimates having been agreed upon, time estimates are changed without all the concerned parties being notified.

[I]   Time Estimating Compared to Scheduling

The following are 10 comparisons between time estimating and scheduling:

1. Time estimating is a consequence of analyzing; scheduling is a consequence of planning.
2. Time estimating is a component of scheduling; scheduling is an integration of sequencing activities, resource planning, cost estimating, and time estimating.
3. Scheduling is based on dependencies, the interrelationships of time, resources, and activities.
4. Times estimates are reviewed by tactical and operational managers, while the strategic manager reviews the schedule.

5. Time estimates are inputs into project management software; scheduling is the automatic output.

6. Time estimates are tasks, while a schedule is a plan.

7. Time estimating is at times an art, while scheduling is at times a science.

8. Time estimating is concerned with an individual activity or groups of related activities, while scheduling is concerned with the complete project.

9. Time estimating is to the schedule what cost estimating is to the budget.

10. Time estimating may be thought of as abstract, while scheduling may be thought of as concrete.

One may think scheduling is scientific because of available techniques and tools such as the Gantt chart (a common overstatement). The scheduling output is only as reliable as the time estimating inputs. The Gantt chart actually is an excellent visual presentation form, but it should not actually be equated to science, which is fundamentally the ability to repeat a measurement of an observable event.

[J] Time-Estimating Criteria, Policies, and Procedures

Time management experts or software tools should be used to develop time estimates. This is a process that can use historical data for establishing benchmarks. Pessimism is better than optimism in doing time estimates. Here are some of the types of information you need to finish this process:

- Criteria for associating cost and time estimates and potential changes
- Criteria for time-estimate formulas
- Criteria for time measurements
- Policy on notifying team members of project time changes
- Procedure for associating time estimates with people, equipment, and material acquisition
- Quality control and validation process for time estimates
- Specific time estimates for handling risks (threats or opportunities)
- Time estimates based on skill types and levels
- Time estimates that reflect the requirements of procurement policies
- Validating methodology for time estimates

[K] Time-Estimating Process

The two basic questions that start the time-estimating process are:

1. How can project milestones be made consistent?
2. What is the agreement on how milestones can be updated?

The first draft of milestones can be based on a specific calendar date, a number of days from when another milestone has been accomplished, or when a specific event is completed. Time should not be considered as a single "measurement." Perhaps a mixture is more practical than saying on day 21 an event will be completed. The important date is the "drop dead" date of the customer.

The milestones as formulated in your planning sessions should be made firm. Many people think of time in working days, but there are many other forms used in scheduling. Only two dates are important: start and finish. Of these two, the finish date is the more important.

A simple action of defining events is to draw a block with the start date at the top of a page of paper. You draw another box with the end date at the bottom of the page. Between these two boxes list all milestone activities and the estimated workdays to complete. Add the workdays of the milestone activities. Is the sum less than the workdays between the start and end dates? If the answer is yes, then you are okay. If the answer is no, then you have a problem in change management.

Resource planning is concerned with three prongs: skill types and levels, equipment, and materials. An important linkage to time is the available skill level involved. Perhaps an expert in a given area can do the activity in a third of the time as a novice. If the skill level is not available, how does the time for training impact your time estimates?

When ordering activities, one can use one timing format or a mixture of timing formats. Have you ever considered when setting up a time estimate that you say that the activity will be completed from *X*-day to *Y*-day?

The end result of time estimating is the schedule. How has the schedule been defined? You can simply have a time line in calendar days with an activity sequence flow chart. There are of course such scheduling concepts as start–end dependencies and lag–lead time relationships.

Cost estimates should reflect time estimates. The cost estimates should reflect the type of time measure used. If the time estimate formula uses plus or minus measures, then cost estimates should reflect this type of formula also.

Use time-management techniques and tools to validate your time estimates. Employ "what if" scenarios to assist in verification of time estimates. Utilize time measurements that reflect the situation of the project.

[L] Method for Determining Time–Cost Trade-offs

There are times when you are required to shorten the time for an activity to be completed. You need to determine the cost factor for doing so. Here is a five-step method for evaluating such trade-offs:

1. Compare the normal activity duration, such as number of weeks, with its defined costs; also compare the potential costs of the shortest duration with the maximum use of resources.

2. Compare incremental scenarios based on varying:
   — Skills available
   — Overtime
   — Equipment
   — Consultants
3. Identify the shortest duration.
4. Determine the availability of resources to do the shortest duration.
5. Determine the impact of change on the project.

[M]   Refining Data by Asking the Correct Questions

Along with bad cost estimates, bad time estimates can destroy a project more quickly than anything else. In fact, most risks are probably caused by inferior estimates (time, cost, or resource). For this reason, you must ensure that you have an excellent—not just good—interrogative process for refining your time estimates.

The responses to the following questions should be based on the goals and deliverables for your project and the tasks to achieve them. Think in terms of plus and minus; think in terms of an optimistic date and a pessimistic date, for both start and end dates, for an activity or a task. The completion point could be a range of days rather than a single day. You still need an absolute date (deadline) at the end of the range, but at least it is a "realistic" date.

MANAGER'S TIP

Unfortunately, an erroneous practice in time estimating is to give duration of days without stating what the production and wait times are.

The fundamental baseline of time estimates should be the critical path. The level of an impact is evaluated from this measurement. The Critical Path Method is the basic technique or tool for time estimates. The following 10 questions consider this technique for time estimate components.

1. What are the basic project assumptions and constraints that affect the time estimating process?
2. How should production time and wait time be noted in a time estimate?
3. When should time estimates be considered at both the activity and task levels?
4. What are the criteria for critical time estimates?

5. How should the time estimates be handled in the scope plan, activity plan, and resource plan?

6. Why is there a need for contingency time estimates?

7. Who approves time estimates?

8. What time dependencies have been considered in doing time estimates?

9. When is it important to consider lag times and lead times in time estimates?

10. What are the criteria for defining a time estimate as optimistic, realistic, or pessimistic?

§ 5.02   MANAGEMENT INVOLVEMENT

[A]   Overview

While time estimating seems more an art than a science, all the management levels can be involved in the defining of reliable time estimates. Everyone looks at the schedule as gospel when it really is not; it is a visual presentation based almost completely on some type of estimate. Time estimating is a major component used in developing the schedule. The chain is only as strong as its weakest link. By following the principles enumerated earlier in this chapter, management can more likely ensure reliable time estimates to achieve customer-defined needs, the project goals.

[B]   Strategic Time Estimating

The strategic manager should ensure the availability of knowledgeable people, including outside consultants, to evaluate the time estimates. The manager should ensure that the project's time-estimating process is consistent with other time-estimating processes in the company. The manager should also assist the tactical manager in resolving any divisional issues on time estimates for the project.

[C]   Tactical Time Estimating

The basic tactical actions of the project manager include the following:

* Ensure there are criteria for defining time estimates, such as:
  — Define the estimates against the project goals
  — Define estimates to average capabilities
  — Do not factor in overtime or possible part-time efforts
  — Time estimates should be done if possible by the person who will do the activity

— Define the time measurements (hours, eight-hour days, or 20-day work months)

- Collect all the estimates before doing a total overview.
- Use technical support of vendors to define any installation or configuration time estimates.
- Establish a process where time estimating becomes more a science than an art.
- Resolve a too-large total of time estimates for the project by beginning with the smallest and working to the largest.
- Set daily project priorities to manage time-estimate issues.
- Analyze time estimates to see possible impacts on the skills, resources, and materials needed for the project.
- Determine with the operational managers what risks might develop with changes to the time estimates.
- Resolve time issues such as getting a required resource well in advance of required date.
- Use project management software to assist in evaluating time estimates.
- Determine how time estimates impact costs (each operational area probably has its own cost per labor-hour).
- Determine how the budget cycle might impact the time estimates, especially those in the fourth quarter.
- Include time estimates for quality control and assurance.
- Determine how time estimates may impact acquisition of outside resources.
- Document issues and discuss at meetings.
- Look for "forgotten" activities that need time estimates such as meetings, training, and documenting.
- Factor procurement requirements into appropriate time estimates.
- Finish the time-estimating process before attempting to do the scheduling process.

[D]   Operational Time Estimating

The basic functions of the operational managers include the following:

- Identify the people knowledgeable to do the time estimates.
- Notify the tactical manager if there is no one available to do certain time estimates.

- Use the criteria created by the project team for developing the time estimates.

- Limit padding (actually, you should have no padding).

- Review time estimates beginning with the smallest to the largest for signs of excess.

- Include time estimates for quality control and assurance.

- Look for "forgotten" activities that need time estimates such as meetings, training, and documenting.

- Review the inputs of the project management software used by the tactical manager for your operational area.

Exhibit 5-1: Time Estimates Checklist

	Attachments
Time estimates by scenario	
Pessimistic	
Realistic	
Optimistic	
Criteria by scenario	
Pessimistic	
Realistic	
Optimistic	
Impacts by scenarios	
Pessimistic	
Realistic	
Optimistic	
Estimates by project goals	
Source ID	
Critical estimates	
Procurement tasks	
Skills development	
Resource tasks	
Material gathering	
Support tasks	

Exhibit 5-1 (*Continued*)

	Attachments
Training tasks	
Documentation tasks	
Production tasks	
Planning	
Design	
Development	
Testing	
Defined assumptions used	
Defined constraints used	
Deliverables accounted for	
Adequate duration	
Schedule requirements used	
Deadline criteria	
Quality	
Control	
Assurance	
Validation	
Field testing	
Resource procurements	
Equipment	
Internal	
External	
Materials	
Internal	
External	
Skills	
Internal	
External	
Project management tools	
Internal	
External	

Exhibit 5-1 (*Continued*)

	Attachments
Development tools	
Internal	
External	
Facilities	
Internal	
External	
Logistics	
Internal	
External	
Training requirements	
Internal	
External	
Documentation requirements	
Internal	
External	
Communications requirements	
Internal	
External	
Risk management	
Project administration	
Special time estimate criteria	
Duration	
Production time	
Wait time	
Calendar days	
Period/effort	
Dependency	
End–start	
Start–end	
Start–start	
Lag time	

Exhibit 5-1 (Continued)

	Attachments
Lead time	
Slack time	
Trade-off considerations	
Part-time staff	
Full-time staff	
Other	
Special variants noted	
Consistency to:	
Scope plan	
Activity plan	
Resource plan	
Manager's approval:	

Instructions for the Time Estimates Checklist

This checklist assists the project team in writing the Project Activity Plan, the project schedule, and the project budget. It is used by each operational manager to do these documents at a group level or departmental level.

Time estimates by scenario: All project time estimates must be given in three forms: pessimistic, realistic, and optimistic. Actual format instructions come from the project team. The estimates should reflect items given in this checklist. A confidence level should be included with each estimate.

Criteria by scenario: There should be objective data to support the three types of estimates. The sources for the criteria include standards, benchmarks, historical records, or project team requirements.

Impacts by scenario: There should be explanations for each of the estimate types. For example, the estimate is pessimistic because no one is immediately available at this time with the skill level to do the task in less than three months. Another example is if the pessimistic estimate happens, then X risk may happen by affecting other estimates.

Estimates by project goals: Estimates should be linked to the projects goals as found in the project scope plan.

Source ID: Identify the person responsible for writing the time estimates, including title, e-mail address, and telephone number. If an external source, also include company information.

Critical estimates: For the listed items, give the justifications for being designated critical.

Defined assumptions: Use the assumptions from the scope plan to develop estimates.

Defined constraints: Use the constraints from the scope plan to develop estimates.

Deliverables: Give links to project deliverables for each estimate.

Adequate duration: Give the criteria for task duration that includes both production and wait times.

Schedule requirements: Use the project schedule requirements as defined by the project team.

Deadline criteria: Use deadline criteria as defined by the project team that is based on the scope plan.

Exhibit 5-1 (*Continued*)

Quality: Give any possible estimates that you consider relevant to the listed areas that might be required for product validation or field testing. Justifications should be included such as reference to a standard or benchmark.

Resource procurements: If a resource (hardware, software, skill, or support materials) has to be acquired from an external source, give estimates for the procurement tasks such as negotiation and administrative times.

Risk management: Consider, if a pessimistic scenario breaks down, the possible time required for correcting.

Project administration: Based on the project team requirements, give estimates. In addition, consider time estimates for giving status reports to operational team by either e-mail or status presentations.

Special Time Estimate Criteria

Each of the following items is of a technical nature to assist you in writing a time estimate:

Duration:

Production time: Actual days of work.
Wait time: Actual days when work is not being done such as weekends and holidays.
Calendar days: Use the Gregorian calendar.
Period/effort: A period is an amount of time, while an effort is the amount of work to complete a task.

Dependency:

End–start: It means that an activity or task must end before another can start.
Start–end: It means that an activity or task must begin before another activity or task can end.
Start–start: It means that one activity or task must start before another.
Lag time: It is the time between two activities or tasks because of the nature of the activities.
Lead time: It is the overlapping time of two activities or tasks.
Slack time: It is the difference between earliest and latest (start or finish) times for an activity or a task.

Trade-off considerations:

Part-time staff: State such as one hour per day or once a week. Justify the use of a part-time staff over the use of a full time.

Full-time staff: Give impacts of having full time over part time. Justify the use of a full-time staff over the use of a part-time one.

Other: Identify if there is a need for a consultant or any other outside staff.

Special variants: Give any additional information that might assist the project team in its responsibilities and minimize further discussions.

Consistency: There should be links in the justifications or impacts to the listed documents.

Scope plan: It is the strategic view of the constraints and assumptions of the project as developed by the project team.

Activity plan: It is a set of definitions for efforts required to achieve measurable results. At the operational level, you consider activities; at the project level, tasks.

Resource plan: It establishes support requirements for a project as to costs, availability, start date and end date (length of time for use plus duration), and technical specifications.

Manager's approval: The manager should be of an appropriate management authority to agree to the time estimate.

Exhibit 5-2: Time Estimating Questions Checklist

Project Name:	Comments
1. Are the time estimates based on skill types and levels?	
2. Are there specific time estimates for handling risks?	
3. Are there time estimates for communicating?	
4. Do the time estimates reflect the requirements of procurement policies?	
5. How do changes in time estimates affect project results?	
6. Is there a validating methodology for time estimates?	
7. What are the criteria for associating cost and time estimates and potential changes?	
8. What are the criteria for a time-estimate formula?	
9. What are the criteria time measurements?	
10. What are the impacts of procurement policies on time estimates?	
11. What are the impacts of the resources on the time estimates?	
12. What are the time increments for the time estimates?	
13. What is the financial impact of expanding or shortening a time estimate?	
14. What is the impact of the quality control and assurance processes on time estimates?	
15. What is the policy on notifying team members of project time changes?	
16. What is the procedure for associating time estimates with people, and equipment and people acquisition?	
17. What is the project's duration?	
18. What is the quality control and validation process for time estimates?	
19. Who determines the time estimates that are used to establish the schedule?	
20. Who should have inputs into or be notified of the time estimates?	

On the CD-ROM

On the CD-ROM are:

1. Exhibit 5-1 Time Estimates Checklist.doc
2. Exhibit 5-2 Time Estimating Questions Checklist.doc
3. Chapter 5 Overview.ppt—Chapter Overview, Time Estimating

Chapter 6

Schedule Developing

§ 6.01   OVERVIEW

[A]   Objectives

At the end of this chapter, you will be able to:

- State a definition for scheduling.
- Identify three types of schedule assumptions.
- Explain five essential terms related to the schedule.

- List six types of information required to support the scheduling activity.
- Identify 10 types of data needed for scheduling.
- Name the four types of activity time start–end dependencies.
- Distinguish between lag and lead times.
- Ask 10 basic questions about scheduling such as: Are budgetary procedures going to impact the schedule? Are there available resources to meet the schedule? Are there realistic milestones? Does the reliability of the time estimates affect the schedule? Have key schedule approvers been identified? How does the ordered activity sequence affect the schedule? How does the schedule meet customer expectations?
- Differentiate between scheduling and time estimating.
- Identify six factors in schedule alignment.
- Develop solutions for schedule slippage.
- State a four-step approach for correcting a schedule.
- Identify how the three managing levels are involved in scheduling.

MANAGER'S TIP

Before reading this chapter, you should read Chapter 5 on time estimates. Put most simply, "A schedule is a formal graphic document of a set of time estimates."

If you have been following the procedures outlined in this book, then you have all the materials necessary to produce a schedule—the result of matching up planning with available resources. At this point, you might think that producing a schedule is just another onerous piece of paperwork, but its importance cannot be overestimated.

The schedule is a graphic representation of time and resource estimates. It is the project plan that is presented to upper management and to clients. If you are working in a situation in which there is a lack of top management interest or communication, then the schedule can help you facilitate buy-in and even collaboration. For the client, the schedule functions as a road map for the project that might have seemed overwhelmingly complex before being evaluated, outlined, and illustrated.

In one case, an intranet for a small company had to be networked in a specific period of time. It would enable communication and collaboration among employees who regularly worked outside the office, as well as for those in-house who worked on projects together.

The systems administrator came up with a simple timetable of tasks and dates that eventually proved inadequate because it did not provide enough detail on activities and resources. The reports to other managers were vague—"running late" or "need a couple of days more." Because there was no concrete, visual measurement of time and tasks, the project ran over schedule.

Practically speaking, the schedule helps you answer two fundamental questions: Where *should* we be on the schedule now? Where *are* we exactly?

[B]   Using Essential Definitions

Because a schedule is, first, a visual presentation of time-oriented efforts of a project and, second, a project standard or baseline for managing a project, there are a large number of essential concepts. Here are 14 essential concepts (the list actually could be longer):

The **schedule** is the duration of the project, including production time and wait time. It is also a production plan for the allocation of tasks with deadlines.

A **critical activity** or task is one which, if not completed, results in project failure.

A **critical path** is when there is no available time for the slippage of the activity or task (that is no slack time).

The **Critical Path Method (CPM)** in its simplest form is selecting the "must" activities and doing them in the shortest possible amount of time, and within the shortest duration.

Duration is the total time involved of an activity or task, including production time and wait time.

The **end–start dependency** means that an activity or task must end before another can start.

An **estimate** is a guess based on opinion or a forecast based on experience. Because a set of time estimates is the basis for any schedule, it is the foundation for project planning.

An **event** is a point in time such as the start or end of an activity or task.

Lag time is the time between two activities or tasks because of their natures.

Lead time is the overlapping time of two activities or tasks.

A **project's duration** is the total number of calendar days involved from start to end, including the project manager's activities in closing the project.

Scheduling is the task that formalizes the time estimates within a calendar structure. It is an integration of sequencing tasks, resource planning, cost estimating, and time estimating.

The **start–end dependency** means that an activity or task must begin before another can end.

The **start–start dependency** means that one activity or task must start before another.

MANAGER'S TIP

Critical chain project management, which focuses on bottom-line results and reduced cycle time, is fast becoming standard practice for project managers. The critical chain or Critical Path Method, when used in conjunction with computer-based collaboration tools, helps make quantitative risk management and effective scheduling possible.

[C]   Schedule Process Definition

Scheduling is the activity that formalizes the time estimates within a calendar structure. To the project manager, it is a plan for managing time, while to business managers it is a commitment. The schedule is a document that at least links the sequences of activities, resource availability, start–end time dependencies, and lag–lead time relationships. The schedule is to time as the budget is to cost.

The schedule can be as elaborate as required. It should be usable. An example of a schedule is a flow chart with milestones and dates. There could also be links to team members and their responsibilities for the project. A schedule should include the quality control milestones and the verification milestones.

This process requires analyzing the milestone interrelationships. The sequence and duration (the period of time to accomplish the activity) of primary and secondary activities also need to be considered. The impact of resource requirements is equally important.

"Developing a schedule" is to "estimating time" as "ordering a set of activities" is to "defining a set of activities." It is an ordering of activities along a time line.

Developing a schedule is the establishment of a *realistic* and *achievable* plan. These are two important criteria. If they are met, all parties involved will have manageable expectations.

Automated time-management software tools are available to develop this type of schedule. Some of the software is very inexpensive, while others can be very expensive. However, a pencil can be as effective as an ink pen as a tool, and it costs much less. A number of manual methods can be used for scheduling. For example, you could write the activities on index cards and then stick them to the wall until a logical order and associations are made. This is a cheap, but very effective, scheduling method.

Time-management software is handy for determining start–end dependencies quickly and giving you visual clues on lag–lead time relationships. This is an activity where fixed time and order activities are combined. A schedule can be presented as a calendar with activities inserted, or it can be an elaborate flow chart with dates placed on the directional arrows.

[D]   Three Types of Schedule Assumptions

Any schedule is based on one of three types of estimates, or a combination of two or all three. The types of estimates are:

1. Pessimistic—assumption is that if something can go wrong, it will
2. Realistic—assumption is that there will be a few problems, but with compromise difficulties will be overcome
3. Optimistic—assumption is that everything will go as planned

The reality of scheduling is that on some activities one position will be assumed, on others another assumption is applied, and on what is left the third assumption is used. Some people believe the project should go ahead even with the pessimistic assumption, although they personally think the project is like the unsinkable R.M.S. *Titanic*. The one person who cannot have a completely pessimistic position is the project manager.

[E]   Essential Scheduling Terms

Any project activity has special terms related to it. Sometimes a term is used in a special instance with an activity, such as *slippage*. One can have a slippage in the schedule or a slippage in the budget. The budget slippage is usually referred to as an overrun or some other appropriate financial term. The following five terms are relevant to scheduling:

1. Critical path
2. Duration
3. Gantt chart
4. Milestone
5. Slack time

A **critical path** exists when there is no available time for the slippage of the activity. The Critical Path Method is identifying critical activities that must be accomplished to achieve project goals and their zero slack date.

Duration is the period each activity will take from start date to end date. An activity may take 10 hours to accomplish, but the 10 hours may cover a duration of five days. Waiting time has to be factored into duration. Duration should not include any thoughts on padding to achieve a moment of glory; it may be more like a day of infamy.

A **Gantt chart** is a visual presentation of activities against time. A Gantt chart is probably one of the most effective methods of presenting a project plan and its progress. A Gantt chart includes a critical path, milestones, and slack time. The Gantt chart is discussed in more detail in Section Two on project tools and techniques.

A **milestone** is a clearly defined date of start or full completion. There are always at least two milestones for a project, start and end. However, there may be groupings of activities that have other milestones, such as the project phases of design, development, testing, and implementation. One could have milestones just for the coding activity. Milestones provide for the project manager a formal mechanism for verifying project status. Milestones can be either internal or external. The internal milestones impact the operational project teams. The external milestones involve the customer.

Slack time is the time differential between the scheduled completion date and the required date. Slack time is used to determine the critical path for a PERT network. For example, if two days of coding are required, the coding can begin anytime within a certain set of seven calendar days and the coding activity end date can still be met. The slack time is five days, not seven.

[F]   Support Data for Scheduling

To support a schedule you need the following:

- Defined project scope
- Activities defined and ordered (put into a logical sequence)
- Activity costs
- Reliable time estimates
- Resources defined, including any special requirements and the time estimates for procuring them
- Essential milestones defined

The schedule could be based on calendar time or on a critical path where the completion of a given event or set of events is important to the completion of project goals.

[G]   Ten Data Types for Project Scheduling

Behind any list of data types there is the assumption that you will have reliable time estimates. This issue was discussed in Chapter 5. The following are 10 types of data you need when you develop a complete schedule:

1. Change notification schedule
2. Communications points scheduled
3. Criteria for changing the schedule
4. Critical path (optional)

5. Quality control and validation schedule
6. Schedule based on the scope definition
7. Time allocated for risk management
8. Time line (calendar, flow chart)
9. Time line for acquiring skills, equipment, and materials
10. Time lines that are consistent and coherent

[H]   Activity Start-End Dependencies Definition

When you have all your support documents and all your reliable estimates, you are ready for the next step. All the activity sequences, activity time estimates, resource estimates, quality control and assurance time estimates, administrative time estimates, training estimates, and documentation estimates need to be calendar-ordered. Next, these require links between the activities according to four types of start–end dependencies. These four dependency types are:

- Start–start
- Start–end
- End–start
- End–end

The *start–start dependency* means that one activity must start before another, or before other activities can be done concurrently. For example, all the "estimating" project activities usually start together and are done concurrently. Activities that can be of the start–start dependency type can usually be grouped together in the project phases:

- Design
- Development
- Testing
- Implementation
- Validation

The *start–end dependency* means that an activity must begin before another activity can end. An example of this is the time-estimating activity really cannot end until the scheduling activity begins. Another example is you must complete the initial procurement process before you can hire a consultant. When the consultant is hired, the first phase of procurement is over.

The *end–start dependency* means that an activity must end before another can start. All the estimating of project activities needs to be defined as completely as possible before you get on with the scheduling activity. This may be considered the most common dependency. Another example is that coding must be completed before implementation, but not before testing.

The *end–end dependency* means that an activity cannot end until another activity has also ended. The obvious case is that testing cannot end before coding has also ended. An activity that has a distinctive problem because of this type of dependency is documentation.

MANAGER'S TIP

A variation on start–end is start–finish. The general ends the war; the racer finishes the race.

[I] Lag Time versus Lead Time

Another element in the schedule is the type of time involved with the start–end dependencies. Lag time is the time between two activities because of the nature of the activities. There is lag time between when you write a documentation plan and complete the documentation plan. Lag time occurs between the time when the training plan is approved and the time when it is implemented. There is nothing optional here, this is reality. There is lag time between the design phase and the testing phase, the development phase.

The lead time is the overlapping time of two activities. How much lead time has to exist with coding and testing?

Start–end dependencies and lag–lead times are based on activities, not availability of resources. The premise is that you have unlimited resources.

[J] Ten Questions to Assist in Scheduling

The core question (can be referred to as the metaquestion) of this activity is, "What is the best way of presenting integrated activities with a time line so that it communicates clearly the expected outcomes?"

HAVE THE WHO'S, WHAT'S, WHERE'S, AND HOW'S BEEN CLEARLY DEFINED AND PLACED IN THE SCHEDULE? This is the activity that also includes the when's. The environmental expectations should be fully defined at this point except for budgetary considerations.

HAVE THE PEOPLE WHO CAN HAVE AN IMPACT ON OR APPROVE THE SCHEDULE BEEN IDENTIFIED? In the schedule, it should be defined when people come into and when people leave the project process. You, the project manager, come into the project at the start date and leave at the close-out date. For you the end date is when the close-out is completed, not when the project goals are achieved.

HAVE THE START AND END TIMES BEEN CONFIRMED? HAVE EXPECTED DELIVERABLES BEEN IDENTIFIED?   The dates for the scope definition are start and end. Other important milestones should be when the customers expect to be given a status report of the project.

ARE THE ESSENTIAL SCHEDULED MILESTONES REALISTIC?   Use time-management techniques and tools (software) to validate the schedule. Use what-if scenarios to assist in verification of time estimates. Use time measures that reflect the situation of the integration.

HOW ARE THE BUDGETARY PROCEDURES GOING TO AFFECT THE SCHEDULE?   The activities leading up to and involved in making changes to the budget should be in the schedule. One of the activities on the schedule is to report on the status of the budget. This may be done at a high level of management, but this activity should be defined.

MANAGER'S TIP

One nervous project manager was so afraid that his project budget would be cut that he purchased all of the equipment required for his project as soon as the project was approved. Due to programming delays, 18 months passed before the timekeeping system was ready for rollout to the customer. Meanwhile, the warranty had expired on equipment that was yet to be unpacked! Now his budget assumed the burden for repair costs for any dead-on-arrival equipment. Even worse, half of the equipment consisted of personal computers. Waiting 18 months would have almost doubled his equipment capabilities!

HAVE THE QUALITY CONTROL EVENTS BEEN INCLUDED AT APPROPRIATE MILESTONES?   Within any schedule the quality control and verification milestones should be clearly defined. The quality control time line may be defined as a separate time line; however, when and where quality control flows into the main part of the integration project must be stated.

ARE HISTORICAL DATA AVAILABLE TO DETERMINE ADEQUATE RESOURCES?   Sometimes the use of historical data can be important in establishing a schedule. For example, you may have kept records on how long it took to do the configuration for various applications in your intranet. The figure(s) can be used as a benchmark(s). A better set of figures, of course, would include information on what skill level was required to do the configurations.

HOW WILL THE SCHEDULE AND ITS CHANGES BE GIVEN TO THE CUSTOMERS?   The schedule should reflect when you or your designates communicate status or significant changes to customers. Marketing may have a program that it forgot to tell you about and it has used your original dates in the schedule to establish its actions. One day may not make a difference to the customer, but 10 days may.

HOW CAN THE FORMULATED SCHEDULE IMPACT THE OUTCOME OF INTEGRATION? The schedule should at key milestones have activities that assess the project's status and determine if there are potential opportunities and threats.

CAN RESOURCES BE ACQUIRED ON TIME?   The schedule should have the flexibility to handle the procurement of outside resources (skills, equipment, and materials). There should be time in the schedule to follow the procedures required to do any procurement.

[K]   Scheduling Compared to Time Estimating

The following are 10 comparisons between scheduling and time estimating:

1. A schedule is a plan to follow, while time estimates are tasks to be done.
2. Scheduling is a consequence of planning; time estimating is a consequence of analyzing.
3. Scheduling is an integration of sequencing activities, resource planning, cost estimating, and time estimating.
4. Scheduling is at times a science, while time estimating is at times an art.
5. Scheduling is based on dependencies, the interrelationships of time, resources, and activities.
6. Scheduling is concerned with the complete project, while time estimating is concerned with an individual activity or groups of related activities.
7. Scheduling is the automatic output from project management software, while time estimates are inputs.
8. Scheduling may be thought of as a concrete process, while time estimating may be thought of as an abstract process.
9. The strategic manager looks at the schedule, while the tactical and operational managers look at time estimates.
10. The schedule is to time estimates what the budget is to cost estimates.

Some people consider scheduling to be "scientific" because of project management tools such as the Gantt chart. The scheduling output is only as reliable as the time-estimating inputs. The Gantt chart is an excellent visual presentation form, but it should not actually be equated to science, which is fundamentally the ability to repeat a measurement of an observable event.

[L]   Aligning the Schedule

One of the goals in the time estimating was to get all the estimates before establishing the schedule. You did this, and now you have completed your schedule. There is one problem; the schedule says it will take six months longer to complete the project than the customer's requirement. If there is a lean schedule, here are six things you might do to realign the schedule:

1. Define whether the date is absolute or flexible.
2. Determine if the project can be done in segments.
3. Diminish functionality.
4. Increase resources (staff).
5. Subcontract.
6. Waive organizational standards.

First, work with the customer to see how concrete the end is. If the customer is going to lose a large sum of money because of project failure, then it is no-go. However, if there is slack time because of a general marketing effort, then a beginning effort can be made.

Second, check with the customer to see if the project can be done in segments. Determine how critical timing is to achieving the project goals. Perhaps one goal can be completed the first quarter, another the second quarter, and then you can get back on a reduced schedule.

Third, consider reducing functionality. Perhaps one feature is critical, other features are needed over a broader period, and there may be one or more features that are just desirable. Determine how the project can be realigned by this analysis.

Fourth, consider adding people. The customer needs to understand the effect on the price. You need to check on availability of resources and working space. It is easier to add staff in the planning stage than after the work begins.

Fifth, consider subcontracting some of the functionality. This is a variation on adding people, except you are going out of house to resolve the problem. You need to consider companies that specialize in the development required. They also may be able to do the development quicker than in-house staff.

Sixth, consider (with higher management's approval) ignoring organizational rules, such as adjusting staff members' hours or limiting paperwork requirements. A person may work better if he or she can come in midday and stay later rather than coming in at the standard hour.

If none of the six possibilities works to realign the schedule to the customer's satisfaction, there is one more option. The option is just say no. The customer will consider you to have more integrity than if you attempted the schedule and failed. In addition, the customer may then reconsider the options.

[M]   Resolving Slippage

Some activity is going to come in late. What are you going to do about it? There are two types of slippage, the expected and the unexpected. The expected slippage is one that you know about *before* the due date. The unexpected slippage is one you learn about *after* the due date. One can manage the first, while the second is a no-no on the part of an operational manager.

The second should be prevented through open discussions at status meetings. This type of failure should be discussed in private with the offending manager. The manager needs to be told why (s)he was not informed. If a slippage happens very near the end of the activity, it is one thing; however, if the slippage was early in the activity, one might consider oneself misled. An unexpected slippage might be considered worse than being late. Not to be informed that a programmer who was expected to work on a project activity quit and a suitable replacement has not been found is a significant example of an unexpected slippage.

Here are some actions you can take to resolve a slippage:

- Consider extension of the schedule.
- Consider overtime as a last resort; the budget quickly overruns.
- Consider with the customer a reduction in the affected project goal; have supporting data.
- Correct in private, but be firm.
- Discover the extent of the slippage's impact; it may be minimal.
- Do not panic.
- Do not throw more resources into the pot to try to correct the slippage; there is the activity learning curve.
- Look for shortcuts or different approaches to accomplish the activity.
- Use project management software to develop various scenarios for possible solutions.

MANAGER'S TIP

Don't count on overtime to meet the finish date. It should only be used for occasional catch-up of a task. Working continual overtime will only cause the people to slow down. In essence, you will be spending more time to achieve your normal 40 hours of result. If the team members become worn out on the project, you will lose still further time training their replacements.

[N]   Correcting a Schedule

You now have a schedule, but you think you might have errors. The following four-step approach can be used to help you make corrections:

1. Analyze the schedule to identify any area that needs correction.
2. Determine the course of action to make the correction.
3. Revise the areas that require correction.
4. Evaluate the new schedule for impacts.

Analysis can be handled in at least two ways. First, have the operational managers analyze their areas against the inputs. Second, use a time-management tool to assist.

The course of action should be according to the type of errors found. The basic assumption is that you have time-estimating errors rather than other types of errors.

In evaluating impacts, you need to consider duration, cost estimates, resource availability, lag–lead times, start–end dependencies, and potential slippage. The fifth step in this approach is to discuss the conclusions with the customer and get the customer's approval before finalizing the schedule to the team.

MANAGER'S TIP

This schedule correction approach, if slightly modified, can be used also for changing or updating the schedule because of customer requests or for other unforeseen reasons.

[O]   Refining Data by Asking the Correct Questions

As the project manager, you should ask the following 20 questions about your tactical scheduling actions. Implied in each question are one or more data type requirements:

1. When applicable, how are vendors to be given the schedule's status?
2. How can resources be made available in accordance with the schedule?
3. How can the company's budget cycle impact the schedule, especially in the fourth quarter?
4. How do you ensure that the schedule realistically reflects the training and documentation requirements?
5. How do varying cost estimates impact the schedule?
6. How does the schedule potentially impact the skills, resources, and materials required for the project?

7. How should resource leveling be used?

8. How was the schedule developed using the project goals?

9. What are the criteria for ensuring that the quality management schedule is appropriate?

10. What are the project assumptions and constraints for developing the schedule?

11. What are the risk criteria that can affect the schedule?

12. What are the schedule alignment criteria?

13. What lag-time and lead-time relationships were defined?

14. What types of project management tools should be used to manage the scheduling process?

15. When should "forgotten" tasks be determined in the scheduling process?

16. When were estimates defined to average capabilities?

17. Where are the links in the schedule for outside resources that are critical to the project's success?

18. Where in the schedule are events that can be impacted by procurement policies?

19. Who defines the start- and end-time dependencies?

20. Why should issues be documented and discussed at meetings?

[P] Using a Schedule Development Checklist

The development of any form or checklist (see Exhibit 6-2: Checklist for Creating a Project Schedule at the end of this chapter) must be based on the basic definition of a schedule; that is, it is the duration of the project, including production time and wait time. It is also a production plan for the allocation of tasks with deadlines. It is a formal, visual, logical, and chronological statement of time estimates for a project's tasks.

You need a schedule that is readable, usable, and reliable for the project team. The schedule becomes one of the fundamental documents of the project, which is used to give status presentations to your upper management and the customers. Perhaps the only forms or checklists you need that are related to a schedule are based on an analytical methodology for determining the basis for these status presentations. This basis can be a simple checklist that leads to complex input. The schedule is a project baseline. You determine:

- What the project variances are.
- How the project variances occurred.
- When the project variances occurred.
- Where the project variances occurred.
- Why the project variances occurred.

Notice that "who caused the variances" is not listed. When you include this item, you get into people issues, which can actually block the success of resolving the variances.

What data do you need? The data come from the scope plan, the activity plan, and the resource plan. A schedule is more that just a time line; a Gantt chart can be considered an example of a basic type of time line. Although the schedule is a visual representation of the relationships of various task sequences, you also need supportive data. The most important task sequence is of course, the critical path. The critical path is derived from the critical tasks done in the least amount of time (that is no slippage).

From your time estimates, you should include support for their assumptions and constraints attached to the schedule. Each activity should be given as duration with production and wait times, not just a dot on a calendar. The schedule should be given in a 24 × 7 mode, because some of the logistic events may occur at any time. Essential technical data for tasks from the time estimates should include:

- End–start dependencies
- Lag time
- Lead time
- Start–end dependencies
- Start–start dependencies

You should develop links—especially to critical resources—using the data developed in resource plan. You need to have a clear notation as to the different types of links by using for example different colors or special icons as determined by the project team. (Do not use red and green, because these two colors carry emotional burdens.) You need links indicating when critical skills, hardware, software, and materials are to be used.

MANAGER'S TIP

In Chapters 7 and 8, cost estimates and the project budget are discussed. There should be appropriate links for critical cost and budget data. For example, you might have links when funding is to occur, who is doing the funding, and how the funding is to be done.

There are three important data types from the resource plan that need to be linked to the schedule. They are:

1. Who (single user or multiple users) is going to use the resource?
2. Where (location) is the resource going to be used?

3. When (production and wait times and duration) is the resource to be used (one time, more than once, or on a continuous basis)?

Exhibit 6-2 is a simple form with an important implied idea. The idea is that, for any activity or task sequence, you should have three timelines: optimistic, realistic, and pessimistic. The basic use of this concept is for the critical path.

The ideas given here on data types associated with the schedule are not considered inclusive. You must consider management abilities, the size of the project, the needs of your customers, the needs of your upper management, and, last but not the least, the abilities and needs of your project team.

The local situation ultimately determines the form of the schedule. However, behind any list of data types, there is the assumption that you have reliable time estimates. (This issue was discussed in Chapter 5.) The following is a short list of 10 data types you can use to refine or enhance a complete schedule:

1. Change notification schedule
2. Communications points schedule
3. Criteria for changing the schedule
4. Critical path with links to skills (who and where) and resources (user and location)
5. Quality control, assurance, and validation timeline
6. Schedule based on the scope plan, activity plan, and resource plan
7. Time allocated for risk management
8. Timeline (calendar or flow chart)
9. Timeline for acquiring skills, equipment, and materials
10. Timelines that are consistent and coherent

§ 6.02   MANAGEMENT INVOLVEMENT

[A]   Overview

Everyone looks at the schedule as gospel when it really is not; it is a visual presentation based almost completely on some type of estimate, primarily time. The schedule is a plan—it should not be considered a commitment by anyone. All management levels have to be involved in the scheduling process. A schedule is a production plan for the allocation of activities with deadlines. A business manager's schedule is a plan to use the least resources to achieve the most profit. A project manager's schedule is a plan to maximize resources to achieve the defined goals in the least amount of time. These two management views occasionally clash.

[B]   Strategic Management and Scheduling

The strategic manager should recognize that the project schedule is a plan, not a commitment, on the part of the project manager. The schedule is viable if all the estimates, not just the time estimates, happen as expected. The manager should ensure that the project's scheduling process is consistent with other scheduling processes in the company. The manager should also assist the tactical manager in resolving any divisional issues on the schedule for the project.

[C]   Tactical Management and Scheduling

The essential tactical actions of the project manager include the following:

- Align the schedule to the customer's expectations.
- Analyze the schedule to see possible impacts on the skills, resources, and materials needed for the project.
- Communicate with vendors if applicable on the status of the schedule.
- Create the schedule against the project goals.
- Define estimates to average capabilities.
- Define the lag-time–lead-time relationships.
- Define the start-time–end-time dependencies.
- Determine how the schedule is impacted if you vary cost potentials.
- Determine how the acquisition of outside resources affects the schedule.
- Determine how the budget cycle might impact the schedule, especially in the fourth quarter.
- Determine with the operational managers what risks might develop with the defined schedule.
- Discuss with the procurement group project requirements.
- Do resource and time leveling.
- Document assumptions and constraints for developing the schedule.
- Document issues and discuss them at meetings.
- Ensure resource availability in accordance with the schedule.
- Ensure that the schedule reflects realistically the training and documentation requirements.
- Ensure the quality control and assurance schedule is appropriate.
- Look for "forgotten" activities that need to be in the schedule.
- Set daily project priorities to manage the schedule.
- Smooth the schedule through a balancing of activities, time, and resources.

- Use project management software to assist in evaluating the status of the schedule.
- Use project management software to validate various potential scheduling scenarios.
- Use the activities to determine the schedule, not the other way around.
- Validate the schedule by getting everyone's concurrence.

[D]   Operational Management Scheduling

The essential functions of the operational managers include the following:

- Communicate to your team their part in the schedule and the significance of their actions.
- Ensure the schedule includes quality control and assurance for your operational area.
- Look for "forgotten" activities that need to be included in the schedule.
- Notify the tactical manager when a known slippage is going to happen to the schedule.
- Review the inputs of the project management software used by the tactical manager for any errors in the schedule for your operational area.

Exhibit 6-1: Schedule Planning Questions Checklist

Project Name:	Comments
1. Are historical data available to determine adequate resources?	
2. Are the essential scheduled milestones realistic?	
3. Are the time lines consistent and coherent?	
4. Can resources be acquired on time?	
5. Have the people who can have an impact on or approve the schedule been identified?	
6. Have the quality control events been included at appropriate milestones?	
7. Have the start and end times been confirmed? Have expected deliverables been identified?	

Exhibit 6-1 (*Continued*)

8. Have the who's, what's, where's and how's been clearly defined and placed in the schedule?	
9. How are the budgetary procedures going to affect the schedule?	
10. How can the formulated schedule impact the outcome of integration?	
11. How will the schedule and its changes be given to the customers?	
12. Is the schedule based on a pessimistic, realistic, or optimistic view?	
13. Is the schedule based on the scope definition?	
14. Is there a change notification process for the schedule?	
15. Is there a quality control and validation schedule?	
16. Is there a requirement for a critical path?	
17. Is there a time line for acquiring skills, equipment, and materials?	
18. Is time allocated for risk management?	
19. What are the criteria for changing the schedule?	
20. What type of time line is required (calendar, flow chart)?	

Exhibit 6-2: Checklist for Creating a Project Schedule

	Attachments
Scenarios for each task:	
Pessimistic	
Realistic	
Optimistic	
Critical path	
Duration	
Production time	

Exhibit 6-2 (*Continued*)

	Attachments
Wait time	
Lag time	
Lead time	
Dependencies	
Start–end	
Start–start	
End–start	
Slack time	
Calendar structure	
Sequence integration	
Tasks	
Resources	
Spending	
Procurement	
Training	
Documentation	
Links to:	
Resources	
Skills	
Responsible people	
Project Scope Plan	
Measurable goals	
Assumptions	
Constraints	
Design and Development Plan	
Activity Plan	
Resource Plan	
Task relationships	
Major milestones	
Deliverables	
Milestones (Gates)	
Deadlines	

Exhibit 6-2 (*Continued*)

	Attachments
Communications milestones	
Logistics	
Location	
Milestones	
Reviews	
Quality events	
Control	
Assurance	
Budget	
Vendor	
Status presentations	
Schedule characteristics	
Readable	
Usable	
Reliable	
Consistent	
Coherent	
Manageable level of details	
24 × 7 mode used	
Resource leveling	
Aligned	
Graphics to highlight events	
Colors	
Icons	
Note indicators	
Company requirements	
Customer requirements	
Gantt chart requirements	
Estimates vs. actual report	

Instructions for a Project Schedule Checklist

This checklist is used to assist the project team to create the project schedule. It is to be used by each operational manager to do a schedule at a group level or departmental level.

Exhibit 6-2 (*Continued*)

When the word activity is used, the reference is at the operational level, while *task* is used in reference to the project schedule. When *event* is used, it is in reference to a point in time such as the start date for an activity or task or for a milestone.

The core question for the design, development, and implementation of any schedule is, "What is the most logical method of presenting integration tasks based on reliable estimates with a time line so that it communicates clearly the measurable project goals?" The essential principle in responding to this question or these instructions is to keep it simple.

The project schedule needs to be approved prior to refining the cost estimates and developing the project budget.

Task by scenario: The task-level detail used must be manageable in that the schedule has to be readable, useful, and reliable. Any detail must be given in three forms: pessimistic, realistic, and optimistic. This means if you have a start–end block, then you must have three sets of dates. The ordering of the scenario is a local issue; however, the ordering of the scenarios must be consistent throughout the schedule and departmental schedules. Another possibility is to have three separate schedules when using a simple linear graphic.

Critical path: A path is critical when there is no available time for the slippage of the activity or task (no slack time). The Critical Path Method in its simplest form is selecting the "must" activities and tasks, doing them in the shortest possible amount of time, and covering the shortest duration. A critical task is a task that if not completed results in project failure.

Duration: The schedule is the duration of the project. It is the total involved time of an activity or task—production time plus wait time. A project's duration is the total number of calendar days involved from start to end, including the project manager's activities in closing the project.

Production time: Since a schedule should use the 24 × 7 mode, production time at an activity level can be stated in hourly or daily increments.

Wait time: It is duration minus production time.

Lag time: This is the time between two activities or tasks because of their natures.

Lead time: This is the overlapping time of two activities or tasks.

Dependencies: A dependency is an event. An event is a point in time such as the start or end of an activity or task.

Start–end: This dependency means that an event must begin before another can end.

Start–start: This dependency means that one event must start before another.

End–start: This dependency means that an event must end before another can start.

Slack time: It is the difference between earliest and latest (start or finish) times for an activity or task.

Calendar structure: A schedule must be related to the Gregorian calendar in contrast to using effort.

Sequence integration: The most important activity or task sequence is the critical path. All other sequences should be related to it.

Tasks or activities: Task sequences are used at the project schedule level, while activities are used at the operational level.

Resources: Use the icons as determined by the project team plus a note indicator. The icon is a visual clue, while the note indicator permits text to be placed in a supplemental document such as details from the resource plan. There may be a number of icons such as for critical hardware, software, materials, and skills.

Spending: As resources.

Procurement: As resources.

Training: As resources.

Documentation: As resources.

Exhibit 6-2 (*Continued*)

Links to: Use note indications and a special link icon as determined by the project team.

Resources: Resources are the tactical ones such as hardware, software, and support materials (do not forget the pencils and paper).

Skills: The link must reference the skill type and its level to a person.

Responsible people: This group of people includes the customer representative, corporate manager for the project, the project manager, the project team, the operational managers, and consultants.

Project Scope Plan: It is the strategic view of the constraints and assumptions of the project as developed by the project team.

Measurable goals: These goals are from the scope plan.

Assumptions: They are predictions that something will be true, an event that ensures project success.

Constraints: They are parameters, limitations or boundaries for the project.

Design and Development Plan: It drives the project Integration Plan that captures all major design and development deliverables and milestones for management tracking and reporting.

Activity plan: At the operational level, an activity plan is a set of definitions. A definition includes the activity's constraints from the scope plan. At the schedule level, the definitions are for tasks.

Resource plan: This is the source document for identifying all the assumptions and constraints for the use of all the resources.

Task relationships: Relationships can be either between different organizations or within one organization.

Major milestones: Use the icons defined by the project team.

Deliverables: They are clearly defined project results, products, or services. They are outcomes.

Milestones (Gates): A milestone is a clearly defined date of start or 100 percent completion. A gate is another term for milestone or a major project event.

Deadlines: They are absolute dates. They are the critical sequence dependencies.

Communications milestones: They are the critical points in the process of getting the correct information to the correct location at the correct time. Note, indicators should be used to reflect the specifics of the event such as a project management review. It is a regularly scheduled performance review.

Logistics: It is the process of getting the correct resource to the correct location at the correct time.

Reviews: All dates or events for management and technical reviews should be noted.

Quality events: The schedule quality events should be in two sequences. The control sequence includes the events for gathering and distributing information for or about the project. The assurance sequence includes the events for validation and testing based on performance.

Budget: Identify critical funding or spending milestones based on the finalized budget. This item is possibly the final act to be completed in the project schedule, beyond updates.

Vendor: A vendor has a product, while a consultant has information or services.

Status presentations: These include customer, upper-level management, and team presentations.

Schedule characteristics: These characteristics may be abstract; thus, agreement as to meanings should be by consensus of the project team.

Readable: The level of detail should not be so broad that an event cannot be identified easily.

Usable: The schedule should be so useful that it is the basis for status presentations.

Reliable: The time estimates have to be valid.

Exhibit 6-2 (*Continued*)

Consistent: The use of icons and colors should be the same, whether on the project schedule or on operational schedules.

Coherent: Events and task sequences should be synchronized.

Manageable level of details: Details at the project schedule level should be tasks, while at the operational level the details are based on activities.

24 × 7 mode used: The Schedule should be given in a 24 × 7 mode because some of the logistic events may occur at any time. In addition, critical tasks such as customer presentations may be identified in hours rather than a day.

Resource leveling: This technique is used to smooth out peaks and valleys for the use of resources.

Aligned: Alignment is another form of leveling, except absolute dates are used.

Graphics to highlight events: Graphic standards are determined by the project team. However, red and green should only be used to highlight a negative or positive situation.

Colors: The colors are determined by the project team. Do not use red or green except to highlight significant negative and positive events.

Icons: The icons are determined by the project team. Icons are an excellent way to distinguish among types of links.

Note indicators: These are determined by the project team.

Company requirements: Based on company policy or standard for a schedule's format.

Customer requirements: A special schedule might be done based on the customer's specified requirements. The requirements are a measurable goal of the project.

Gantt chart requirements: A Gantt chart is a visual presentation, a horizontal bar chart, of activities or tasks against time. A histogram is the opposite of a Gantt because vertical bars are used to represent values.

Estimates vs. Actual Report: This report should be updated at milestones and prior to any review briefing with the customer or upper-level management.

On the CD-ROM

On the CD-ROM are:

1. Exhibit 6-1 Schedule Planning Questions Checklist.doc

2. Exhibit 6-2 Checklist for Creating a Project Schedule.doc

3. Chapter 6 Overview.ppt—Chapter Overview, Schedule Developing

Chapter 7

Cost Estimating

§ 7.01   OVERVIEW

[A]   Objectives

At the end of this chapter, you will be able to:

- State a cost-estimating definition.
- Identify seven impacts of cost estimating on the project's success.
- Recognize seven cost-estimating principles.
- Identify 10 data types for cost estimating.
- Ask 10 basic questions about cost estimating such as: Who funds the

various project activities? Are there cost estimates for quality control activities? How are cost estimates merged into the budgetary process? Are the cost estimates realistic? Who are the experts that assist in the cost estimates? How reliable are the cost estimates? Have the time estimates been linked to cost estimates?

* Differentiate between a cost estimate and a budget item.
* Ask two core questions for cost management.
* Identify three documents that assist in cost management.
* Identify five steps for determining cost–time trade-offs.
* Identify how the three managing levels are involved in cost estimating.

MANAGER'S TIP

The legendary failures of many dot-com startups were captured in the recent documentary film *Startup.com,* which detailed the rise and fall of govWorks. com. The company's Web-based service enabled local governments to offer online services, everything from obtaining permits and licenses to paying taxes. The company rolled through $40 million worth of venture capital in 18 months, unable to overcome the expense of unanticipated client needs, high operating costs, and a frozen equity market.

One of govWorks' cost-related problems that could have been solved earlier by asking the right questions was the decision to host applications in-house. This decision proved extremely expensive and time-consuming. With the company's first large restructuring and subsequent layoffs, they moved to the ASP (application service provider) model. They hoped to be able to cut costs substantially by using an ASP.

But it was too little, too late. Their competitors were offering the same services for less money or, in some cases, for free. By January 2001 the company had filed for Chapter 11 bankruptcy.

By following the checklist and questions described in this chapter, a project manager can avoid at least some of the potential cost-driven pitfalls inherent in any project.

[B] Using Essential Definitions

All prior discussions on estimates are relevant to this chapter, especially those in Chapter 5 on time estimates. The following seven definitions; however, are essential to any discussion about cost estimates:

Cost estimating is the process of establishing or defining the amount to be budgeted for a task based on constraints and assumptions from the project goals for the duration of the task, the average skills required for completing the task, and the resources required for completing the task.

An **estimate** is a guess based on opinion or a forecast based on experience. Cost, time, and resource estimates are the foundations for project planning.

Padding is an informal action such as adding time or cost to an estimate, which should not take place. Any such additions to estimates should be formalized in a contingency plan.

A **resource** is anything that supports the project. This includes, in general terms, money, skills, materials, time, facilities, and equipment.

The **Project Cost Updates** document updates the initial project cost estimates at each major phase of implementation with comparison to the Initial Budget Estimate.

[C]   Definition of Cost Estimating

Cost estimating is like time estimating in many ways. Cost estimating is the process of establishing or defining the amount to be budgeted for an activity based on constraints and assumptions from the project goals. Cost is estimated for the duration of the activity, the average skills required to complete the activity, and the resources required to complete the activity.

One of the difficulties of cost estimating is hidden expense. For example, travel costs can be allocated in many different budgets without reflecting direct costs to any project. Hidden expenses happen frequently in a large corporation, but they can also be seen in a company of fewer than 20 people.

Cost estimating should be done in parallel to activity sequencing and time estimating. It should be completed before the budgeting activity has begun. Each major activity to meet identified *measurable* goals should have a defined cost estimate. People who are familiar with the project goals should do the estimating. It may be important even to get outsiders (vendors) to assist in doing these cost estimates.

Cost estimates should also be done in the context of the scope plan goals and resource plan. Cost estimating needs to consider both tangibles and intangibles. A tangible cost is using known rates (hourly, weekly, monthly, or fixed) for the services of people involved in the project. A related intangible cost is the impact of the skill levels of the same people. An expert might cost more in the long term than a novice. Considering that you might pay an expert $50 per hour and a novice $10 per hour, the expert would have to produce at a rate five times as fast as the novice does. The intangible is the quality comparison; if the expert produces a higher quality product, then that person may well be worth the extra cost. Thus, it is very important to evaluate tangible costs against potential intangible costs.

Cost management has software tools that parallel time management tools. A good project management tool should have both. The features required for cost management in such a software program are discussed in Section Two on project tools and techniques.

[D]   Seven Impacts of Cost Estimating

Since many cost estimates are tied to time estimates (labor being the best example), one might expect this activity to be another place where a project might fail. The signal for a cost-estimate failure will of course show up in the budget.

You should keep an accounting of activity spending so you can readily identify cost-estimate failures. The technique is straightforward. The formula is:

$$\text{Variance cost (VC)} = \text{estimated cost (EC)} - \text{actual cost (AC)}$$

Total the variances. The analysis should be as detailed as possible so you can identify specific issues.

A cost-estimate failure usually occurs because of an unrealistic time estimate. No business manager or customer ever believes a project will cost as estimated. When you get a negative response to project cost estimates, you need to respond with strong supporting justification. Remember, a business manager's view is to minimize costs to maximize profits.

Cost management, like time or risk management, is a critical process of the project. This is another area where the use of project management software can be of great value. One can set up scenarios to study the impacts of cost changes. A cost change can ripple through the budget either positively or negatively very quickly.

The cost estimates can affect a number of items or events in the project process, including:

- Activity sequencing
- Budget cycle
- Project benchmarks
- Resource planning
- Risks
- Schedule
- Time estimate

You can see from this list why cost estimates, along with time estimates, may be a core reason for a project's failure. Can you do cost management if your data, and time estimates, are faulty? Bad cost estimates are like thieves in the night. When formally developed, cost estimates, as determined by activity defining and sequencing, cost estimating, and resource defining, are used to create budget items. Remember, when a cost estimate makes it to the budget it is now ensconced in your project—or more accurately, entrenched.

The report that a strategic manager first flags on any project is the monthly budget report or analysis. If you are required to revise your budget on a quarterly cycle, bad cost estimates can impact the receiving of funds. Bad cost estimates substantially increase the potential for risks.

Cost estimating can be more of an art than a science. As has been said, many cost-management software packages are available to assist in doing your project. You need to do a number of scenarios, or "what ifs," to get an early view of possible consequences of under- or overestimating costs. For example, you might consider what would happen if there were 20 percent reduction in the budget in the third quarter of the year.

[E] Seven Cost Estimating Principles

When developing cost estimates, you should follow seven principles to make cost estimating more of a science than an art. The following is a list of these principles that might assist you in this activity:

1. Get the person who is to do the activity to do the estimating.
2. If no one is knowledgeable about the activity within the group, ask an outside expert.
3. Base cost estimates on average production.
4. Do all the original cost estimates, and then do a total.
5. Revise cost estimates from the least to the largest.
6. Do not factor in the possibilities of the increase or decrease of prices in developing the original cost estimates.
7. Get knowledgeable and objective people to review cost estimates.

When you get an estimate from the person who is responsible for the activity, you should get not only an estimate but also a commitment. This action also adheres to the principle of "ask an expert."

One expert you can consult is the vendor that has a product you need to achieve a project goal. That vendor will have historical data and cost ranges, of what it took to install and configure the product in question into another system. If the vendor does not desire to give you this data, perhaps you could talk to other project managers who have interacted with the vendor.

By using average costs, you at least tone down one of the areas of failure, optimism. Human resources should have data on the average cost for a labor classification such as the one you, the project manager, have on your programmers. This also sets a minimum expectation when a better-than-average worker is available. You would also expect any contractor to cost more. Remember, if a contractor's fee is $50 per hour and an in-house novice with similar skills is paid $25 per hour, then the contractor has to accomplish more than twice as much in the same period for the dollar (assuming that the quality of the output is the same).

By waiting until all cost estimates are available, you have a level playing field. There is no pressure to make the final estimates lower. In addition, a sense of fairness will exist throughout the group.

It may seem easier to adjust the largest cost estimates first. You should challenge the higher estimates after the lower estimates are changed and there are no significant results. Do not say, "this is too much," but ask questions that can lead to either further justifications for the estimates or a lowering of the estimate.

You would not factor in the possibilities of potential price changes in getting the original cost estimates. These possibilities are really constraints of the budgetary activity.

Review of the cost estimates should be by knowledgeable people who are not a part of establishing the original cost estimates. This team should be looking for "padding." Using the 80–20 rule, one might expect padding on the larger estimates to run about 20 percent of total cost estimates. One needs to look at one's own experience in this area. This does not mean you should automatically remove 20 percent of all the cost estimates.

MANAGER'S TIP

If there is padding, it should be an up-front activity and be labeled for what it is, a contingency fund.

[F] Ten Data Types for Cost Estimating

Cost-management software tools should be used to develop cost estimates. There is the need also to use historical data for establishing benchmarks.

The following are 10 of the types of data you need when you have finished your cost estimates:

1. Cost estimates based on skill types and levels rather than headcount
2. Cost estimates that reflect the methodical nature of procurement
3. Criteria for associating cost and time estimates and potential changes
4. Criteria for establishing cost measures
5. Criteria for formulating cost estimates
6. Methodology for validating cost estimates according to the goals of your project
7. Policy on notifying others of cost changes to the project process
8. Procedure for associating cost estimates with people, and equipment and people acquisition
9. Quality control and validation cost estimates (suggested 10 to 20 percent of total cost estimates)
10. Specific cost estimates for handling risks (threats and opportunities)

[G]   Basic Questions for Cost Estimating

Whenever possible, questions for cost estimating should be based on identified benchmarks, such as a measurable activity or task. These questions need to reflect managing of actual, specific expenses (costs) against planned costs (budget). By asking questions about the cost-estimating process, you can formulate the data types required for your management forms and checklists for this area.

The responses to the following questions should be based on the goals and deliverables for your project and the activities or tasks necessary to achieve them. Think in terms both of an optimistic cost and a pessimistic cost, and then determine a reliable median cost. Cost estimate should be a range rather than a single value. You will still need an absolute total at the end of the range, but at least you will have a value that is pessimistic. This principle can be used to reduce padding and to create a financial contingency plan.

MANAGER'S TIP

Unfortunately, one common cost-estimating practice is to give a value without stating the impact of production and wait times.

In Chapter 5, the approach used for developing questions on time estimates reflected the importance of impacts. The following questions reflect the general cost-estimating process to define data types:

HOW DOES THE ACCOUNTING CHART OF ACCOUNTS AFFECT THE COST-ESTIMATING PROCESS?   A chart of accounts can be organized in many ways. Each line in the budget can be numbered or labeled. The important idea is that cost estimating should reflect the structure of the chart of accounts. The budget structure is just one of many plans that impact how a project is viewed by business managers.

WHO IS GOING TO FUND THE VARIOUS PROJECT ACTIVITIES?   Is there a reporting system that links the appropriate people to the project costs and to the people with budgetary control? You should always think of linkages in terms of cost estimates and budgets that should reflect these costs. Some people may confuse your daily IS costs as being a part of the project process.

HOW DO COST ESTIMATES REFLECT FINAL PROJECT EXPECTATIONS?   Ensure that the total of the estimates is not greater than the customer's cost expectations. Identify what can be done as to functionality and service expectations within cost constraints. Sometimes it is better to have half an apple than none. The half of an apple should be negotiated and approved.

TO WHAT DEGREE ARE COST ESTIMATES BASED ON RELIABLE, DEFINED TIME ESTIMATES?   Cost estimates should reflect time estimates and should reflect the type of time measure used. If the time estimate formula uses plus or minus measurements, the cost estimates should also reflect this type of formula.

WHAT ARE THE TYPES OF INPUTS THAT NEED TO BE CONSIDERED? All cost estimates should have associated time estimates. The time estimates do not have to be detailed out to everyone. However, those responsible for time estimates and budgetary planning should be involved. You may ask, "Why should every cost estimate have a time estimate?" A set of activities may require more expenditures than expected as a whole.

WHAT ARE THE IMPACTS OF THE BENCHMARKS AND VALIDATION PROCESS ON PROJECT COSTS? A specific amount of cost should be allocated for quality assurance control. You should set a benchmark of 10 to 20 percent. This percentage is of the estimated total cost for the project. This task should be among the first tasks of the cost-estimating process.

SHOULD RESOURCES BE INTERNAL ONLY? Cost estimates should reflect skill levels rather than headcount. When cost estimating, use the basic categories of resources: skills, equipment, and materials. You should first consider cost estimates against labor classifications (such as a Java programmer) rather than against a skill level. This gives you a baseline, salary range, for establishing a cost estimate for a given skill level.

WHAT ARE THE COSTS FOR INFORMING PEOPLE ON THE STATUS OF THE PROJECT? There are two basic parts to any communicating system: cost status and budget status. Criteria should be established as to who sees what and when they see it.

DO THE KNOWN COSTS OUTWEIGH THE KNOWN OR POTENTIAL THREATS OR OPPORTUNITIES? You should have cost estimates for risk management in each of the major phases of your project. If you have no threats to the project in a given phase, you have generated an opportunity.

WHAT ARE THE HOURLY OR DAILY RATES FOR OUTSIDE SERVICES FOR A SKILL OR EQUIPMENT? Your cost estimates may be seriously impacted when there is a delay in acquiring any required skills, equipment, or materials. It is a good idea to be pessimistic rather than optimistic on cost estimates in the area of procurement.

Other questions you might ask include:

- How have possible increases or decreases in prices been factored into the process of developing the original cost estimates?
- How should cost estimates be reviewed?
- What are the objective criteria for establishing reliable cost estimates?
- What critical estimates are based on the results of a Critical Path Method action?

- When should an outside expert be used to do cost estimating?
- When should cost estimates be reviewed?
- Where in the process should base cost estimates be determined on average production?
- Who is to do the cost estimating for an activity or a task?
- Who should review the cost estimates?
- Why should all individual cost estimates be determined before doing a total estimate?
- Why should the revised cost estimates be from the lowest to the highest?

MANAGER'S TIP

As stated in the prior chapters, each of these questions could be reformulated in the context of any of the six metaquestions—how?, why?, when?, where?, who?, and what?

[H]   Cost Estimating versus Budgeting

Here are 10 comparisons between cost estimating and budgeting:

1. Cost estimates are inputs into budget, while budget items are inputs into the table of accounts.
2. Cost estimates are looked at by tactical and operational managers, while the budget is looked at by the strategic manager.
3. Cost estimates are tasks, while a budget is a plan to be followed.
4. Cost estimating is a component of budgeting; budgeting is the formal structuring of many activities that include activities of the project at one level of the corporate budget.
5. Cost estimating is a consequence of analyzing; budgeting is a consequence of planning.
6. Cost estimating is at times nebulous, while budgeting is at times precise.
7. Cost estimating is concerned with an individual activity or groups of related activities, while budgeting is concerned with the complete project.
8. Cost estimating is to the budget as time estimating is to the schedule.
9. Cost estimating is viewed as an abstract process, while budgeting is viewed as a concrete process.
10. Cost estimating uses the duration of a single activity or a group of related activities, while budgeting is the method you use to frame the spending plan within a calendar usually based on monthly increments and accounting categories.

One of the issues of the corporate world is that business managers forget that an estimate is a guess, not a fact. They also tend to forget that a budget or a schedule is a plan, not a commitment. There is a major contrast between the thinking of business managers, who think in terms of commitment, and project managers, who tend to think in terms of plans. Many project issues can find their origins based on these contrasting viewpoints.

You have to ensure that your cost estimates are as precise and realistic as possible because the customers and the associated managers will always think of the concrete form of the budget, their perceived bottom line. Only one budget is meaningful. It is the one at the highest level. As a project manager, you need to understand how the corporate budget process is managed. You can then factor this into the cost estimates and their related time estimates.

Many of the contrasts above could have been summarized as the project manager's view and the business manager's view. There is also the tendency to say we estimate the costs but we plan the budget. Sorry, we estimate both.

The budget process within a corporation is hierarchical. It starts with the president's budget, the vice-presidents' budgets, and so on down the line until your project budget items are included somewhere in the "great tree-house." You need to be aware of which line items are the most important so you can get your project costs on those lines.

One final point about cost estimates: You should never give a casual one. You may find later that it has been considered a commitment and a budget item.

[I] Two Core Questions on the Cost-Estimating Process

There are two questions that you must answer yes to before continuing:

1. Have the project cost definitions been made consistent?
2. Has a list for cost responsibility been formulated?

Your scope plan must be clear on funding because it can become very complex. It can become a key factor in getting your project terminated. There should be clear definitions and understandings of the funding policies and invoicing practices of the doers and the receivers. A large corporation can have multiple layers of sources of funds. Those at a high level of funding are sometimes surprised at how "their" money is being used. It is important to ask, "Are all levels of funding authority in agreement with this project?"

A number of software packages can assist in defining your cost. You should consider ways to improve cost even if software is not available, because the opportunity might rise up and shake your hand! All types of costs should be considered: human (actual and potential), materials, and time. In addition, costs can be divided into design, development, implementation (production), and, most important, quality and verification controls.

An important costing activity is the determination of how the budget issues are handled. You use cost estimates to formulate a budget. A budget is a plan in which costs are organized into debits and credits (expenses and revenues).

Resource planning requires that you seriously consider skill types and skills required for success. Is it better to pay $50 an hour to an expert or $25 an hour to a novice? Are the people involved in the project full time or part time? It can be surprising how many different categories into which resources can be divided that can impact cost estimates.

As you order your activities for the project process, the availability of funding should be used. Have costs been divided over all essential phases of the project process? Never take from the quality control activities to try to improve another part of the schedule. This type of action has a way of biting you in places where it hurts.

All time estimates should have associated cost estimates. The time and cost estimates do not have to be detailed to everyone. However, those responsible for time and cost estimates and budgetary planning should be involved. You may ask, "Why should every time estimate have a cost estimate?" A set of activities may require more time than expected or cost more than the total of the individual items.

An integral part of a schedule is defining the activities involved in cost management. This undertaking may be done at a high level of management, but all activities should be defined.

Cost estimates can go into one budget line or into many. The usual case is at least three budget lines. The resources of the project can be divided into salaries, equipment, and materials. You probably also need to have a separate line for vendor or consulting costs.

[J]   Three Basic Types of Cost-Management Documentation

You could have any number of documents based on sound cost-management principles. Recognize that good cost management probably is a blending component of any management process. Here are three examples of related documents:

1. Project Cost Update
2. Initial Budget Estimates
3. Initial Funding Requirements

Project Cost Update

This document updates initial project cost estimates at each major phase of your project in comparison to the Initial Budget Estimates. The concern here is how the costs (actual expenditures) and revenues go into the budget (the financial plan). The costs are usually reported on a monthly basis.

Initial Budget Estimates

This document provides a view of the expected development costs. The estimate is usually based on the scope plan of the project. The document gives estimates for direct labor as well as capital and expense requirements. Remember, the indirect costs should be considered as important as direct costs. This document is updated in the Project Cost Update.

Initial Funding Requirements

This document is for monitoring and reporting project costs at each major phase of the project. There should be comparisons to the Initial Budget Estimates document used to establish financial targets and expected milestones and deliverables. This document can also be included in the Project Cost Update.

[K] Method for Evaluating Cost–Time Trade-offs

On occasions you may be required to reduce cost by extending the time for an activity to be completed. You need to determine the time factor for doing so. Here is a five-step method for evaluating such trade-offs:

1. Compare the normal activity duration such as number of weeks with its defined costs and the potential costs with an extended duration with the minimum use of resources.
2. Compare incremental scenarios based on varying:
   — Skills available
   — Overtime
   — Equipment
   — Consultants.
3. Identify the longest duration.
4. Determine the resources needed to have the longest duration for the activity.
5. Determine the impact of change on the project.

[L] Using a Cost-Estimates Checklist

Invalid cost estimates are considered one of the three major causes of project failure. However, the source of the failure may be because of two factors: invalid time estimates (Chapter 5) and the assumption that costs are discrete data; that is, you do not need a range of costs. Exhibit 7-1: Cost-Estimates Checklist is used to consider both of these problems.

Exhibit 7-1: Cost-Estimates Checklist

	Attachments
Cost estimates by scenario	
Pessimistic	
Realistic	
Optimistic	
Criteria by scenario	
Pessimistic	
Realistic	
Optimistic	
Impacts by scenarios	
Pessimistic	
Realistic	
Optimistic	
Estimates by project goals	
Source ID	
Critical path estimates	
Procurement	
Hardware	
Software	
Consultants	
Special materials	
Skills	
Training	
Procurement	
Internal Resources	
Support tasks	
Documentation tasks	
Production tasks	
Planning	
Design	
Development	
Testing	

Exhibit 7-1 (*Continued*)

	Attachments
Noncritical path estimates	
Procurement	
Hardware	
Software	
Consultants	
Special materials	
Skills	
Training	
Procurement	
Internal Resources	
Support tasks	
Documentation tasks	
Production tasks	
Planning	
Design	
Development	
Testing	
Defined assumptions used	
Defined constraints used	
Deliverables accounted for	
Budget requirements used	
Deadline criteria	
Time estimates inputs	
Quality	
Control	
Assurance	
Validation	
Field testing	
Resource cost tools	
Equipment	
Internal	
External	

Exhibit 7-1 (*Continued*)

	Attachments
Materials	
Internal	
External	
Skills	
Internal	
External	
Approx. headcount	
Project management tools	
Internal	
External	
Development tools	
Internal	
External	
Facilities	
Internal	
External	
Logistics	
Internal	
External	
Training cost totals	
Internal	
External	
Documentation requirements	
Internal	
External	
Communications cost totals	
Internal	
External	
Travel	
Risk management	
Project administration	

Exhibit 7-1 *(Continued)*

	Attachments
Cost-Estimates Criteria	
Links to time estimates	
Incremental spending periods	
One time	
Monthly	
Quarterly	
Vendor pricing	
Fixed	
Variants from fixed	
Dependency	
Project goals	
Project milestones	
Task milestones	
Learning curve	
Special event	
Trade-off considerations	
Cost-benefit analysis	
Part-time staff	
Full-time staff	
Other	
Contingency plan	
Special customer support	
Special variants noted	
Consistency to:	
Scope plan	
Activity plan	
Resource plan	
Project schedule	
Business Justification	
Commercial Specification	

Exhibit 7-1 (*Continued*)

	Attachments
Design/Development Plan	
Market Analysis Report	
Trial (Beta) Strategy	
Request for Proposal	
Funding source approval	

Instructions for a Cost-Estimates Checklist

This checklist is to produce consistency between the project requirements and the operational or functional areas. Ultimately these estimates are first compiled at the functional level and then consolidated as required in the project budget.

Cost estimates by scenario: All project cost estimates must be given in three forms: pessimistic, realistic, and optimistic. Actual format instructions come from the project team. All the estimates need to reflect items given in this checklist. A part of this task is to get a draft set of estimates. Second, these estimates are refined using outside assistance, if necessary. Third, refine the estimates to determine if they are affordable for the customer. As a part of the refinements, a confidence level should be stated for each one.

Criteria by scenario: There should be objective data to support the three types of estimates. The sources for the criteria include time estimates, resource estimates, corporate billing policy, standards, benchmarks, historical records, or project team requirements.

Impacts by scenarios: There should be explanations for each of the estimate types. For example, the estimate is pessimistic because no one is immediately available at this time with the skill level to do the task; thus, an outside source must be procured. Another example is if the pessimistic estimate happens, then X risk may happen.

Estimates by project goals: Estimates should be linked to the projects goals as found in the project scope.

Source ID: Identify the person responsible for writing the time estimates, including title, e-mail address, and telephone number. If the source is external, also include company information.

Critical path estimates: For the items listed give the justifications for being designated critical.

Noncritical path estimates: For the items listed give the formulae and their sources plus relevant standards or benchmarks for estimates.

Defined assumptions: Use the assumptions from the scope plan to develop estimates.

Defined constraints: Use the constraints from the scope plan and the time and resource estimates to develop estimates.

Deliverables: Give links to project deliverables for each estimate.

Budget requirements: Use the project budget requirements as defined by the project team. Check for rules of aggregation of cost estimates.

Deadline criteria: Use deadline criteria as defined by the project team that is based on the scope plan. The estimates might be affected by milestones, such as spending must completed by X event.

Time estimates inputs: There should be objective data to support any time estimate. If the duration of a realistic time estimate for a linked task is too short or too long for your function, what are the potential impacts? For example, if X training course is more than two weeks in length, there will be serious impacts such as Y.

Quality: Give any possible estimates that you consider relevant to the listed areas that might be required for product validation or field tests. Justifications should be included such as reference to standards or benchmarks.

Exhibit 7-1 (*Continued*)

Resource cost totals: If a resource (hardware, software, skill, or support materials) has to be acquired from an external source, give estimates for the procurement tasks such as negotiation that includes travel and direct administrative costs. Internal costs refer to having to budget costs to another corporate functional groups such as Training or Documentation.

Travel: Give costs as to airplane, hotel, meals, and car rental. Justify requirements based on data given earlier with this form.

Risk management: Consider if a pessimistic scenario breaks down, the possible costs required for correction.

Project administration: Based on the project team requirements, give estimates. In addition, consider cost estimates for giving status reports to operational team by either e-mail or status presentations. It is possible that all of these costs are indirect.

Special Cost-Estimate Criteria

Links to time estimates: Define links as they relate to costs. In addition, give links as appropriate to the project schedule.

Incremental spending periods: You must give spending increments based on the project schedule. Quarterly can be defined by the project team as either a three-month period of the project's duration or as a calendar quarter.

Vendor pricing:

  Fixed: Justify the reasons a price is fixed for such items as hardware or training courses. Determine if the vendor is "buying the job."

  Variants from fixed: Give the justifications for cost for a lesser item and a better item. In addition, consider the cost impacts of not getting the product.

  Dependency: When appropriate, give the dependency requirements for the listed items. An example is a goal that must be completed before spending is required. A second example is spending that must be done before a milestone or event can be started. Give the cost impacts if a learning curve shortens or lengthens the time.

Trade-off considerations:

  Cost-benefit analysis: When appropriate, work with the marketing group to do an analysis that serves as a standard for the estimate.

  Part-time staff: State such as one hour per day or once a week. Justify the part-time effort.

  Full-time staff: Give impacts of having full-time over part-time staff. Justify the use of full-time staff over part-time staff.

  Other: Identify if there is a need for a consultant.

Contingency plan: Give justifications for including a contingency amount and the potential requirements. This plan formalizes padding.

Special customer support: Include the possible "hidden" costs for corporate training; also include travel.

Special variants: Give any additional information that might assist the project team in its responsibilities and minimize further discussions.

Consistency to: The listed documents should be used to define the environment for all costs estimates. Cost estimates should not be finalized until the project schedule is completed.

Scope plan: It has the strategic view of the constraints and assumptions of the project as developed by the project team.

Activity plan: It has a set of definitions for efforts required to achieve measurable results. At the operational level, you consider activities; while at the project level, you consider tasks.

Resource plan: It establishes support requirements for a project as to costs, availability, start date and end date (length of time for use plus duration), and technical specifications.

Project schedule: It formalizes the time estimates within a calendar structure. It is an integration of sequencing tasks, resource planning, cost estimating, and time estimating.

Exhibit 7-1 *(Continued)*

Business Justification: It is the general rationale for making the financial investment.

Commercial Specification: It is an evolution of the Business Justification. It identifies the market need and gives adequate requirement and limitation data for the design and development group(s).

Design/Development Plan: It drives the project Integration Plan that captures all major design and development deliverables and milestones for management tracking and reporting.

Market Analysis Report: It documents and verifies market opportunities and justifies the features, services, and applications for the project goals.

Trial (Beta) Strategy: It identifies the software and hardware elements in the project that are a part of any trial.

Request for Proposal (RFP): Ensure there is a consistency between the requirements of the RFP and the vendor's response. Ensure that response adheres to the requirements of this checklist.

Funding source approval: The funding source or sources must give a written agreement to the cost estimates.

Even when there is a single piece of hardware with a "fixed" catalog value, there has to be a cost estimate that includes the three scenarios, pessimistic, realistic, and optimistic. The pessimistic estimate would include the effects of not having the hardware, while the optimistic considers having an even better piece of hardware, if it is available. The estimate also has to consider the factor of how fixed is "fixed." Exhibit 7-1 and its instructions show you how to consider these situations when doing cost estimating.

If you consider especially the pessimistic scenario for a cost estimate, then you have a basis for a contingency plan. Within a company, there is usually a broad policy on the creation of an annual group budget by head-count (employees) rather than by skill levels. It is recognized that the corporate budgetary policy might distinguish between a junior programmer and a senior programmer but will ignore the reality that there might be major skill differences within each group. Because the factor of skill levels is important to the project management process, the checklist instructions show you how you consider this issue. A contingency plan might be a pessimistic cost-estimate scenario of the loss of an essential skill. You would have to factor in the cost by using a temporary worker from an outside source.

MANAGER'S TIP

The first assumption for the design and development of the checklist and its instructions is that there must be a separate project budget, even if in actuality the various budget items are "hidden" within the IS group's budget because of corporate constraints. You must have a separate management document so you can properly manage the financial issues.

MANAGER'S TIP

WARNING: Shoddy cost estimates impact the project budget in the same manner as inferior time estimates impact the project schedule. However, there is one big difference: Upper-level management tends to view a schedule as a management tool but a budget as a document set in stone unless management wants to change the document. This actuality must be considered a major constraint for any project cost estimating.

---

§ 7.02   MANAGEMENT INVOLVEMENT

[A]   Overview

To many people—and in particular this attitude seems to exist among business managers and customers—anyone can do cost estimates and the process really does not take that much effort. In fact, many people feel that estimating can be done casually. However, budgeting is a complex activity. As the old saying goes, "Garbage in, garbage out."

All the management levels should be involved in the defining of reliable cost estimates. Everyone looks at the budget as the truth when it really is not; it is actually a formalized visual presentation based on estimates. The budget format comes from a set of evolved accounting rules, experiences, and the needs of the highest level of management to comprehend the bottom line quickly.

Cost estimating is the major activity used in developing the budget. The budget is structured in the context of corporate marketing goals. The chain is only as strong as its weakest link. When the IS project involves the integration of the Internet, the corporate intranet, and external customer and vendor involvement as a single enterprise network, the link needs to be strong.

[B]   Strategic Management and Cost Estimating

The strategic manager should ensure the availability of knowledgeable people, including outside consultants, to evaluate the cost estimates. This does not mean having the vendor verify the cost estimates for the vendor's product or component of the project (this is the tactical manager's job). The manager should ensure that the project's cost-estimating process is consistent with other cost-estimating processes in the company. The manager should also assist the tactical manager in resolving any divisional issues on cost estimates for the project.

[C]   Tactical Management and Cost Estimating

The essential tactical actions of the project manager include the following:

- Ensure there are criteria for defining cost estimates such as:
  — Define the estimates against the project goals
  — Define estimates to average capabilities
  — Do not factor in potential changes in costs
  — Cost estimates should be done if possible by the person who will do the activity
  — Define the cost measurements (hours, eight-hour days, or 20-day work months)
- Analyze cost estimates to see possible impacts on the skills, resources, and materials required for the project.
- Collect all the estimates before doing a total.
- Determine how cost estimates impact time estimates (each operational area probably has its own cost per hour).
- Determine how cost estimates may affect acquisition of outside resources.
- Determine how the budget cycle might influence the cost estimates, especially those in the fourth quarter.
- Determine with the operational managers what risks might develop with changes to the cost estimates.
- Document issues and discuss them at meetings.
- Establish a process in which cost estimating becomes more a science than an art.
- Factor procurement requirements into appropriate cost estimates.
- Finish the cost-estimate process before attempting to do the budgeting process.
- Include cost estimates for quality control and assurance.
- Look for "forgotten" activities that need cost estimates such as training or documentation.
- Resolve a too-large total of cost estimates for the project, beginning with the least amounts and working up to the largest amounts.
- Resolve cost issues well in advance of the "spending" date.
- Set daily project priorities to manage cost-estimate issues.
- Use project management software to assist in evaluating cost estimates.
- Use technical support of vendors to define any installation or configuration cost estimates.

[D] Operational Management and Cost Estimating

The basic functions of the operational managers include the following:

- Identify the people knowledgeable to do the cost estimates.
- Include cost estimates for quality control and assurance.
- Limit padding; actually, you should do no padding—use a contingency fund.
- Look for "forgotten" activities that need cost estimates such as training or documenting.
- Notify the tactical manager if no one is available to do certain cost estimates.
- Review cost estimates beginning with the least amount to the largest for signs of excess.
- Review the inputs of the project management software used by the tactical manager for your area to check for any corrections.
- Use the criteria from the project team for developing the cost estimates.

Exhibit 7-2: Cost-Planning Checklist

Project:		Date:			
Preparer:					
			YES	NO	EST.
PROJECT/SYSTEM LABOR COSTS					
Definition					
Design					
Impact on legacy infrastructure					
Software integration					
Documentation					
Training					
Tool support					
Configuration					
Quality control					
Support					
HARDWARE COSTS					
Planning					
Capital					

Exhibit 7-2 (*Continued*)

	YES	NO	EST.
Training			
Installation			
Maintenance			
Legacy implications			
SOFTWARE COSTS			
Planning			
Operating system			
Installation			
Documentation			
Training			
Maintenance			
Legacy implications			
Support applications			
COMMUNICATIONS COSTS			
Planning			
Capital			
Equipment			
Installation			
Maintenance			
EXECUTION COSTS			
Travel and living			
Consultants			
Training			
Office supplies and materials			
CLIENT COSTS			
Team member involvement			
Meetings			
Training			
IMPLEMENTATION COSTS			
Travel and living			
Staff support			
Labor costs			
OTHER			

On the CD-ROM

On the CD-ROM are:

1. Exhibit 7-1 Cost Estimate Checklist.doc

2. Exhibit 7-2 Cost Planning Checklist.doc

3. Chapter 7 Overview.ppt—Chapter Overview, Cost Estimating

Chapter 8

Budget Developing

§ 8.01   OVERVIEW

[A]   Objectives

At the end of this chapter, you will be able to:

- State a definition for a budget.
- Ask 10 basic questions about budgeting such as: Do the project duration and the budget duration match? Have internal and external costs been budgeted? Have the results of risk management been considered for the budget? How and to whom should the financial information be given? Are there one or more budgets to manage project spending? Where do

the quality control costs go in the budget? Who handles the merging of cost estimates into the budgetary process?

- Identify 10 types of support data for budgeting.
- Identify three types of budgetary support documents.
- Differentiate between budgeting and cost estimating.
- Differentiate between a project budget and a business budget.
- Identify five steps in refining cost estimates.
- State five reasons for developing a bad budget.
- List seven consequences of a too-low budget.
- Identify six areas that can be refined in the budget.
- Identify how the three managing levels are involved in budgeting.

Like the schedule, the project budget is a visual representation; it illustrates the various cost estimates that make up the financial underpinnings of the project. But when projects start to run over time and cost, the project manager must make crucial decisions that may not have been factored into the original budget planning.

The budget, like the schedule, is an overall set of estimates that is not set in stone but must be defined and refined, sometimes while managing the project. Such a possibility must be part of any contingency planning.

Practically speaking, a budget helps you keep tabs on one fundamental question: *Are cost estimates correct?*

MANAGER'S TIP

For example, a midsized software development company specializing in financial services applications began work on a new product for its banking clients. After six months of development, the project was running over the original time and budget estimates. The project and product managers insisted on training more developers in order to roll out the product, but the cost of the high learning curve set the project back even further and the budget had to be completely revised. Eventually, a new project manager whose view was more in line with that of company management was brought onboard.

[B] Using Essential Definitions

Because a budget is, first, a visual presentation of the cost-oriented efforts of a project and, second, a project standard or baseline for managing a project, it involves a large number of essential concepts related to budgeting. Here are eight of the essential concepts (the list actually could be longer because any project document probably has financial data that is relevant to the project budget):

A **baseline plan** is the initial approved point from which any deviations will be determined with standards and benchmarks.

The **budget** is a plan in which costs are organized into debits and credits (expenses and revenues). It is a formal plan that uses a chart of accounts to give structure to estimates for expenses and revenues.

Budgeting is taking cost estimates and entering them into a formal financial structure.

An **estimate** is a guess based on an opinion or a forecast based on experience. Cost, time, and resource estimates are the foundations for project planning.

Headcount is a factor used by business managers in planning an annual budget but should not be used by project managers.

The **Initial Budget Estimates** provides a view of the expected development costs. Estimates are usually based on the Preliminary Project Specification. This document is updated in the Project Cost Updates.

Padding is an informal action, such as adding time or cost to an estimate, that should not take place. Any such estimates should be formalized as in a contingency plan.

Skill level is a factor used by a project manager in planning the project's budget, rather than using headcount.

[C]   Budget Definition

A budget is a formal plan that uses a chart of accounts to give structure to estimates for expenses and revenues. An IS project budget may be formal in that it is linked through other business budgets to the corporate budget. It can also be informal in that the budget is used as a project plan and management tool and its budget items are formally located in one or more business budgets.

The project budget could become important historical and benchmark data. It is recommended that any technical upgrades to your information system should be included in your operations budget. An IS project is an activity to support a customer's needs, not support operational needs. There needs to be a separate budget for any major project. When changes to a budget are needed, there should not be a mixing of the issues of the project with those of the day to day operations. You, the IS administrator, wear two hats, the business manager and the project manager. You have to think differently as to budget issues with each hat.

MANAGER'S TIP

A budget deals in dollars. A cost estimate reflects potential effort based on available skill levels, time requirements, and duration (work time plus wait time).

Because of the differences between the perceptions of a project budget and a business budget, one should try to get the project budget outside of the general budget reviews. The project should be considered as an external or separate corporate effort. The important concern is how do the project's accomplishments affect the corporation's bottom line over a period of time, not just one year.

Your budget needs to specify the cost estimates as to individuals, equipment, materials, and support activities (quality, risk management, documentation, and training). The results of this process could be entries in the budgets of the approving management authorities within a corporation if you cannot have your own project budget.

Budgeting is to cost estimating what scheduling is to time estimating. A similar relationship exists between activity sequencing and activity defining. Budgeting takes cost estimates and groups and consolidates them into a formal structure (the budget). As stated earlier, a budget is a plan or prediction of expenditures and revenues for a given period, usually a year in length for a company. Analyzing your spending is an excellent management tool for refining future expenditures. Your project budget is specific to the length of time (duration) it takes you to do the project.

[D] Ten Basic Questions for Resolving Budget Issues

A budget is an itemized plan of revenues and expenditures for a given period. The period here is the length of time to implement the original project goals. Your project budget can be linked to other budgets and it is important to define those linkages. The answers to the questions should be relevant to the project budget and these other budget links.

To answer these questions, the responses from cost estimating (Chapter 7) should also be used. The metaquestion of this activity is, "How do I organize project cost estimates into a formal structure?"

IN WHOSE BUDGET (CHART OF ACCOUNTS) DO THE COST ESTIMATES GO? You need to know the organizational structure of the budget to determine where the cost estimates are going. It is possible to have several different types of budgets. There must be one consistent and coherent project budget even if it is *not* a part of the formal budget structure. It should adhere to the defined project goals.

HOW ARE VARIOUS BUDGETS INTERRELATED?   The important links are the cost estimates to budget lines or items. It is also important that budget expenditures and revenues reflect the time line of the project cycle.

HOW MANY BUDGETS ARE AFFECTED BY THIS PROJECT?   The scope plan is important for the budgeting activity. It can be used as a basis for structuring the cost estimates by month and budget line. The scope plan may point to a special line in the budget. Some corporate budget structures are very elaborate, to say the least. Remember the "rollup" principle. Your project may be entered in your manager's budget as a single line or multiple lines. You need to be aware of the type of rollup so you can explain variances in budgets.

WHAT IS THE DEFINED DURATION OF THE PROJECT?   Is more than one corporate budget cycle involved? A project budget is based on the duration (work time plus the wait time) of the project cycle. If there are other budgets to be considered, you must define the project budget's impacts on them. More and more projects seem to be scheduled for less than a year. In addition, there is a tendency for a project's start and end dates to fall in the same year.

HOW ARE PROJECT COST ESTIMATES TO BE ALLOCATED?   Cost estimates can go into one budget line or into many. The usual case is at least three budget lines. The resources of the project can usually be divided into salaries, equipment, and materials. It is recommended the project budget be as granular as is feasible.

HAS THE QUALITY PROCESS BEEN COST ESTIMATED AND BUDGETED?   It is recommended to have at least two budget lines for the quality process. The lines are control and assurance. You may also wish to divide these two lines into salaries, equipment, and materials.

HOW ARE INTERNAL AND EXTERNAL RESOURCES BUDGETED?   The buying of equipment for the project may go in a budget line different from leasing the equipment. The salaries of corporate employees would certainly go on a different line than payments to contractors. An important question is, "Are the other corporate budget lines associated with an employee's compensation included in the project's budget?"

HOW AND TO WHOM IS FINANCIAL INFORMATION GIVEN?   There may be special requirements in a budget for such items as postage and shipping expenditures. It is important to have knowledge of the procedures for communicating with the appropriate people who post expenses to a budget when you are in a corporate environment. It is likely to happen more than once that some expenditures get posted to the wrong line in a corporate budget related to a project. Usually this error takes more than several months to correct.

HAVE POTENTIAL THREATS AND OPPORTUNITIES BEEN FACTORED INTO THE BUDGETARY PROCESS? In one or more budget lines there should be factored in an amount for risk management. The most logical line is the allocation of money for contractors. Another line to consider if one is established is for quality control and assurance. Your project may need more testing than you estimated.

WHAT ARE THE IMPACTS ON THE BUDGETARY PROCESS FOR OUTSOURCING ACTIVITIES? One of the most difficult budgetary issues is the paying of contractors. Where in the budget the expenditure appears is important but also when the expenditure is paid. If you have to set up your budget to meet certain financial milestones, a late payment can have an impact on the project status. You need two change notices for the following situation: You stated you were going to spend a certain amount on contractors in the first quarter of the year (corporate budget). However, the expenditure did not appear in the budget until the second quarter because of the procurement procedures.

[E]   Budgetary Support Data

The budgeting activity is to take cost estimates and enter them into a formal financial structure. A budget is to cost as a schedule is to time. At the end of the cost-budgeting activity, you should at least have the following:

- A budget or budgets that are consistent to the project's goals and objectives that reflect the customer's needs
- Budget lines for support functions such as documentation and training
- Links defined between the project's budget and any other budgets
- Procedure for handling the payments for outside resources
- Procedure for handling the project's budget cycle when it impacts another budget over several of its cycles
- Procedure for making changes and updates to the budget reporting system as relevant to the project
- Separate budget line for risk management or an identified component of another budget line
- Separate budget lines for quality control and verification (optional)
- Statement on which budget lines are impacted (this is for all involved budgets)

[F]   Three Budgetary Management Documents

Given below are three budgetary documents that can assist you in controlling the budget for your IS project. Actually, they would be useful all the time. Recognize that good budgetary management is the result of good cost management. These documents are for both cost and budgetary management.

Remember, costs are the actual expenditures. The budget is the formal structure for accounting for the costs.

1. Initial Budget Estimates
2. Initial Funding Requirements
3. Project Cost Updates

Initial Budget Estimates

This document provides a view of the expected project costs. The estimate is usually based on the scope definition of the project. The document
gives estimates for direct labor as well as capital and expense requirements.
Remember, the indirect costs should be considered as important as direct
costs. This document is updated in the Project Cost Updates.

Initial Funding Requirements

This document monitors and reports project costs at each major phase
of the project. There should be comparisons to the original funding document
used to establish financial targets and expected milestones and deliverables.
This document can also be included in the Project Cost Update.

Project Cost Updates

This document updates initial project cost estimates at each major phase
of your project in comparison to the Initial Budget Estimates. The concern
here is how the costs (actual expenditures) and revenues go into the budget
(the financial plan). The costs are usually reported on a monthly basis.

[G] Budgeting versus Cost Estimating

Here are 10 comparisons between budgeting and cost estimating:

1. A budget is a plan to be followed, while cost estimates are tasks.
2. Budget items are inputs into the chart of accounts, while cost estimates
   are inputs into the budget.
3. Budgeting is a consequence of planning; cost estimating is a consequence of analyzing.
4. Budgeting is at times precise, while cost estimating is at times nebulous.
5. Budgeting is concerned with the complete project, while cost estimating
   is concerned with an individual activity or groups of related activities.
6. Budgeting is the formal structuring of many activities that includes activities of the project at one level of the corporate budget, while cost estimating is a component of budgeting.

7. Budgeting is the method you use to frame the spending plan within a calendar usually based on monthly increments and accounting categories, while cost estimating uses the duration of a single activity or a group of related activities.

8. Budgeting is viewed as a concrete process, while cost estimating is viewed as an abstract process.

9. The budget is important to the strategic manager, while cost estimates are important to the tactical and operational managers.

10. The budget is to cost estimating what the schedule is to time estimating.

[H]   Project Budget versus Business Budget

You need either an informal or formal project budget. Most likely you will have to create your own informal budget—that is, a document that is based on your corporate chart of accounts and that combines all the various formal budgets related to the project. An unfortunate practice is to enter individual project budget items as one combined item in your IS group budget or in the formal budget of each participating group of the project team.

To comprehend a budget in the context of its inputs of cost estimates, you must be aware of some of the differences between a project budget and a business budget. The following 10 comparisons show some of the differences:

1. A project budget cannot easily determine unpredictable peak periods, while a business budget can be created to manage peak periods such as Christmas sales or end-of-quarter requirements.

2. A project budget cannot survive on underplanning, while a business budget might (which is the reason for third and fourth quarter reviews of budgets).

3. A project budget does not have to consider long-term benefits, while a business budget usually does.

4. A project budget is concerned with achieving goals, while a business budget's focus is profit.

5. A project budget needs monies to maximize resources, while the business budget baselines for minimum resources.

6. A project budget needs to reflect skill requirements, while a business budget considers headcount.

7. A project budget relies on contract services more than a business budget.

8. A project budget requires a place for contingencies, while a business budget usually does not.

9. A project budget usually has limited financial histories to use as an estimating tool, while a business budget usually has at least last year's budget to use for planning or financial histories with similar functions.

10. A project budget usually reflects costs for highly skilled personnel, while a business budget hides skill differences.

One of the issues of the corporate world is that business managers forget that an estimate is a guess, not a fact. They also tend to forget that a budget or a schedule is a plan, not a commitment. A major contrast between the thinking of business managers and project managers is the first thinks in terms of commitment while the second tends to think in terms of plans. Many project issues can find their home based on these contrasting viewpoints.

You have to ensure that your cost estimates are as precise and realistic as possible because the customers and the associated managers will always think of the concrete form of the budget, their perceived bottom line. Only one budget is meaningful within a corporation. It is the one at the highest level. As a project manager, you need to understand how the corporate budget process is managed. You can then try to factor this understanding into the cost estimates and their related time estimates.

Many of the contrasts above could have been summarized as the project manager's view and the business manager's view. There is also the tendency to say we estimate the costs but we plan the budget. Sorry, we estimate both.

MANAGER'S TIP

Several years ago, partners at a large international accounting firm decided to implement a popular new technology to deliver an online magazine to subscribers. Weeks before the launch, the company that produced the technology teetered on the edge of bankruptcy, foiled by an unstable and technologically restrictive product despite advertising spin and good word of mouth. The online project had to be redesigned for delivery using a different technology. It blew the budget and precipitated one of the worst scenarios possible for a project manager.

The essential assumption of this chapter and the checklist in Exhibit 8-1: Checklist for Project Budget Items for the design and development of budgetary items is that a separate project budget must exist. It does not necessarily have to be a part of the formal budget structure of the company, but having it so would make project management—and perhaps even the managing of your IS financial issues—much easier.

The checklist assists you in your design and development of a budget. You might also use the company's format to assist you. A project budget gives the visual financial status of your project and supportive evidence in a set of documents. It includes the source of funds, the amount to be spent by major

Exhibit 8-1: Checklist for Project Budget Items

	Attachments
Budget methodology	
Corporate budget requirements:	
Table of accounts	
Item locations	
Item aggregation	
Spending increments	
Input requirements	
Reporting structure	
Reporting requirements	
Funding sources:	
Customer	
Internal (IS)	
Other	
Scenario type:	
Pessimistic	
Realistic	
Optimistic	
Link types to estimates by:	
Pessimistic	
Realistic	
Optimistic	
Milestones:	
Pessimistic	
Realistic	
Optimistic	
Links to project goals	
Links to deliverables	
Source ID	
Critical path items	
Procurement	
Hardware	

Exhibit 8-1 (*Continued*)

	Attachments
Software	
Consultants	
Special materials	
Skills	
Training	
Procurement	
Internal Resources	
Support tasks	
Documentation tasks	
Production tasks	
Planning	
Design	
Development	
Testing	
Contingency	
Noncritical path items	
Procurement	
Hardware	
Software	
Consultants	
Special materials	
Skills	
Training	
Procurement	
Internal Resources	
Support tasks	
Documentation tasks	
Production tasks	
Planning	
Design	
Development	
Testing	

Exhibit 8-1 (*Continued*)

	Attachments
Links to assumptions	
Links to constraints	
Deadline impacts	
Time estimates inputs	
Quality items	
Control	
Assurance	
Validation	
Field testing	
Resource items	
Equipment	
Internal	
External	
Materials	
Internal	
External	
Skills	
Internal	
External	
Headcount equivalent	
Project management tools	
Internal	
External	
Development tools	
Internal	
External	
Facilities	
Internal	
External	
Logistics	
Internal	
External	

Exhibit 8-1 (*Continued*)

	Attachments
Training cost totals	
Internal	
External	
Documentation cost totals	
Internal	
External	
Communications cost totals	
Internal	
External	
Travel	
Customer support	
Training	
Data gathering	
Time requirements	
Vendors	
Functional	
Goal	
Deliverable	
Time requirements	
Payment requirements	
Dependency links	
Project goals	
Project milestones	
Task milestones	
Learning curve	
Special event	
Risk management	
Project administration	
Special variants noted	
Consistency to:	
Scope plan	
Activity plan	

Exhibit 8-1 (*Continued*)

	Attachments
Resource plan	
Project schedule	
Business Justification	
Commercial Specification	
Design/Development plan	
Baseline plan	
Change management	
Update requirements	
Slippage rules	
Links to other budgets	
Funding source approval	
Estimates vs. Actual Report	

Instructions for a Project Budget Checklist

This checklist may be used during the general estimating process; however, it cannot be completed until there is an approved project schedule. Time has cost.

There is one question for project budget design, "What method should I use so the project's budget is minimally impacted by the business budget cycle?" This checklist is the framework for answering this question.

A major assumption for project budget design is that there should be three budgets: pessimistic, realistic, and optimistic. The realistic budget is the project budget. The other two budgets are the basis for change and contingency management.

A second assumption of the project budget is it is more than a list of budget items and the period when they will be funded or spent. There must be a set of support documents. Unfortunately, the project manager or an essential player might be lost from the project and there are no written parameters for then managing the budget.

Use this checklist to keep track of the documents you need to create the budget. In the Attachments column, name the document that contains the information for the item listed in the first column.

Budget methodology: Use the "bottom-up" approach if budgeting can be done at the task level. However, if fund allocation is tight, then use the "top-down" approach to allocate funds at the functional level.

Corporate budget requirements: Before designing your own budget, check for special corporate requirements and exceptions. In particular, check the listed items. If there is a requirement for the formal project budget to be a part of the corporate structure, ensure you can define as many separate project budget items as possible from IS group budget items. You still need to create a set of informal project budgets.

Reporting requirements: It is important to know corporate, customer, and project team requirements for information. These requirements affect the level of detail (table of accounts) for the budget.

Funding sources: When possible, each source should be identified on a separate budget line. "Other" means such things as the training group pays for customer training because of a marketing agreement.

Exhibit 8-1 (*Continued*)

Scenario type: Unfortunately, the basic attitude is that you have only one formal budget. Changes and updates can require a large amount of effort. By having three budgets up front, it saves administrative time during the project's duration.

Link types to estimates by: There needs to be a document that gives the source or responsible person for the cost estimates.

Milestones: The milestones help determine when there is to be funding and spending and the incremental amounts.

Links to project goals: Each budget item should have a link to one or more project goals as found in the scope plan.

Links to deliverables: When it is appropriate, there should be links from budget items to deliverables, this includes training and documentation.

Source ID: Identify the person responsible for the budget item, including title, e-mail address, and telephone number. If an external source, also include company information.

Critical path items: The budget items for the critical path determine the fundamental design of the project budget. When there is no expenditure for a listed item, then $0.00 should be given on the checklist. It may be required to break down the list further such as production or testing hardware.

Contingency: It is the rational preparation for change. A contingency plan is the preparation for a pessimistic scenario or worse to become reality.

Noncritical path items: These items can be changed or even possibly can be deleted without risk to the project. If this assumption is incorrect, then there needs to be a supporting document as to the possible amount of change or the impacts of deleting the budget item.

Links to assumptions: Use the assumptions in the scope plan and in cost estimates to determine a budget item and when amounts will be funded or spent.

Links to constraints: Use the constraints in the scope plan and in cost estimates to determine a budget item and when amounts will be funded or spent.

Deadline impacts: When amounts will be funded or spent is absolutely affected by deadlines since they are absolute dates or events.

Time estimates inputs: These inputs are used to determine when amounts for a given budget item will be funded or spent. You never take a budget item amount and divide it by the monthly increments of the project's or a task's duration.

Quality items: Budget items for quality tasks should be divided by at least the four listed items. When there is only one line, it is difficult to determine impacts. In addition, the tasks by different groups may be either internal or external.

Resource items: Amounts for various resource types should be detailed when possible, especially if there is more than one funding source. When there is no expenditure for a listed item, then $0.00 should be given on the checklist.

Training: Integrate appropriate items in the training group's budget into the project budget. In addition, create special budget items for training done outside the training group.

Documentation: Integrate when appropriate in the related documentation group's budget items into the project budget. In addition, create special budget items for training done outside the documentation group.

Communications: Budget items such as cost to communicate with customer about the project's status would be here. Travel might be included here or under the travel budget item.

Travel: Budget items for travel should be broken down into at least the four categories.

    Customer support: This item might be here or under communications. You should also include car rental, hotel, and meals.

    Training: Use only if customer training is given in a project goal.

    Data gathering: There may be a special requirement to go to a vendor's location. In this case, the budget item can be here or located under budget.

Exhibit 8-1 (*Continued*)

Time requirements: If there is a direct cost, amounts should be defined. Indirect costs are never put in a budget. The costs for direct and indirect administrative efforts are one item in a standard budget. The corporate financial group usually states for a given head or a certain type and level, the budget factor is $175 per hour. This amount covers all the various administrative tasks and travel time, say, of a manager or programmer.

Vendors: The budget items can be broken down to function or deliverable. A budget support document should state goal, time for funding or spending, and payment requirements.

Dependency links: When appropriate, a document should be written that includes the appropriate listed items.

Risk management: There needs to be a budget item for potential risk corrections. This amount is a contingency, a known padding factor. An amount not spent might be moved to another budget item that has slippage if required when not spent during the month. A slippage is a form of risk.

Project administration: If there is a corporate rule that certain administrative activities or tasks are to be considered direct, then this budget item should be in the project budget. For example, your costs for being a project manager might be here and your costs for being an IS manager would be given in the IS budget.

Special variants: There are always issues not covered in this checklist that need to be considered in the project budget.

Consistency to: The listed documents should be used to define the environment for all cost estimates. Cost estimates should not be finalized until the project schedule is completed.

Scope plan: This plan is the strategic view of the constraints and assumptions of the project as developed by the project team.

Activity plan: This plan is a set of definitions for efforts required to achieve measurable results. At the operational level, you consider activities; while at the project level, you consider tasks.

Resource plan: This plan establishes support requirements for a project as to costs, availability, start date and end date (length of time for use plus duration), and technical specifications.

Project schedule: This plan formalizes the time estimates within a calendar structure. It is an integration of sequencing tasks, resource planning, cost estimating, and time estimating.

Business Justification: It is the general rationale for making the financial investment.

Commercial Specification: It is an evolution of the Business Justification. It identifies the market need and gives adequate requirement and limitation data for the design and development group(s).

Design/Development plan: It drives the project Integration Plan that captures all major design and development deliverables and milestones for management tracking and reporting.

Baseline plan: It is the initial approved point from which any deviations will be determined using standards and benchmarks.

Change management: The procedure for changing the budget should be documented.

Update requirements: The procedure for updating the budget should be documented.

Slippage rules: This applies to when a budget item is overspent. The procedure for managing a slippage should be documented.

Links to other budgets: Rather than including the training group's budget items that directly affect the project, there can be a support document that gives these items.

Funding source approval: The funding source or sources must give written approval on all or part of the budget as is appropriate.

Estimates vs. Actual Report: This should be done after the financial group sends an update of funding and spending. No review briefing should be held with the customer until this report is completed. The exception to this is that budget issues are not on the agenda.

task groups, and the month in which it is to be spent. If the financial components of a project are "hidden" within single or multiple lines of an IS budget, you have to struggle to keep matters correct. When you are asked to revisit your IS budget on a quarterly basis by your upper-level management, how do you distinguish easily between the amounts that belong to the project and the amounts that belong to the IS group? If an edict comes down from upper-level management that you must cut all budget lines by 10 percent, what do you do? If you make cuts automatically, how does it impact the project? The checklist in Exhibit 8-1 gives you a tool to lessen the impact of such an edict, and it assists you in protecting the budgetary items for the project.

MANAGER'S TIP

Using the methodology described above, the author kept up with 18 different sized projects at one time. At the end of the year, I knew within $50 what was actually spent on each project by funding source, and by the group as funded by the corporation.

[I]   Refining Cost Estimates

Before putting together the budget, you need to analyze closely the cost estimates. The following are five steps that can be used:

1. Perform a "rough cut" using cost-management software to create various scenarios (at this step you may be doing across-the-board percent cuts).

2. Do a more reliable review with experts and a more granular analysis of tasks.

3. Carry out fine-tuning.

4. Discuss the estimates with strategic manager.

5. Get budget approval and resolve ways to cut the budget.

MANAGER'S TIP

Remember, you begin with the lowest estimates and work toward the highest estimates.

[J]   Five Budget Bears

Besides the usual events that might affect your budget in the long term, such as acts of God or quarterly budget reviews, there are some pressures, which

I call hungry bears, that may be lurking during the time you are trying to assemble a budget. The following are five of these bears:

1. Forgotten activities, resources, or materials
2. Not enough time to refine estimates
3. People desiring funds that are unrealistic
4. Quotes from vendors that range far apart
5. Senior management, especially a manager who wants to be a hero at the expense of the project, who wants the budget compressed

The basic consequence of being unable to resist the budget bears is having a too-low budget. Some specific risks can come out of the situation. Remember, a risk is an event that can be disastrous to the project. The following are risks that might arise because of a too-low budget:

- Project failure
- Costs going upward
- Low morale, resulting in lower productivity
- Shortchanging on the quality of resources, equipment, and materials
- Quality of work going in a downward spiral
- Rework of performance errors being impacted
- Risk management becomes a firehouse

[K]   Refining the Budget

You believe you have reliable cost and resource estimates and you put forth your budget to the customer and upper management. The reaction is that the budget is too high. You silently think to yourself, "But they agreed to the cost and resource estimates." Your task is to do a budget alignment similar to a schedule alignment. The following are six areas you need to analyze in this process:

1. Capital spending
2. Cash flow
3. Contingency funding
4. Expenses
5. Overhead
6. Staff charges

On capital spending, have you accepted a capital cost that really belongs to the customer? If the equipment is to be turned over to the customer, then you need to treat this situation as a flow-through and not as a budget item.

On cash flow, you need to adjust customer payment milestones so their frequencies cover outgoing costs. The cash inflow must equal or exceed the cash going out.

On contingency funding, you need to analyze the contingencies for emergency travel, consultants, and training. All of this funding should be overt, not covert.

On expenses, you need to evaluate your extraordinary expenses such as travel or special supplies. Do reports really need to be bound and in four colors? You need to consider lower-cost alternatives.

On overhead, you need to consider if certain costs can be paid for by other company funds rather than the project. Say, for example, a person needs to be trained to assist on some specific project activity; however, after the project the person's training will be used in long-term operational tasks. Perhaps the operational group should be paying for the training.

On staff charges, you need to reduce rates per hour, but they are fixed according to corporate policy. You see that a certain activity needs a novice employee, but the operational manager has placed a top runner on the activity and is charging accordingly. You should negotiate to have a lower staff charge. You do need to be aware of how this action impacts the project.

§ 8.02   MANAGEMENT INVOLVEMENT

[A]   Overview

It is easy for most people to see that all levels of management need to be involved in the budgetary process—or more specifically the project budgeting activity. The confusion comes as to what part each level plays. One first must recognize that the strategic manager and the operational managers treat the project budget as a business plan and perhaps as a commitment strategically, while the project manager views the project budget as a plan. Many a career falters on these different views. It has been shown earlier why the views differ. It is the obligation of all these managers to be aware of these differences and negotiate changes based on these different budgetary assumptions.

All the managers should ensure there is a process in place to get the most reliable estimates possible for any activity duration, resource requirements, and potential costs. The budget should reflect money for the critical support functions of quality control, risk management, training, and documentation.

All managers should be aware that any spending that is reflected in the project budget is for:

- Deliverables as specified in the project plan; no "hidden" add-ons such as "the customer will really like this feature"
- Invoices that reflect the vendors' commitments
- Resources defined in the project plan and other project documents such as third-party commitments
- Delays in spending for a particular area of concern, along with reasons
- Overspending for a particular month, that is, a delay from an earlier month or an overage that might be in a future month's allocation or a real overspending

[B]   Strategic Management and the Budget

The strategic manager should not consider a project budget a commitment but a plan. This manager should try to get from higher management an acceptance that the project budget is a separate management tool and should not be treated the same as the operational budgets are during quarterly reviews. This is especially true if the project is to resolve a customer's needs more than a specific corporate need.

If this treatment cannot be achieved, then the strategic manager needs to work with the project manager and other business managers to ensure a consistent process for funding the budget. There may be funds for the project in the budgets of marketing, training, quality control, and documentation. When the quarterly reviews happen, how do changes to these budgets impact the project? Each group may have a different percentage of reduction of budget in a given quarter. What are the impacts?

[C]   Tactical Management and the Budget

On one occasion the project manager *must* act as a business manager. This occasion is not an activity of project management. The occasion is the negotiation of who pays for the activities. The timing of payments affects the budget's schedule and the spending by month.

MANAGER'S TIP

If the customer pays, then the customer should give you, the project manager, the authority to spend and to manage the project budget.

The essential tactical actions of the project manager include the following:

- Be aware of events that affect monthly budget reports (especially validate time-sheet inputs).

- Be aware of the impact of each vendor's invoicing cycle (you spend in the second quarter, the vendor's invoice appears in the fourth quarter).
- Ensure that cost estimates are correctly entered by category or subcategory (refine the cost estimates into as many budget items as possible).
- Ensure that operational managers do monthly budget status reports.
- Ensure that cost estimates are reliable.
- Ensure that resource estimates are reliable.
- Ensure that time estimates are reliable.
- Ensure that predicted spending is reliably given by month (do not divide the total by 12).
- Ensure you have a budget to manage project administration.
- Hold a monthly meeting on budgetary issues.
- Identify funding for contingencies such as emergency travel.
- Identify capital costs.
- Seek the lowest staff charges.
- Seek to reduce extraordinary costs such as travel.
- Use project management software to evaluate spending prior to any monthly budget report (assist in identifying possible input errors or omitted spending, late invoices).

[D]   Operational Management and the Budget

The basic functions of the operational managers include the following:

- Be aware of the monthly budget constraints that affect your project efforts.
- Ensure that cost estimates are reliable.
- Ensure that resource estimates are reliable.
- Ensure that time estimates are reliable.
- Ensure that if your employees do time sheets, they need to reflect only the effort directed toward the project.
- Inform the tactical manager as soon as possible of any budgetary issue.
- Review with the tactical manager the results from the project-management software.
- When you have a budget that includes project spending, then you need to treat those items as a project manager would, not as a business manager.

Exhibit 8-2: Budget Questions Checklist

Project Name:	Comments
1. Are there budget lines for support functions such as documentation and training?	
2. Are there separate budget lines for quality control and verification?	
3. Has the quality process been cost estimated and budgeted?	
4. Have links between the project's budget and any other budgets been defined?	
5. Have potential threats and opportunities been factored into the budgetary process?	
6. How and to whom is financial information given?	
7. How are internal and external resources budgeted?	
8. How are project cost estimates to be allocated?	
9. How are various budgets interrelated?	
10. How do I organize project cost estimates into a formal structure?	
11. How many budgets are affected by this project?	
12. In whose budget (chart of accounts) do the cost estimates go?	
13. Is the budget consistent with the project's goals that reflect the customer's needs?	
14. Is there a procedure for handling the payments for outside resources?	
15. Is there a procedure for handling the project's budget cycle when it impacts another budget over several of its cycles?	
16. Is there a procedure for making changes and updates to the budget reporting system as relevant to the project?	
17. Is there a separate budget line for risk management or an identified component of another budget line?	
18. Is there a statement on which budget lines are impacted (complex budget)?	
19. What are the impacts on the budgetary process for outsourcing activities?	
20. What is the defined duration of the project?	

On the CD-ROM

On the CD-ROM are:

1. Exhibit 8-1 Checklist For Project Budget Items.doc

2. Exhibit 8-2 Budget Questions Checklist.doc

3. Chapter 8 Overview.ppt—Chapter Overview, Budget Developing

Chapter 9

Controlling Quality

§ 9.01   OVERVIEW

[A]   Objectives

At the end of this chapter, you will be able to:

- Define the two basic components of the quality process.
- State 10 reasons for having a quality product.
- Identify 20 sources for errors in an IS project.
- Identify 10 things that can be measured for cost consequences by quality assurance and control.

- Answer three core questions about your quality control process for the project.

- Ask 10 basic questions about quality control such as: Have quality resources and activities been budgeted? Have quality control checks for each major component and project milestone been determined? How and to whom should the quality control information be given? Is the quality control internal, external, or both? What are the critical performance criteria for determining project success? Who should handle quality control?

- Identify the nine components of a quality assurance and control plan.

- State 10 questions that could be asked by a peer review.

- Identify the three functions essential to configuration control.

- List five ISO standards for quality.

- Identify how the three managing levels are involved in quality control.

MANAGER'S TIP

The Y2K phenomenon, as it became known, left a legacy in the IS world that continues to resonate deeply. It demonstrated the need for disaster recovery plans and for tight quality assurance (QA), especially in the present environment, where there is a constant challenge to work on faster schedules and in exponentially more complex environments. Unfortunately, many small- to medium-sized firms have still not learned this lesson.

As an example illustration of the importance of QA: Public Service Electric and Gas, New Jersey's largest power utility, set up a permanent quality assurance department to test all new software. The objective was to replicate the successful team of QA engineers who performed tests on the Year 2000 work of programmers. Previously, programmers had done all testing of the utility's software.

Quality management issues can be viewed as either a cost center or profit maker for any business. It is costly because you must hire highly skilled professionals to do the work, who must be involved from the initial project phase onward. In addition, any failure to meet customer requirements can be costly on the business side. But QA that maintains a quality standard for your products or services is profitable because it helps brand your company as professional. An active quality management program can bring you huge savings by identifying serious errors in your products or services before they are released to the market.

[B] Using Essential Definitions

The five essential concepts that are the basis for any discussion on a quality control and assurance program are the following:

Quality assurance is based on performance. It is the establishing of performance standards, then measuring and evaluating project performance against these standards. This component of quality management considers measurable deviations in performance during a project.

A **quality audit** is an independent evaluation or test of some component of the project by qualified personnel.

Quality control is the component of quality management that considers the system or development processes of a project. It is the tasks used to meet standards through the gathering of performance information, inspecting, monitoring, and testing.

Quality management is the process that uses control and assurance to prevent risks and, if a risk occurs, to minimize it.

The **Quality Plan** defines the role of quality control and assurance in all phases of the project process.

[C]   Quality Control Process Definition

There are two basic components of the quality process: assurance and control. Quality as defined by those in the profession as "conformance to specification." Another way to state the purpose of the quality process is that it seeks to minimize performance errors.

Assurance is based on performance. It is the establishing of performance standards, then measuring and evaluating project performance against these standards. Finally, assurance acts on performance deviations.

Control acts to meet the standards through the gathering of performance information, inspecting, monitoring, and testing.

The essential word is *performance*. This means the project activities should be evaluated against the following by quality assurance and control:

- Project goals
- Standards, such as ISO
- Corporate standards
- Standards established by the project team during the planning phase
- Schedule
- Budget

Quality assurance and control can affect a number of areas, including:

- Customer satisfaction
- Design improvement
- Development improvement
- Implementation integrity
- Testing guaranty

The project manager should use quality assurance and control to bring light to the darkest corner of any closet.

[D]   Gold Medaling with a Quality Product

Having a quality product can be summarized in two words: customer satisfaction. However, what do these two words mean? The following are 10 characteristics that reflect customer satisfaction with a quality product:

1. Quality demonstrates an awareness of customer needs. In one sense, quality means that the product does what the customer desires.

2. Quality equates to control. There need to be checks and balances that usually take the forms of standards and benchmarks.

3. Quality is commitment. It is the obligation of any project team member to state when an activity as defined cannot be accomplished.

4. Quality is measurable. When a customer uses the product, the customer can validate functionality against product specifications.

5. Quality is support for the effort even when there are disagreements. The project cannot be accomplished by a single person and the team is only as strong as its weakest link.

6. Quality means avoidance of cost for things unnecessary. This initiative does not mean turning out a cheap product but focusing on spending for what is required.

7. Quality means having the right skill at the right place and at the right time. The goal is to have minimal performance errors. This result is most likely to be achieved through consistency to the defined project goals and the actual production.

8. Quality means there is some form of communication between you and the customer. Communications can establish a bond of confidence.

9. Quality requires metrics so analysis can be done to determine degree of success. When the customer knows there are product metrics, a sense of product integrity can be established.

10. Quality revolves around coordination. All parties involved in the project should be integrated as a team.

[E]   Twenty Sources for IS Errors

There are many, many sources for errors. Most are found in the general operational process, such as the following:

1. Activity sequencing error
2. Coding error
3. Database format error
4. Documentation error
5. Equipment being below standards

6. Failure to give timely reports
7. Feature not being a part of a project goal
8. Hardware incompatibility
9. Material not meeting standards
10. Network component incompatibility
11. Not using appropriate standards
12. Operating system incompatibility to system infrastructure
13. Project activity not being defined in the schedule
14. Report layout in error
15. Requirement specification in error
16. Resource received not being in accordance with specification
17. Skill level not valid
18. Software incompatibility
19. Training objective not meeting a project goal
20. Vendor product incompatibility to system

Why do you want these errors eliminated? It improves customer satisfaction. Errors cost dollars, expensive dollars. You might eliminate some or even most of the errors without quality assurance and control; however, you will have no baseline to identify the extent of your accomplishment.

[F] Measuring Cost Consequences

During the project management activity of validating cost estimates, besides using project management software, you, the project manager, can also use quality assurance and control to measure cost consequences. The following are 10 examples of the types of cost consequences that could be analyzed:

1. Adding staff, equipment, or materials
2. Comparing two vendor products
3. Eliminating certain training components
4. Eliminating certain types or components of user documentation
5. Limiting or decreasing debugging time
6. Limiting or decreasing testing time
7. Performing maintenance after product release
8. Performing customer service
9. Resolving an incompatibility problem
10. Revising software or hardware requirements because of a revision of a project goal

[G] Three Core Questions about Your Quality Control Process

The following are three questions you need to answer so the dark things in the night do not attack your project:

1. Have the quality standards been made consistent?
2. Has a quality control system been established?
3. Have verification activities been formulated?

Benchmarks of the quality and performance of the project should be established at your earliest planning sessions, not after the project is nearly completed. What are the realistic expectations of your customer(s) for the project? Get them in writing. You should be as specific as possible about expectations. Everyone will be happier when the project is completed.

Benchmarks should be clearly formulated in the definition of the goals and objectives of the project and the use of standards. The use of external appropriate benchmarks or standards for project activities and for evaluation of the end goal would make your project more valid to the world. This validation can be significant to your customers and perhaps to yourself.

The forefront of defining project activities should be quality control. Do you know of a project that was completed without a change? You must have activities that show how you handle change. You must establish benchmark actions at the beginning of the project for validating the product. This point is not negotiable because you need a consistent point to have project control.

When you plan your resources, you have to look at all the resource types and, in particular, how the resources affect the quality of your project. If a new skill requirement is identified halfway into the project cycle, has a process been defined that can handle this issue? What skills are required to do adequate controlling and verifying of a project sequence and the status of the project?

Across any activity sequence there must be quality control activities. Are there also validation activities in the activity sequence? You should never say, "We could do all of the quality control at the end." Monitoring is a continuous act, not a random act.

Time estimating can sometimes be more of an art than a science. There is time-management software available to assist in controlling your project. Doing time estimates for quality control can be tricky because you are checking for project errors. A specific amount of time should be allocated for quality control. You should set a benchmark of about 20 percent of the estimated time for the project. This task should be at the beginning of the planning phase.

A specific cost estimate should be established for quality control. You should set a benchmark of between 10 and 20 percent. This percentage is of the estimated total cost for the project. This task should be among the first tasks of your project planning.

The quality control and verification milestones should be clearly defined within any schedule. The quality control time line may be defined as a separate time line; however, when and where quality control flows into the main project cycle must be stated.

It is recommended to have at least two lines in your budget for quality control: Assurance and Control. You may want to divide these two lines into Salaries, Equipment, and Materials.

[H]   Ten Basic Questions on Project Quality Control

Usually an IS group has a separate quality control team. The following questions look at the issues of this team's linkage to the project team. Many IS quality control teams look only at product testing or code control, but in a project situation this team needs to extend itself across group boundaries.

HAS A COMPREHENSIVE QUALITY CONTROL PROGRAM BEEN DEFINED, INCLUDING STANDARDS AND BENCHMARKS? The basis for defining the quality control process is through related standards and benchmarks. There need to be specified quality control points throughout the entire project process. An example of quality control is a review of the scope plan and definition to verify coherence. The quality control process should be defined separately from the testing and more as the validating process.

HAS THE QUALITY PROCESS BEEN COST-ESTIMATED AND -BUDGETED? It is recommended to have at least two budget lines for quality: Control and Verification. You may also wish to divide these two lines into Salaries, Equipment, and Materials.

HAVE THE QUALITY CONTROL EVENTS BEEN INCLUDED AT APPROPRIATE MILESTONES? The quality control and verification milestones should be clearly defined within any schedule. The quality control time line may be defined as a separate time line; however, when and where quality control flows into the main part of the integration project must be stated.

WHAT IS THE NECESSARY TIME FOR QUALITY VALIDATION? Quality control activities need to be established throughout the schedule. There should be validation activities in the activity sequence. Never schedule all of the quality control for the end or last phase of the project.

WHAT ARE THE CRITERIA FOR DOCUMENTING QUALITY CONTROL ACTIVITIES? Some people think the writing group does all documentation, which is far from the truth. As it has already been alluded to, there is a need for project documentation by the entire project team. There need to be criteria or standards for product design and development documentation. These types of documentation are the foundation for the customer documentation developed by the writing group. Therefore, a planning activity that has to be done is establishing documentation requirements and deciding who is responsible for writing each document and perhaps even editing it.

WHAT ARE THE QUALITY CONTROL PROCEDURES THAT NEED TO BE IN THE ACTIVITY PLAN? There should be quality control procedures to cover all activities, not just the results of operational activities. The quality control team can be used as an objective resource for viewing project status as long as they do not get too involved in red tape.

WHAT ARE THE QUALITY CONTROL PROCEDURES THAT ENSURE CORRECT SEQUENCING? Quality control considerations are universal to all activities. You need to establish quality control activities linked into all project sequences. There need to be validation points through the project.

WHAT ARE THE STANDARDS AND BENCHMARKS FOR QUALITY CONTROL? As used here, a standard is usually an external and an industry-accepted document for achieving quality for one or more of the project-defined expected goals. Benchmarks are specific technical levels of excellence. These standards and benchmarks should be collected and placed in a location that is available to any team member.

WHAT IS THE IMPACT OF THE QUALITY CONTROL AND ASSURANCE PROCESSES ON TIME ESTIMATES? Quality control should have a specific amount of time allocated. You could set a benchmark of approximately 20 percent of the estimated time for the project. This task has to be a part of your original estimating process.

WHAT QUALITY CONTROL POLICIES, BENCHMARKS, OR STANDARDS HAVE TO BE FOLLOWED? Has it been determined the impact of outside policies such as federal rules or standards, on the project? Remember, any large company, and some small companies, may have different procedures for contracting outside people, for leasing equipment, and for buying materials. You need to define project activities that ensure that these policies are followed.

[I]   Quality Plan Requirements

This plan defines the role of quality control in all phases of the project process. It also defines the deliverables, functions, and specific activities required of quality control to ensure the successful completion of the project. Quality procedures that are specific to the project should also be identified in an appendix.

There should be a set of quality metrics that defines how a new application is measured, attained, and controlled. These metrics are also included in the project plan with the quality procedures.

The Quality Plan also summarizes the staff, resources, and equipment required by quality assurance and control to perform specific activities and to support a new application.

The Quality Plan should be updated before each major phase review to reflect changes.

[J] Importance of Peer Reviews

Beyond the traditional quality assurance and control group, there has been the more recent development of peer reviews. This is another aspect of team management. A peer review is a technical meeting called for one purpose, to review a deliverable. There should be a final review of each deliverable, and one for the complete set of deliverables.

MANAGER'S TIP

Management (this includes the project manager) should be absent from the technical review, so it does not turn into individual performance reviews.

The peer review needs to ask a number of hard technical questions. Depending on the type of deliverable, the following questions might be asked:

- Does it meet corporate benchmarks?
- Does it meet appropriate standards?
- Does it technically fulfill project goals?
- Does it meet operational requirements?
- Does documentation correctly state technical requirements?
- Have training courses been developed to correctly cover technical issues?
- Does it meet functional requirements?
- Does it meet protocol requirements?
- Does it meet security requirements?
- Does the help function assist the customer in resolving technical issues?

One of the requirements for doing time estimates was to allocate time for meetings. Peer reviews need their appropriate allocations. There are many types of peer reviews, including:

- Capacity plans
- Coding
- Documentation
- Implementation plan
- Internet working plan
- Project plan
- System design
- System development
- Testing plan
- Training
- "X" technical plan (example, vendor technical specification)

Each peer review has its own deliverable. This deliverable should be treated with the importance that is its due. The deliverable could impact either the project schedule or the budget or both; usually it is both. Specific technical statements should be made about the product. This should not be a design meeting.

[K]   Consequence of Configuration Control

Configuration control is important to everyone, whether it be hardware or software. "Everyone" here includes the customer. When customers say the product is too hard to use, they usually mean there is a configuration problem. Configuration as used here means issues involving the correct version, not the values or parameters used to make a product work correctly.

At the project level, the team relies on deliverables from each other. When a team member works for a time on a deliverable and then finds out it is an incorrect version and the work has to be redone, is there frustration?

To eliminate this type of frustration, the project should have a process, method, or mechanism that does the following:

- Identifies deliverable versions
- Describes differences between or among versions
- Ensures that any team member can get the most recent version

When you have a mechanism with the above three functions, you have a management and control tool. It is essential to have all three. The version should be displayed outside of the product so the team member can instantly determine version level.

[L]   Quality and the ISO

The International Organization for Standardization (ISO) is a consortium that sets quality standards in a variety of areas. The following five ISO standards are important to quality:

- ISO 9000 is a quality system standard for any product, service, or process.

- ISO 9001 is a quality system standard for design, production, and installation of a product or service.

- ISO 9002 is a quality system model for quality assurance in production and installation.

- ISO 9003 is a quality system model for quality assurance in final inspection and testing.

- ISO 9004 is a set of quality management guidelines for any organization to use to develop and implement a quality system.

[M]   Using a Quality Management Program Checklist

As has been stated quite a number of times, invalid time and cost estimates are two of the primary reasons for the failure of most projects. The actual reason for project failure may be because of the lack of an early warning system. An early warning system is, in reality, an effective quality management program that has two major functions: control and assurance. Most managers say they have a quality control program: actually, they probably have a loosely defined framework that is not integrated into the project management process. Too many project managers rely purely on the corporate and IS quality groups to handle project issues without direction. The rationale is that these groups know their jobs, so why should the project manager need to tell them anything?

The big failure is when a quality group is not brought into the very beginnings of a project, and is usually called upon only when there is a problem or pain caused by a potential risk. You do preventive maintenance on your car, should you not do the same for a project? When a quality group sits too far from the project manager, their input is overlooked until the traditional events for validation and testing are to occur. Unfortunately, these are the times when project managers usually find the dark goblins in the closet.

Two of the essential items in the creation of time and cost estimates are reliable and relevant standards and benchmarks. Exhibit 9-1: Checklist for a Quality Management Program and its instructions should assist you in integrating the quality functions into these efforts. Without this integration, you should expect risks and possible project failure.

Exhibit 9-1: Checklist for a Quality Management Program

	Attachments
QUALITY CONTROL	
Source ID	
Document identification:	
Scope plan	
Activity plan	
Resource plan	
Schedule	
Budget	
Standards	
Benchmarks	
Verification	
Testing	
Time estimate criteria	
Cost estimate criteria	
Resource est. criteria	
Skill criteria	
Technical procedures	
Technical policies	
Procurement procedures	
Procurement policies	
Communications	
ISO standards	
PMI standards	
Customer satisfaction criteria	
Critical path criteria	
Identify skill criteria:	
Pessimistic	
Realistic	
Optimistic	
Establish tasks criteria:	
Planning	

Exhibit 9-1 (*Continued*)

	Attachments
Design	
Development	
Production	
Testing	
Task sequencing criteria	
Determine reviews requirements:	
Time estimates	
Cost estimates	
Resource estimates	
Project adm. criteria	
Assumptions:	
Criteria	
Validation criteria	
Constraints:	
Criteria	
Validation criteria	
Determine field test criteria	
Identify training criteria:	
Validation	
Testing	
Identify documentation criteria:	
Validation	
Testing	
Identify quality support tasks	
Variances criteria:	
Time	
Cost	
Resources	
Variance reporting criteria	
Risk management criteria	

Exhibit 9-1 *(Continued)*

	Attachments
Specify random inspection criteria:	
Equipment	
Materials	
Skills	
Project management tools	
Development tools	
Facilities	
Logistics	
Training	
Documentation	
Communications	
Specify audit criteria:	
Equipment	
Materials	
Skills	
Project management tools	
Development tools	
Facilities	
Logistics	
Training	
Documentation	
Communications	
Vendors:	
Assist writing RFPs	
Gather performance history	
Gather validation criteria	
Gather testing criteria	
Dependency identification:	
Project goals	
Project milestones	
Task milestones	

Exhibit 9-1 (*Continued*)

	Attachments
Learning curve	
Special events	
Consistency determination criteria:	
Scope plan	
Activity plan	
Resource plan	
Project schedule	
Project budget	
Business Justification	
Commercial Specification	
Design/Development Plan	
Baseline Plan	
Field Introduction	
Gather change management criteria:	
Identify update requirements	
Describe slippage rules	
Contingency plan criteria	
Resource-leveling assistance	
Gather logistics criteria	
Gather modeling data	
QUALITY ASSURANCE	
Source ID	
Review viability responses	
Confirm project adm. criteria	
Analyze skills:	
Pessimistic	
Realistic	
Optimistic	
Validate document usage:	
Scope plan	
Activity plan	

Exhibit 9-1 (*Continued*)

	Attachments
Resource plan	
Schedule	
Budget	
Standards	
Benchmarks	
Verification	
Testing	
Time estimate criteria	
Cost estimate criteria	
Resource est. criteria	
Skill criteria	
Technical procedures	
Technical policies	
Procurement procedures	
Procurement policies	
Communications	
ISO standards	
Customer sat. criteria	
Authenticate tasks criteria:	
Planning	
Design	
Development	
Production	
Testing	
Assist in field testing	
Validate training performance	
Verify documentation:	
Customer	
User	
Technical (IS)	
Reports	

Exhibit 9-1 (*Continued*)

	Attachments
Do quality support tasks	
Validate and test assumptions	
Validate and test constraints	
Assist in reviews:	
Time estimates checklists	
Cost-estimates checklists	
Resource estimates	
Task identification checklists	
Task sequencing	
Critical path	
Contingency plan	
Approve risk management criteria	
Do variance reports	
Perform random inspections:	
Identify variances and causes:	
Time	
Cost	
Resources	
Equipment	
Materials	
Skills	
Project management tools	
Development tools	
Facilities	
Logistics	
Training	
Documentation	
Communications	
Perform audits:	
Identify variances and causes:	
Time	

Exhibit 9-1 (*Continued*)

	Attachments
Cost	
Resources	
Equipment	
Materials	
Skills	
Project management tools	
Development tools	
Facilities	
Logistics	
Training	
Documentation	
Communications	
Project management process	
IS procedures and process	
Manufacturing	
Other support groups	
Vendors:	
Review RFP responses	
Analyze performance history	
Confirm validation process	
Confirm testing process	
Confirm dependency usage:	
Project goals	
Project milestones	
Task milestones	
Learning curve	
Special event	
Consistency validation:	
Scope plan	
Activity plan	
Resource plan	

Exhibit 9-1 (*Continued*)

	Attachments
Project schedule	
Project budget	
Business Justification	
Commercial Specification	
Design/Development Plan	
Baseline Plan	
Field Introduction	
Validate change management process	
Validate update process	
Validate slippage usage	
Do feedback reports	
Assistance resource leveling	
Analyze logistics criteria	
Assist in model development	
Validate and test deliverables	

Instructions for Checklist for a Quality Management Program

Quality management is the process that seeks to prevent risks and minimize them, if they do occur. The Quality Plan defines the tasks of quality management's two functions, control and assurance, in all phases of the project process.

It is the purpose of this checklist to assist in the writing of the plan.

The guiding principle for responding to this checklist is that quality control creates the map, while quality assurance drives a route based on the map.

This comprehensive checklist should be used to the level of detail that produces an effective and efficient quality management for the project.

QUALITY CONTROL: It is the quality management component that considers the system or the development of a project's processes. It has tasks used to gather performance information requirements—that is, standards and benchmarks.

Source ID: Identify the person responsible for the budget item, including title, e-mail address, and telephone number. If the source is an external one, also include company information.

Document identification: This task results in a distributed document that identifies the location of listed documents and the methods of acquisition. There should be brief descriptions of the relevance of documents to the project. Two optional project process document sets are the ISO and PMI standards. The International Organization for Standardization (ISO) is a consortium that sets process standards in a variety of areas. The Project Management Institute (PMI) is a professional organization that studies and promotes project management through its standards. The standards should be more than technical; they should include the requirements for stakeholder satisfaction (customer, management, and team), financial variances, and the impacts of innovation on the project and on the IS infrastructure as to interoperability, reliability, and scalability.

Exhibit 9-1 (*Continued*)

Critical path criteria: A critical project task is one, that, if not completed, results in a potential project failure. The task with this item is to identify the criteria used to define the term *critical*. Second, the task is to assist in the design and development of the critical path. Third, the task is to distribute the path criteria as required by the project team.

Identify skill criteria: The task is to gather information so there is consistency in the method of defining skills on three levels (pessimistic, realistic, and optimistic).

Establish tasks criteria: The task is to develop criteria that distinguish between a task and an activity for the project schedule for the listed project phases.

Task sequencing criteria: The task is to gather information to ensure that task sequencing is done in a consistent manner so project goals are completed.

Determine reviews requirements: The task is to gather objective criteria and any special customer, company, or project team requirements to ensure that the three major types of estimates meet any relevant standards or benchmarks.

Project adm. criteria: The task is to define administrative criteria to ensure that the project process uses a systematic and sequential set of tasks to achieve a set of measurable and realistic goals. The results should include essential tasks of the project manager, the project team, and the operational managers. One of the project management techniques that must be considered in the development of criteria is the Program Evaluation and Review Technique (PERT). It combines statistics and network diagrams.

Assumptions: In general, they are predictions that something will be true, either an action or an event that ensures project success. First, this task assists in defining any criteria (pessimistic, realistic, and optimistic). Second, this task establishes the criteria that are used to validate or test project components as to performances or results. Third, these assumptions and their validation requirements are organized into a document and distributed as required.

Constraints: In general, they are parameters, limitations, or boundaries for the project such as the project schedule or the project budget. First, this task assists in identifying any constraints (pessimistic, realistic, and optimistic). Second, this task establishes the criteria that are used to validate or test if these constraints are being used in the project process. Third, these assumptions and their validation requirements are organized into a document and distributed as required.

Determine field test criteria: The task is to gather data for the Trial (Beta) Strategy that identifies the software and hardware elements in the project that are a part of any trial. Also the where, the when, the how, and by whom should be included in the strategy. This provides a clear identification of the testing requirements plus the extent of the resources and capabilities for a trial.

Identify training criteria: The task is to gather data for doing validation testing of defined project goals and results for formal and informal training. The task includes identifying required skill levels to training events.

Identify documentation criteria: The task is to gather data for doing validation testing of defined project goals and results for customer, user, and technical support documents. The task includes identifying document links to project goals.

Identify quality support tasks: The task is to do any special tasks indirectly implied from the project goals or by the project team not given in this checklist.

Variances criteria: The task is to gather the criteria for determining normal and risk variances. A variance is any deviation from the planned work, whether it is costs, time, or resources.

Variance reporting criteria: The task is to gather data on methods for writing variance reports. Other data to be included would be when they should be completed, why they should be written, and for whom they should be given.

Risk management criteria: The task is to gather the benchmarks for determining risks and potential scenarios that foreshadow them. A risk is a performance error that can have a significant or disastrous impact on the success of a project or major activity. It is not just a problem. A scenario is a set of possibilities that could happen to cause a risk.

Exhibit 9-1 (*Continued*)

Specify random inspection criteria: The criteria are for an independent evaluation or test of a part of listed project components by qualified personnel. *Independent* here means evaluation by either QA or an outside consultant. The criteria should be distributed as required by the project team.

Specify audit criteria: The criteria are for an independent evaluation or test of one of the listed project components by qualified personnel. *Independent* here means evaluation by either QA or an outside consultant. The criteria should be distributed as required by the project team.

Vendors:

Assist writing RFPs: The task is ensure a Request for Proposal is consistent with related project goals and milestones, technical performance requirements, quality process, skill-level requirements, and competitive position.

Gather performance history: *Performance* as used here means that there are objective data that demonstrates that the vendor can act at the level of work required by the RFP.

Gather validation criteria: This task is to identify methods for validating information from vendors against project goals.

Gather testing criteria: This task is to identify methods for testing information from vendors against project goals.

Dependency identification: Dependency means that a task has to be completed before or after another one. For example, coding has to be completed before code testing can be completed. Less obvious is that a code test has to be written before code testing. A document should be a collection of dependencies for at least the listed items and distributed in accordance with the project team's instructions.

Consistency determination criteria: The task is to identify the data links between the listed documents so that what is stated is the same sequentially throughout the documents.

Baseline plan: This task is to define the initial approved point from which any deviations are determined using standards and benchmarks. This document or parts of it will be distributed as approved by the project team.

Field introduction: The task here is to assist in the writing in the Trial (Beta) Strategy.

Gather change management criteria: The task is to classify the parameters required to make changes to the project estimates, in particular those that directly affect the schedule and budget as to who, what, why, when, where, and how.

Identify update requirements: Here you describe the parameters required to make updates to the project estimates, in particular those that directly affect the schedule and budget as to who, what, why, when, where, and how.

Describe slippage rules: The task is to define a potential schedule or budget slippage and how and when it should be reported. Budget slippage happens when a budget item is overspent. Time slippage is expected when you know about it before the due date, while it is unexpected when you learn about the fact after the due date.

Contingency plan criteria: Here you prepare a document of potential causes and solutions using pessimistic scenarios or worse with the potential that they will become reality. In addition, the document identifies time and cost estimates that have a contingency value.

Resource-leveling assistance: The task here is to do leveling that is the technique of smoothing out peaks and valleys for the use of resources in a project schedule.

Gather logistics criteria: The criteria should ensure that the logistics process gets the correct resource to the correct location at the correct time. The criteria should be published as required by the project team.

Gather modeling data: The task is to define the data requirements for doing models or simulations to ensure theoretically that process results as defined by required project goals can be validated prior to project completion. However, more preferable is validation before project development begins.

Exhibit 9-1 (*Continued*)

QUALITY ASSURANCE: This function is based on performance. It uses defined performance benchmarks to measure and evaluate project task performances. This component of quality management considers measurable deviations in performance during a project in a systematic manner. All tasks imply the need for measuring effects on IS interoperability; reliability; scalability; resource management (effectiveness and efficiency); and, perhaps most importantly, quality of performance.

Source ID: Same as QC instruction.

Review viability responses: The task is to assist the project manager in the responses from the project viability process before any review by upper-level management.

Confirm project adm. criteria: The task is to validate the defined administrative criteria, which are being used to ensure that the project process is systematic and sequential to achieve the project's measurable goals. The validation includes the project administrative tasks of the project manager, the project team, and the operational managers. While this checklist does reflect the more specific tasks of the project management process, a broad set of project administration areas needs to be monitored and evaluated. The areas include planning, organizing, systematic processing for nontechnical areas (financial, communications, and change and risk management), and control management (resources, cost, and time).

Analyze skills: The task is to analyze the skill requirements and the demonstrated abilities of the person holding the skill.

Validate document usage: This task should use inspections and audit to determine if project stakeholders are adhering to criteria relevant to the project as found in the listed documents.

Authenticate tasks criteria: Here you authenticate that tasks drive the project-level processes, while activities drive the operational-level processes.

Assist in field testing: The task is to ensure the process in the Trial (Beta) Strategy is followed. In addition, the task includes when technical expertise is available to give support in the completion of the test.

Validate training performance: Here the task is to validate that formal and, when possible, informal training meet the project goals and, that it produces the required skill levels to achieve realistic estimates.

Verify documentation: The task is to validate that the listed document types are written in accordance with project goals and requirements.

Do quality support tasks: The task is to do any special tasks implied from the project goals not given in this checklist.

Validate and test assumptions: First, this task randomly validates and tests any critical assumptions. Second, this task confirms the assumptions for validating or testing project components as to performance or results. Third, the results are organized into documents as required and distributed.

Validate and test constraints: First, this task validates and tests critical constraints. Second, this task determines how the criteria are being used in the project process. Third, the results are organized into documents and distributed as required.

Assist in reviews: For the items listed, the task is for QA to have a review member that determines that estimates, tasks, and plans reflect the project goals as stated in the scope plan.

Critical path: This task is to assist in the review of the critical path plan. Second, this task is to report to the project team on negative and positive deviations from the criteria as to adherence to the critical path.

Contingency plan: This task first gives assistance in reviewing the document. Second, it validates the need for a particular part of the plan to go into affect.

Approve risk management criteria: Here you analyze the benchmarks for determining risks and potential scenarios that foreshadow them and determine if all goals have been covered. In addition, the task includes verifying the project process against the benchmarks.

Exhibit 9-1 (*Continued*)

Do variance reports: The task here is to complete reports for the project team on variances of standards and benchmarks as found in inspections and audits. This task uses the data gathered by QC as to the method for writing variance reports. Other data would include when they should be completed, why they should be written, and for whom they should be given.

Perform random inspections: It is an independent evaluation or test of part of a project's component by qualified personnel. It is a partial audit. The task includes using QC criteria and doing this task before milestones or critical events.

    Identify variances and causes: Anytime this task is performed all related estimates (time, costs, and resources) have to be considered.

    Perform audits: It is an independent evaluation or test of some component of the project by qualified personnel. It is more complete than an inspection. An audit is accomplished at a milestone or major event for the listed items.

Identify variances and causes: Anytime this task is performed all related estimates (time, costs, and resources) have to be considered.

Other support groups: Examples of other support groups are marketing and human resources. These groups are only audited as to their performance based on the scope plan.

Vendors:

    Review RFP responses: The task is to assist in the analysis of any RFP response as to how it reflects the stated requirements and criteria in the RFP.

    Analyze performance history: The task is to analyze performance data to ensure that the vendor has demonstrated at the level of work required by the RFP.

    Confirm validation process: The task is to verify the vendor's stated validation process from the RFP response.

    Confirm testing process: The task is to verify the vendor's stated testing process from the RFP response.

    Confirm dependency usage: The task is to validate or test stated dependencies.

Consistency validation: The task is to ensure what is stated in any document is used consistently through the other listed documents. The baseline in all cases is the scope plan.

Baseline plan: This task is to validate or test for any deviations based on criteria from this plan.

Field Introduction: The task is to assist in the process as given in the Trial (Beta) Strategy.

Validate change management process: The task is to validate the change process as to how it is being managed in accordance with the defined project standards and benchmarks.

Validate update process: The task is to validate the update process as to how it is being managed in accordance with the defined project standards and benchmarks.

Validate slippage usage: The task is to validate the slippage management process as to whether it is being managed in accordance with the defined project standards and benchmarks.

Do feedback reports: The task is to provide feedback on any task listed in this checklist as required by the project team or relevant quality standards.

Assistance resource leveling: Here you provide assistance in using leveling to smooth out peaks and valleys in the use of resources in a project schedule.

Analyze logistics criteria: The analysis is to validate that the criteria are being followed so that the logistics process is getting the correct resource to the correct location at the correct time.

Assist in model development: The task here is to use the criteria established by QC to assist in modeling or simulation.

Validate and test deliverables: This task is to ensure that all deliverables as defined in the project goals are as promised in the scope plan. Any deviations are to be reported to the project team.

The Checklist for a Quality Management Program should be used to identify the most intangible effects on the IS infrastructure and the project's results. These intangibles include innovation, interoperability, reliability, scalability, stakeholder satisfaction, and production quality. When these intangibles are ignored, there is the potential for long-range effects beyond the project's duration with the IS group. In addition, all forms of information gathering should be considered: formal technical meetings, review briefings, reports (paper, e-mail, and bulletin boards), and, perhaps the most powerful form of information gathering, hallway conversations.

A special task that specifically relates to the IS group is for quality management to determine technical performances for configuration management. All hardware and software have to be integrated correctly. One of the most dangerous activities is when a programmer does "cut and paste," which means taking a piece of code created for one specific function and replicating it for some other function to meet a project's goal. The technical performance requirement is to determine the effects of this replicated code—it might cause a database value to be processed incorrectly or might change the code processing sequence.

§ 9.02   MANAGEMENT INVOLVEMENT

[A]   Overview

There is one fixed rule for all managers involved in the project: Do not let quality slide when deadlines are too close for comfort. To do so will take you out of the frying pan and put you into the fire.

Quality requires a long-term view of success, not a short-term gain. Quality can seem to be a nebulous activity until near the end of the project. Each manager must recognize that the quality of a project can result in an improved view by the customer as to the corporation's integrity and thus improve the bottom line. Quality lessens the need for customer service—that is, the type that has to resolve product bugs in the field.

[B]   Strategic Management and Quality Control

The strategic manager has to ensure that there is an effective quality assurance and control effort for the project. The project quality mechanism should also be consistent with the corporate quality program. How important are ISO 9000–9004 certifications to you?

The strategic manager needs to establish an appropriate battlefield for excellence. One of the four cornerstones is quality. The other cornerstones are a realistic schedule, a viable budget, and solid risk management.

[C]   Tactical Management and Quality Control

The essential tactical actions of the project manager include the following:

- Place quality planning at the top of the project agenda.
- Ensure there are significant time and cost estimates for
  — monitoring activities
  — testing deliverables
  — evaluating performance
  — measuring performance
  — correcting performance deviations, errors
- Guarantee there is time for peer reviews.
- Have a configuration control mechanism.
- Create an appropriate reporting system on quality issues.
- Assure that quality issues stay at the deliverable level rather than being considered personal.
- Have separate lines in the budget for quality assurance and control.
- Have a location where all standards and any other quality-related documentation are available to all.

[D]   Operational Management and Quality Control

The essential actions of the operational managers include the following:

- Support the tactical manager to ensure there is an appropriate quality program for the project.
- Ensure that the best technicians attend the peer reviews.
- Manage deliverables so they adhere to the configuration control mechanism.
- Report promptly on quality issues and resolutions.
- Support quality assurance and control in its function so that it will not be obtrusive on the day-to-day project operations.

Exhibit 9-2: Activity Audit

Project Name:		Date:	
Preparer:		**Activity:**	

Core Evaluation:				
Performance:	ON	ABOVE	BELOW	(Circle One)
Budget:	ON	OVER	UNDER	(Circle One)
Schedule:	ON	AHEAD	BEHIND	(Circle One)
Overall Status:	Positive		Negative	(Circle One)

Factors:

Things done above standards/benchmarks:

Things done below standards/benchmarks:

Recommendations:

Additional comments:

Exhibit 9-3: Quality Control and Deliverables Questions Checklist

1. Have the quality standards been made consistent?	
2. Has a comprehensive quality control program been defined, including standards and benchmarks?	
3. Has the quality process been cost-estimated and budgeted?	
4. Have the quality control events been included at appropriate milestones?	
5. What are the criteria for documenting quality control activities?	
6. What are the quality control procedures that ensure correct sequencing?	
7. What are the quality control procedures that need to be in the activity plan?	
8. What are the standards and benchmarks for quality control?	
9. What is the necessary time for quality validation?	
10. What quality control policies, benchmarks, or standards have to be followed?	
Questions on a deliverable	
1. Does the documentation correctly state technical requirements?	
2. Does it meet appropriate standards?	
3. Does it meet corporate benchmarks?	
4. Does it meet functional requirements?	
5. Does it meet operational requirements?	
6. Does it meet protocol requirements?	
7. Does it meet security requirements?	
8. Does it technically fulfill project goals?	
9. Does the Help function assist the customer in resolving technical issues?	
10. Have training courses been developed to cover correctly technical issues?	

On the CD-ROM

On the CD-ROM are:

1. Exhibit 9-1 Checklist for a Quality Management Program.doc
2. Exhibit 9-2 Activity Audit.doc
3. Exhibit 9-3 Quality Control and Deliverables Questions Checklist.doc
4. Chapter 9 Overview.ppt—Chapter Overview, Controlling Quality

Chapter 10

Managing Risks and Opportunities

§ 10.01   OVERVIEW

[A]   Objectives

At the end of this chapter, you will be able to:

- State a definition for a risk.
- State a definition for risk management.
- List 10 types of impacts caused by risks.
- Identify eight different categories of risks.
- Answer two core questions on the risk-management process.
- Ask 10 basic questions about risk management such as: What are the cost estimates for risk-management activities? What are the criteria for a

risk that may affect project activities? What are the documentation requirements and standards for risk management? What are the time estimates for risk-management activities?

- Discuss that risk and opportunity are different faces of the same coin.
- Identify the requirements for two risk-management documents.
- Discuss a scenario for installing a firewall as to risk management.
- Identify how the three managing levels are involved in risks and oppor-
tunities.

MANAGER'S TIP

Recently an e-mail spun around in Internet circles admonishing Hotmail users
that their e-mail could be read by any semiskilled hacker. Indeed, there are
a couple of sites that give specific instructions on how to do so. For those
who rely on Web e-mail because it provides easy access from almost any
Web browser, the realization that opportunity and risk are two faces of the
same coin comes as a blow.

In a world of increasing technological complexity, the project manager
who tries to manage risk effectively may turn to new technologies for help,
but introducing such new factors may bring different forms of risk. So it is
with the ASP (Application Service Provider) model, which increases the distribution of applications and limits the amount of physical software and hardware, thereby lowering costs to customers and possibly increasing confidence if the company is small or the costs too high. But ASPs also bring
concerns about security and reliability.

The ASP purveyor owns the actual software and licenses the product,
but the data resides on the ASP's server. The customer rents, or uses for free
in the case of Hotmail, the use of the ASP and accesses it from a remote
location. Hotmail functions as an ASP because you can access it from a Web
browser; however your e-mail sits on their server, not on your local machine.
If the ASP does not protect your e-mail adequately, the e-mail could be vul-
nerable to security concerns. A good ASP has a secure data center and redundancy connections to ensure reliability.

In addition, there are different kinds of ASP models—from Web-based
applications that are built and run by the same company, to ASP-enabled
solutions that are built by one company and hosted elsewhere. The type of
model to use depends entirely on the size and needs of the business. The
project manager would do well to use the questions and checklists discussed
in this chapter to evaluate risk when choosing an ASP or, as a matter of fact,
in any project situation in which risk is paramount.

[B] Using Essential Definitions

There are three essential concepts for this discussion:

A **risk** is a performance error that can have a significant or disastrous impact
on the success of a project or major task. It is more than a problem; its effect
can have an adverse or disastrous consequence on the project's outcome.

Risk management is the activity in which you identify a risk, assess a risk, and allocate resources to resolve the risk.

Risk analysis is a technique, tool, or method for assessing either quantitatively or qualitatively (or both) the impacts of an identified risk or a potential risk identified through a scenario.

[C]   Risk Management Definition

A risk is not just any problem, bug, or variance. A risk is a performance error that can have a significant or disastrous impact on the project's success.

Risk management involves three functions:

1. Identify the risk.
2. Assess the risk.
3. Allocate resources to resolve the risk.

Risk management is resolving or managing both negative and positive opportunities. Risk management was developed as a tool to minimize liabilities. A risk is a problem that will adversely affect the project. An opportunity is a situation that will positively affect the project in time, money, resources, or all three, in a significant manner.

Risk management is a generic management tool in that there are no special tool definitions for this activity. It is applicable across all phases of the project process. Risk management can begin when a customer comes to you to discuss an idea for a project. Notice the word *idea*. The customer may think there is a project. You need to ask the customer a minimum of three questions:

1. Is there money in the customer's budget for the project?
2. Has the customer formed a project definition and appropriate milestones?
3. Does support exist by all affected parties for the project?

A "no" to any of these questions is a flag that there is a risk. The project is an idea. Risk management in this case is asking the correct questions to ensure there is a potential project, not just an idea.

[D]   Types of Impacts Caused by Risks

A risk could have a disastrous effect on a project, especially one built on sand. Some of the impacts of risk include:

- Attitudes (internal and external)
- Changes in organization structure
- Customer relationships

- Financial success
- Project success
- Resource allocations
- Responsibilities
- Safety
- Security
- Vendor relationships

One major area of risk is procurement. Because of the historical action of putting the risks on the supplier, there has been an evolution—though it might be called a revolution—as to the guiding principle between the customer (purchaser), you, and the vendor. Procurement, in particular for the U.S. Department of Defense (DOD), follows the principle that the reimbursable mode is up to the agreed scope definition and then a fixed price. DOD only pays for the defined project deliverables. For any additional deliverables, the DOD pays a fixed price. A defined project deliverable may be reimbursable based on a cost range rather than a fixed cost.

The goal of risk management should be to share the risk impacts when possible in an equitable manner. There should not be a "dumping on" one party unless it is clearly shown that the party is the only party causing the risk. The reality is that this situation rarely happens.

[E] Categories of Risks

Risks come in all colors and shapes. There are at least eight common categories of risk and you can easily add to them based on your specific project goals. Here is a short list of project risks:

1. Customer
    — Financial support becomes unavailable
    — Not participating in agreed-upon reviews
    — Response time to questions is not timely
    — Seems to have new interpretations of goals
    — Skill resources availability degrades
2. Delivery
    — Product does not meet functional requirements according to standards or the project goals
    — Product has incompatibility issues
    — Product has interoperability issues
    — Product's requirements exceed available capacity
    — Product's response time is inadequate

3. Equipment
   — Does not meet specifications
   — Limited availability
   — Missed delivery date

4. People
   — Lacking in skills required
   — Not available at time required
   — Not available because of job change

5. Physical
   — Critical computers or hardware fail
   — Data stolen
   — Facility lost through fire or another catastrophe
   — Virus infects some critical data

6. Scope
   — Customer identifies the need for additional effort
   — New requirements are identified
   — An operational area introduces new functionality without approval by the project manager

7. Technology
   — Technical assumptions are not factual
   — Technical constraints cannot be overcome
     Technology is not understood clearly
   — Technology is too new

8. Vendor
   — Financial failure
   — Not participating in agreed-upon reviews
   — Response time to questions is not timely
   — Seems to have new interpretations of goals
   — Skill resources availability degrades

[F]   Core Questions on the Risk-Management Process

To establish a risk-management process, you need to ask yourself two core questions:

1. Do you have a list of constraints (guidelines) and assumptions for handling potential threats and opportunities?

2. Are there identified fixed points in the project cycle for assessing risks?

When planning the scope of your project, you have to think in terms that a risk is a threat. However, you can be one of those unique people who see a way to turn a situation into an opportunity. Perhaps it takes six months to develop a product, and then someone has invented a utility that shortens the time in half or less. Does this affect the project? Of course it does. Just think of the example of the utilities that can be used to create a Web page in hours rather than days. Are they as simple as the vendors say?

When you define the project scope, you should establish how to handle threats and opportunities. Unfortunately in risk management, most people think of only the threats to the project. What if someone comes up with an idea that a component of a hardware product or a software application can be omitted and the product or application still achieve the customer's expectations? This is an opportunity. A pebble thrown into the sea could become a tidal wave. This is a nice metaphor, but not reality. Perhaps you see the point anyway.

There should be defined activities for handling threats. There should also be activities that handle opportunities if they arise. A simple activity rule would be: "Until a threat (an opportunity) reaches a certain threshold (your definition), no action shall be taken."

Risk assessment is important when resources are being planned. You need to determine what are the minimum skill-level requirements. Notice that headcount requirement is not used. Perhaps for some activities a novice can do them, while for other activities an expert is needed. Remember, a lack of a skill can be turned into an opportunity.

There should be a priority list of the essential or critical tasks required in your project so that you can evaluate potential threats and opportunities. A minimum recommendation is that you plan at least one risk review during each phase of the implementation or integration. Quality control should always be on the outlook for risks and could be responsible for risk-management activities.

You should have cost and time estimates for risk management in each key phase of integration. If you have no threats to the project in a given phase, you have generated an opportunity.

The schedule (ordered activities plus time) should have at each essential milestone an activity that assesses the project's status and determines if there are potential threats and opportunities. How can the formulated schedule impact the outcome of the project? Time analysis is a major component in risk management.

In your budget, there should be a separate item for risk management. The most logical line is the one to allocate money for contractors. Another line to consider, if one is established, is for quality control and verification. Your product may need more testing than you estimated.

[G]   Ten Basic Questions on Risk Management

The following questions are asked in the context of the project goals. The customer's needs are paramount. Questions need to be asked about the qualifications of the team and characteristics of the process.

WHAT ARE THE CRITERIA FOR RISK MANAGEMENT THAT MAY IMPACT ACTIVITIES?   The first set of criteria is not necessarily based on sophisticated risk analysis but on the experiences of the team. If the team lacks experience, perhaps it is advisable for an outside expert to give advice on these criteria.

ARE THERE ANY TRAINING REQUIREMENTS FOR THE RISK MANAGEMENT?   One should not necessarily expect the quality team to be trained already to assess and monitor a new product and in particular to do risk assessments and evaluations. They may have to go to a class on protocols or a new standard related to the product. They may be experts on the quality process, but not technically knowledgeable of the assumptions and constraints of the product to be developed.

DOES THE PROJECT SCHEDULE HAVE APPROPRIATE LINKS FROM THE QUALITY CONTROL SCHEDULE TO ALL OTHER AREAS OF THE SCHEDULE?   A performance error can happen anywhere in the project process. The quality assurance and control group needs to evaluate and assess the error's potential as a risk. Because of these two requirements, quality needs to have links into all project activities.

WHAT ARE THE DIRECT-COST ESTIMATES FOR RISK-MANAGEMENT ACTIVITIES?   There is the managing of risks *after* they are identified, and managing them *before* they happen, to minimize damage. Direct-cost estimates should be for the prevention of risk. This is for the risk-management structure and ongoing process. There should also be contingency funds for resolving risks. This amount is determined by the significance of the project's results. While risk management is the responsibility of everyone, you may wish to associate your risk-management responsibilities with the quality group. You need to factor in cost estimates for risk analysis and evaluation.

WHAT ARE THE DOCUMENTATION REQUIREMENTS AND STANDARDS FOR RISK MANAGEMENT?   You need to establish in the planning phase criteria for when a performance error becomes a risk. Risk criteria should be established against the project goals and against appropriate standards. You should have a risk form that should be available to everyone to be used in risk analysis and evaluation. This is so everyone can be familiar with the types of information to be gathered for risk management. Finally, but not the least, any IS risk-management policies and procedures should be fully utilized in the project.

WHAT ARE THE ESSENTIAL PROJECT ACTIVITIES FOR MANAGING RISKS? If you identify risk management as an associated responsibility of quality assurance and control, then the general activities may seem straightforward. There may also be special risk-management tasks generated because of the project goals and the failure to achieve any one of them. Ultimate responsibility for risk management resides in the hands of the project manager.

WHAT ARE THE RESOURCES REQUIRED FOR RISK MANAGEMENT? Resource requirements for risk management should be an extension of the resources for quality assurance and control. There may be special equipment required to handle risk potential based on the project goals.

WHAT ARE THE SKILLS AND THEIR LEVELS REQUIRED FOR RISK MANAGEMENT? The project goals should assist in developing the skill definitions. There are the technical skills to resolve certain types of risks; however, there may be other types of skills also required. Early in the planning phase, there should be a list drawn up of potential risks by the project team. This list should focus on the technical risks rather than other areas. This list could be used to identify the other required skills.

WHAT ARE THE TIME ESTIMATES FOR RISK MANAGEMENT? There should be some slack time allocated for major groups of activities to resolve minimal risks. A large risk requires a complete evaluation of the project's status. Time is then defined as how long it takes you to control a disaster.

WHAT PROCEDURES, STANDARDS, OR POLICIES GOVERN RISK MANAGEMENT? The first standards that should be brought to the table are those IS standards involving risks. Other standards are those that assist in defining the project goals. Project risk management should be consistent with any existing corporate policies, procedures, or standards for risk management.

[H] Risk and Opportunity as Twins

A risk is an adverse effect on a project; it is disastrous. There seem to be only checks for risks, but none for opportunities. An opportunity is not a simple change to the project process but should be a significant affirming result to the project process that improves the company's bottom line. A risk or an opportunity can begin as a ripple and turn into a tidal wave. Both have to be managed. Thus, when you establish criteria for a risk, you must do the same for an opportunity. For every risk there may be a matching opportunity if you look deeper into the dark closet. The danger, of course, is the possibility that an opportunity is a disguised risk.

Most people think of risks only as threats to the goals. What if you find a new product that can ease your project goals by tenfold? Let us do some dreaming. Is this a risk? It is similar to finding out that the configuration for a product is going to take twice as long as originally anticipated. You say no. Have you considered the implication of the new product on your whole project? Do you have to set new expectations? Do you now have the opportunity (read as requirement) to add additional functionality and services to your project?

[I]   Documenting Risks and Opportunities

Because risks come in two forms, threats and opportunities, both should be equally documented. Given here are examples of two important risk-management documents:

1. Business Justification
2. Risk Assessment

Business Justification

The Business Justification shows how the achieved goals of the project will improve your company's bottom line and make more effective financial relationships with either another company or with your vendors or customers. In this light, doing a Business Justification and sharing it with others is necessary perhaps for your survival or at least your good health. The Business Justification assures that the current view of the project performance meets previous commitments and management expectations. The document may have a one or more year(s) view of:

- Revenues
- Maintenance costs
- Investment
- Return on investment (ROI)
- Customer impact

Risk Assessment

It is important that any risk assessment consider both threats and opportunities. All involved parties should review the Risk Assessment. When there are too many people to do the review, there should be representatives from each component. Perhaps only one or two key vendors should do the review for all the others. A risk assessment should be done at least at every major project phase.

The Risk Assessment should be against established thresholds. An example of a threshold is that no action is taken until a certain number of errors are found over a given period.

[J] Refining Data by Asking the Correct Questions

You should ask as many questions as necessary to clarify a risk-management environment; however, the following six questions must be asked up front:

1. What are the criteria for a risk?
2. Who defines the risk criteria?
3. When are the risk criteria applied?
4. Where in the project process are risk criteria applied?
5. How are the risk criteria applied?
6. Why has the potential risk happened?

Perhaps the first data type you need for risk management is a set of risk categories. Risks come in all colors and shapes. There are at least eight common categories of risks, and you can easily add to them based on your specific project goals. Section 10.01[E], "Categories of Risks," contains a short list of project risk categories. With these risk categories and the six core questions above, you can make your first major step in identifying important risk data types and data requirements.

You can rewrite the above core questions and risk categories to reflect an opportunity. For example, the customer risk category could be stated as follows:

- Additional financial support becomes available
- Willing to participate in additional reviews
- Response time to questions exceeds expectations
- Accepts the interpretation of goals throughout the project
- Increases available skill resources

While you may consider the above situations pure fantasy, you must consider them at least on a theoretical basis. Considering any unexpected situation is the basis of risk management.

After you have examined the core questions, you have to ask questions about the risk-management process you are going to use. If you have been thorough after this activity, you are ready to determine your data types and data requirements. In addition to the Ten Basic Questions on Risk Management listed previously, here are some questions to ask on the risk-management structure and process:

- How does a contingency plan impact risk management?
- How do cost estimates impact risk management?
- How will the risk management tasks be funded?
- Where in the project budget is risk management allocated?
- Where in the project process will there be assessments for risks?
- Who (which individual or group) is responsible for managing risks?

MANAGER'S TIP

When *risk management* is used in the above questions, it is implied that risks and opportunities are discussed. When *risks* is used, it can be replaced by *opportunities*.

[K]   Risk-Management Scenario: Installing a Firewall

The following is a template for thinking about the risks involved in the installation of a firewall into your IS network. It details how to minimize not only the risks but also the potential portals to disaster.

First, you need to be aware of the potential types and levels of security risks that may already be present in your system before you identify your requirements. Second, you need to know what would be the role of a firewall in your IS network. A formal definition of a firewall is it is used to guard your private network, your intranet, from the public network, the Internet. About all you should get from this definition is that it is a guardian between two types of networks. What you really need is to acquire from a variety of firewall vendors their specifications. Then you need to do an analysis to consider, first, what these firewalls have in common and, then, how they differ. You then compare this analysis against your list of potential risks.

You also need to know what types of risks a firewall cannot mitigate. For example, they are not effective against backdoor types of risk such as "worms" in e-mail attachments nor against the risk from a disgruntled employee.

One concern of identifying the security level is the level of integration of your intranet with the Internet. There is a different level of security for just using an Internet service such as e-mail, and having a Web-based intranet.

Another concern is determining the types of data that require protection. The position that all data must be protected at the same level is unrealistic. You may consider "moats" of firewalls around certain strategic data that if lost could cause a major crisis for the company. You may not need to protect training and customer documentation files, but financial data and marketing strategies need to be protected.

A consideration of the type of firewall required is to compare the importance of the data against the likelihood of attack. There is a belief that most attacks are never noticed.

The following is a short list of other types of security concerns:

- Financial status
- Motivation of attacker
- Reputation of company
- Safety
- Type of attacker (for example, a young person or a spy)

A common question when the issue of risk management arises is, "Should we have a formal risk assessment?" A security professional probably would say yes; however, it is most likely that your IS group has been concerned with risks from day one and managing risks has become a part of the day-to-day operations. Risk management should be ingrained in IS policies and procedures. Such issues may arise when the IS project is for another corporate organization.

There are three ways to do security analysis:

1. Intrusion testing

2. Brainstorming

3. Security engineering procedures

Intrusion testing is usually used when you have an established security system and you have a known security breach. This method would not be used during project planning. However, designated members of a tiger team could be involved in the second method, brainstorming. The early stage of project planning usually takes on the characteristics of structured brainstorming. Structured engineering procedures should be integrated into the activities of the project risk-management team.

For the integration of a firewall into your IS network you have to do all the project functions described in previous chapters. The project context is the defined expectations of the firewall to protect the selected data and to provide the level of security needed. You have to do the following:

- Define activities.
- Sequence the activities.
- Do cost, time, and resource estimates.
- Do a schedule.
- Do a budget.
- Manage and control the project events.

§ 10.02   MANAGEMENT INVOLVEMENT

[A]   Overview

Each manager must recognize that the results of a quality product with minimal performance errors can be an improved view by the customer as to the corporation's integrity and thus can boost the bottom line. As mentioned in Chapter 9, a quality product lessens the need for customer service to resolve product bugs in the field. There needs to be a commitment by all of the managers to analyze and evaluate identified risks quickly and with integrity. Resolve the risk rather than spend time to search for someone to blame.

[B]   Strategic Management and Risk Management

Certainly, the strategic manager becomes involved when an impacting risk is identified; however, as with the quality control process as a whole, the strategic manager should emphasize the effort to minimize errors, not fight fires. This manager needs to support the project manager in cross-divisional areas to ensure a complete and comprehensive risk-management program.

[C]   Tactical Management and Risk Management

The following are essential actions of the project management:

- Discuss risk potentials at all scheduled meetings, and make this a fixed agenda item.
- Identify people to correct and do quick technical analyses of risks.
- Identify people who can do evaluations of issues.
- Ensure that risk management has the time in the schedule to do a proper job.
- Ensure that there is funding in the budget for risk management, distinctive from the quality assurance and control functions.
- Ensure that there are skilled personnel to handle risk evaluations.
- Ensure that there is a contingency fund to handle significant risk issues.
- Ensure that there are criteria developed during the planning phase for identifying risks.
- Be responsible for risk management.
- Have a risk-management program that involves external resources.
- Identify any special equipment that may be required to do analyses of potential risks as determined during the analysis and evaluation of the project goals.

[D]   Operational Management and Risk Management

The tasks of an operational manager for risk management include the following:

- Identify policies, procedures, benchmarks, and standards that assist in minimizing performance errors during the planning, design, development, and implementation phases for your component of the project.
- Support the project manager's efforts in risk management.
- Document risk issues in your area.
- Identify personnel in your area who can assist in minimizing performance errors.
- Assist the quality group in the analysis and evaluation of any identified risk in your operational area.

Exhibit 10-1: Checklist for Risk-Management Tasks

First line of defense, basic parameter definition:
1. What are the criteria for a risk?
2. Who defines the risk criteria?
3. When are the risk criteria applied?
4. Where in the project process are risk criteria applied?
5. How are the risk criteria applied?
6. Why has the potential risk happened?
Second line of defense, risk category, identification:
1. Customer
2. Delivery
3. Equipment
4. People
5. Physical
6. Scope
7. Technology
8. Vendor

Exhibit 10-1 (*Continued*)

Third level of defense, detailing the process:
1. How does a contingency plan impact risk management?
2. How do cost estimates impact risk management?
3. How will the risk-management tasks be funded?
4. What are the direct-cost estimates for risk management?
5. What are the documentation requirements for risk management?
6. What are the essential project tasks for managing risks?
7. What are the resources required for risk management?
8. What are the skills and their levels required for risk management?
9. What are the time estimates for risk management?
10. What are the training requirements for risk management?
11. What procedures, benchmarks, standards, or policies govern risk management?
12. Where in the project budget is risk management allocated?
13. Where in the project process will there be assessments for risks?
14. Where in the project schedule are there appropriate links from the quality control schedule?
15. Who (an individual or a group) is responsible for managing risks?

Exhibit 10-1 (*Continued*)

Fourth line of defense, use of model and simulations:
Statistical models
Simulations
Risk assessments
Fifth line of defense, performance criteria identification:
1. Acceptable plus or minus measurable variances
2. Assumptions
3. Audit criteria
4. Communications criteria
5. Confidence levels
6. Constraints
7. Criticality criteria
8. Dependency management
9. Distortion possibilities
10. Effectiveness
11. Efficiency
12. Logistics criteria
13. Qualitative impacts
14. Quantitative impacts

Exhibit 10-1 (*Continued*)

Instructions for a Risk-Management Tasks Checklist

These instructions should be done twice. The first time is to define risk management, while the second time is to define opportunity management. This is done simply by replacing the word *risk* with the word *opportunity*.

First line of defense, basic parameter definition: Use the responses for other checklists and ensure that there is consistency among the responses. The responses to the first four questions should be stated in a risk-management section of the scope plan.

1. What are the criteria for a risk? An example response, a criterion for a risk is in the event that the confidence level for a pessimistic scenario might become greater than 80 per cent.

2. Who defines the risk criteria? An example response: The project team with assistance by members of the IS quality team do the defining.

3. When are the risk criteria applied? An example response: Risk criteria are applied by quality management group with consent of the project team.

4. Where in the project process are risk criteria applied? An example response: The location is determined by the negative degree of not meeting standards and benchmarks for X number of interrelated tasks or to the critical path.

5. How are the risk criteria applied? An example response: Risk criteria are applied as a part of the quality management process.

6. Why has the potential risk happened? The response to question should include what, when, where, and how. It should not include an individual whom.

Second line of defense, risk category identification: When the phrase *risk criteria* is used, it means a set of criteria. The listed areas must be considered in completing a set of risk criteria. Examples for each are given as a starting point. Each operational area and the critical path must be reviewed for these risk areas.

1. Customer
   - Financial support becomes unavailable
   - Not participating in agreed-upon reviews
   - Responses to questions are not timely
   - New interpretations to goals
   - Skill resources availability degrades

2. Delivery
   - Product does not meet functional requirements according to benchmarks, standards or the project goals
   - Product has incompatibility issues
   - Product has interoperability issues
   - Product has portability issues

3. Equipment
   - Does not meet specifications
   - Has limited availability
   - Has missed delivery date

Exhibit 10-1 (*Continued*)

4. People
   - Lacking in skills required
   - Not available at time required
   - Not available because of job change
5. Physical
   - Critical computers or hardware failure
   - Data stolen
   - Facility lost through a catastrophe
   - Virus infects critical data
6. Scope
   - Customer identifies the need for additional effort
   - New requirements are identified during development
   - An operational area introduces a new function that has not been approved by the project team
7. Technology
   - Technical assumptions are not factual
   - Technical constraints cannot be overcome
   - Technology is not understood clearly
   - Technology is too new
8. Vendor
   - Financial failure
   - Not participating in agreed-upon reviews
   - Responses to questions not timely
   - New interpretations of support and goals
   - Skill resources availability degrades

Third level of defense, detailing the process:

1. How does a contingency plan impact risk management? An example response: The contingency plan should minimize the effects of padding. There should be a determination of the possible amount of padding.

2. How do cost estimates impact risk management? An example response: Shoddy cost estimates impact the project budget and potential funding requirements. Thus, consideration of risk impacts needs to be a part of any estimate review.

3. How will the risk-management tasks be funded? An example response: Risk management tasks will be funded from the contingency fund.

4. What are the direct-cost estimates for risk management? An example response: Direct-cost estimates for any full- or part-time employees and the funding are found in the contingency plan.

5. What are the documentation requirements for risk management? An example response: Documentation requirements might be either in the form of project or customer documents and the documentation that gives the specifics on the management of an identified potential risk.

Exhibit 10-1 (*Continued*)

6. What are the essential tasks for managing risks? An example response: The essential tasks are defined in accordance with the first and second lines of defense as formulated with the Checklist for Risk-Management Tasks.

7. What are the resources required for risk management? An example response: The general resources are all stakeholders, but specific resources are the project manager, the project administrative team, and identified members of the quality management function.

8. What are the skills and their levels required for risk management? An example response: Originally skill levels are determined by the areas with the highest potentials of risk. Second, skills levels have to be determined when a specific risk is identified and possible solutions have been defined.

9. What are the time estimates for risk management? An example response: The time estimates are blocks of time with funds in the contingency plan and noted as special events in the project schedule.

10. What are the training requirements for risk management? An example response: The training requirements are to have a person or persons who can create risk models and simulations, and use risk-analysis techniques and tools.

11. What procedures, benchmarks, standards, or policies govern risk management? An example might be that a part of the quality management process is to collect and use procedures, benchmarks, standards, or policies that govern risk management.

12. Where in the project budget is risk management allocated? An example response: Risk management costs are allocated in the budget line for contingency.

13. Where in the project process will there be assessments for risks? You may want to review the status of a milestone's interrelated tasks for potential risks at the completion of any major operational milestones.

14. Where in the project schedule are there appropriate links from the quality control schedule? The links may be determined by the project team and by assistance of the quality management function.

15. Who (an individual or a group) is responsible for managing risks? An example response: Everyone is responsible for identifying risks, but the project manager is ultimately responsible for managing and solving risks.

Fourth level of defense, use of models and simulations:

Statistical models: This type of model uses mathematical distributions to define the performance of an activity or task.

Simulations: A simulation is a process to imitate the physical components of your system.

Risk assessments: A technique, tool, or method for assessing, either quantitatively or qualitatively (or both), the impacts of an identified risk.

Fifth level of defense, performance criteria identification:

1. Acceptable plus or minus measurable variances: It is any deviation from the planned work, whether it is costs, time, or resources.

2. Assumptions: An assumption is a prediction that something will be true, either an action or an event that ensures project success. A characteristic of a risk is for a positive assumption to fail.

3. Audit criteria: Criteria developed for an independent evaluation or test of some component of the project by qualified personnel to determine variances.

Exhibit 10-1 (*Continued*)

4. Communications criteria: Criteria used to define the best method for using the communications process for different categories of risks. This means determining who gives and receives the information on a potential risk, what data is to be given, when there is to be communication, and how the information is to be given (e-mail or a briefing).

5. Confidence levels: A percentage level for a scenario for a pessimistic, realistic, or optimistic scenario to occur as described should be given.

6. Constraints: A constraint is a parameter, limitation or a boundary for the project plan such as the budget or the schedule. A characteristic of a risk is for a task to go negatively beyond a constraint.

7. Criticality criteria: They are used to determine if a position on the team where the individual in this situation has skills; usually technical that if not available to the project puts the project at risk.

8. Dependency management: This management type is concerned with nonadherence to start–end, start–start, and end–start dependencies and how this may generate risks.

9. Distortion possibilities: It is the misrepresentation of the situation, whether it is a fact, experience, or a feeling.

10. Effectiveness: It is the attained measure of quality to complete the activity or event. It is also the skill set required to define goals and to accomplish them.

11. Efficiency: It is the measurement of output based on amount of input. It is also the skill set that can accomplish a task with a minimum of input to get a maximum of output.

12. Logistics criteria: They are used to define the process of getting the correct resource to the correct location at the correct time.

13. Qualitative impacts: Task performance must be identified as to how well it is being performed. Because a task is supposedly completed does not necessarily mean it was done correctly. This type of failure can generate long-range failures.

14. Quantitative impacts: The amount of resources that went into the completion of a task may be excessive. A determination needs to be done to determine if a potential risk has been generated.

Exhibit 10-2: Risk Management Activities Questions Checklist

Project Name:	Comments
1. Are there any training requirements for the risk management?	
2. Does the project schedule have appropriate links from the quality control schedule to all other areas of the schedule?	
3. What are the criteria for risk management that may impact activities?	
4. What are the direct-cost estimates for risk management activities?	
5. What are the documentation requirements and standards for risk management?	
6. What are the essential project activities managing risks?	
7. What are the resources required for risk management?	
8. What are the skills and their levels required for risk management?	
9. What are the time estimates for risk management?	
10. What procedures, standards, or policies govern risk management?	

Exhibit 10-3: Contingency Planning Form

Project Name:		Date:	
Preparer:			

Potential Risks	Solution Options	Notes

On the CD-ROM

On the CD-ROM are:

1. Exhibit 10-1 Checklist for Risk-Management Tasks.doc

2. Exhibit 10-2 Risk-Management Activities Questions Checklist.doc

3. Exhibit 10-3 Contingency Planning Form.doc

4. Chapter 10 Overview.ppt—Chapter Overview, Managing Risks and Opportunities

Section Two

Project Management Tools and Techniques

This section looks at selected tools and techniques for improving IS project management. It is not about the day-to-day operational uses of these tools, however. You are probably extensively using the tools already. It is important to be able to present these tools in a user-friendly manner when you see that a tool or a set of tools can resolve a customer's needs.

This section's primary focus is to demonstrate how the IS project team discussions can be enhanced for:

- Activity planning
- Resource planning
- Time estimating
- Cost estimating

The discussions in this section might be used as starting points for more detailed discussions. The information is related to the information given in Section One.

Chapter 11

Project Modeling

§ 11.01 OVERVIEW

[A] Objectives

At the end of this chapter, you will be able to:

- List six general types of models.
- Explain the importance of modeling for an IS project.
- State differences between "what if" and architectural models.
- List the essential characteristics of an extrapolation model.
- List the essential characteristics of a simulation model.
- List the essential characteristics of a statistical model.
- Make a determination as to the best type(s) of modeling for your project.
- Identify how the three managing levels may be involved in modeling for your project.

[B]   Model Definition

A model is defined as an imperfect reflection of reality. There are many types of models. The following are six of the generalized types:

1. A display
2. A person
3. A preliminary pattern
4. A scaled version of a larger object
5. A style of an item
6. A system description

Obviously for IS project management, the last type—a system description—is the one of highest interest. However, all of the others could be used. The model has to be presentable to others to show a vision of the results such as an interface layout. One could use a person as a model to demonstrate necessary skill requirements. One could lay out an event pattern. A preliminary software demonstration is a scaled version of the final product. One can demonstrate the inputs and outputs of a product to show it has a user-friendly style.

You probably have written down in various documents the components of a model of your informational system. Since you are a successful project manager or desire to be one, you probably have also mentally integrated these components as an entity.

IS project management can be divided into five management areas:

1. Accounting
2. Configuration
3. Fault
4. Performance
5. Security

As a project manager, you need to consider these five areas when answering the question, "Is this project viable?" Any IS project may affect all of these areas, some more than others. From this notion, we might get the following questions, which really require a model to establish definitive answers:

- How might this project affect the network's bandwidth and other traffic resources?
- How might this project affect the network's configuration variables?
- How might this project impact the network for the development of new errors and the basic system runtime?
- How might this project affect performance standards?
- How might this project affect the present security operations of the system?

The focus of a model can be highly specialized, such as an organizational chart, which is a model of organizational relationships. A project management organizational chart might include additional information as to project activity relationships and responsibilities. The complexity of this model is raised a notch or two.

MANAGER'S TIP

Modeling has its own jargon. An analog model for a computer system might be the interface layout, a physical presentation. An iconic model is equivalent to a software demonstration, a scaled-down version of the project's results. A symbolic model is a representation of the product's properties and relationships. A dynamic model permits you to do "real-time" scenarios that can be used to manage a project.

A model can be developed to analyze time, resources, and costs outflows. Throughout the rest of this book there are many "modeling moments," that is, examples are given that can be considered in a system model—which should be the ultimate goal. The object of project management is to play the game of "what if" continuously. The use of Gantt charts and PERT/CPM techniques are just forms of specialized administrative project management modeling. This chapter looks at some of the theoretical underpinnings of modeling.

A model for an IS project manager will establish the clearest reflection of the project events, interactions, and results so that all the team members, including the customers, have a sense of direction and assurance that risks are minimized. If the model cannot do this, then you should not waste your time or frustrate everyone else with a sense of inadequacy.

You need to have two different models. First, you need a model to manage the project. Second, you need a model or models to comprehend the effects of the project on the information system and the effects of the information system on the project.

[C]   Modeling Definition

System modeling might be viewed from three perspectives:

1. Extrapolation (extending historical data)

2. Simulation (process imitation)

3. Statistical (relationships defined by mathematical data)

As discussed in Chapter 18, your legacy infrastructure might be either concrete (hosts, applications) or abstract (speed, time). An informational system as an entity cannot be viewed as a single type of infrastructure. Thus, the complexity of modeling has moved up a notch or two.

Below are additional random thoughts on impacts that should be considered in doing modeling.

- Two core network principles—simplicity and scalability—are rapidly going down the drain. They have already been replaced by complexity and segmentation.

- Users are more in number and in a remote access environment. They have more experience and have the intense desire to push the envelope of applications, such as using e-mail heavily.

[D] What-If versus Architectural Modeling

A what-if model might be used for presenting simulations, developing predictions, and showing dynamic interrelationships. A commonly used what-if model is the project beta or demonstration. An essential characteristic is to have a method for managing changing variables. A what-if model might be considered prescriptive, that it has "oughtness." That is, it shows what ought to be done in given instances.

In contrast to the what-if model, the architectural model is descriptive, an inventory of reality. A common IS architectural model is a cabling blueprint. It is a scaled depiction of your real wiring situation. Probably the most common architectural model is the basic organizational chart, a presentation that gives you a sense of individual and group relationships. One should recognize that a business organizational chart is probably hierarchical or a tree, while a project management organizational chart shows the interrelationships based on project activities. There should be many interconnecting arrows to reflect the dynamic relationships during a project.

You will use both types during an IS project. First, a simple what-if model is required during the "should this project happen" phase that is the initial project discussion between the responsible strategic manager and you as the project manager. It may be only an extrapolation model using historical and descriptive IS data available and comparing the customer's defined goals or needs against this data. Second, architectural models might be developed to reflect time, resource, and cost estimates. An obvious model is the use of the Critical Path Method that is discussed in more detail in Chapter 13.

MANAGER'S TIP

Chapter 1, § 1.04[D], contains a discussion of the question, "Is the project viable?"

[E]   Extrapolation Modeling

Extrapolation modeling is the theoretical process of extending historical data. The extension can be either linear or nonlinear. An example of linear extension is using the bandwidth of a given set of users and their average utilization percentage, then changing the average utilization percent and calculating the number of new users. An example of nonlinear extension is the plotting of your traffic loads.

Extrapolation modeling is not reliable. Very few events, if any, move in a linear fashion. It is not good for predicting bandwidth utilization or latency. It is an excellent way to open the mind for possibilities and consider new questions in a new light.

During a project, one probably does more extrapolating than anything else. When you do the following activities, you are extrapolating:

- Doing cost estimates
- Estimating time
- Doing resource estimates
- Using the 80–20 principle
- Defining risks
- Evaluating priorities

All of these require historical data or experiences in the areas being extrapolated. You should always remember the major limitation of this type of modeling: The interpretation of events of the past is not an exact reflection of the potentials of the future. With the extrapolation model, you should use as many outside benchmarks and standards as possible in reaching conclusions, which may really only be educated opinions.

[F]   Simulation Modeling

Simulation is a process to imitate the physical components of your informational system. Simulation has a counterpart: emulation. Emulation is a process to imitate the physical components and the infrastructure. The infrastructure is your concrete and abstract legacy that includes software and traffic. Emulation is not discussed here because of its complexity. A vendor usually uses emulation to validate the performance of its product.

A simulation can be a process to imitate the administrative components of your project. When you have a budget and start changing the figures to determine what-ifs, then you have a simple financial simulation. An economic simulation is the use of essential variables that impact the financial well being of a large social organization such as a multinational corporation. If your corporation uses financial simulations, you should become familiar with the principles used so that when you do project financial simulations, they are as consistent with the financial goals of the corporation as possible.

Simulation uses prior historical performance data or performance data from a similar system to your own (a highly unlikely scenario). Simulation modeling comes in two flavors: discrete and state-change.

The discrete model uses mathematical distributions (raw or massaged) in a systematic series of equations. The result for a network might be bandwidth and latency predictions. The discrete model is used with production processes. Definable items such as network device counts, traffic counts, and throughputs are used in this simulation model. An advantage of a discrete model is that equilibrium of user input values can be established quickly.

The state-change model is concerned with conditions and events that can change the state of your enterprise network. Example states that might be considered are bridge on- or off-line, traffic low or high, or amount of application usage. This model is commonly used in the realm of statisticians. This model is good for determining possible configurations.

MANAGER'S TIP

A disadvantage of the state-change model is the requirement to include all conditions to get a realistic result.

In both models, the device models can be either deterministic or statistically random (technically stochastic). Deterministic processes are extrapolated and linear. A view of reality shows that your enterprise network does not work linearly—traffic does not flow smoothly, it flows in bursts.

MANAGER'S TIP

An extrapolated model can be very sophisticated; it can use such things as numerical analysis, probability, differential and partial equations, dynamic and complex analyses, and optimization. It can also be very practical just by using historical data and experiences of the project team and consultants. Both have the same limitation: A linear situation cannot predict a nonlinear situation.

[G] Statistical Modeling

Before one can comprehend what a statistical model is, one needs to comprehend what a statistic is. A working definition is that statistics are numerical estimates that probably are a random variable. The essential word in this definition is *numeric*. You use numbers to establish predictions with a statistical model.

One type of statistical model uses mathematical distributions to define such events as traffic streams. One develops a set of simultaneous equations that are solved by using a computer. The results are bandwidth and latencies. One can determine such things as optimal performance configurations, performance breakpoints, and minimal resource requirements. Honestly, a statistical model is complex and may be more than a bit confusing. When you want to do a networking statistical model, you should consider hiring a consultant.

To build a network traffic model, you need to have an extensive amount of historical statistical data available:

- Bandwidth used
- Circuit
  — Availability in percent
  — Busy number (average, maximum)
  — Failures (average, maximum)
  — Use in percentage
- Number of calls (real, virtual)
  — Attempted
  — Blocked (failure, traffic)
  — Completed
  — Disconnected
  — Preempted
  — Queued
- Number of packets
  — Blocked
  — Delivered
  — Processed
  — Transmitted
- Call queue
  — Probability
  — Size
  — Time
- Averages
  — Buffer use
  — Call length
  — Message delay
  — Packet delay
  — Packet queue time

More items could be added to the list. This list is given to assist you in selecting a tool that could do a custom-designed simulation model. A weakness in the model is you may have numbers but you do not necessarily know how they were determined.

MANAGER'S TIP

Because of the complexity of a statistical model, you might desire to use this technique when you perceive that the project might significantly impact an essential component of the informational system such as traffic.

[H]   Reasons for Using Modeling

You are going to do pragmatic modeling the moment you use historical data and experiences to establish cost, time, and resource estimates. To do sophisticated modeling requires a yes to one question: "Will the model assist the administration or management of the project?" Chapters 12 to 15, on project management tools, emphasize the pragmatic aspect of modeling.

MANAGER'S TIP

The modeling experiences of the author tend to be more pragmatic than theoretical. Thus, the book's presentation has a built-in bias.

---

§ 11.02   MANAGEMENT INVOLVEMENT

[A]   Overview

The moment any manager uses historical data and experiences to establish cost, time, and resource estimates, the manager is modeling at some level. No manager should shy away from modeling because of the misconception of complexity. Any successful manager does modeling on the fly; it is usually called an educated guess. This is just a basic form of extrapolation. Modeling requires a use of benchmarks and of standards to integrate historical data and experiences to minimize the randomness of a prediction.

Modeling is not an individual effort but a team effort.

[B]   Strategic Management and Modeling

The strategic manager should ensure that the tactical manager has adequate historical data and people with the appropriate experiences available to do sophisticated modeling, if required. All the things that were stated in Section

One about the responsibilities of the strategic manager as to the developing of cost, time, and resource estimates are applicable here also.

[C]   Tactical Management and Modeling

The tactical manager has to answer the essential question about modeling: "Will the model assist in managing the project?" When doing even simple extrapolations, the tactical manager must ensure that there are adequate historical data and people with the appropriate experiences available to reach realistic conclusions and decisions. The IS tactical or project manager must be able to identify descriptive data that can be used in making project management decisions such as a cabling inventory. Any financial modeling should be consistent with any corporate model.

[D]   Operational Management and Modeling

An operational manager should be aware that any operational model has to be integrated into a system or project model. An operational model is a one-eyed view of an imperfect reflection of reality. An operational manager needs to comprehend the importance of extrapolated modeling using historical data and the experiences of the team.

On the CD-ROM

On the CD-ROM is:

1.   Chapter 11 Overview.ppt—Chapter Overview, Project Modeling

---

Chapter 12

Gantt Charts and Schedules

§ 12.01   OVERVIEW

[A]   Objectives

At the end of this chapter, you will be able to:

- Define a schedule.
- Compare Gantt charts to other scheduling tools.
- Describe the basic features and functions of a Gantt chart.
- Establish the criteria for the use of a Gantt chart for project activity sequences, time estimates, resources, costs.
- Construct a simple Gantt chart.
- Correct a Gantt chart because of scheduling issues.
- Identify how the three managing levels may be involved in Gantt charting for your project.

[B] Schedule Definition

A schedule is a tool that should not set project activities in concrete. If the schedule is not flexible, then the schedule rather than the project manager controls the project. It is based on time estimates using experiences or even unreliable opinions. The schedule unfortunately may be seen by business managers as written in concrete. A project schedule should be written with a pencil and you should have an eraser at hand. The issue is not to use the eraser too quickly.

A schedule can be as elaborate as required to implement your project. It should also be useable. This chapter considers the use of the Gantt chart as one of the scheduling tools for project management. Remember, a schedule should include the quality control milestones and the verification milestones.

[C] Gantt Charts versus Other Scheduling Charts

There are many scheduling tools and techniques in addition to Gantt charts. The following are three of these:

1. Calendars
2. Listings
3. Milestones

Gantt charts are excellent for a visual presentation or overview of project timelines in the horizontal bar mode. They are good for simple projects, but because they do not illustrate activity relationships, they are weak for complex projects. However, Gantt charts should never be ignored in the earlier stages of project planning. They can be used to compare the project's actual progress against the original definition.

MANAGER'S TIP

Henry Laurence Gantt developed this technique at the turn of the twentieth century for presenting project tasks. Gantt was an American engineer and social scientist.

Calendars that are annotated can be helpful to the project manager in establishing daily personal management and administrative priorities. One could, for instance, use different colors to signify various activity time lines such as one color for software development and another for documentation development. Large calendars that can be displayed for everyone to see can also be used as a motivating tool.

Listings are really checklists. They are also very good in the early stages of project planning. By putting a listing in an electronic document or work-sheet file, one can quickly sort the list as required. A listing can easily be sent as an e-mail attachment to another person for approval or changes and then returned quickly. A listing is an excellent method for notifying large numbers of people of data in a very straightforward manner.

Milestones—also known as gates, or more ominously as deadlines—are the highlights of the project rather than the details that are expected in Gantt charts, calendars, or listings. They are excellent for executive summaries and establishing important quality control and assurance points. The use of mile-stones is a communication method, not a management method.

In a complex project you might use all four of these methods. In a simple project you might only use one or two, but in all cases you would want to use the Gantt charts because of the ability to present data visually. While there are tools available for building Gantt charts, including plug-ins for Microsoft Excel, you can do simple Gantt charts that are effective with-out these tools. (See § 12.01[F] "Constructing a Simple Gantt Chart," later in this chapter, which shows how to build a Gantt chart using Microsoft Excel.)

[D]   Basic Features and Functions of a Gantt Chart

A Gantt chart is a visual horizontal bar chart of a project's time lines. The first column is tasks, while the other columns are dates. The date columns are as refined as required for the project. However, one might find it easiest to use weekly increments such as July 1, July 8, and so forth.

MANAGER'S TIP

While the usual Gantt chart is thought of in terms of tasks in comparison to time lines, one might also do a chart that compares tasks to costs. The point is to have a visual bar chart that is horizontal.

The activities are listed by priority and sequence. The period of an activ-ity is represented by a bar with its start and end dates being the parameters. The bars usually come in two colors. It is recommended to use a light color to represent percentage of activity completion. Other features that you might include within a Gantt chart are:

- Milestone symbols
- Overdue indicators
- Legend, to note details such as review type
- Notes

MANAGER'S TIP

Depending on the version of Microsoft Excel used, there might be a limit to the number of columns available if you were to do a column for each day of the project. Check the product documentation for exact details. In addition, how do you handle the dates for weekends unless the project activities run seven days a week?

In all cases, the Gantt chart should be easy to comprehend. For example, a chart for a project lasting a year might be broken up into monthly increments (sections) rather than having one long chart for presentations.

MANAGER'S TIP

A weakness of the Gantt chart is that it does not show activity relationships. One might consider the use of a network diagram, such as PERT, to show these relationships.

If you decide to do a Gantt chart using Microsoft's Project, there are many opportunities for designing and developing your own style. Some of the possibilities include the following:

- Editing
  — Text
  — Headings
  — Bar height
  — Bar style (color, shape, or pattern)
  — Link line appearances
- Formatting
  — Text and heading styles
  — Activity (task) categories
  — Bars
  — Time scales
  — Gridlines
- Sorting a view
- Copying
  — Graphics between Gantt charts
  — Graphics from other Microsoft products
  — Graphics to other Microsoft products

[E]   Establishing the Criteria for a Gantt Chart

While a Gantt chart might be considered only as a set of project time lines, it might be used to present visually the four fundamental areas of a project:

1. Project activity sequences
2. Time estimates
3. Resources
4. Costs

How can a Gantt chart assist with these areas, since primarily it is a bar chart? One uses the chart to organize the activities determined by the time estimates, and then one can annotate the chart to reflect when special resources are to be used in the project time line and where major costs are required. Through symbols, one might indicate the following during the project cycle:

- Milestones, including important resource deliverables
- Critical path activities
- Start and end dates of basic activities
- Variances in dates
- Slack time

When a Gantt chart is used effectively, it can in a simple manner display the means for tracking the three areas of interest of the customer and of management: schedule, performance, and cost. As to the schedule, one can see the start and end dates for major activities. Performance as to percentage of work can be displayed through the shading of the bars. Cost status can be pointed to by using milestone symbols. You might create a Gantt chart with just spending activities.

Beyond these results, what other results can you achieve with an effective Gantt chart? The following are five potential positive results from using Gantt charts:

1. Determine contractor status.
2. Identify activities where the time line can be reduced.
3. Establish better priority and precedence standards for activities.
4. Develop a visual methodology for giving executive summaries.
5. Develop ways to reduce decision-making time.

A negative aspect of using a Gantt chart is that you cannot do predictions. One might use network analysis that includes activity interdependencies to achieve this requirement.

[F]   Constructing a Simple Gantt Chart

There are nine steps in constructing a simple Gantt chart in an Excel worksheet:

1. Starting with the second column, place the project time line across the first row (days, weeks, and so forth).

2. Beginning with the second row, list the tasks (major tasks could be made bold and subtasks normal) in the first column.

3. Using the color option, format the rows to represent the durations of tasks in a dark color (update using a light color).

4. Select the cell or cells you want to format.

5. Click Format on the Menu bar.

6. Click on Cells.

7. Click on Patterns.

8. Under Cell Shading Color, click colored box of preference.

9. Click on OK.

See Exhibit 12-1: Sample Gantt Chart in Excel, for a sample chart.

Exhibit 12-1: Sample Gantt Chart in Excel

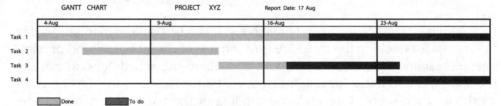

MANAGER'S TIP

It is recommended that you not use red and green as contrasting colors, because they carry a high emotional significance. People who are color blind also have trouble telling the difference between red and green.

[G]   Correcting a Gantt Chart

When you identify an error in a Gantt chart, you would use the following four-step approach, as you would for any scheduling error:

1. Identify any area that needs correction.

2. Determine the corrective action.

3. Revise the areas that require correction.

4. Evaluate the new chart for impacts.

You should have the operational managers analyze their areas against the corrections. Course of action should be according to the type of errors found. The basic assumption is that you have time-estimate errors rather than other types of errors.

See Chapter 6 for more details on the concepts involved with scheduling.

§ 12.02   MANAGEMENT INVOLVEMENT

[A]   Overview

All managers have an interest in the use of Gantt charts. A Gantt chart can be a simple tool that displays activities in comparison to time lines, or spending activities in comparison to cost estimates. The Gantt chart is a simple project management tool; however, it can be elaborated upon through use of symbols, legends, and notes.

[B]   Strategic Manager and Gantt Charts

The strategic manager should make it clear to the project manager, especially a new one, that there is a need for a standardized executive summary. This manager should state the expectations and the potential uses of the Gantt chart.

[C]   Tactical Manager and Gantt Charts

The tactical manager should expect contractors and, in some cases, consultants to present Gantt charts as a part of their proposals. This action should give you a visual list of proposed activities and the expected amount of time per activity according to each contractor. You might use the chart to evaluate the proposed price for work from the contractor. These charts become a standard format or environment for contractors and consultants to report their status.

As the project manager, you should use the Gantt chart method to assist in the following actions:

- Develop initial project plan.
- Refine the project plan.
- Track project status.
- Revise project activity requirements.
- Report project status.

The project manager should research the possibility that the corporation has a standard for Gantt chart design. If true, this should be used so the project's status can be presented in the context of similar projects.

[D]   Operational Managers and Gantt Charts

Operational managers should work with the project manager to develop a standard method and symbols for the project's Gantt charts so there can be an easy integration of data. Operational managers should do Gantt charts for their areas for basic project planning—that is, the project activities that are their responsibility. It makes life easier if there is a common, visual presentation tool.

The five areas that assist the tactical manager when using a Gantt chart are also applicable for any operational manager. Using a Gantt chart can simplify communications downward to an operational team or upward to the tactical and strategic managers. An operational manager must consider how the information in a Gantt chart can be presented as an executive summary.

On the CD-ROM

On the CD-ROM are:

1. Exhibit 12-1 Sample Gantt Chart in Excel.xls

2. Chapter 12 Overview.ppt—Chapter Overview, Gantt Charts and Schedules

---

Chapter 13

PERT/CPM Techniques

§ 13.01   OVERVIEW

[A]   Objectives

At the end of this chapter, you will be able to:

- Describe the positive side of PERT/CPM techniques.
- Describe the negative side of PERT/CPM techniques.
- Describe the basic features and functions of PERT/CPM techniques.
- Establish the criteria for the use of PERT/CPM techniques for: project activity sequences, time estimates, resources, costs.
- Explain basic PERT/CPM terminology.
- Identify how the three managing levels may be involved in the use of PERT/CPM techniques for your project.

[B]   Positive Side of PERT/CPM Techniques

Program Evaluation and Review Technique (PERT) was developed for the United States Department of Defense in the late 1950s. Specifically, it was developed by the consulting firm of Booz, Allen, and Hamilton for the U.S. Navy's Polaris submarine project, Polaris Weapon System. The project manager was Admiral Hyman Rickover.

The Navy established four requirements for PERT. Briefly stated, the four requirements were as follows:

1. Rules must be in place to logically establish events and activities in sequence.
2. Activities must be clearly visualized.
3. There must be three basic time-estimate levels:
    - Optimistic
    - Probable (most likely)
    - Pessimistic
4. There must be the ability to compute critical path and slack time.

MANAGER'S TIP

The time estimates used in PERT have been given statistical definitions. Optimistic time (o) improves only one in twenty while pessimistic time (p) exceeds this ratio. Probable is the most likely value of occurrence (m). A common formula for determining an activity's mean duration (d) is:

$$d = (o + 4m + p)/6$$

From these requirements flowed some advantages. Some of them are as follows:

- The project manager is forced to consider in detail personnel assignments.
- Useful details are given to resolve complex issues.
- Three potential timelines are demonstrated.
- The critical path is identified and marked by essential milestones to achieve defined goals.

The basic reason for using PERT is that a given project might be considered a series of activities that are unique from any other project. This means that while one might speak to common types of activities, the details are different. This position requires program control that is logical with the ability to evaluate quickly and a technique to review and revise project activities with a minimum of disruption. Yes, the four key words that PERT stands for appear in this reason.

In any IS project, whether it is in the design, development, or implementation phase, there are at least four categories of activities that must be managed. These four categories are:

1. Activities are interdependent.
2. Some activities are performed at the same time.
3. Some activities must be completed prior to others.
4. All activities require some type of resource (skills, equipment, or materials).

From this logic comes the idea that some activities are more important, or more critical, than others. Knowledge of this critical path's activities and duration can be used to control and manage the project's direction.

PERT/CPM techniques enable you to blend two areas that impact an IS project: project management and system engineering. Many IS project managers tend to think as system engineers rather than as project managers. What is system engineering? There is no single definition, but here is one working definition: "System engineering is the attempt to integrate and to synthesize entire systems to act as one entity." As an IS project manager, you have an information system that must handle technical, administrative, accounting, documentation, and training issues among others. Your entity is the corporation. Your system is the IS network. PERT recognizes that activities within an entity are interdependent. Critical Path Method (CPM) recognizes that all activities are important but some are more important than others.

The expectations from an IS project are usually the same as for system engineering. The following are five types of common expectations:

1. Technical design and development is significant.
2. There is a high degree of technical complexity.
3. Failure will not be tolerated.
4. Performance is the major criterion for success.
5. There is a high potential for risks.

PERT/CPM techniques were developed to resolve problems that come out of these expectations. You must be able to think in various ways. One must be able to explain an IS project in a variety of terms and positions. If you need solutions for a project issue, you might search on the Web using either *project management* or *system engineering* as key words. Both should lead to ideas on how to use PERT/CPM techniques.

MANAGER'S TIP

What Is Systems Engineering?

Systems engineering is an interdisciplinary approach and means to enable the realization of successful systems. It focuses on defining customer needs and required functionality early in the development cycle, documenting requirements, then proceeding with design synthesis and system validation while considering the complete problem:

- Operations
- Performance
- Test
- Manufacturing
- Cost & Schedule
- Training & Support
- Disposal

Systems Engineering integrates all the disciplines and specialty groups into a team effort forming a structured development process that proceeds from concept to production to operation. Systems Engineering considers both the business and the technical needs of all customers with the goal of providing a quality product that meets the user needs.

Source: International Council of Systems Engineering

When the idea is raised about the use of CPM, you usually get a question such as "why?" You cannot give an answer such as "the contract says so." You have to give an answer that expresses the potential that the project can be managed better and that communications can be easier because the core activities of the project have been identified. With the use of CPM, you can make a decision that requires project change more quickly. Notice this will only be true if you have computerized the input from the results of the CPM analysis and are able to update changes frequently. Frequency depends on the project's dynamics.

MANAGER'S TIP

Yes, you can do a project without using project management techniques. However, if you want to reduce risks and use less effort over the course of the project, then just try it. This statement is given here on the discussion on PERT because it is a technique that can initially be a challenge.

An IS administrator as an IS project manager has a distinct advantage over other project managers when it comes to the use of PERT/CPM. PERT is based on networking concepts. When you create an electronic network, you must be concerned with critical paths and software and hardware interdependencies (interoperability and compatibility). Performance and time are also critical to network stability. In addition, as a part of the general management of a network, you also accumulate historical data. This is a reminder that when working with managers in other areas, they do not usually have this type of background or experience. They may collect data but it is not usually system data, as it is for the IS group.

PERT is also beneficial in developing scenarios for evaluating project changes, or risk analysis. You, for instance, might do performance and resource trade-offs. You might also be able to identify potential project bottlenecks.

A person who is statistically oriented can determine the probabilities for meeting activities at a given milestone. Statistics assist in smoothing out uncertainty.

PERT, as a visual presentation, can assist you in discussions with customers and project team members about apparent issues on the project. It becomes a standard of communications. What is necessary is an acceptance of all parties to use this technique.

[C]   Negative Side of PERT/CPM

The issues with PERT/CPM are not with the concept, but in the early 1960s, it was the lack of computer power. Today a basic workstation probably has more computing power than any mainframe of that time.

Issues that have occurred since PERT's introduction include these 10 concerns:

1. Early forced federal government compliance.
2. Early software that was based on linear principles
3. Need for resource extensions (1962)
4. Introduction of the "earned-value" concept (1963)
5. Labor-intensive
6. Need for customer orientation definition (1990s)
7. Complexity
8. Rigidity
9. Technique may produce too much detail
10. Time-intensive

Without going into historical details, here are a few of the evolutionary steps of PERT/CPM:

- PERT/CPM (1958–1959)
- PERT/Cost (1962)

- Cost/Schedule Control System Criteria (C/SCSC) (1967)
- Earned Value Management (EVM) (1996)

A detailed discussion of this evolution is beyond the scope of this book. However, here is a brief outline of the 32 criteria of the Earned Value Management guidelines within five categories. These criteria are a revision of the 35 of the C/SCSC. They are only given here as a perspective of areas you must consider in IS project management when working with the federal government, but you should always use the invented wheel rather than trying to do your own thing. For further thought here are the 32 EVM criteria quoted from *Earned Value Management Implementation Guide,* Department of Defense approved December 14, 1996:

ORGANIZATION

- Define the authorized work elements for the program. A work breakdown structure (WBS), tailored for effective internal management control, is commonly used in this process.

- Identify the program organizational structure, including the major subcontractors responsible for accomplishing the authorized work, and define the organizational elements in which work will be planned and controlled.

- Provide for the integration of the company's planning, scheduling, budgeting, work authorization, and cost accumulation processes with each other, and as appropriate, the program work breakdown structure and the program organizational structure.

- Identify the company organization or function responsible for controlling overhead (indirect costs).

- Provide for integration of the program work breakdown structure and the program organizational structure in a manner that permits cost and schedule performance measurement by elements of either or both structures as needed.

PLANNING, SCHEDULING, AND BUDGETING

- Schedule the authorized work in a manner that describes the sequence of work and identifies significant task interdependencies necessary to meet the requirements of the program.

- Identify physical products, milestones, technical performance goals, or other indicators that will be used to measure progress.

- Establish and maintain a time-phased budget baseline, at the control account level, against which program performance can be measured. Budget for far-term efforts may be held in higher-level accounts until an appropriate time for allocation at the control account level. Initial budgets established for performance measurement will be based on either internal management goals or the external customer negotiated target cost including estimates for authorized but undefinitized [sic] work. On government contracts, if an over target baseline is used for performance measurement reporting purposes, prior notification must be provided to the customer.

- Establish budgets for authorized work with identification of significant cost elements (labor, material, etc.) as needed for internal management and for control of subcontractors.

- To the extent it is practical to identify the authorized work in discrete work packages, establish budgets for this work in terms of dollars, hours, or other measurable units. Where the entire control account is not subdivided into work packages, identify the far term effort in larger planning packages for budget and scheduling purposes.

- Provide that the sum of all work package budgets plus planning package budgets within a control account equals the control account budget.

- Identify and control level of effort activity by time-phased budgets established for this purpose. Only that effort which is unmeasurable or for which measurement is impractical may be classified as level of effort.

- Establish overhead budgets for each significant organizational component of the company for expenses which will become indirect costs. Reflect in the program budgets, at the appropriate level, the amounts in overhead pools that are planned to be allocated to the program as indirect costs.

- Identify management reserves and undistributed budget.

- Provide that the program target cost goal is reconciled with the sum of all internal program budgets and management reserves.

ACCOUNTING CONSIDERATIONS

- Record direct costs in a manner consistent with the budgets in a formal system controlled by the general books of account.

- When a work breakdown structure is used, summarize direct costs from control accounts into the work breakdown structure without allocation of a single control account to two or more work breakdown structure elements.

- Summarize direct costs from the control accounts into the contractor's organizational elements without allocation of a single control account to two or more organizational elements.

- Record all indirect costs which will be allocated to the contract.
- Identify unit costs, equivalent units costs, or lot costs when needed.
- For EVMS, the material accounting system will provide for:

  (1) Accurate cost accumulation and assignment of costs to control accounts in a manner consistent with the budgets using recognized, acceptable, costing techniques.

  (2) Cost performance measurement at the point in time most suitable for the category of material involved, but no earlier than the time of progress payments or actual receipt of material.

  (3) Full accountability of all material purchased for the program including the residual inventory.

ANALYSIS AND MANAGEMENT REPORTS

- At least on a monthly basis, generate the following information at the control account and other levels as necessary for management control using actual cost data from, or reconcilable with, the accounting system:

  (1) Comparison of the amount of planned budget and the amount of budget earned for work accomplished. This comparison provides the schedule variance.

  (2) Comparison of the amount of the budget earned [sic] the actual (applied where appropriate) direct costs for the same work. This comparison provides the cost variance.

- Identify, at least monthly, the significant differences between both planned and actual schedule performance and planned and actual cost performance, and provide the reasons for the variances in the detail needed by program management.

- Identify budgeted and applied (or actual) indirect costs at the level and frequency needed by management for effective control, along with the reasons for any significant variances.

- Summarize the data elements and associated variances through the program organization and/or work breakdown structure to support management needs and any customer reporting specified in the contract.

- Implement managerial actions taken as the result of earned value information.

- Develop revised estimates of cost at completion based on performance to date, commitment values for material, and estimates of future conditions. Compare this information with the performance measurement baseline to identify variances at completion important to company management and any applicable customer reporting requirements including statements of funding requirements.

REVISIONS AND DATA MAINTENANCE

- Incorporate authorized changes in a timely manner, recording the effects of such changes in budgets and schedules. In the directed effort prior to negotiation of a change, base such revisions on the amount estimated and budgeted to the program organizations.

- Reconcile current budgets to prior budgets in terms of changes to the authorized work and internal replanning in the detail needed by management for effective control.

- Control retroactive changes to records pertaining to work performed that would change previously reported amounts for actual costs, earned value, or budgets. Adjustments should be made only for correction of errors, routine accounting adjustments, effects of customer or management directed changes, or to improve the baseline integrity and accuracy of performance measurement data.

- Prevent revisions to the program budget except for authorized changes.

- Document changes to the performance measurement baseline.

The implications of these 32 criteria are discussed in § 13.02, entitled "Management Involvement." It is recognized that most readers might never be involved in federal government IS projects; however, you should have a broad knowledge of general project management (product, construction, and IS). You should recognize that the DOD has formulated usually specialized project management from shipbuilding to computer networks.

PERT has also had to evolve because of the evolution of society and business. This may be considered the negative side of PERT, but it does represent the ingenuity of system engineers and project managers to adapt. Whatever else may be said about PERT/CPM techniques, they do require a significant learning curve to use well.

[D]   Basic Features and Functions of PERT/CPM Techniques

PERT and CPM have their own unique definition of duration. PERT uses *ranges* of durations. CPM uses *averages* of durations based on historical data.

PERT, like any project management tool, has its own jargon for developing activity network diagrams. The basic terms include the following:

- Event, node
- Job, activity
- Immediate predecessor
- Immediate successor
- Initial node, terminal node

- Duration
- Earliest start time
- Earliest finish time
- Latest start time
- Latest finish time
- Critical path
- Total slack

For most of the terms you can easily formulate a logical definition; however, one of these needs to be explained now because of its importance. Slack time is the difference between earliest and latest (start or finish) times for an activity or event. Total slack is the amount of time that can be lost without delaying the project's overall schedule. There is no slack time on the critical path.

These terms are discussed in more detail in § 13.01[F], which discusses PERT/CPM examples. The focus of this chapter is to highlight the basic concepts involving PERT rather than detailing the use of PERT. The learning curve to use PERT might be significant for some individuals. An ideal situation is to hire a consulting firm, but your responsibility as a project manager is to comprehend what PERT/CPM techniques might do for you to enhance the management and control of the project.

MANAGER'S TIP

For technical details on this subject, you might consider Project Management with CPM, PERT, and Precedence by Joseph Moder, Cecil R. Phillips, and Edward W. Davis (Blitz Pub. Co. 1995).

While PERT and CPM can be spoken of in the same breath, they represent opposite viewpoints about activities. PERT assumes that activities are random and have a high degree of probability to change. CPM assumes that activities are fixed and are predictable. CPM uses sequential and dependent activities rather than parallel activities as are used in PERT. Another way of stating this is CPM relies on historical data, while PERT works with the unknown. The core phrase when working with PERT is the use of the "best guess."

MANAGER'S TIP

Probably one of the most difficult things with project management is that one has to work with estimates (time, cost, and performance), especially true with PERT, that business managers want to turn into concrete definitions. There is a series of Dilbert cartoons by Scott Adams that expresses this idea clearly.

What should you expect from PERT/CPM software at a minimum? The following four basic functions or capabilities should be available with any PERT/CPM software:

1. Calculate earliest and latest dates.
2. Plot network activity diagrams.
3. Print out reports.
4. Recalculate data based on new input.

CPM uses one of two methods for representing activities and events. Which method to use is a matter of preference, and you might use both. The two methods are:

1. Activity on arrow
2. Activity on node

Both use circles and arrows. With the activity-on-arrow method (AOA), the activity is represented by the arrow, while the circle represents the event. With the activity-on-node method (AON), the activity is represented by the circle, while the arrow represents precedence between the activities.

A variation of the activity-on-node method is to use boxes to identify network precedence. This method is becoming more common in CPM software.

[E]   Criteria for Using PERT/CPM Techniques

While a Gantt chart might be considered only as a set of project time lines, it might be used to present visually the four fundamental areas of a project:

1. Project activity sequences
2. Time estimates
3. Resources
4. Costs

Because you rarely have precise time estimates, there are formulae available to smooth random variation. To find out more on this subject you might consider materials on project management from the U.S. Navy. Shipbuilding is a very complex project; consequently there have been many technical techniques developed to achieve better control and management for any project, including the one for informational systems.

MANAGER'S TIP

These statistical tools are not discussed here because normally you would not need them. If you are a project manager for a very large and very complex IS project, you should be aware that someone, somewhere, uses these tools, usually for a federal government project. Construction and engineering companies also use these tools.

When developing criteria for planning project activities, you might consider the three fundamental things that make up a system. These three things are basic also to a programming model:

1. Components (input, process, and output)
2. Attributes (characteristics)
3. Relationships (links)

All activities can be interrelated for a common goal. Your problem as a project manager is to control and manage the impacts on your IS network, and PERT is a tool that can assist in this accomplishment. Notice it is *a* tool, not *the* tool.

A component's properties can affect the system's components as a whole. A metaphor is to watch what happens when one throws a stone into a pond and watch the resulting ripples. You must ensure during a project that the system is still greater than the parts of the project.

Attributes and relationships should be clearly defined. They actually should be measurable when possible. If they are not measurable, you should have a precise reason why they are not.

The optimization of the system should be a goal of the project. This means all associated technical parameters are defined and there is assurance that all interfaces (functional and physical) are compatible.

[F] Basic Terminology of PERT/CPM Techniques

The terminology of PERT/CPM techniques is expressed in symbols since we are working with a visual tool. We can state so-and-so is an event or activity, but what do they look like in a PERT activity diagram or network? See Exhibit 13-1. In the illustration:

- The circle represents an event.
- The arrow represents an activity.
- The number in the circle represents an event number.
- The text above an activity arrow represents the duration.

In Exhibit 13-1, event 8 has to be completed prior to the completion of event 4. The events are numbered without necessarily meaning sequence. It takes two weeks to complete customer documentation after testing is completed.

Exhibit 13-1: Basic PERT Terms: Event and Activity

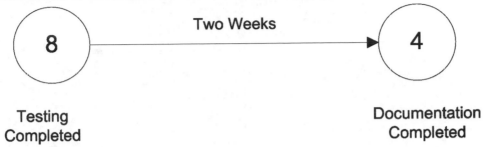

Two Weeks

Testing
Completed

Documentation
Completed

As in Exhibit 13-1, you might have one activity flow into another activity; however, there are two other scenarios: Two or more activities flow into one other, or one activity flows into two or more activities.

The PERT term for the first scenario is "sink," while for the second it is "burst" (see Exhibits 13-2 and 13-3).

One of the weaknesses of a Gantt chart is that the relationships among events cannot be shown. This is possible with PERT. The next figure is a simple Gantt chart with just the bars and event numbers. Exhibits 13-4, 13-5, and 13-6 show this Gantt chart converted to a basic PERT activity diagram with potential relationships. Durations between activities are omitted. Note that Exhibit 13-6 is the same as 13-5 but with the critical path shown with bold arrows. Exhibit 13-7 is a Gantt chart created using Microsoft Visio, to give you an idea of what one looks like created with project management software.

Exhibit 13-2: Sink Scenario

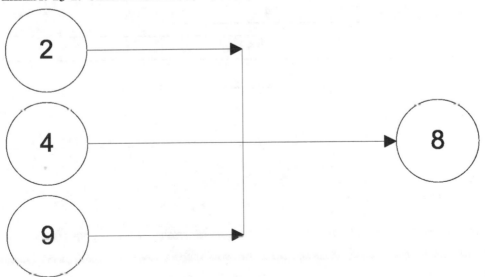

Exhibit 13-3: Burst Scenario

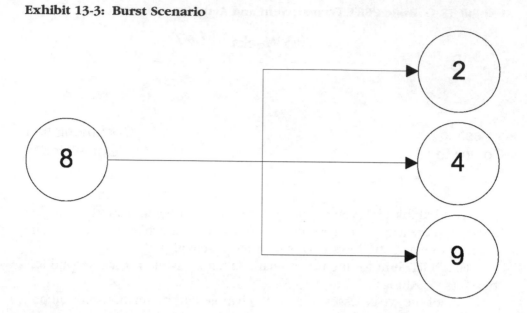

Exhibit 13-4: Basic Gantt Chart

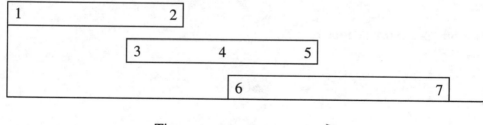

Exhibit 13-5: Gantt Chart Converted to a Basic PERT Chart

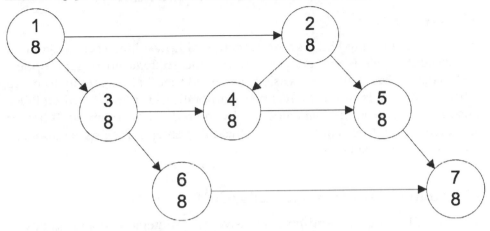

Exhibit 13-6: Critical Path on a PERT Chart

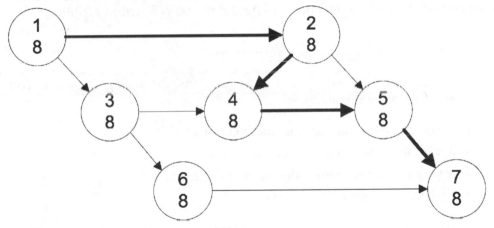

Exhibit 13-7: Gantt Chart Using Visio

ID	Task Name	Start	Finish	Duration	Jan 2003													
					3	4	5	6	7	8	9	10	11	12	13	14	15	16
1	Task 1	1/3/2003	1/6/2003	2d														
2	Task 2	1/6/2003	1/9/2003	4d														
3	Task 3	1/7/2003	1/14/2003	6d														

§ 13.02　MANAGEMENT INVOLVEMENT

[A]　Overview

One difficulty in using PERT is the perception of how it impacts management involvement. PERT is end-item oriented. Some strategic managers, upper-level management, have on occasion perceived that their capability to make decisions on core issues that affect their corporations is removed when PERT is used, especially in the mandated use by the federal government. Whether this perception is true is not important; that this perception exists is important to any IS project manager.

[B]　Strategic Manager and PERT/CPM

Because PERT is labor- and time-intensive, the strategic manager needs to make a commitment that when PERT is used, its chart will be a living and enforceable document. The manager also needs to make a commitment for training support for personnel within the IS group. The strategic manager should require a briefing to formulate types of executive summaries needed. Finally, the strategic manager must support the project manager to resolve potential risks that are identified using the scenario function of PERT.

[C]　Tactical Manager and PERT/CPM

You can use CPM to assist you in your relationships with contractors. You have the following possibilities:

- A way for determining alternate solutions
- A way for determining potential delays
- A way for determining valid payment requests
- Easier communication process

Like any powerful project management tool, a PERT/CPM application has a learning curve. It is suggested that you have a person on your staff who uses this tool and is statistically oriented to assist you in the general control and management of the operational tasks or activities of the IS network. Since you are responsible for a complex system with many interdependent components that have numerous attributes with a multitude of functional and physical links, the use of a PERT application is logical.

If you are already using PERT when you are responsible for an IS project, then you might overlay external data to the appropriate time lines. You also have a visual presentation to use for communicating requirements, and a set of time estimates that have been validated through experience.

When preparing a schedule using PERT/CPM, you need to identify a person or persons who are most knowledgeable about the activities. They need to comprehend the conditions of the activities and the performance requirements of the activities. The project supervisory team should participate and approve the schedule because they are the ones who are going to be held accountable.

Remember that software only speeds up the opportunity to do scenarios. It does not manage the project; you do. In addition, remember to remind higher-level managers and customers that you have to input the data before you can use the software effectively. The secret of success will always be experience.

The following is a seven-step process if you decide to use PERT/CPM:

1. List activities; do not consider resources.
2. Revise activities list by priority (precedence) and interdependency or interrelationships by developing activity network diagrams.
3. Review activity network diagrams with appropriate operational managers.
4. Convert the activity network diagrams to a PERT chart by including the duration of the activities.
5. Identify the critical path (revise until appropriate for the project).
6. Identify the plan using limited resources.
7. Make the PERT chart a living document.

When using PERT, you must always consider three minimums for any schedule:

1. Cost
2. Risk
3. Time

Your use of PERT also has at least four constraints:

1. Absolute defined milestones or deadlines
2. Spending and revenue restrictions
3. Resource restrictions
4. Strategic manager's approval

Section One of this book detailed what actions are expected of you as an IS project manager. Based on that information and the 32 criteria of EVM, the following 16 specific actions are required by you even if your customer is not the federal government:

1. Define the work elements.
2. Identify the project organization structure.

3. Integrate the company's processes with each other.

4. Establish cost and schedule performance measurements.

5. Sequence work based on interdependencies.

6. Identify all indicators such as milestones and performance goals.

7. Establish and maintain a time-phased budget baseline.

8. Identify budget items by significant cost elements (labor, materials, so forth).

9. Identify the activities in discrete work packages.

10. Identify when an activity is not measurable as a level of effort.

11. Establish overhead budgets for each significant organizational indirect cost.

12. Reconcile cost estimates with actual costs.

13. Record direct costs in accordance to standard budgetary practices.

14. Identify all indirect costs, which will be allocated to the project's budget.

15. Develop monthly reports, especially for budget status.

16. Prevent revisions to the project budget except for authorized changes.

[D] Operational Managers and PERT/CPM

Any operational manager needs to be involved in the seven-step process for developing a PERT chart. The manager needs to verify that all tasks for the operational area are noted and that all activity durations are correct. All managers need to work with the tactical manager to ensure that the project PERT chart is a living, viable document.

On the CD-ROM

On the CD-ROM are:

1. Exhibit 13-1 PERT Activity Data Survey.doc (on CD-ROM only)

2. Chapter 13 Overview.ppt—Chapter Overview, PERT/CPM Techniques

---

Chapter 14

Risk Analysis

§ 14.01   OVERVIEW

[A]   Objectives

At the end of this chapter, you will be able to:

- Define risk.
- Identify 10 types of impacts on a project caused by risks.
- Identify eight categories of risks.
- List 20 sources of risks.
- Define risk analysis.
- Describe the basic features and functions of a risk-analysis model.
- Establish the criteria for a risk-analysis model for your project that includes: project activity sequences, time estimates, resources, costs

- Identify how the three managing levels may be involved in the development of a risk-analysis model for your project.

MANAGER'S TIP

Luck 1 a: a force that brings good fortune or adversity b: the events or circumstances that operate for or against an individual 2: favoring chance

---

[B]   Risk Definition

A risk is not just any problem, bug, or variance. Risk is the potential of a problem occurring. A risk is a performance error that can have a significant or disastrous impact on the project's success.

Risk management involves three functions:

1. Identify the risk.
2. Assess the risk.
3. Allocate resources to resolve the risk.

Risk management is resolving or managing both negative and positive opportunities. Risk management, a specialized form of project management, was developed as a mechanism to minimize liabilities. A risk is a potential issue that might adversely affect the project. A risk is not a dark cloud in the sky; it is a big, bad monster lurking in the dark. An opportunity is a situation that might have a significant positive effect on the project in time, money, resources, quantity, or all four.

It is important that any risk analysis consider both threats and opportunities. The risk analysis should be against established thresholds. A very simple, but common, example of a threshold is that no action is taken until a certain number of errors are found within a given constraint.

MANAGER'S TIP

Usually an electronic risk-analysis tool focuses on the threat mode. However, through a reverse of variables one can develop scenarios for opportunities. If the customer decides that you have an extra six months to complete the project, you can input this variable into a risk-analysis model and look for opportunities. In this case, one might also find risks because of the unavailability of resources beyond the original finish date.

[C]   Ten Types of Impacts Caused by Risks

A risk will have a disastrous effect on a project that does not have an adequate control system or process. Ten impacts of risk include:

1. Attitudes (internal and external)
2. Changes in organizational structure
3. Customer relationships
4. Financial success
5. Project success
6. Resource allocations
7. Responsibilities
8. Safety
9. Security
10. Vendor relationships

A major area of risk is procurement. Because of a long history of putting the risks on the supplier, there has been an evolution in the guiding principle between the customer (purchaser), you, and the vendor. Procurement, in particular the U.S. Department of Defense (DOD), follows the principle that the reimbursable mode is up to the agreed scope definition and then a fixed price. (Please see § 10.01[D].)

[D]   Eight Categories of Risks

Risks span the complete spectrum of a project. The following is a list of eight core risk categories, each having subcategories:

1. Customer
2. Delivery
3. Equipment
4. People
5. Physical environment
6. Scope
7. Technology
8. Vendor

One can easily produce examples for each because of a lack of resources or skills or a failure to meet a time estimate. Here is an example for each of the eight categories that represents a risk:

1. The customer goes bankrupt and can no longer financially support the project.
2. The deliverable turns out not to be compatible with the customer's system.

3. A critical piece of equipment that is to be used in the project does not meet the defined specifications.

4. People critical to the project quit the company.

5. The facility is lost through an act of nature such as a flood.

6. An operational manager decides to assist the project's customer by adding a function that is not a part of the approved project's scope.

7. Critical technology does not happen at the time expected.

8. The vendor goes bankrupt and cannot deliver critical goods.

You can see from this list that one might have a risk at anytime from anywhere. A basic element of risk analysis is the development of scenarios such as the above. A risk-analysis tool permits you to develop solutions prior to actual risk events. In addition, when a known risk happens, a risk-analysis tool can assist you in identifying potential solutions. All solutions require trade-offs.

MANAGER'S TIP

Not all risks become reality. There is much potential in our world that does not occur. Driving to work today, I saw clouds that indicated the potential of rain. Dark clouds don't indicate a certainty of precipitation, but they do indicate a greater potential than a clear sky. I perceive an increased risk that I will get drenched on the long walk across the company parking lot, so I carry an umbrella with me. The odds are that it will not rain. The weather reporter says the clouds will pass. I can even see patches of blue sky between the massive dark clouds. Still, to reduce my risk of being drenched, I carry an umbrella.

MANAGER'S TIP

Some risks can be reduced almost to the point of elimination. A hospital could install a backup generator system with the goal of ensuring 100 percent electrical availability. This machine will protect them against the risk of electrical blackouts and brownouts. It also introduces new risks such as the generator failing to start automatically when the electricity fails. It also does not protect the hospital against a massive electrical failure internal to the building.

Some risks are unavoidable and you can only take steps to reduce their impact. You cannot prevent an important team member from leaving the company in the middle of a project, but you can require that all work be well documented, so that the next person will be able to quickly pick up where the worker left off.

[E]   Twenty Sources for Potential Risks

Most sources for potential risks obviously start at the operational level. Loss of control of risks happens at the tactical level. Just to give a flavor of the potential sources, the following list of 20 potential risks is provided:

1. Activity sequencing in error

2. Coding error

3. Database format error

4. Documentation error

5. Equipment falling below standards

6. Failure to give timely reports

7. Feature not being a part of a project goal

8. Hardware incompatibility

9. Material not meeting standards

10. Network component incompatibility

11. Not using appropriate standards

12. Operating system incompatibility to system infrastructure

13. Project activity not being defined in the schedule

14. Report layout in error

15. Requirement specification in error

16. Resource received not being in accordance with specification

17. Skill level not being valid

18. Software incompatibility

19. Training objectives not meeting a project goal

20. Vendor product incompatibility to system

The previous examples of potential sources do not necessarily in themselves represent risks. A risk is determined by the degree of consequence. If an error seriously threatens a project, you have a risk.

[F]   Risk-Analysis Definition

Risk analysis is a technique, tool, or method for assessing, either quantitatively or qualitatively (or both), the impacts of an identified risk or a potential risk identified through a scenario. Risk management is the course of action you use to solve the risk.

When you use risk analysis, you are comparing alternatives to determine trade-offs for actions, durations, resources, or skills.

The comparison might come in three flavors: optimistic, pessimistic, and realistic. This concept is the basis of PERT. If you have read Chapter 13 on PERT, you have already been introduced to a form of risk analysis. We all have a rational criterion for risk analysis in the work environment: If the risk is worse than 50 percent, forget it. There are many exceptions to this criterion, such as startup companies and in one's personal life (betting on winning the lottery).

While risk analysis may seem arcane, you will do risk analysis even if you do not do the project. The place for risk analysis is in the preproposal review that asks the question, "Is the project viable?" See § 1.04[D] for the 20 types of questions you should ask about the project. Those 20 items imply an underpinning of management experience.

One can approach risk analysis from many different viewpoints. Any approach might include these core steps:

1. Develop a model.
2. Identify unknown qualities or quantities.
3. Analyze the model through scenarios or simulations.
4. Decide on a solution.

There is one risk you might never think of, but all project managers experience it. It is the risk that business managers think that when you do risk analysis you are an alarmist. Business managers tend to consider risks serious only when they happen. You overcome this by doing the following:

- Documenting all risks
- Keeping management informed
- Presenting measurable recommendations
- Making sure management comprehends the consequences
- Keeping a neutral position by never saying, "I told you so"

[G]   Features and Functions of a Risk-Analysis Model

A model is a reflection of reality. Throughout any design or development process you need to consider the components of your network; all of these components make up the infrastructure. The components come in two flavors: concrete and abstract. (See Chapter 18 for details on legacy software and hardware.) Knowing what the components are and their places in the network is key to modeling, determining what tools you need, establishing protocols that implement integration, identifying interconnectivity issues, and establishing the roles of the service and access servers.

You may ask, "How do I model the abstract?" The abstract for a network includes such things as stability and performance. One always has some measurable data, standards, or benchmarks to explain these abstractions. One might need to consider that one either has three network maintenance personnel per day (eight-hour shifts) or has two network maintenance personnel per day (12-hour shifts). In addition, do you have them for three, five, or seven days? You use risk analysis to determine the impact of the loss of one or more of these people during a critical activity of the project. Notice the word *critical.* You do not use risk analysis such as this scenario for any activity in which these people are not available and their absence does not cause risk.

A model is a theoretical environment with as much data as possible to reflect reality adequately for decision making. A scenario is a set of possibilities that could happen to cause a risk. The possibilities are uncertainties. These uncertainties include:

- Resource availability
- Skill availability
- Duration of an activity or a set of activities
- Cost of activities
- Doubtful milestones

A risk-analysis tool uses qualitative and quantitative distribution functions to identify potential risks in these areas and any of the potential sources for risks as discussed in § 14.01[E]. As with PERT you need a person who is statistically oriented to assist in interpreting a risk-analysis model. There are many types of distribution types. A very short list includes:

- Chi-square
- Extreme value
- Histogram
- Pareto
- Poisson

One distribution type that is discussed in detail is found in Chapter 13 on PERT. Why are statistics the basis of these distribution types? Risk is probability. For example, it was stated in § 13.01[B] that an optimistic date can only be improved 1 in 20 times, or 5 percent of the time. You want to use a risk-analysis tool to help you to minimize potential risks. Think of risk-analysis odds like the odds in a game of craps. The odds of throwing snake eyes (pair of ones) are statistically known (1 in 36). A risk-analysis tool helps you to resolve factors more complex than determining odds when you are throwing two six-sided dice. The principle is the same.

MANAGER'S TIP

A nice feature in a risk-analysis tool, but not required, is the capability to produce random values and produce graphics of various scenarios for you.

While one may not comprehend the underlining theory of a distribution function, one can come to grips quickly with colored graphics. An important feature of any risk-analysis tool is to have summary graphics so they can be used in presentations to the project team, strategic manager, or the customer. It is amazing that when you use red to indicate criticality, your audience gets the point quickly and usually without asking theoretical questions. The resulting questions are very practical. Some of the types of graphics that you should have in a risk-analysis tool include:

- Critical path indices
- Cumulative curves
- Histograms
- Multiple distribution graphs
- Range summary graphs
- Relative frequency distribution graphics

MANAGER'S TIP

There are plug-in risk-analysis tools available to work with some versions of Microsoft Project.

There is one goal of any risk-analysis tool. Its result should be an easily read distribution of the probability of the possible values.

[H] Surveys and Checklists for Creating a Risk-Analysis Model

For a risk-analysis model to have validity, you must have adequate input, step one of the process. One way to develop input is create either a survey or a checklist for determining how to establish the input. Any survey or checklist must consider four areas:

1. Activity sequences
2. Duration of activities
3. Resource availability
4. Spending and revenue expectations

The following is a set of 20 survey questions that might assist you in the creation of a risk-analysis model:

1. Have all operational activity sequences been identified?
2. Have all training activity sequences been identified?
3. Have all milestones been identified?
4. Have all documentation activity sequences been identified?
5. Have all quality control points been identified?

6. Are there standards or benchmarks for comparing activity durations?

7. Have operational cost estimates been identified?

8. Have indirect-cost estimates been identified?

9. Have all revenue dates been identified?

10. Have skills availability been identified?

11. Have deliverable dates been identified?

12. Have status report dates been identified?

13. Has a critical path been established?

14. Have critical equipment requirement dates been established?

15. Have critical material requirement dates been established?

16. Are there "slippage" dates?

17. Have software infrastructure benchmarks (configuration, compatibility, and so forth) been identified?

18. Have hardware infrastructure benchmarks (interoperability, portability, and so forth) been identified?

19. Have the dates, equipment, and resources been entered from all vendors and consultants?

20. Have skill-level benchmarks been identified?

Exhibit 14-1 is a checklist that is similar to the survey above. Assign a value to the Likelihood and Impact columns; the scales to use are from 0 to 10, with 0 as extremely unlikely and 10 as a sure thing. You may also use the scores of 0 for no chance, 1 for low, 2 for medium, and 3 for high. Multiply the two values together to get a score for that item. You can now sort the items by the score to see where you need to spend most of your time; the higher the score, the more attention you should pay to that area. You can also sum the scores for all the items to calculate a risk value for the entire project. By keeping records of every project, you'll begin to develop a history of project risk that you can then use to refine your handling of risk on future projects. Using information from Chapter 18, this checklist is for the core hardware infrastructure of an IS network.

This detailed checklist is given here for a number of reasons. First, one needs to comprehend the level of detail required to do adequate risk analysis. Second, while many of these items may not be required for a given project, they should be considered for any project. If you do not have adequate equipment diagrams for a project that has important IS network hardware enhancements, you might have a potential risk. Third, this is a template for other checklists for budget definitions, skill definitions, and so forth.

Exibit 14-1: System Hardware Risk Analysis

Project:		Date:		
Manager/Team Leader:				
Item	**Likelihood**	**Impact**	**Score**	
Hosts				
Mainframe				
Server (each of your server types should be listed)				
CPUs				
Mainframes				
Operating systems (each type should be listed)				
Intermediate Nodes				
Bridges				
Firewalls				
Gateways				
Hubs				
Routers				
Switches				
Terminals (all appropriate types should be noted)				
Workstations (note all appropriate types)				
Peripheral Nodes				
Faxes				
Printers				
Applications				
Operations (all appropriate ones should be noted)				
User (all appropriate ones should be noted)				
Code				
Executable (identify areas of impact)				
Source (identify areas of impact)				
Databases				
Buffer size				
Cache				
Number of users (users impacted by project)				

Exibit 14-1 (*Continued*)

Item	Likelihood	Impact	Score
Disk			
Cache			
Controller speed			
Drivers			
Load balance			
GUI Components			
Servers			
System			
Memory Components			
Cache type			
Size			
Speed			
Protocols			
Intranet			
Internet			
System			
Server Protocols			
Chat			
Directory			
E-mail			
File			
News			
Search			
IS Tools			
Blueprints			
Equipment diagrams			
Inventories			
Management			
Performance analyzers			
Policies			
Process flowcharts			
Protocol analyzers			
Wiring route map			

§ 14.02   MANAGEMENT INVOLVEMENT

[A]   Overview

While it is the responsibility of the tactical manager to control and manage risks, it is the responsibility of the operational managers to minimize risks. In addition, it is the responsibility of the strategic manager to support the need for risk analysis and management across corporate divisions.

[B]   Strategic Manager and Risk Analysis

The strategic manager must acknowledge risk analysis as a proper project management and control tool or technique. This manager should also expect to be kept regularly informed on the status of potential and identified risks. The strategic manager should support the acquisition and use of risk-analysis tools, including PERT/CPM.

   The strategic manager is involved with the tactical manager at the inception of the project when they meet to discuss the question, "Is this project viable?" The strategic manager must recognize that risk analysis is not necessarily the use of arcane tools and techniques. It can simply be the comparison of alternatives with experiences used in the evaluation. This may not be the most reliable method of doing risk analysis, but may be more common than the use of risk-analysis tools.

[C]   Tactical Manager and Risk Analysis

You have to remember that the customer and management only know that you are behind schedule, they do not think of the why. The reason, most of the time, is a risk that is real and requires that you have to take critical time and resources to solve.

   You have to control the risks; you cannot let the risks control you. A risk may be beyond your direct control in any of a hundred project closets, but once it is out, you are the person that has to solve the risk.

   As project manager, you can do at least two things to minimize potential risks:

1. Establish measurable objectives, benchmarks, and performance standards.
2. Prepare for potential risks by using a risk-analysis tool.

   You need to handle risk analysis in a positive manner. You should ask, "How can we resolve this risk if it happens?" You should not ask, "What can go wrong?" The word *wrong* implies a moral decision. One should use the word *incorrectly* since it implies a potential measurable standard or benchmark.

You must evaluate regularly identified potential risks and define new ones with the use of risk-analysis tools and techniques. You control and manage risks through the following:

- Team meetings
- Informational conferences with the strategic manager and customers
- Project status reports
- Risk-analysis tools to develop solutions to potential risks

You need to overcome the attitudes in the corporate environment that risks are not discussed until they happen and that doing risk analysis is an alarming activity. Reassure upper management by doing the following:

- Documenting all risks
- Keeping management informed
- Presenting measurable recommendations
- Making sure management comprehends the consequences
- Keeping a neutral position by never saying "I told you so"

[D]   Operational Managers and Risk Analysis

Each operational manager must recognize that when the tactical manager does risk analysis, it is not a threatening act. It is the responsibility of the operational managers to minimize the risks and to support the tactical manager in managing the risk's solutions. Any insight into identifying a potential risk should be seen as a positive, not a negative.

Because any formal risk-analysis tool requires valid input, it is the responsibility of each operational manager to review the data. In addition, as new data is developed, it should be given as input to the risk-analysis tool. A part of this action is to be involved in risk-analysis discussions at project team meetings and also to keep the operational team informed.

On the CD-ROM

On the CD-ROM are:

1. Exhibit 14-1 System Hardware Risk Anaslysis.doc

2. Chapter 14 Overview.ppt—Chapter Overview, Risk Analysis

Chapter 15

Learning Curve Analysis

§ 15.01   OVERVIEW

[A]   Objectives

At the end of this chapter, you will be able to:

- State two reasons for the importance of learning curve analysis.
- Describe the basic features and functions of learning curve analysis.
- Establish the criteria for a learning curve analysis for your project that includes project activity sequences, time estimates, resources, costs.
- Design a checklist for learning curve analysis.
- Identify five limitations to learning curve analysis.
- Identify how the three managing levels may be involved in using a learning curve analysis for your project.

[B]   Importance of Learning Curve Analysis

It is widely recognized that incorrect time estimates are a major downfall of many projects. Perhaps one of the factors for incorrect time estimates is not comprehending the importance of learning curves. The original definition of a learning curve is that whenever the quantity of units manufactured doubles, then the average time to produce a unit is reduced by a constant percentage. This concept can be more broadly applied to developing information systems; as a person or team has more experience developing a certain type of system, the time and resources required to produce each new system should decrease.

Learning curves may be like the weather; everyone talks about it, but they think they can do nothing about it. While one cannot turn learning analysis into pure science, there are techniques and tools for making it a more predictable process.

A learning curve can be called a number of different names: experience curve, startup capability, or progress potential. Whatever the name, one can usually see the negative results of underestimated learning curves through missed deadlines or production inefficiencies, both of which affect direct labor costs.

One might not be sure about resolving the learning curve issue because it is usually associated with repetitive tasks, and most project tasks or activities are unique. Sorry, unless you are doing a network from scratch, a project within itself, you have experiences and historical data to assist in doing learning curve analysis. If you are going to install a new server for a customer, you already have a file server. How many work-hours with how many people of a given experience did it take to do the installation? If you are going to install a new software application, have you installed a similar type of application? An initial step in doing learning curve analysis is simply looking for IS system data that parallels the present IS project whenever possible.

MANAGER'S TIP

The ideas discussed in this chapter were influenced by the tenets put forth by Peter Senge in his book *The Fifth Discipline: The Art and Practice of the Learning Organization* (October 1991). A corporation (Senge) or a project team (author) needs to be a "learning organization" that uses "system thinking." A basic model from Senge is "team learning." A project's efficiency might be affected by the interaction of learning experiences of the team as a whole.

[C]   Features and Functions of Learning Curve Analysis

Any learning curve tool should assist a project manager in preparing and presenting analyses with minimal effort. The tool should also assist you in focusing on solutions for resolving standard or normal learning curve issues. Not all learning curve issues can be completely resolved, but they certainly can be minimized.

Unlike most studies of this type, the original study of learning curves did not come from the military but from the aircraft industry. It is interesting that the results of the early studies on learning curves are similar to the concerns of project management. Both are focused on the following:

- Activity sequencing
- Activity durations
- Allocation and utilization of resources
- Costs and resulting revenues

MANAGER'S TIP

T. P. Wright published the first learning curve analysis article in the *Journal of Aeronautical Science* (February 1936). His theory of developing cost estimates for repetitive tasks has evolved to the handling of tasks such as those required to create a space shuttle.

A basic idea from these studies that might seem contrary to an application in IS project management is that "repetitive experience produces efficiency," but if you use parallel experiences from general IS operational tasks, you can apply this principle in this area. Learning curves are usually defined by percentage (%) with 100 percent being a flat curve. The basic premise is, as the percentage of the learning curve goes down, efficiency goes up.

There are a number of steps you have to do when you use a learning curve analysis tool. Here are six possible steps:

1. Establish parameters.
2. Gather data.
3. Input data into the tool.
4. Calculate the learning curve.
5. Create charts.
6. Do a forecast.

Calculating the learning curve includes deciding on such parameters as correlation, coefficient, curve values, intercepts, and slope. You then can run regressions. At this point, you are asking, "Where is my statistical person?" It has to be recognized that with the use of any project management tool, you need someone on the project team who is strong in statistics. It still is your responsibility to comprehend the output and then present it to the team and to the strategic manager.

Exhibit 15-1: Sample Learning Curve is a very simple example of determining the learning curve for a particular process. The units can be workstations, function points, and so on. The graph shows that as the team gains experience with the process, the cost per unit decreases. Of course, much more accurate models can be created using more advanced statistical techniques.

Exhibit 15-1: Sample Learning Curve

	First Project	2nd Project	3rd Project	4th Project	5th Project
# of units	100	150	200	250	300
Cost/unit	$150	$125	$100	$85	$75
Diff vs. 1st Project	$ -	$25	$50	$65	$75
	Savings	$3,750	$10,000	$16,250	$22,500

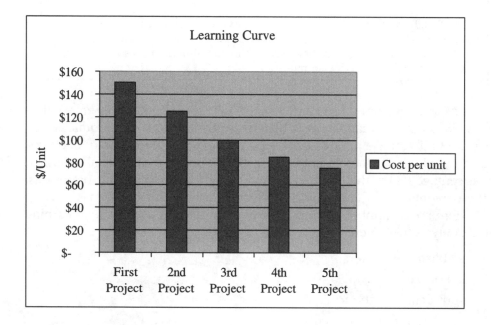

Learning curve analysis is not only done for operational activities, but one must also consider the impact of classroom education or training of the project team and ultimately with the customer's training. You do not just hand off project results to a customer; there is classroom training and documentation. You should turn to the two operational managers of these areas to assist in developing appropriate learning curve analyses. These analyses give additional justifications for the expenditures of time, resources, and materials (all three represent direct project costs) for customer training and documentation.

MANAGER'S TIP

IT training costs exceed $10 billion a year in the United States, but in fact, direct training expense is normally far less than the cost of the employee's time during the training.

With measurable performance goals, perhaps you can easily answer the question that any student might have upon entering a classroom, "What can I learn here?" If a student knows what is expected, perhaps the learning curve might be made shorter.

[D]   Criteria for a Learning Curve Analysis

As one establishes criteria for a learning curve analysis, one must have a reference point. A learning curve is a graphical representation of repetitive tasks that when done on a continuous basis lead to a reduction in activity duration, resources, and costs.

If you asked for learning curve analyses to be done for the classroom, what type of data would you expect to be required for these activities? The following four broad areas are possible:

1. Environment
2. Input
3. Processes
4. Output

Environmental considerations are the influences prior to entering the classroom, those in the classroom, and after leaving the classroom. A place to look for this type of data is in the IS customer service group. Has customer service improved because of training? Now, how is this data applicable to determining project efficiency?

Input would be to consider the experience levels of the students prior to entering the classroom and their performance levels after leaving the classroom. It is recognized that there is a hidden factor of the students' attitudes toward the training and the workplace. One should consider specifically any data related to students from the project's customer.

Processes include what type of training style was used to convey data of a similar nature required for the project. Should seminars or a formal classroom setting be used? There is one project requirement: training objectives should be stated in measurable terms. If this practice is implemented, you may not get the data you want for this project, but you will have data for the next project.

Output is any type of factor that the student might have experienced that could impact the instructional process. A factor such as a possible "reduction in force" can impinge on project efficiency.

An important concept of education is the use of just-in-time training. This means the immediate application of the principles, techniques, and concepts in the work environment. This approach might be very effective for project management. It has been shown that after a six-month period, students tend to retain only 70 percent or less of the information acquired in the classroom.

One can readily see that there may be many hidden factors in doing a learning curve analysis. You might ask, "Why should I waste my time on this activity?" The answer might be that the act of identifying factors might be very helpful in solving potential risks. A risk may develop because of a team member's attitude rather than through inexperience.

How should one look at documentation? Data might be available in the IS customer service group that either points to the lack of good documentation or the inability of the customer's group to read and understand it. You can consider the same four areas for documentation as with training.

What is important for project management is not the theoretical premise that repetitive experience improves efficiency or the learning curve but the identification of parallel experiences to improve a project's overall efficiency. When you use learning curve analysis—more than with any other project management tool—you must look for informational bridges.

[E]   Checklist Design for Learning Curve Analysis

How would you begin a learning curve analysis? I would hope that after reading this far into the book that you answered you would begin with developing a set of measurable performance criteria. Your goal when doing a learning curve analysis is to work with the premise that as a person's performance level improves, so does the person's efficiency. This premise becomes the foundation for any learning curve analysis checklist.

You need to identify performance, training, and miscellaneous factors to assist in the learning curve analysis. A miscellaneous factor might be the work environment. If it would be better for a person to work a random shift rather than a fixed shift, then you might have a solution for improving that person's efficiency. What does this have to do with learning? Unless a person is dead, one continues to learn. Perhaps a person learns less at some times than at others.

Actually, one person may retain and may be able to retrieve data better at different times from another person. One person may do better in a morning training class than another person simply because of the body's circadian rhythm.

A number of factors might be considered in the development of a learning curve analysis. Recognize that the factors do interact with one another. The following 10 factors might serve as a core outline for an analysis:

1. Compensation potentials

2. Corporation environment for the transfer of learning

3. Degree of specialization

4. Measurable performance goals
5. Production processes
6. Project stability
7. Quality control definitions
8. Resource mix
9. Task methodologies
10. Use of standards and benchmarks

In addition to these 10 factors, you should look for comparisons to the present project and data from prior projects such as the following:

- Project duration
- Customer
- Types of deliverables
- Team members
- Product comparison
- Resource availability
- Environment
- Product differences

[F]   Five Limitations to Learning Curve Analysis

If a learning curve analysis has its limitations in the general corporate environment, perhaps they are accented in a project. Do not jump to faulty conclusions based on any data you have from a learning curve analysis; variables interact most dynamically. The following five limitations are especially true for project management:

1. Learning curve predictions are better for the long term rather than the short term.
2. A learning curve is not continuous.
3. Marketing decisions may impact the learning curve.
4. The data for one product may not be so viable for the project as thought.
5. The cost data available might not be reliable.

§ 15.02   MANAGEMENT INVOLVEMENT

[A]   Overview

All management levels should consider the use of learning curve analysis as a long-term effort rather than just as a short-term effort such as for an IS project. Since most IS projects are evaluated on performance, the use of learning curve analyses might play a valuable role in the management and control of such a project.

[B]   Strategic Manager and Learning Curve Analysis

The strategic manager should support the project manager's efforts in using learning curve analysis to develop a foundation for long-term benefits. Perhaps techniques can be tested to improve repetitive tasks so costs might be lower. Since learning curve analysis requires the involvement of groups outside of IS, the strategic manager should give demonstrated support for any effort in this area.

[C]   Tactical Manager and Learning Curve Analysis

You need to frame solutions to learning curve issues in terms of whether comprehension and training are improved a certain percentage. If so, then it is expected there will be a potential percentage (range) of improvement in production efficiency for this activity. It is important to give a range rather than a fixed percentage because you do not want to make a commitment to an absolute figure to the strategic manager and other upper-level managers. Remember that time and cost estimates become concrete to these same business managers, unless they want to change them.

You may need someone who has knowledge of statistics to manipulate the learning curve data for the project. However, it still is your responsibility to comprehend the output and then present it to the team and to the strategic manager.

You should work with the two operational managers from training and documentation to assist you in developing appropriate learning curve analyses. These analyses give additional justifications for the project costs of time, resources, and materials for these two areas.

For further information on learning curve calculations for cost estimating, you might read either of Rodney Stewart's books, *Cost Estimator's Reference Manual,* Second Edition (March 1995), or *Cost Estimating,* Second Edition (January 1991).

[D]   Operational Managers and Learning Curve Analysis

Two important operational managers who see significant results from learning curve analyses are those in training and documentation. There was an earlier discussion in this chapter on potentials for these managers and learning curve analysis. In addition, any manager who is involved with repetitive tasks should be concerned about this technique. While a programming manager may not first think coding is repetitive, a closer analysis may reveal that it is more repetitive than you think. How often and in what manner do programmers apply the rules of the programming (coding) language used?

On the CD-ROM

On the CD-ROM are:

1. Exhibit 15-1 Sample Learning Curve.doc

2. Chapter 15 Overview.ppt—Chapter Overview, Learning Curve Analysis

Chapter 16

Documentation

§ 16.01   OVERVIEW

[A]   Objectives

At the end of this chapter, you will be able to:

- Distinguish between administrative project documentation and support project document types.
- Explain the reasons for the project procedural manuals or guidelines.
- Identify eight impact types on documentation by three constraints.
- List 19 potential documents that can be used the management of a project.
- Describe the basic content for 19 project management documents: Market Analysis Report, Business Justification, Commercial Specification, Organizational Chart, Project Proposal, Project Specification, Content Agreement, Schedule, Design and Development Plan, Initial Budget Estimate, Initial Funding Requirements, Quality Plan, Trial Strategy, Field Introduction Requirements, Training Strategy, Communications Plan, Risk Assessment, Third-Party Documents, Project Manager's Log

- Identify four important impacts on the Communication Plan.
- Identify how the three managing levels use the different types of documentation.

Well-written documentation presents a clear, accurate picture of the process or system documented. The documentation detail must be tuned to the technical skill level of the reader, who should be able to understand a system or operation from reading the documentation. This is especially true when users are nontechnical people. Yet, user documentation is often left until the last minute, written hastily by nonprofessional writers, and most often is considered an after-the-project nicety rather than a requirement of the project itself. For these reasons, documentation explaining a computer system's use and internal workings must be an integral part of any project. This effort will be budgeted and the assigned funds to be used for documentation only. Users of computer systems will approve all documentation developed for their use.

Technical documentation of a system's internal workings is the starting point for programmers to investigate problems or make changes to the system. This documentation is best written during system rollout so as to capture a fresh understanding of how the system works. Without technical documentation, every debugging effort must start with a time-consuming analysis of how the system works—where each data element originates from, how data is manipulated, and so on.

Every company keeps some sort of documentation library today. In some cases, it is in a dusty bookcase. More often, manuals and system documentation are scattered around the various work areas and programmer cubicles. All of these documents vary in how current they are. In many cases, no one knows what another person may have on their shelves and must search around even to borrow an old book. Most hardware and software vendors would be very happy to provide their documentation electronically (on an optical disk or via an Internet link), since printing mounds of manuals only distracts them from what they do best.

A well-maintained documentation library will provide an IT manager with ready access to the latest information, which will save on storage space since so many copies of so many things are not floating around, and greater agility for responding to user problem reports.

MANAGER'S TIP

Well-written software documentation is the bread and butter of a helpdesk. When users call, helpdesk analysts can answer most questions if they have access to current user documentation and can look up more detailed questions in the system documentation. The more information the helpdesk has, the fewer distractions that will be passed on to your technical staff. And the callers appreciate the quick answers to their questions!

[B]   Administrative and Support Project Documentation Types

The document types discussed in this chapter are not necessarily a comprehensive set nor is it expected that you would use all of these types for every project. You need to identify the types of data you may want to develop for the history and benchmarks of your project. Some of the documents you should expect will provide input for others. For some documents, you will provide the output. Committees may develop some documents. You need to be familiar with all possibilities so you are prepared to ask for the information and be prepared to give information to others when you determine this information exchange is needed for the success of the process.

An example of a project supportive document is the Business Justification. Once there is agreement that it includes sufficient data to continue with the project, this document becomes stable. It is used in many other documents as the justification for the development of activities and the acquisition of resources.

An example of a project administrative document is the schedule. The document is a living document throughout the life cycle of the project. The IS project manager uses this document to manage and to control the project. When this document is not used properly, then the IS project manager loses control. Perhaps a clear distinction between a supportive and an administrative document is to what level this document is used by the IS project manager to steer the project's direction.

[C]   Procedural Manuals or Guidelines Trend

Perhaps your company is developing its own project life-cycle manual or guidelines. This book's assumption is that procedural manuals are general rather than corporate-specific. As an IS project manager, you need to be aware of existing manuals or potentials for such development by working with your strategic manager to gather such data across divisional boundaries. Here are three reasons for this process:

1. Work definitions are clear.
2. Estimation standards are used, in particular for pricing.
3. Benchmarks are in place for incremental funding.

If your company follows this process, you need to work with procedural manual developers to create standard forms and checklists, especially for IS projects. Perhaps through corporate project procedures, your work will be made easier; for example, a jargon may be used that upper-level management will comprehend. Here are five potential benefits to this process:

1. Standard documentation is assured.
2. Paperwork is minimized.

3. Communication issues are eased.

4. A project team is unified.

5. A broader basis for data analysis is provided.

[D] Impacts on Level of Documentation

There are eight impact types using three constraints that determine the level of documentation output. These constraints are cost, time, and performance (skills), the basic project management resources. This paradigm might be used to analyze any project output level (see Table 16-1).

The paradigm illustrated in Table 16-1 permits you to determine the level of documentation. Whenever you have a variable *performance,* you may expect a lengthy document and get a short one, or vice versa. You may expect documents for presentation to upper management and not get them.

When *time* is variable, then what was planned today may not be valid tomorrow. If a time estimate for a document is given a range of three to five months, the document will probably be designed for the three-month benchmark and finished in five months.

When *cost* is a variable, you may have expected a simple black-and-white document on standard paper and you may get a multiple-color glossy. Any cost estimate that is variable for a document probably will be on the high side.

Impact Type 4 is a theoretical position that any project manager would like to have because it is close to the business manager's paradigm of budgeting. You may start at this level but conflicting forces will cause you to do a trade-off to another impact type. Impact Type 8 is a situation with no controls.

Table 16-1: Impact Types on Documentation Output

Impact Type	Cost	Time	Performance
1	Fixed	Variable	Variable
2	Fixed	Fixed	Variable
3	Fixed	Variable	Fixed
4	Fixed	Fixed	Fixed
5	Variable	Fixed	Variable
6	Variable	Variable	Fixed
7	Variable	Fixed	Fixed
8	Variable	Variable	Variable

MANAGER'S TIP

If you manage an IS project as a whole, then the project usually follows impact Type 6. Cost and time overruns may be acceptable, but not performance.

[E]   Potential Project Documents

Depending on the type of IS project involved, you might use just a few of these documents or you might need to use them all in a major effort that includes external corporate customers and vendors. Whatever the case, you will need the basic data from these documents. It is plausible that more than one Web server has been developed with just the Business Justification that a rival corporation has one, so we must have one also. As an IS project manager, you might look at the rival's Web site to determine the parameters of the requirement or you could ask of business management, "What business goals need to be achieved with the Web site?"

After a moment of laughter, you actually need to sit down with the strategic manager—that is, the manager accountable for the end project—and do a preproject review. This review was discussed in § 1.04[D], which considers the question "Is this project viable?"

MANAGER'S TIP

Several software vendors provide tools that simplify the collection of information for documentation and make it available over the corporate intranet. Some packages to check out include Zavanta from Comprose, Inc. (www.comprose.com) and onGO DMS from Uniplex Software (www.uniplex.com).

Two factors usually determine the number and size of documents: first, the requirements for data that come out of the preproject preview, and second, the requirements established by your corporation for project documentation. The following list includes only some of the document types that might be required in a large corporation:

- Market Analysis Report
- Business Justification
- Commercial Specification
- Organizational Chart
- Project Proposal
- Project Specification
- Content Agreement
- Schedule

- Design and Development Plan
- Initial Budget Estimate
- Initial Funding Requirements
- Project Cost Update
- Quality Plan
- Trial (Beta) Strategy
- Field Introduction Requirements
- Project Support Plan
- Customer Documentation Strategy
- Training Strategy
- Communication Plan
- Business Justification Updates
- Risk Assessment
- Third-Party Documents
- Project Manager's Log

An important aspect of documentation is that the more clearly it is written the closer you come to achieving expected goals. One purpose of documentation is to try to eliminate hidden agendas and to give you, the IS project manager, control of the project. Many a failed project has been managed well but was without proper documentation.

There are many different types of projects, but there is one common principle: Document the measurable activities you are going to do, and then document that you have achieved the measurements.

Market Analysis Report

The Market Analysis Report documents and verifies market opportunities. It can be global in nature or segmented into localized conditions. This report should be in agreement with the viability of project goals. The report should include how your project is to be introduced into the marketplace.

The report should justify project goals for the applications, features, and services. Base this input on such things as the following:

- Competition
- Customer needs
- Inferred commitments for special functions
- Market opportunities
- New governmental regulations
- Product surveys

The report should include adequate descriptions of the input so there is sufficient information to make design decisions. The report should also include revenue gains. The counter to this is a statement on revenue losses, if this project is not implemented.

A life-cycle statement identifies the various stages of this version of the computer system's market cycle such as introduction, growth, maturity, and replacement. It explains impacts on existing products by the introduction of the project's defined goals.

Business Justification

The Business Justification is the financial investment rationale for doing the project. Some of the following questions should be answered to develop the initial justification:

- How do this project's goals affect already established market policies and strategies?
- What are the impacts on your system?
- What are the requirements for success?
- What is the business (nonprofit) opportunity?
- What is the financial (revenue) opportunity?
- When must the goals be completed?

The Business Justification may include:

- Competition data
- Concept (as compared to definition)
- Distribution strategy
- Impact on products
- Market need
- Market window
- Required functions and characteristics
- Return on Investment (ROI)

For upper-level management to make decisions, a cost–benefit analysis might be included. It is important for the IS project manager to get necessary support, especially when the project crosses multiple business functions. One should expect to see a time line that shows the cost of obtaining the product, the value of having it, and the cost value (benefit) position.

Commercial Specification

The Commercial Specification is an evolution of the Business Justification and identifies the market need. The specification gives adequate requirement and limitation data for the design and development group(s). There should be design flexibility to achieve expectations. The Commercial Specification describes the expected *what* for the project's goals.

The Commercial Specification describes in *detail* the project requirements and the targeted market. The key to a successful system would include:

- Application of the project
- Customer participation
- Customer verification plans
- Design constraints
- Distribution methods
- Project maintenance
- Enterprise support requirements
- Key performance requirements and features
- Life cycle
- Market historical background
- Market window
- Portfolio information
- Special interfaces
- Standards
- Success criteria for the project
- Target costs versus revenues
- Usage of the project

This is a suggested unordered list. A one-page spreadsheet for a very large project can be effective and successful. For example, in one company, it took just three people to do such a spreadsheet, but they were very experienced people with a strong knowledge of the specific market.

Organizational Chart

There should be an organizational chart of the team, along with a description of major project responsibilities. The detail should be included in an appendix. There must be a detailed statement of the project manager's responsibilities. All other responsibility statements should be linked to this description. The format of the chart should be at your discretion or in accordance with corporate policy.

An organizational chart is usually a center of political intrigue because some people consider it a flag for potential promotion when someone is labeled a project leader or an operational manager. In the earlier days of project management, the tree organizational chart was used and temporary relationships were identified, which in some cases became permanent relationships after the project's end. This hierarchy resulted in issues about titles and power. Perhaps the best chart is a circular one with all the team members on it and a line from each identifying that person's project responsibilities. Very few people will be full-time on a project, even a large one. One might even use broken lines rather than solid lines in the chart. The essential point of a project's organizational chart is to show dynamic relationships and potential responsibilities.

The focus of a project's organizational chart is the project manager. This document needs to delineate the project manager's responsibilities, at a minimum:

- Prime position in the project
- Ability to resolve cross-functional conflicts
- Authority to cross-divisional boundaries to manage and control the project
- Control of project funds
- Final approval on project plan
- First in the project, last out of the project
- Participant in management decisions
- Prime liaison to customer
- Project team's voice
- Selector of subcontractors

Project Proposal

The Project Proposal is a formal response to the Commercial Specification that describes the requirements for a project. This proposal may include the following information:

- Commercial Specification compliance
- Definition of preliminary functions
- Hardware requirements
- Installation requirements
- Maintenance requirements
- Software requirements
- Software strategy

- Summary of commercial information
- Target costs based on preliminary development definition
- Testing requirements
- Verification requirements

Project Specification

The Project Specification is also a formal response to the Commercial Specification that specifies the requirements for a project. This specification may include the following types of information:

- Project definition from a technology (hardware and software) element point
- Project definition from a user, and external viewpoint
- Project estimated costs
- Project introduction strategy
- Project operational description
- Specific testing requirements
- Standards requirements
- Updates to the Proposal for the project

There should be a section on possible noncompliance. The section describes deviations from the Commercial Specification. It should be determined if noncompliance is permanent or temporary. When the noncompliance is permanent, the changes should be noted in the Design and Development Plan for a project through the change management process.

Content Agreement

The Content Agreement is the written "contract" between the development group and the marketing group as to the content and functions of the network. This document should include the following:

- Hardware requirements (availability status)
- How end users use the project's functional results
- Software features and requirements
- Start and end dates for completion of the project

Schedule

A schedule is a tool, not something that came off Mount Sinai. It is based on time estimates using experiences that in some cases may only be opinions.

The schedule and the budget that are seen by business managers are written in concrete. A project schedule should be seen as written with a pencil that can be erased as necessary.

The schedule can be as elaborate as required to implement your project. It should be useable. An example of a schedule is a flow chart with milestones and times. There could also be links to key players and groups and their responsibilities to the implementation of the project goals. A schedule should include the quality control milestones and the verification milestones.

One aspect of a schedule is the development of a critical path. One formal technique is called Critical Path Method (CPM), which is usually used in conjunction with another scheduling tool, Program Evaluation and Review Technique (PERT). Both of these techniques are discussed in more detail in Chapter 13. A highly simplified definition of a critical path is achieving the "must" requirements in a minimum of time. The critical path is a piece of concrete; it is a schedule in the truest sense in that it cannot be modified without approval by the customer.

Design and Development Plan

The Design and Development Plan drives the project Integration Plan that captures all major design and development deliverables and milestones for management tracking and reporting. The document may include the following items (if applicable):

- Project goals
- Project definition
- Project software structure description
- Project hardware structure description
- Project user definition
- Project market (summary from Project Specification)
- Risk assessment
- Responsibilities defined
- Resources defined
- Project milestones
- Verification dates

Initial Budget Estimate

The Initial Budget Estimate provides a view of the expected development costs. The estimate is usually based on the Preliminary Project Specification. The document gives estimates for direct labor as well as capital and expense requirements. Remember, the indirect costs should be considered as important as direct costs. This document is updated in the Project Integration Cost Update.

The Initial Budget Estimate might include a number of different types of cost estimates or parameters for developing these costs. Here are five possible cost types that might be considered in a project:

1. General—rough estimates that could be in a –50% to a +50% range
2. Definitive—clearly identified costs that could be in a –5% to a +5% range
3. Capital—level defined by the corporation with costs in a –15% to a +15% range
4. Feasibility—level determined by project size with costs in a –25% to a +25% range
5. Appropriation—level determined by criticality of project with a –20% to +20% range

The goal of the cost estimates is to lower the range for each based on experiences, standards, and benchmarks.

Initial Funding Requirements

The Initial Funding Requirements is a document for monitoring and reporting project costs at each major phase of implementation. There should be comparisons to the original funding document used to establish financial targets and expected milestones and deliverables. This document can also be included in the Project Cost Update.

Project Cost Update

The Project Cost Update document updates initial project cost estimates at each major key phase of implementation with comparison to the Initial Budget Estimate. The concern here is how the costs (actual expenditures) and revenues go into the budget (the financial plan). The costs are usually reported on a monthly basis.

Quality Plan

The Quality Plan defines the role of quality control in all phases of the project process. It also defines the deliverables, functions, and specific activities required of quality control to ensure the successful completion. Quality procedures that are specific to each project goal should also be identified in an appendix.

There should be a set of quality metrics that defines the various measures by which the quality of a new application is measured, attained, and controlled. This is also included in the project plan with the quality procedures.

The Quality Plan also summarizes the staff, resources, and equipment required by the quality control group to perform specific activities and to support a new application.

The Quality Plan should be updated before each major phase review to reflect changes.

The following five areas might be defined in separate documents but can be included in the Quality Plan as appendices:

1. Quality Policy
2. Quality Objectives
3. Quality Assurance
4. Quality Control
5. Quality Audit

A quality policy states the "what," promotes consistency, gives a view for outsiders (good for ISO 9000 compliance), specifies guidelines, and provides methods for updating the policy. This document is usually written by experts in this area. However, a corporate policy could be modified by the project team.

Quality objectives have to be measurable, realistic, comprehensible, and specific as to deadlines. The objectives specify the policy. Quality objectives should advance the project's progress, not frustrate it.

A quality assurance system identifies appropriate standards and benchmarks, seeks to eliminate risk through prevention, collects data for continuous improvement, maintains performance measures, and establishes criteria for quality audits. Quality assurance is the formal set of activities that ensure that the stated project goals meet the stated quality standards and benchmarks.

A quality control program determines items or events to be controlled, establishes the standards, provides the measurement tools, analyzes the test results, monitors any measuring devices, and writes the process documentation. Quality control is the formal set of activities that monitors the stated project process and ultimately is responsible for certifying that this process was successful.

A quality audit system identifies areas that can be improved, identifies that data collection is adequate, checks for product safety, and ensures that all applicable laws are followed.

Trial (Beta) Strategy

The Trial (Beta) Strategy identifies and locates the software and hardware elements in the project that are a part of the trial. It specifies when and by whom the trial should be conducted. This document provides a clear identification of the testing requirements plus the extent of the resources and capabilities to test.

Field Introduction Requirements

The Field Introduction Requirements document reflects the strategy and detailed plans to verify conformance to specification and functionality as defined in the Project Specification. This document should be concerned with such events as how the customers become users of the project.

Project Support Plan

The Project Support Plan ensures that the project is supportable in a market environment and should include a process for customer support. It defines the logistic support requirements of the project. This is the plan for the product after development that requires maintenance, service, and support (technical, documentation, and training). At least nine areas need to be considered:

1. Facilities
2. Hardware support
3. IS support
4. Maintenance support
5. Personnel
6. Supply support
7. Technical data (documentation)
8. Training
9. Transportation process

Customer Documentation Strategy

The Customer Documentation Strategy document provides how timely and quality project documentation becomes available. There really is a triad in quality: control, documentation, and training.

The strategy contains activities, schedules, and estimates that develop into a plan. The strategy is developed out of a set of negotiations among the product management group, the marketing group, and the development group. The strategy might include the following:

- Key activities
- Schedule
- Manpower requirements
- Cost estimates
- Production process

Training Strategy

The Training Strategy document can have two components: internal requirements and customer (external) requirements. The strategy should show how training is to be designed, developed, implemented, and verified. The emphasis of the strategy should be based on the customers' needs and expectations.

The strategy might include the following:

- Key activities
- Schedule
- Manpower requirements
- Cost estimates
- Implementation process

Communications Plan

The Communications Plan should include as a minimum:

- People doing the reporting
- People who receive the reports
- Types of reports to be sent
- When reports are sent (specific dates or after an event occurs)
- How reports are sent

The Communications Plan should have a global component as well as "local" communications processes. You may desire to have a local form where your developers communicate to each other on status.

Business Justification Update

This document assures the current view of the implementation of any project goals that have performance criteria meet previous commitments and management expectations. The update may have a one or more year(s) view of:

- Revenues
- Maintenance costs
- Investment
- Return on Investment (ROI)
- Customer impact

Risk Assessment

It is important that any risk assessment consider both threats and opportunities. The Risk Assessment should be reviewed by all the components of the team. The review should include at least representatives from each component (your group, marketing, and project users). A risk assessment should be done at least at every major phase of the project.

The risk assessment should be compared to established thresholds. An example of a threshold is that no action is taken until a certain number of errors are found.

MANAGER'S TIP

A good source for risk management is the Department of Defense's Directive (DoDD) 4245.7-M. This directive provides a standard for identifying technical risks, especially during the transitional period from development to production. It gives methods for reducing risks.

Another recommended guideline is the Office of Naval Acquisition Support Pamphlet (ONAS P) 4855-X, "Engineering Risk Assessment." This pamphlet gives guidelines for appropriate managers to monitor risk corrections.

The risk assessment might include considerations for the following risk types:

- External risks
  — Predictable (borrowing rate)
  — Unpredictable (natural hazards such as tornadoes)
- Internal
  — Technical (technological changes)
  — Nontechnical (labor strike)
  — Legal (patent acquisitions)

Business Affiliate Plan

The Business Affiliate Plan provides information when the project is to be developed by a third-party developer. The plan can consist of the following:

- Explanation for the need for a third-party developer
- How the third party doing the development qualifies
- What part the third party plays in the marketing program
- Training requirements
- Documentation requirements
- Quality control system description

Third-Party Market Agreement

The Third-Party Market Agreement provides the plans where the project is to be marketed by a third party. This agreement may include the following:

- Product content
- Delivery schedules
- Marketing strategy
- Verification strategy
- Documentation strategy
- Training strategy

Third-Party Service Plan

The Third-Party Service Plan provides how the project is to be serviced by a third-party developer. The question is, "Will the third party do customer service?" The plan may include the following details:

- Customer training
- Customer documentation
- Diagnostic tools
- Support process

MANAGER'S TIP

Do not forget ongoing maintenance, a service, if there is a lack of internal programming expertise.

Project Manager's Log

The Project Manager's Log is an electronic to-do list. It can be as simple as a Word document with a set of dates, each with a priority list. As action is taken, a comment about the action is noted such as, "I talked to John Smith about activity X and he said it is on schedule." At the end of the day, that day's actions are moved to the bottom of the file so the latest date is always at the top of the list. You can read what your priorities are for the next work-day. You can use the Find function to check for any occurrence of "John Smith" or any other item of interest. You also have a historical record of your administrative project duties, and you can also cite to other files such as conference minutes.

[F] Importance of the Communication Plan

All the measurable data gathered and all the clearly defined activities and estimates will mean absolutely nothing if they are not communicated to the correct people at the correct time. The plan should cover formal and informal, written and oral situations. The direction of the communication can be lateral, upward, or downward.

The communication process is affected by a number of factors. The plan needs to reflect ways to resolve these factors. Here are five important factors, out of many, that affect the process:

1. Business environment
2. Communication skills
3. Creditability
4. Frame of reference
5. Team member relationships

There are also barriers to the communication process. Many are similar to the factors. Here are five important barriers:

1. Communications skills
2. Evaluation skills
3. Feedback
4. Listening skills
5. Preconceived ideas

A number of internal and external forces can affect the communication process. Here are 10 such factors:

1. Business environment
2. Indirect communications
3. Memo management
4. Mixed messages
5. Partial transmission of data
6. Political environment
7. Power games
8. Restriction of data
9. Stereotyping
10. Technological environment

The method of communication also plays a significant role in the process. A visual presentation might convey something differently than a nonvisual one. One can reread a written presentation but not a spoken one. Different senses can have different effects on the communication process.

§ 16.02   MANAGEMENT INVOLVEMENT

[A]   Overview

Project documentation seems to be one of the most difficult areas for the various manager types to define their roles. However, the rule of involvement is easy:

- Strategic managers *monitor.*
- Tactical managers *seek consistency.*
- Operational managers *input measurable data.*

[B]   Strategic Manager and Documentation

The strategic manager and other interested upper-level managers should use the executive project summaries to monitor results. Formal structured feedback should be given, based on results. The strategic manager should give directions as required to ensure that corporate policies are followed, such as ensuring that the project's Quality Plan is consistent with the corporate one. This manager should resolve cross-divisional issues for documentation. For example, the documentation or training groups might have policies contrary to the project's requirements, such as a different format for documents or for the training to be given. The essential action is monitoring, not involvement in the details of the documents. This manager should state clearly what is required to ensure adequate monitoring.

[C]   Tactical Manager and Documentation

The tactical manager has the responsibility to develop executive summaries, a decoding of the technical jargon, so the strategic manager is comfortable with the project's status. You should use the documentation as a tool to control the project, but not to suppress initiative. You should keep the strategic manager informed immediately of the possibility that project documentation might sink. The difficult issue is to manage across divisions documentation requirements and standards. Many of the writers of the project documentation may be new to the project environment versus the business environment, and if also interested in project results, may be enthusiastic and cloud issues with details. Of course, you might have the reverse situation and not be able to find the details because of high-level highlights. You must distinguish between the support and the administrative types of documents. You must recognize when a document should be closed and another continue.

[D]   Operational Manager and Documentation

An operational manager has to recognize the need to compromise between documentation for a business goal and a project goal. Any operational manager needs to consider project documentation as a project team member rather than as an individual business manager. One should recognize the parallel dynamics of a project versus the usually hierarchical dynamics of a business. Any operational manager should lend her or his experiences to ensure that the documentation reflects the measurable goals of the project. Also when a milestone is achieved, the operational manager should ensure that the documentation reflects the accomplishments of the project to that milestone.

Exhibit 16-1: Documentation Checklist

Document	Yes	No	Start Date	End Date	Source
Market Analysis Report	❑	❑			
Business Justification	❑	❑			
Commercial Specification	❑	❑			
Organizational Chart	❑	❑			
Project Proposal	❑	❑			
Project Specification	❑	❑			
Content Agreement	❑	❑			
Schedule	❑	❑			
Design Development Plan	❑	❑			
Initial Budget Estimate	❑	❑			
Initial Funding Requirements	❑	❑			
Quality Plan	❑	❑			
Trial (Beta) Strategy	❑	❑			
Field Introduction Strategy	❑	❑			
Training Strategy	❑	❑			
Communications Plan	❑	❑			
Risk Assessment	❑	❑			
Third-Party Documents	❑	❑			
Project Cost Update	❑	❑			
Project Support Plan	❑	❑			
Customer Documentation Strategy	❑	❑			
Business Justification Update	❑	❑			
Other	❑	❑			
Notes:					

Exhibit 16-2: Project Report Form

Project		From Date:	
Preparer:		To Date:	

Schedule Status:	ON AHEAD BEHIND (Circle One)

Any Change to Project Goal:	Change Request by Customer/by Business:

Potential Issues:

Potential Impacts of Change:
  Time:
 	
  Cost:
 	
  Resources:
 	
  Performance:
 	
  Other:
	Approval Authority/Standard/Benchmark:

	Steps Required to Make Changes:

Comments:

On the CD-ROM

On the CD-ROM are:

1. Exhibit 16-1 Documentation Checlist.doc

2. Exhibit 16-2 Project Report Form.doc

3. Chapter 16 Overview.ppt—Chapter Overview, Documentation

Chapter 17

Miscellaneous Software Packages

§ 17.01   OVERVIEW

[A]   Objectives

At the end of this chapter, you will be able to:

- Identify four reasons for the use of general software applications for project management.
- List 10 potential project management requirements that might be made easier using a software application.
- List seven uses for administrative (office-type) applications project management.
- Identify 10 functions or features an office application might have to be useful for project management.
- Use Microsoft's Excel to do four simple examples for project managing: project activity sequences, time, resources, costs.

- Use Microsoft's PowerPoint to do four simple examples for project management.

- Use Microsoft's Word to do four simple examples for project management.

- Identify how the three managing levels might use Microsoft Office applications for your project.

[B]   Importance of General Software Applications

If you are unfamiliar with project management–specific applications, it is sometimes feasible to consider using standard spreadsheet, graphic, and word processing applications as project management tools. They might even be more useful to the project team as a whole than software specifically designed for project management. This approach does not preclude the use of a project management tool by the tactical (project) manager. In fact, this type of tool is necessary for doing what-if situations. This point about using a project tool was made earlier in Chapter 12 on Gantt charts and in Chapter 13 on PERT/CPM techniques.

MANAGER'S TIP

This chapter uses Microsoft's Excel, PowerPoint, and Word as points of discussion. The principles are the same for any spreadsheet, graphics package, or word processor. The use of packages from a single vendor makes the work easier because of product compatibility, interoperability, and portability issues.

MANAGER'S TIP

I have time-managed over a dozen documentation projects at one time using just one Microsoft Excel spreadsheet. It was also necessary to have an enforced time-sheet policy.

With support software applications, the team might develop a communications standard more easily. It is probable that your corporation already has standards for doing presentations using PowerPoint.

MANAGER'S TIP

Whatever presentation software is the agreed application of use, there should be a standard as to look. As project manager, you should be able to select slides to create an executive summary presentation with a minimum of changes. Nonstandard backgrounds and fonts can distract from the importance of the data.

Many books have been written on the use of general software applications, so you have available a potential database for acquiring the experiences of many people from many sources on these applications. In addition, you need to consider that in all likelihood some people within your organization are very knowledgeable about the applications and can be of assistance to the project team.

To summarize the above, the following are significant reasons for using general administrative types of applications for project management:

- Availability
- Familiarity
- Potential standards
- Many resources, including books and the Internet

[C]   Project Management Requirements and Software

Software may assist project management in four general areas:

1. Activity sequencing
2. Time estimating
3. Cost estimating
4. Resource defining

These areas are not just the responsibility of the tactical manager; the operational managers also have to be involved. No amount of software, however, can make up for a lack of project leadership. The use of any software needs to be determined by the project duration, resources, and the skills available to handle the tools. The following are 10 specific examples of project management requirements in which software might assist in the analysis of the many variables of a project (for example, the four areas above produce these 10 variables):

1. Cost analysis with variances
2. Critical paths
3. Data summaries
4. Forecasting
5. Graphic reports
6. Reports
7. Resource planning
8. Risk analysis
9. Scenarios ("what-if")
10. Time analysis with variances

With any project tool or a set of administrative applications, you might use them to do the following:

- Analyzing
- Monitoring
- Planning
- Predicting
- Reporting
- Scheduling
- Tracking

From the previous two lists, the following are software features and functions you need to consider:

- Control mechanism for time, costs, and resources
- Cost effectiveness through either purchase or lease
- Dates, calendar, and schedule
- Graphic display such as the Gantt chart
- Memory requirements for maximum efficiency
- Networking schema
- Report generator
- Sort capability
- System capacity adequate for a number of project activities
- Update capability

[D]   Four Project Management Examples with Excel

In this section, we look at four very simple examples of using Excel to assist you in managing and controlling a project for these core areas:

1. Project activity sequences (database)
2. Time (Gantt chart)
3. Resources (database)
4. Costs (spending analysis)

Constructing an Activity Sequence Database

Prior to using a project management tool such as PERT, you need to have an excellent sense of all your activity and pertinent data, such as the following:

- Measurable name ("write code" is too general, "code for a specific function or feature" is somewhat better)
- Operational group code (P for programming, D for documentation, T for training, PT for programming test, and so forth)
- Priority level to assist in developing a critical path; either 1, 2, and 3, or H (high), M (medium), and L (low)
- Start date
- End date
- Work requirement (hours or days)
- Cost estimate
- Special hardware requirement (Y or N)
- Documentation requirement (Y or N)
- Training requirement (Y or N)
- Optional notes (any special consideration)

The steps for constructing this database are as follows:

1. On the first row, label the columns with data from above such as task, group, priority, and so forth.
2. Beginning with the second row, enter the data as you receive it; you do sorting later.
3. At any time you can highlight *all* the cells with data and do a sort.
   a. Click on data on the Menu bar.
   b. Click Sort.
   c. Select your sort options, up to three columns in either ascending or descending order.
   d. Click on OK.
   e. If you want to keep this sorted worksheet, do a File Save As with a new file name.

You can determine many things from this basic database. Here are five of the sort possibilities:

1. *Group* and *start date* give you task order by group.
2. *Start date* gives you all tasks in order
3. *Work requirements* can give you shortest task to longest task or in reverse.
4. *Cost estimates* can give you from the least amount to the largest amount, or vice versa.

5. You can do sorts so you identify readily all tasks that have special requirements such as hardware, documentation, and training.

You might also total the work requirement and cost-estimates columns, then in the cell one down, divide this total by number of tasks to get an average. After a sort, you can find the median value for either of these columns.

Because you have readily available start and end dates, you can easily produce a Gantt chart and in addition have the input to do PERT. This type of database makes it easy for operational managers to verify their data.

An additional method in constructing this database is having the team agree on a template and input, and then have each operational manager construct his or her own worksheet. At that point, you can then merge all the worksheets as one.

MANAGER'S TIP

Remember not to use red and green as contrasting colors because they carry a high emotional significance and may be difficult to read by someone who is colorblind.

Constructing a Simple Gantt Chart

There are nine steps in constructing a simple Gantt chart in an Excel worksheet:

1. Starting with the second column, place the project time line across the first row (days, weeks, and so forth).
2. Beginning with the second row, place the tasks (major tasks could be made bold, and subtasks, normal).
3. Using the color option, format the rows to represent the durations of tasks in a dark color (update using a light color).
4. Select the cell or cells you want to format.
5. Click Format on the Menu bar.
6. Click on Cells.
7. Click on Patterns.
8. Under Cell Shading Color, click colored box of preference.
9. Click on OK.

Constructing a Resource Database

A resource database can be built on the same principle as the activity sequence database. By having the operational managers each do a worksheet that identifies resources, in particular staff members, you have a tool for determining if a skill is actually going to be available for a task. It is possible, surely due to an oversight, that a task is scheduled but the person with the required skill is not available. This database, with the activity sequence database, might assist you identifying any such occurrences.

This database might include the following information:

- Person's name
- Available start date
- Available end date
- Associated task
- Group code
- Allocation of time
- Cost estimate
- Special requirements (training or equipment; enter none if none required)

A person might require several rows in the database if there are special requirements or more than one set of availability dates. By doing sorts you can easily identify all the team members who need training and the type of training required. There should be a standard on how special requirements are to be entered into the worksheet.

Constructing a Spending Analysis Worksheet

A spending analysis is not a budget analysis. A spending analysis looks at the total spending estimates for project administration and each of the operational areas and the variance by month. A budget analysis would provide more detail in specifying budget lines.

An Excel worksheet would be constructed in the following manner:

1. Beginning on the first row, second column, enter the month in which the project begins. (It doesn't have to be January.)
2. In the first column, second row, enter **project adm.** and then in the following rows enter each operational area.
3. Fill in the estimates for spending per month per group.
4. Make a summary row of estimates by month.
5. In the column after the months, make a summary of estimates by group.
6. Skip a row or two.
7. Copy the information from the first column.
8. As actual spending figures come in from each group, enter in this row.

9. Create total spending row and spending to date column.

10. Skip a row or two.

11. Copy the information from the first column set.

12. In the cell next to *enter project adm.* enter =*sum* (cell of project adm. variance/B2).

13. To make the cell display percentage:

    a. Click on Format on the Menu bar.

    b. Click on Number.

    c. Click on Percentage.

    d. Check to see that Decimal Place box has 2.

    e. Click OK.

When the variance is less than 100 percent, you keep going; but when it is greater than that and you are surprised, you need to resolve the issue *yesterday*. The practical goal is to have an overall variance percentage of less than a hundred.

[E] Four Project Management Examples with PowerPoint

A PowerPoint presentation can be used to present an attitude rather than a set of facts. In reality, there are many types of presentations. The following four types of presentations are important to you as a project manager:

1. Executive summaries
2. Team meetings
3. Data gathering
4. Customer presentations

In all cases, you should develop presentation standards. Using standards for presentations has its advantages:

- When a Web page is used, there is a common look and feel as to data presentation.
- Operational presentations can be merged into presentations for executive summaries with a minimum of administrative changes, or slides can be created quickly through cut-and-paste.
- Through experience, one can create new presentations quickly.
- Through experience, the audience can expect a certain consistency of informational flow.

To assist you in developing standards, PowerPoint includes a number of templates. There are templates for slide design, color schemes, and animation schemes. A search of the Internet will find many different design templates for just about any possible look you can imagine.

MANAGER'S TIP

Some of these templates use a serif font type such as Times New Roman. It is recommended that you use a sans serif font such as Arial. Displayed and Web pages are easier to read with a font such as Arial. In addition, the team should consider any corporate standards there may already be for PowerPoint presentations.

Presentations for Executive Summaries

An important function of an executive summary is to persuade. You need to present bottom-line issues in a top-level manner. Significant points of project status should be comprehensible quickly. You do not create a slide with details but use color to make the slide easier to read. For example, if you wanted to present the status of all the operational areas as to schedule, you could simply list them on the slide in various colors as follows:

- Green—Ahead of schedule
- Yellow—On schedule
- Red—Behind schedule

With this technique, you do not have to have a chart with days ahead or behind, then do an analysis. You get someone's attention in a hurry. You can use the note function to give detailed information at the presentation, or to give to the strategic manager after the presentation.

Executive summary presentations should be short. If you have a half-hour presentation, plan to speak for no more than 15 minutes with 8 to 12 slides. If you do speak for the full half hour, do not expect the audience to believe you have delivered a professional presentation.

There should be an emphasis on graphics rather than text. By using the graphic capabilities of Excel, one can develop a professional-looking executive summary.

In addition, there is a simple thing you can do to make an executive summary easier to present: Ask the strategic manager for his or her expectation for the presentation. I have seen where a corporate vice-president defined his presentations' expectations (standards) to his globally located directors. At the quarterly meetings, the presentations were consistent in tone and one could easily compare common situations (the budget) among the different divisions.

Presentations for Team Meetings

A basic task of a project manager is to manage and control events. You can use PowerPoint presentations for this task during team meetings. While you should have sent out the meeting's agenda earlier, it is an excellent idea to have it as a presentation. By using the transition feature, you can bring up one point at a time. In addition, in the presentation you can give the time allocated for each item so that there is an even flow on all the items rather than having a rush at the end or running the meeting overtime.

As said earlier, use a sans serif font such as Arial. In addition, put only a few items per slide. What is readable on your monitor may not be readable in the conference room. Consider the size of the meeting room; what looks good as a 14-point font on your screen should probably be a 24-point font to be easily read on a projection screen.

The most important time for a PowerPoint presentation is the first meeting. This presentation will set the tone for all further meetings. If it demonstrates that you know the direction of the project and points to the requirements to be considered to achieve success, you have made a big step forward.

In the first presentation, you need to outline project needs in these areas (project scope foundation):

BENCHMARKS

- Performance
- Validation
- Risk
- Data
  - Historical
  - Marketing

TIME PARAMETERS

- Start date
- Milestones
- End date

SELECTION CRITERIA

- Skills
  - Type
  - Level
- Time lines

- Resources
  - — People (skills)
  - — Equipment
  - — Materials

COMMUNICATIONS

- Reports
- Documentation
- Training

TEAM

- Customers
- Support
- Technical
- Management
- Marketing

The presentation should continue with the requirements for the scope definition:

METHODOLOGY

- Resources
- Integration
- Communications
  - — Who
  - — When
  - — How
  -   Why
  - — Where
- Risk analysis
- Support services

COSTING

- Direct
  - — Human
  - — Time

— Equipment

— Materials

- Indirect

TIMING

- Responsibilities
- Support
- Management
- Customers
- Technical

QUALITY CONTROLLING

- Design
- Development
- Implementation
- Testing
- Validation

All other project meetings will be a variation on one or more of the areas above. There will be meetings for data gathering, for discussion of status, and so forth; but this first meeting sets the framework for all the others to the project's conclusion.

Presentations for Data Gathering

You will have a number of data-gathering meetings. You can present a series of slides for a form, to show how it should be filled out. Do not give one slide with one completed form, but a slide per box on the form or a set of related boxes.

You also may use presentations to stimulate brainstorming as to the types of data required. You can use either key words such as "code activities" or questions such as "What code activities are required for this piece of the product or project?"

Presentations for Customers

The presentations should reflect what the customer is getting for funds expended. Unless there is a special request for it, minimize the technical terminology. The presentations should be user-friendly. The key principle is to use a minimum of words in large fonts and dynamic, positive graphics. One should use graphics when possible to express the goals of the project. Do not give technical details about how a new server goes into the network for accounting; show a graphic of the IS network, highlighting the parts of the network that are impacted by the installation of the new server.

If the status of time is to be discussed, use Gantt charts with colors other than red and green. Do not use PERT/CPM activity diagrams.

Don't conclude from the above recommendations that you should speak down to the customers because they may not be technically literate. This conclusion is far from the truth. You should do presentations that reflect the *customer's* position, the one in need, and the one with the money.

MANAGER'S TIP

For any presentation, a copy of the presentation should be printed and passed out for the meeting. The timing of the distribution of this documentation depends on the presentation itself. For example, for team member meetings the copies of the presentation should be passed out before the meeting, so the team members have time to prepare comments and questions. Also during the presentation team members can take notes on the slides that are being presented. For customer meetings, you may wait to pass out copies until after the presentation. This delay ensures that your audience is listening to you at your pace and not looking ahead to the end of the presentation.)

[F]   Four Project Management Examples with Word

There is a tendency to think of the use of Word as a text editor (word processor) only. However, as a project manager, you can use Word as a valuable communications tool for project status. Beyond examples given, think of ways you can use it with e-mail. Status reports can be sent to all the team members quickly.

Linking and Embedding Excel Tables into Word Project Reports

Summary tables discussed in the Excel worksheet examples could be either included or linked into a Word document. There are two methods for creating a table:

1. From the Menu bar, choose Table → Insert Table.
2. From the Standard bar, click the Insert Table button (icon).

For you as the project manager, the insertion of a table is not so important as the linking of an Excel worksheet to a Word document. Why is this feature important to you? This technique permits you to keep data updated on a regular basis without necessarily having to rewrite a new weekly or monthly status report. If modifications are required, you do the changes in the Excel worksheet rather than worrying about the editing process in Word. Again, you should link from the spending analysis worksheet, not from the document to the worksheet. This method permits you to generate a report without the consumption of a large amount of time.

Here are the nine basic steps for linking an Excel worksheet to a Word document:

1. Open the Excel worksheet that you want to link to the Word document.
2. Highlight (select) the data to be linked.
3. Click the Copy button, or press Ctrl+C.
4. Open the Word document that is to receive the linked data.
5. Place the cursor at the location where data is to appear.
6. From the Menu bar choose Edit → Paste Special.
7. In the Paste Special dialog box, click the Paste: radio button.
8. Select the method the worksheet is to appear in the Word document.
9. Click OK.

MANAGER'S TIP

The link between the worksheet and the document must be broken from the worksheet file.

You can select any data or all of the data from an Excel worksheet to create a special status report. The opposite of linking is embedding data. Embedding is the storing of a single Excel file's data in the Word document. In addition, embedding permits you to edit the data within the Word document.

MANAGER'S TIP

The binder feature of Microsoft Office permits you to have one file with Word, PowerPoint, and Excel. This feature may not be available in products from other vendors.

When should you use linking? When should you use embedding? Linking might be used for any of these reasons:

- The file size needs to be small.
- The file needs to be updated dynamically.
- Data needs to be controlled.

MANAGER'S TIP

All receivers of the file must have the same software used to create the data and the document. (This requirement means the version of the application might be significant.)

Embedding might be used for any of these reasons:

- The file is to be given to other team members.
- Use of a single file is convenient.
- Data may be edited by a receiver of the file.

MANAGER'S TIP

Remember, you lose control of data accuracy if you embed data in a document and a file's size with embeds becomes too large.

Using a Newsletter

The use of a newsletter is both creative and a positive method for presenting project information. It was stated in § 16.01[F] that all the measurable data gathered and all the clearly defined activities and estimates will mean absolutely nothing if they are not communicated to the correct people at the correct time. In addition, the direction of the communication might be lateral, upward, or downward.

The communication process is affected by at least five factors:

1. Business environment
2. Communication skills
3. Credibility
4. Frame of reference
5. Team member relationships

A newsletter might assist you in smoothing out the impact of these factors because the method of communication can play a significant role in the informational process. A newsletter may give you a more positive environment to present project information than e-mail. In addition, e-mail can be more easily misinterpreted than a printed newsletter. Team members can be praised for their successes in a more public manner. While a newsletter may take more time, it does look more professional than any e-mail. A newsletter might be used to keep motivational slogans and important milestones in the forefront. In addition, production requirements might be presented using humorous cartoons or some dynamic graphics.

MANAGER'S TIP

E-mail is a "delivery system." A newsletter can be either printed and distributed or sent by e-mail as an attachment. If the newsletter is distributed as an e-mail attachment, it could be an Adobe file so changes cannot be made as the document is sent along.

Using a Web Page

You might create a special Web page on your intranet to have links to a server that includes documents, worksheets, and presentations. Word documents can quickly be converted to HTML documents by selecting File → . Save as HTML.

As an IS project manager, you should have team members who are skilled in this technique. What is important here is the idea of using a special Web page for assisting in the communication process.

Using Word to Create Project Forms

Word can be used to create both printed and electronic forms and checklists. Is this capability valuable? On the CD-ROM that comes with this book there are a number of forms and checklists that might be used with your project.

As shown in earlier chapters, you need to have checklists to standardize the gathering of data and to ensure that all the known basic data are identified and common processes are completed. Forms need not be elegant, but they should be professional looking.

Any well-written book on Word should give you the dozen or so core steps it takes to create a form. It is important before you start to have either a sketched or an existing form as a guideline.

§ 17.02   MANAGEMENT INVOLVEMENT

[A]   Overview

Not all managers may be involved in the direct use of office-type applications for project management. However, all managers are affected by the communication process generated by the output, whether they are givers, presenters, or receivers of data. All of them should be concerned with how office-type applications can be used to assist in a better communication process.

[B]   Strategic Manager and Support Software Applications

The strategic manager should work with the tactical manager in defining the executive summary expectations. The strategic manager should make the tactical manager aware of any standards or templates available for output from Microsoft Office applications.

[C]   Tactical Manager and Support Software Applications

There is one error that will do you in quicker than anything else. It is not a too-small font. It is not too-crowded slides. It is not a presentation without graphics. It is not a presentation with either too few or too many slides. It is a misspelled word. I have seen a group vice-president ignore a presentation once he saw a misspelled word.

The second danger is poor grammar, but you can get away with it more than you think you can. Most will not realize that the Queen's English dictates "data are" rather than "data is," but be careful.

You need to consider 11 questions when using office-type applications to do project management:

1. Is an application available for all to use?
2. How effective can I be with different applications to get the most for the least amount of effort?
3. Are there standards available on output of the applications?
4. What are the criteria for an executive summary presentation?
5. What are the criteria for a customer status report presentation?
6. Do I have available someone skilled in one or more of the office-type applications?
7. What standards are required so operational inputs can be used easily, and merged together to develop project reports?
8. What templates are required to create presentations?
9. How can I use a newsletter effectively?
10. How can I use a Web page for project management?
11. What is the cost of application?

[D]   Operational Managers and Support Software Applications

Operational managers should first consider how they might use the output generated from the office-type applications for their teams. Second, they should be involved in the development of standards since they will be the basic source for information that is used in presentations, checklists, forms, databases, and so forth.

In many ways, the operational managers can apply the ideas in this chapter to their operational groups on a smaller scale, if not to the project, at least to their day-to-day business management.

On the CD-ROM

On the CD-ROM is:

1. Chapter 17 Overview.ppt—Chapter Overview, Miscellaneous Software Packages

---

Section Three

Support Project Management Analysis

This section describes three important types of analysis: legacy software and hardware, profitability, and the abstract IS network infrastructure. Scalability, interoperability, and portability are the foundations of the discussion. In addition, the information in these chapters is related to Sections One and Two.

Chapter 18

Legacy Software and Hardware

§ 18.01   OVERVIEW

[A]   Objectives

At the end of this chapter, you will be able to:

- Define IS infrastructure.
- State the essential reason why legacy software and hardware have to be considered in any IS project.
- Identify basic concrete infrastructure components.
- Identify basic abstract infrastructure components.
- Identify basic interconnectivity issues such as bandwidth, device configuration, network configuration, protocol implementation, and traffic loads.

- Identify the basic issues for service servers: chat, directory, e-mail, news, and search.

- Identify the fundamental issues for access servers: certification, firewalls, gateways, proxies, routers, and Web.

- Use a method to evaluate browsers.

- State three reasons for considering alternate browsers.

- Identify how the three managing levels might be involved in legacy issues for an IS project.

[B]   IS Infrastructure Definition

IS infrastructure is another area that sets IS project management apart from general project management. An IS infrastructure is both concrete and abstract. The concrete components are easy to define; they are any hardware or software involved in the transmission of electronic data across a server-based network. Hardware can be workstations, servers, or cables. Software is applications, system management tools, or graphical user interfaces, or GUIs. The abstract components are really descriptions of functionality of the IS network such as stability, interoperability, and compatibility. Then you have bandwidth—is it concrete or abstract? It might be considered a definition that relates the concrete and the abstract.

MANAGER'S TIP

Telephony and television are both concerned with data transmission; however, neither type in a traditional sense is based on server architecture or protocols.

[C]   Legacy Infrastructure and IS Project Management

Any IS project affects the legacy infrastructure (network). The impact on your legacy infrastructure has to be a major consideration when you do a preproposal review of a project and ask the question, "Is the project viable?" You should have a checklist to assist you in this review, because the obvious may be overlooked. The areas that may be overlooked easily are the abstract ones, but the impacts on these may be the ones that bring risk to the project. Remember, legacy is the state of your network one minute ago.

MANAGER'S TIP

This chapter's focus is to assist you in developing the checklist for the preproposal review. See Chapter 1 for the types of questions you should be asking during this review.

[D]   Concrete Components

Concrete components or objects give the structure to the IS network. They are things you can see either with your eyes or with GUIs (management tools).

The most important component is the people. These are the users (internal and external, customers, vendors), technicians (support, development, maintenance), administrative support (training, documentation, procurement, finance, and so on), and you. Without people there is no need for an IS network. An associated component is the organization. The organization (the corporation, the company, or the division) has its policies, goals, practices, locations, and financial sources.

The primary components or objects of the hardware structure can be categorized as hosts, central processing units (CPUs), intermediate nodes, and peripheral nodes. The structure can be visualized using either the client-server or the object-oriented paradigm. Whichever paradigm is used, the fundamental visualization process is the same. One paradigm divides the structure into types of "actors," the other is a world of object types. The process is a breakdown from the highest compound name down to the lowest level, the actor's or object's simple name.

Software components include databases, development tools, GUIs, applications, server software, protocols, system kernel, and code (source and executable).

The lists shown in Tables 18-1 to 18-13 are arbitrary. They should help you to more easily visualize your infrastructure and create your own unique

Table 18-1: Host Components of an IS Network

Hosts	Functionality
Mainframe	The central processing unit (CPU) of a computer system
Servers	The components in a distributed environment that act for a set of clients as functions, such as access, or as a service, such as a newsgroup

Table 18-2: CPU Components of an IS Network

CPUs	Functionality
Mainframes	The central processing units that do not include remote devices or peripherals
Operating Systems	The basic software that defines the fundamental operations of a computer such as inputs and outputs

Table 18-3: Intermediate Nodes Components of an IS Network

Intermediate Nodes	Functionality
Bridges	Used to connect two or more networks and forward packet data between them
Firewalls	Used to prevent unauthorized access into a network, maybe either software or hardware
Gateways	Used to perform format translation from one system to another
Hubs	Used as central points to move data from one network to another
Routers	Used to direct the path flows of network traffic
Switches	Used to divert data from one network to another
Terminals	Used as access points or to transfer data—modems, printers
Workstations	Used as points of data manipulation by a person

Table 18-4: Peripheral Nodes Components of an IS Network

Peripheral Nodes	Functionality
Faxes	Facsimile devices used to forward images of printed matter from one location to another
Printers	Devices that produce printed matter

Table 18-5: Application Components of an IS Network

Applications	Functionality
Operating systems	Used to do the basic functions of the computer
User	Used to extend the abilities of the user such as word processors or spreadsheets

Table 18-6: Code Components of an IS Network

Code	Functionality
Executable	State of a programming language that does the operations
Source	State of a programming language as written

Table 18-7: Database Components of an IS Network

Databases—Proprietary and Public	Functionality
Buffer	Space to store data so it can be transmitted smoothly through the network
Cache	CPU fast storage buffer
Number of users	Users include people, servers, peripherals

Table 18-8: Disk Components of an IS Network

Disk	Functionality
Cache	Disk fast storage buffer
Controller	Moves data between the system memory and permanent storage
Drivers	Software used to define specific functions between two network components such as a workstation and a printer
Load balance	Process of defining adequate flow of data traffic

Table 18-9: GUI Components of an IS Network

Graphical User Interface	Functionality
Server	The visual component that permits you to see a structured view of data
System	The visual component that permits an administrator to see a structured view of data flow

Table 18-10: Memory Components of an IS Network

Memory	Functionality
Cache	Memory fast storage
Size	Virtual RAM or ROM
Speed	Degree of effective accessibility

Table 18-11: Protocol Components of an IS Network

Protocols	Functionality
Intranet	Protocols such as Ethernet and Token-Ring overlaid with TCP/IP
Internet	TCP/IP Suite
System	Protocols based on LAN or WAN traffic

Table 18-12: Server Components of an IS Network

Server Protocols	Functionality
Chat	Internet Relay Chat (IRC)
Directory	Lightweight Directory Access Protocol (LDAP)
E-mail	Post Office Protocol (POP), Standard Mail Transfer Protocol (SMTP), Interactive Mail Address Protocol (IMAP)
News	Network News Transport Protocol (NNTP)
Search	Z39.50 Standard—Wide Area Information Server (WAIS)

Table 18-13: Tool Components of an IS Network

Tools	Functionality
Blueprints	Network maps—process flows, detailed wiring routes, equipment locations, structure representations, and geographical views.
Equipment diagrams	Used for performance tuning and design refinements
Inventories	Used for resource accountability—hardware (spares control) and software (version control)
Management	GUIs to identify bottlenecks and assist in real-time maintenance. Aid in cleaner configurations.
Performance analyzers	GUIs to tighten vendor specifications as to operational performance standards
Policies (disaster, security)	Standards for expected network failure rates and recovery times for various failure types
Process flow charts	Either in electronic or in written format. Ability to meter data movement (traffic levels and types) from any two points in the network
Protocol analyzers	GUIs to establish the effectiveness of protocol configurations and to determine if traffic is within stated standards.
Wiring route map	Documentation to adhere to TIA/EIA standards

checklist to resolve the question, "Is the project viable?" This checklist should assist you in answering these general questions:

- Does this affect [the component]?
- How extensively does this project affect [the component]?
- What changes may impact [the component] because of the project?
- Why does this project affect [the component]?
- What location(s) is (are) affected by the project?
- When do the project's results affect [the component]?

Most of the questions seem straightforward. The last question means: Do the project results impact the infrastructure at a given hour each day or a given day of the week, say Saturday?

[E]   Abstract Components

Abstract components are the purposes, utilities, and flows of the IS network. They are things you cannot see either with your eyes or with GUIs (management tools). Both the concrete and the abstract are important for understanding the configuration of a system. The abstract components are the results of trying to describe the concrete capabilities.

Within the administrative planning process, you can have a question such as, "How complex is it to maintain the application or the tool?" With this technique, you can see how many basic questions you can develop to ask vendors, users, and your development team. To assist you further, Table 18-14 are two dozen abstractions to go with the concrete items previously given.

Table 18-14: Abstract Components of an IS Network

Abstraction	Definition
Accessibility	The degree to which a user can use a system or the process for entering a system
Compatibility	The degree to which the system components interact successfully with one another
Complexity	The degree to which the system architecture has been developed. Two computers connected is simple; 100 computers, both mainframe and personal, is complex.
Cost	Amount to be paid to maintain and use a system—visual and hidden

Table 18-14 (*Continued*)

Abstraction	Definition
Design	The plan of the system—purposeful and haphazard
Environment	The conditions or circumstances of the system
Flaws	Things in the system that are not a part of the design plan
Functionality	The number of functions or abilities within a system
Interoperability	To what degree the various system components work with one another successfully
Integration	The process of organizing the various components to act as one
Maintainability	To what degree maintenance updating is required to ensure user requirements of the system
Optimization	To what degree the components contribute efficiently to the ultimate capabilities
Platform dependency	To what degree the system components require a particular software or hardware environment
Purpose	The goal of the system as defined by the users
Reliability	To what degree the various components continue to function at the required level
Redundancy	To what degree duplicate components are required to ensure a continuous flow of data
Scalability	The degree to which one can add to a system without a major change in design
Security	The degree to which system data is protected
Sophistication	From a user view, how simple or user-friendly the system is
Speed	The amount of time required to move data from one point in a system to another
Stability	To what degree a system can be run without breakdowns—minor and major
Time	The interval between the start and finish of an operation
User friendliness	The degree to which a user can work without getting frustrated
Wiring infrastructure	The wiring structure that connects all the network components

[F]   Interconnectivity Issues Defined

Interconnectivity may be the fundamental issue that has to be resolved for any IS project. The issue certainly involves configuration, and any time a new protocol is added to enhance the network, this issue includes a huge potential for risks.

Interconnectivity issues vary from device to device and from vendor to vendor. However, you should consider common basic performance issues for any device. Below are 10 issues:

1. Bandwidth
2. Communication latency
3. Device configuration
4. Network configuration
5. Network segmentation
6. Protocol implementation
7. Protocol mix
8. Traffic loads
9. Transmission latency
10. Wiring infrastructure

For any interconnectivity device from any vendor, ensure that you comprehend the claims and, if necessary, ask for validation to your satisfaction. Remember that the performance specifications given are based on a particular configuration, load, protocol implementation, and to a specific level of IS network integration.

Gateways

A standard definition for a gateway is a server that performs protocol conversion between different types of networks and applications. For an IS network, consider a gateway to be the access server from an intranet to the Internet. Its counterpart would be the firewall that can be considered the entrance into your intranet from the Internet. The following are some of the functions or characteristics of a gateway:

- It is bidirectional.
- It can be a major bottleneck if it is not configured correctly.
- It can have multiple ports.
- It handles multiple protocol translation.

Three of these points are technical; however, the configuration point needs to be considered seriously in any preproposal review of the project.

Is the customer getting a new server and/or does the customer want to use an existing server but with special requirements? When the customer is asking for a gateway, does this mean there is also a requirement for a firewall? With this question come all the questions as to level and type of security.

Bridges

A bridge is a signal repeater that filters traffic between local area network (LAN) segments. The segments can be different types, such as one can be an Ethernet and the other a Token Ring. The following are functions or characteristics of a bridge:

- It is bi-directional.
- It buffers packets.
- It builds tables that indicate nodes by bridge port.
- It can have multiple ports.
- It can be slow on large networks with many nodes.
- It can impact latency negatively.
- It can use too much bandwidth.
- It can impact Internet performance positively.
- It has limited addresses.
- It uses the same overhead for small and large packets.

The following are two questions you need to resolve in the preproposal review when you see that this component is affected by the project:

1. How will the new requirement for bandwidth impact my legacy bandwidth?
2. What new tools are required to manage the packet transmissions?

Hubs

A hub, or concentrator, concentrates multiple network connections into a manageable configuration. Some of the functions or characteristics of a hub are:

- It does not check packet address.
- It functions as a passive wiring concentrator.
- It may have backplanes to increase bandwidth.
- It has varying performance based on configuration.
- It is useful for broadcasts and multicasts.

The hub becomes important for projects that require multicasts. Also important is the consideration of the impacts on the network as to bandwidth and other traffic issues.

Repeaters

A repeater replicates a decaying transmission signal to extend the signal's normal transmission length. The following are some of the functions or characteristics of a repeater:

- It is bi-directional.
- It boosts poor-quality signals.
- It drops simultaneously arriving packets.
- It enforces protocol specification on excessive designed networks.
- It enhances the chances for corrupt data.
- It increases overall bandwidth utilization.
- It operates bit by bit at the physical level.
- It does not depend on a protocol.

A repeater is important for any project where stable data transmission is critical. As with many of the other network components, one must also define bandwidth requirements.

Routers

A router is an interconnectivity device that forwards data packets from one LAN to another or from one WAN to another. A router differs from a bridge in that it processes protocols at the data and network layers of the OSI model. The following are some of the functions or characteristics of a router:

- It is bi-directional.
- It can act as a firewall for segmented traffic.
- It can have multiple ports.
- It can handle multiple protocols.
- It can create broadcast storms.
- Compacts protocol information to forward packets to their destinations
- May cause performance degradation because of a high potential for buggy software
- Is much slower than a bridge
- Provides traffic filtering, forwarding, and routing
- Is slower than a repeater
- Can be a source for transmission latency

- Is susceptible to network-level protocol translations
- Uses the same overhead for small or large packets
- Has a variety of protocols

If the idea arises to use a router for security, one should consider alternate solutions. When speed is a concern, a router should be considered after either a bridge or a repeater.

Switches

A switch can come in at least two flavors—matrix, or network, and virtual. Because of the dynamic changes in this area, there are many different types of implementations. A matrix or network switch is fundamentally a shared media technology that acts like a wiring concentrator. A virtual switch may be the ultimate in microsegmentation technology because it includes only nodes (source and destination) in a temporary (virtual) network. The virtual switch is based on telephony technology.

[G]   Service Servers Defined

A server can be defined as any device not on the client side of the network. Perhaps it can be narrowed to two functions—a service or an access. For a project customer, you may have to explain that there may not be five physically different basic Internet servers, but there are five virtual servers. In other words, a service server is a metaphor for a network device that handles one or more network services.

There are five "basic" service servers that most users think of as the intranet or the Internet. These service servers are:

1. Chat
2. Directory
3. E-mail
4. News
5. Search

A difficulty in defining a service server is there is no simple way to view a service. The basic services can be viewed from one or more of the following four perspectives:

1. Application
2. Communications
3. Database
4. Storage

The big issue, of course, is legacy software design and technology. There can be significant differences between software written in 1997 and 1999 (upward compatibility, but not downward). There can even be configuration issues within a specific version of software. It might be as simple as one person using Times New Roman 12-point font, while another person uses Arial 10-point font. There are graphics in the document that have to appear in a particular position on a page. The correct positioning probably may not happen because of this one configuration difference.

MANAGER'S TIP

The manuscript for this book was written in Times New Roman 11-point font. If this manuscript had been done using Times New Roman 12-point font, there would have been an additional one to two pages for every 10 pages in the original manuscript.

Chat Servers

One of the earliest tools of online services was the ability to chat. The Internet Relay Chat (IRC) protocol is used. Why is this protocol important in an IS network? By setting up groups with special interests that are made up of people in diverse areas and locations, perhaps new ideas can be developed to improve corporate productivity. Also there may be an increase of team sense across the corporation—an elimination of "them" and "us."

The technical issues involved are installation, maintenance, and available platforms. Above these issues are administration and control. A technological issue is the amount of bandwidth required.

There have been significant technological changes in the chat environment; among them is the development of a graphical interface. Changes that are coming include Virtual Chat and the use of Java applets to enhance the system.

When determining the requirements for a chat system these items should be in the mix:

- Sales support requirements
- Real-time support needs
- Desire for special interest groups
- Policy for employee awareness on corporate direction and issues

Directory Servers

The ideal directory server is to have a single entry point that controls all employee information. The system would have an access privilege procedure.

Some people should be able to see a person's telephone and department numbers. Only people in Human Resources should be able to retrieve the full information. Besides tracking employee information, a directory service should keep up with application resources, server configuration, server operation, and of course, access data. Based on local requirements, this information should be available from any terminal.

The controlling protocol for directory services is Lightweight Directory Access Protocol (LDAP). It is a multiple platform and operating system protocol. Legacy data can be used to enhance the environment with the ability to use a single login.

E-Mail Servers

The secret success of e-mail service is not just the sending of basic mail quickly and efficiently but also how well attachments can be sent. The big issue is, should you use shareware or commercial products?

The following are a few areas you need to consider if you are new to e-mail service:

- Account administration
- Client tools
  - Searching
  - Spelling and grammar checking
  - Uses POP3 (SMTP) or IMAP
- Directory (includes aliases)
- LAN and WAN server protocols
- Platform requirements
- Post Office Protocol (POP), Standard Mail Transfer Protocol (SMTP), and Interactive Mail Address Protocol (IMAP)
- Remote access
- Server options

News Servers

While you might be thinking of the already-established newsgroups on the Internet, you might want to consider an internal news server using push technology. There is nothing better than home delivery.

News servers use the Network News Transport Protocol (NNTP). This is the protocol used to distribute USENET (the Internet news forum) posts. A major concern is to have filters to eliminate redundancy and focus on the news service required for your users.

One tool you should consider is the installation of a newsreader as a supplement to the news service. The major browsers have reading options.

There has to be a balance between service and administrative requirements. An impact area is your decision as to the availability of internal and external newsgroups.

Search Servers

Because of technological advances in search engines, users of your enterprise network also expect to have such a utility available to them. One way to define the criteria for your search engine is to look at the many available on the Web. In the reality of the virtual world, there are bottom-line criteria you need to consider when buying:

- Price (per site, per individual, both)
- Index size to database comparison
- Maintenance, such as re-indexing time
- Installation size (server and terminals)
- Platforms (Windows NT, Unix, Solaris)
- Number of releases and how often

A search engine usually has two major components: indexer and interrogator. A good indexer can handle your HTML, ASCII, and RTF files. The concern should be what impact the index algorithm has on memory requirements. The interrogator should have an excellent filtering algorithm so results are returned quickly and are ordered by significance.

Besides the basic short-term financial considerations and system requirements, long-term financial concerns and functions also need to be considered. They may not appear to affect your budget today, but they can affect not only the budget year after year but also how users see and use the system. A short list of financial concerns and functions includes:

- Access controls
- Configuration requirements
- Cross-intranet searches
- Directory requirements
- Hardware interoperability
- HTML conversion time
- Installation time
- Programming requirements
- Scalability (For small networks that become large, will software still function?)

- Search (Boolean) logic
- Software interoperability
- Support time and requirements
- Updating software
- User-friendliness

There are issues about search engines that you need to make clear to the customer when a search engine is an essential component of the project. Search engines may overlook certain types of sites:

- Educational and research sites
- International sites
- New sites
- Sites with few links

The results of a number of studies show the most popular search engines only cover 60 to 70 percent of the available sites. There are also many dead sites. A trend is toward the use of metasearch engines that combine and sort findings for several search engines.

Issues

The following are some of the implementation issues for an IS network and its services caused by software design and technology:

- Shareware versus commercial application versions
- Software version
- Software configuration
- Different implementations of the same service
- Different service protocols
- Single servers versus server clusters

While the remarks here use e-mail for examples, they are applicable in principle to any service. These items can seem unimportant, but they may be the items that keep you up at night.

You may select shareware because it is free. The hidden cost is that you may need a very knowledgeable and experienced programmer of the service to handle local requirements. How do you spell the programmer's name? Dollars!

One should consider the importance of the software version issue given above. For example, suppose a user writes a document using the latest version of a word processing software and sends the document for review to another user who has an earlier version of the software. The result is likely to be a reviewer unhappy with the writer when he tries to print the document. You might get back a comment like, "Have you tried printing this?" There are now two unhappy users wondering why there is not one version of the word processing software (read any application).

There can even be configuration issues within a specific version of software. For example, a person uses Times New Roman 12-point font while another person uses Arial 10-point font. Graphics in the document have to appear in a particular position on a page. This positioning probably may not happen because of this one configuration difference. The best way to understand this is to take a document with the first font type and change it to the second. This can catch you in e-mail attachments and with the problem just described above.

Two implementations of a service may be distinctly different. One implementation may use a text command such as Print, while the other one uses a printer icon. It might get more sophisticated when new types of icons or drop-down menus are used in implementing functions. There are a number of e-mail servers and they all handle attachments differently.

The use of different protocols is tricky, especially in e-mail. It is not just the use of the protocols given in the "E-Mail Servers" section listed previously, but special LAN and WAN protocols that have to be considered.

The last issue to be considered here is a recent development. Traditionally, when a service was new, the first step was to have a server for a single application or service. As its usage grew, the next step was to put two or more services on one server. This created work, which ensured that the installation of one service did not change the system configuration of an already-installed service. A more recent development has been to have server clusters supporting a service or set of services.

What is a server cluster? It is the configuration of two or more servers so they appear as one to both the users and the client applications. This idea strives to improve fault tolerance, to increase availability time, and to enhance scalability.

There is no discussion of server clusters here because this is a rapidly changing technology. You do need to know what the basic architectures or models are, if approached by a vendor on this subject. The three architectures are:

1. No share
2. Share disk
3. Share memory

MANAGER'S TIP

It seems that when you use a common vendor's set of products for the back bone of your network, the more likely there will be security breaches.

[H]　Access Servers Defined

A server can be defined as any device not on the client side of the network. The word *access* implies a "going into"; however, access servers can involve throughput, input, output, and checking or verification.

There are at least six "basic" access servers in the domain of the IS administrator. Access servers usually take their names from the fundamental function they each perform. These six access servers are:

1. Certification servers
2. Firewalls
3. Gateways
4. Proxies
5. Routers
6. Web servers

There are three major issues involved in the implementation of access servers in an IS network. They are legacy, optimization, and security. This section discusses some of the implementation and maintenance concerns you may have about these six basic access servers you probably use.

Certification Servers

Certification servers become most important in an IS network because this is a developing environment where people who want to play mischief might be able to do damage. Certification is a technique in which all parties involved in data exchange can "trust" one another. The basic principle of certification is to have an intermediary party trusted by at least two parties certify that a public key can be shared by them so there can be secure data exchange.

As the size of the parties grows, there has to be a certification authority. This authority signs a public key that acts as proof of trust. As the concept of certification has evolved, so has a protocol. An application has been developed that supports the Secure Socket Layer (SSL) protocol. The trend is to use digital certificates for two-way authentication. This type of authentication has been around for a time in Lotus Notes.

Beyond the SSL protocol there is the use of the X.500 directory services and the X.509 specification of the International Telecommunication Union (ITU). Digital certificates are stored in an X.500-based directory. The fields of an X.509, version 3, are:

- Version
- Serial number
- Algorithm identifier

- Issuer
- Period of validity
- Subject
- Subject's public key
- Signature

The driving force behind X.509 is RFC 1244 "Site Security Handbook." This area is rapidly changing because of the need for new requirements. It is highly recommended to check both the specification and the Request for Comment for updated information.

Firewalls

A firewall server is a fortified gateway. A certification server can be a support component of your security system in conjunction with a firewall. To keep the evil doers out, most firewalls perform the same functions, but the implementation can vary from vendor to vendor. The four important functions are:

1. Fortified operating systems
2. Internet Protocol (IP) filtering
3. Isolating strategies
4. Proxy servers

Implementing a firewall may require at least a security consultant, significant expenditures, and a minimum of two pieces of hardware with associated software. The hardware requirements are as follows:

- Bastion host (guards the intranet structure)
- Screen router (does packet filtering)

You may actually have the requirement for a series of firewalls. This need is determined by your decision as to what level of system security is necessary. You have to have at least an external firewall between the intranet and the Internet. This means one on each intranet in your IS network. In addition, you may need one or more firewalls to protect proprietary resources such as financial data.

Where do you look for further ideas on the use of firewalls in your enterprise network?

- Application layer of the TCP/IP protocol suite
- Network tunneling
- Secure Socket Layer (SSL) protocol
- X.500 standard

Gateways

The term gateway has been around for a long time. It probably was used first to convey the functions of a router. It is a point of access—to the Internet or to an intranet.

A gateway performs bi-directional protocol conversions between heterogeneous (unlike) networks. The integration or implementation issues revolve around which layers of the OSI Reference Model are required for protocol conversions and where these conversions take place. To add to the confusion, a gateway operation can take place at any layer. There is one last confusion: Gateways come in both hardware and software varieties.

There is a basic question you need to ask vendors about their gateways: "What networking protocols do you use?" If they start discussing connections to a particular operating system or to an environment, they do not have a gateway.

Why should you consider a gateway? There are three general functions:

1. File transfers
2. Management support
3. Remote log-on

Proxies

A proxy is a separate storage facility (database) to handle frequently used applications or data. It is a substitute for the real thing. When a proxy supports a set of multiple IP address identities, it is sometimes referred to as a virtual Web server. A proxy server can have many different functions, among which are the following:

- Assist in security processing within a firewall
- Increase a server's responsiveness
- Increase a server's security architecture
- Distribute processing workload
- Forward a browser's request

Here is a simple example of when you might use a proxy server in your IS network:

1. The user launches the browser.
2. The user types in a URL.
3. The request goes to a proxy server.
4. The request goes to the Internet.

This process should be transparent to the user. The user thinks the connection to the Internet is direct. This process gives you a firewall and a way to control where a user may get to on the Internet. If a proxy server configured correctly, you can eliminate users going to their favorite sport site or other nonproductive sites.

MANAGER'S TIP

In one instance a large corporation blocked telephones for time and weather, and to the local bookie, and reduced outside calls by at least 30 percent. If this screening is possible for telephone numbers, what would similar screening do for your Internet traffic?

What are some of the criteria you might consider in buying a commercial proxy server product?

- Ability to reduce traffic flow
- Access restriction options for users
- Caching scheme
- Data distribution process
- Dependability
- ISP requirements
- Maintenance
- Resource management
- Security
- Service control
- Speed

Routers

There are many different routers, but the one that should be included in any discussion of firewalls, gateways, and security is the screening router. The functions of a screening router are based on the network (Internet Protocol) and the transport (Transmission Control Protocol) layers of the OSI (Open Systems Interconnection) Reference Model (1978) of the International Organization of Standards (ISO). A screening router acts as a controller of traffic on network segments. This activity in turn controls the service types on each of these segments. If there is a service compromise, the result is thus limited.

Screening routers are also known as packet filter routers. This secondary name comes from their capability to discriminate between packets. Packet filtering is based on the protocol criteria from the OSI Reference Model. Packet filtering is based on the following:

- Source port number
- Destination port number
- TCP flags (usually ACK and SYN)

MANAGER'S TIP

When speed is a concern, a router should be considered after either a bridge or a repeater.

Web Servers

The Web server may be of interest to many potential customers within your corporation. A way to prepare for this situation is to do a presentation so the customers might clearly define their requirements for this server. The presentation should not be technical; instead, it should emphasize potential uses and pitfalls. One area that has to be discussed is potential security risks. This discussion is when you get a clear definition of the desired security level and type of requirements.

To consider the long-range issues of a Web server, one needs to raise questions on user types and potential number, scalability, and fault tolerance (reliability). The following are four scalability areas that need to be considered:

1. Amount of memory for users
2. Additional processing requirements
3. Additional disk storage
4. Additional enhancement to parameters

When long-range needs are considered, the original server can be designed to manage scalability.

Fault tolerance needs to be considered in the context of criticality. Some companies that have gone into the electronic commerce business, in particular stock market trading, have probably learned some important lessons on the value of fault tolerance.

Optimization and Access Servers

Each network has its own unique optimization issues because of legacy software configurations and hardware architectures. Ten common optimization issues should be considered in the implementation and maintenance of your IS network:

1. Cache size
2. Control file locations
3. Disk fragmentation
4. Hard disk seek and access times
5. Improper allocation of resources

6. Load balance

7. Memory fragmentation

8. Partitioning

9. Processing priorities

10. Processing scalability

Network optimization is one of the areas that sets IS project management apart from general project management. Any time there is an addition or an upgrade to the informational system that affects network optimization, these issues have to be considered in doing project activity planning—in addition to the normal cost, time, and resource estimates. Any impact to a network's optimum configuration because of a nonoperational project, such as adding a server for an accounting group, should be considered in the context of the project, not as a day-to-day operational issue.

[I]   Browser Issues Defined

The browser was probably the most dynamic area of change in all of Internet technology. The introduction of a user-friendly graphical user interface and the associated technologies set the groundwork for the rapid growth of intranets. This section looks at evaluating this core software technology and the implications of the use of browsers in your IS network.

A basic definition of a browser is a graphical user interface (GUI) that enables you to look at data on the Internet and at data on your IS network. The browser concept has evolved so that it should also be a user-friendly interface to user services: e-mail, chat, news, search and directory. The browser definition is now at the desktop stage.

Every other browser is evaluated against the two major browsers (Internet Explorer from Microsoft and Navigator from Netscape). Perhaps the two big ones also need to be evaluated more closely, by you in particular, in the implementation of the use of Java applets. The following section discusses evaluation criteria, while the section following that discusses reasons for considering alternative browsers. For example, have you considered the question, "Do your users' desktops have the memory to handle one of the big two browsers?"

Browser Evaluation Criteria

This section does not have a goal of defining the best browser, but it is designed as an evaluation process for selecting one or more browsers. While functionality among browsers may be very similar, the functions may be handled differently. A simple test is to run an HTML document with a variety of tags and font types and sizes using two or more browsers. See the differences

Table 18-15: Matrix for Browser Analysis

	Browser A	Browser B	Browser C
Criteria 1			
Criteria 2			
Criteria 3			
Criteria 4			
Total			

in appearance and other modes of presentation. One of the "little" things may probably be the handling of fonts. Just to add to the confusion, select various font configurations within one browser and see the how the HTML document outcome changes.

Before the evaluation criteria are given, a few suggestions for using the criteria will be mentioned. Draw a matrix such as the one shown in Table 18-15. In each box use the numbers from 1 to 4.

- 1 = unsatisfactory
- 2 = poor
- 3 = good
- 4 = satisfactory

MANAGER'S TIP

You do not use an array of options. You need to make a specific decision.

When you finish the evaluation, make a total of each column and compare the browsers. The higher the number, the better the potential for the browser. However, if an essential criterion is unsatisfactory, you will need to consider an alternative, either as to the browser or as to what the criteria mean to the customer. In addition, you can give weight to each criterion. For example,

- 0 = not required
- 1 = nice to have
- 2 = required

Any kind of scheme is fine, just try to make the scheme unbiased. There is much emotional baggage involved when selecting one of the big two browsers.

The following criteria are in an alphabetical list. You should establish the priority as recommended above.

- Availability
- Conferencing
- Disk size requirements
- Display capabilities
  — Forms
  — Frames
  — Tables
- Documentation
- E-mail client support
- Font controls
- Foreign language support
- General performance
- Graphic handling
- Help capabilities
- HTML support
- Java support
- Load time
- News support
- Platform requirements
- Platform support differences
- Plug-in capability
- Printing capabilities
- RAM requirements
- Scripting support
- Security
- Stability
- Usability

- User-friendliness
- Vendor support
- Video capabilities

Some of these 30 evaluation criteria may be more important than others. The required criteria might be disk and memory size requirements, platform capabilities, HTML handling, and user-friendliness. As you look over the list, the same criteria appear as those for almost any application you have on your IS network.

Alternative Browsers

At first glance, it may appear to be easy to have only one browser. It all changes when you consider the platforms for remote access and, of course, your legacy hardware of older desktops. It is important to weight each of the criteria for its implications in having a balanced IS network.

There are browsers available that are very good for site development but not for general uses. Some browsers may work better on one platform than another.

As a part of your network structure, you may need to consider organizational groups and how they interact with other groups or the special needs they may have. Are you going to use a browser's e-mail capabilities or use one of the many e-mail applications available? These are just some of the questions you need to ask yourself when applying your browser policy. There may be many more questions you can ask but if you use the criteria above and acknowledge perhaps the need for more than one browser, you are far down the road to success in this area.

§ 18.02   MANAGEMENT INVOLVEMENT

[A]   Overview

All the managers are involved in the impact of a project on legacy software and hardware. The range is from capital budget concerns to the nuts-and-bolts technical concerns.

[B]   Strategic Manager and Legacy

The strategic manager needs to know the impact of a project when it affects the capital budget. Are there funding sources for capital? This question has to be raised during the project viability preproject survey.

[C]   Tactical Manager and Legacy

The tactical manager needs to comprehend the implications on the legacy software and hardware of the IS network created by any project. While hardware and software were the focus of this chapter, there are two other pieces of legacy that have to be considered in any project: documentation and training. It is the responsibility of the operational managers of these two areas to give the details, but the tactical manager must ask the questions about these areas.

[D]   Operational Managers and Legacy

When it comes to the nuts-and-bolts level, the IS operational managers need to analyze the project's goals to detail the impact on any IS legacy software and hardware. Most of the non-IS operational managers do not have to be concerned with legacy except those in documentation and training. How do legacy changes impact these areas? There may be new configuration values that have to be documented and the use of the values has to be added to one or more training courses.

On the CD-ROM

On the CD-ROM is:

1. Chapter 18 Overview.ppt—Chapter Overview, Legacy Software and Hardware

---

Chapter 19

Profitability Analysis

§ 19.01 Overview

    [A] Objectives

    [B] Profitability Analysis Definition

    [C] Basic Features and Functions of Profitability Analysis

    [D] Criteria for Profitability Analysis

    [E] Constructing a Profitability Analysis

§ 19.02 Management Involvement

    [A] Overview

    [B] Strategic Manager and Profitability Analysis

    [C] Tactical Manager and Profitability Analysis

    [D] Operational Managers and Profitability Analysis

§ 19.01 OVERVIEW

[A] Objectives

At the end of this chapter, you will be able to:

- Define profitability analysis for project management.
- Describe the basic features and functions of profitability analysis.
- Establish the criteria for the use of a profitability analysis for project activity sequences, time estimates, resources, and costs.
- Construct a simple profitability analysis.
- Identify how the three managing levels may be involved in profitability analysis for your project.

[B] Profitability Analysis Definition

One might think profitability analysis is something only done by the financial and the marketing groups or by the strategic manager. Why should an IS project manager be concerned with profitability analysis? You have to work

407

with business managers who think in terms of the bottom line, profit, or the top line, revenues. Especially when the project is specifically for the corporate information system, you do have to construct the project plan to demonstrate how the company will benefit from the project. The benefit may not be direct revenues but in terms of measurable productive labor-hour savings. You might also consider that if you do the IS project now, you will not have to update other components of the system for an additional period at a certain savings to the corporation.

MANAGER'S TIP

Benefit analysis is done prior to a project being approved; the project plan isn't developed or constructed to demonstrate profitability. Putting together a budget to successfully complete the project and bringing the project in on budget is an important objective of the project manager.

Business success can be measured by many different metrics such as market share, return on assets, and earnings per share. One way to improve any of these values is to improve efficiency or create economies of scale. Thus, one can look at profitability analysis as a technique for determining gained efficiencies after completion of an IS project.

What things are available to you in project management to develop simple project profitability analysis? The results of this analysis should be expressed to higher-level management in terms of efficiency, or dollars. Two things can assist in developing return on investments (ROI): standards and benchmarks.

A standard states that if you do this, you will accomplish that. A benchmark states that if you are below or above a certain level or point, you get a specific result. In both cases if you improve on a standard or a benchmark, you have increased your efficiency. The standard or benchmark may have a formula that might assist in determining the level of efficiency.

MANAGER'S TIP

Profitability analysis is usually an unmentioned component of project management. The project manager only has responsibility for controlling the costs for the project implementation, not whether or not the results of the project meets the projected benefits. If the project has been approved by using some form of profitability analysis, the project manager may see during the project that these benefits may not be realized and can bring this matter to management's attention so they can make the necessary decisions concerning the project.

Tools are available to give feedback on project costs. The discussion here is a preproject scenario. These tools can assist in insuring project profitability, which is project revenues less project spending.

[C]   Basic Features and Functions of Profitability Analysis

When you do a profitability analysis, there are five areas you need to analyze:

1. Costs
2. Outputs
3. Quality
4. Time
5. Customer satisfaction

Do these sound familiar? Each of these is a concern of project management. Therefore, if you combine or merge techniques for cost analysis, quality assurance and control, and time analysis, you have the basis for a profitability analysis process.

How do you analyze customer satisfaction? That always seems to be a nebulous activity. Someone in your corporation is always trying to quantify and qualify customer satisfaction. You do have an advantage in this area if you have established measurable project goals with the customer. You might be able to define very specific profits to the customer because of the achievement of these goals. These measurable goals become benchmarks for doing a profitability analysis.

[D]   Criteria for Profitability Analysis

The first step in developing criteria for a profitability analysis is to ask five questions:

1. What are the measurable resources, materials, and equipment required for the project (inputs)?
2. What are the measurable activities with associated durations and costs (process)?
3. What are the measurable consequences of the project (outputs)?
4. How reliable are the data from the above questions?
5. What standards and benchmarks might one use to do a profitability analysis of the IS project?

In developing your criteria, you might consider two different scenarios. The first scenario is the worst-case, while the second is best-case scenario. If you want to take a page from PERT, you might also consider a middle-of-road scenario.

Another method is to use the appropriate standards and benchmarks available for the project that you want to do. They may give helpful formulae for reliable estimates of the results of the actions taken by the project.

[E]   Constructing a Profitability Analysis

As stated earlier, profitability analysis is usually a function of the financial group, the marketing group, or the strategic manager. As a project manager, you need to see the implications of spending on revenue. Here is a very simple example: When you spend $100,000 on a project, where does the profit start when the profit on an IS widget is a certain amount?

- If each IS widget returns $50—profit starts at widget 2001
- $80—widget 1251
- $150—widget 668
- $49.95—widget 2003

Of course, many other factors are omitted such as marketing and distribution costs. Notice that a nickel difference in price requires the sale of two additional widgets.

If you want to do a profitability analysis for an IS project that does not sell a widget to a customer, then you have to think in terms of efficiency. A measurable item is the number of production hours as compared with the number of labor-hours saved over a given period. Another scenario is the cost to the corporation if there is a security breach to the accounting group or any other group within the corporation. The second example requires the assistance of the concerned group for such an IS project. Getting a secure server, for example, is usually initiated by that group.

To return to the first scenario, you need to do a preproposal analysis as discussed in Chapter 1, except all the questions have to be in the context of the core question: "How profitable will this project be over time?" The definition of time or duration of cost recovery must be realistic when it is given to the strategic manager. There might be two parts to the conclusion:

1. Amount that can be recovered in the budgetary year
2. Amount that can be recovered in the next budgetary year

Profitability is determined by the difference between production-hours expended through the project and the labor-hours saved. Profitability analysis may be easier for an IS project manager than a marketing manager because of the amount of historical data that is generated for operational reasons.

Let us return to the original questions that were generated around the question, "Is the project viable?" It has been stated that a project manager has to view cost, time, and resources differently from business managers, but the first step is the responsibility of business management, not project management. Your responsibility as an IS project manager is to make the conclusions of the preproposal review valid.

Below are the original preproposal questions on project viability rewritten to reflect the notion of profitability:

1. What are the costs for potential materials and equipment to achieve project results?
2. What are potential resource costs to achieve the project results?
3. Are potential costs going to be too high to achieve project results?
4. Are there appropriate project savings justifications to achieve project results?
5. What are the costs for the appropriate skills to achieve project results?
6. Are there budgetary monies available to achieve the project results?
7. What are the costs for the project tools to ensure control to achieve project results?
8. Do the project results meet the strategic financial goals of the company?
9. Do the project results reflect enough efficiency to save a significant amount of labor-hours?
10. How may project results impact any product pricing?
11. How may project results meet future informational system needs?
12. How stable is the IS organization to limit project costs?
13. How stable is the technology required to limit project costs?
14. How will the results impact the return on investment (ROI)?
15. Is the recovery period for project production costs realistic?
16. What are the events that can increase project costs?
17. What are the events that can decrease project costs?
18. What are the possible financial impacts on the information system as a whole?
19. What are the possible financial restraints that can affect the project?
20. What is the level of formal authority required to fund this project?

Most of the questions have only been slightly modified from the original ones. Several of the questions have not been changed. The focus of the questions has been changed from the general viability of the project to the financial consequences of the project. If you do have a project that is internal to the information system and your customer is a strategic business manager, you will have to answer both sets of questions.

You have available a large set of tools for answering the previous questions:

- Historical data on the informational system
- Benchmarks

- Standards
- Time estimates
- Resource estimates
- Cost estimates

The estimates are the results of analyses of the historical data. The key to the use of these tools is to remember that excellent performance achieves efficiency, which means saved labor-hours or profit over a specific time. This might be called a return on investment.

Besides the answers you develop for your profitability analysis, it is equally important to present a credible presentation. The following 10 points need to be considered in constructing the profitability analysis:

1. Executive summary
2. Presentation order
3. Measurable objectives
4. Analysis parameters
5. Duration to recover project costs
6. Impacts on the financial goals of the corporation
7. Cost recovery model
8. Quality impacts (IS general improvements)
9. Quantity impacts (IS technical improvements)
10. Security impacts

§ 19.02   MANAGEMENT INVOLVEMENT

[A]   Overview

While profitability analysis is a technique or tool that is used before doing an IS project, all levels of managers are involved. Why? Because all are involved also in any preproposal analysis to answer the question, "Is the project viable?" The strategic manager has to make a business decision. The tactical manager has to construct the profitability analysis, and the operational managers have to give input.

[B]   Strategic Manager and Profitability Analysis

The strategic manager needs to work with the IS tactical manager to develop a profitability analysis that can be presented to higher-level management, if necessary. This manager should assist in identifying potential sources within the corporation that may have done profitability analysis and point to any corporate standards in this area. Perhaps most important, the strategic manager should state the expectations for the profitability analysis when the subject is first discussed. The strategic manager should have a body of experience in resolving issues about the acquiring of profits.

[C]   Tactical Manager and Profitability Analysis

When doing a project profitability analysis, you have to act with your business manager hat on, but when you do the project, you use the analysis as a standard for achieving project goals. You are the person responsible for constructing the analysis. You need to answer the 20 questions given in § 19.01[E] on constructing a profitability analysis. You need to ensure that you have reliable data from the operational managers. Finally, you need to write an effective report or create an effective presentation.

[D]   Operational Managers and Profitability Analysis

The operational managers have two responsibilities in the constructing of a profitability analysis. First, they need to ensure that the input is reliable. Second, they should review the report for accuracy for their areas and for impacts on their areas.

On the CD-ROM

On the CD-ROM is:

1.   Chapter 19 Overview.ppt—Chapter Overview, Profitability Analysis

---

Chapter 20

Analysis for Scalability, Interoperability, and Portability

§ 20.01   OVERVIEW

[A]   Objectives

At the end of this chapter, you will be able to:

- Ask three core general questions on scalability, interoperability, and portability to IS project management.
- Identify 20 related abstract components of the IS infrastructure.
- Ask questions about scalability in the context of other abstract infrastructure components for an IS project.
- Ask questions about interoperability in the context of other abstract infrastructure components for an IS project.
- Ask questions about portability in the context of other abstract infrastructure components for an IS project.
- Identify how the three managing levels may be involved resolving scalability, interoperability, and portability issues for your project.

[B]   Importance of Scalability, Interoperability, and Portability

The terms scalability, interoperability, and portability have become recent buzzwords for networking, in particular for use with Java software. However, they are concepts that have been around for a long time in association with words such as *modularity,* both software and hardware. These terms also represent a part of your abstract IS infrastructure. The notion of infrastructure is discussed in detail in Chapter 18.

As part of the process of deciding if a project is viable, you might ask these three questions, all directly related to the terms:

1. What impact does this project have on the size of the IS network (bandwidth, traffic, hardware requirements, and so forth)?

2. What are the requirements to ensure the new product interacts with my IS network or the customer's network?

3. What network components are usable with the new product or what will be included in the project that will be usable on my IS network?

While you may use an abstract term to express an aspect or component of your IS infrastructure, the questions you ask relate to the concrete components. In addition, you would not discuss with customers, such as the accounting group, the scalability aspect of a new server they perceive they need. Rather, you would discuss the importance of record file growth or security protection.

MANAGER'S TIP

You would never think of making this pedantic statement to a customer: "We need to improve the network's interoperability and portability so there will be no future crisis in scalability." The customer would just frown and say "Ugh!"

These infrastructure components interact with all the other such components on the IS network. The following is a short list of 20 abstract components that exist in any IS network.

Accessibility	Measure of effort required by a user to use a system or to enter a network
Compatibility	Stage to which the system components interact successfully with one another
Complexity	Size of the network system architecture—two computers connected is simple; 100 computers, both mainframe and personnel, are complex
Cost	Amount to be paid to maintain and use a network—visible and hidden

Design	Plan of the system—purposeful and hap-hazard
Environment	Network's conditions or circumstances
Functionality	Extent of system's functions or capabilities
Integration	Process of organizing the various components to act as one
Maintainability	Grade of maintenance updating that is required to ensure user requirements of the system
Optimization	Level to which the system components reach their ultimate capabilities
Platform dependency	Degree to which the system components require a particular software or hardware environment
Purpose	Goal of the system as defined by the users
Redundancy	State, hardware or software, required to duplicate components to ensure a continuous flow of data
Reliability	Scale to which the various components continue to function at the required level
Security	Level to which network data must be protected
Sophistication	From a user view, how simple or user-friendly is the system
Speed	Amount of time required to move data from one point in a system to another point
Stability	Degree to which a system can run without minor or major breakdowns
Time	Interval between the start and finish of an operation
User-friendliness	Degree to which a user can work without getting frustrated

[C]   Related Abstract Components of the IS Infrastructure

Because scalability, interoperability, and portability do not stand alone, you need to consider how they interact with other abstract components as well as appropriate concrete components of the IS infrastructure when considering any customer's project. Since the interactions for concrete components may be product-specific and because abstract components are common to all IS networks, only this type of interaction will be discussed in this chapter. In addition, the importance of these concepts is sometimes forgotten: Is it not difficult to sell a customer on a larger server than required now because of the need for a server that should be scalable?

[D]   Scalability Interaction

A basic definition for scalability is to what degree a network can be enhanced without a major (fundamental) change in design. With this definition, how can you use scalability in relationship to other abstract infrastructure components to assist you in managing and controlling an IS project?

The following is a set of questions or statements you might ask or state when talking to an accounting customer about a new server to handle personnel records and the need for protection from the possibility of hackers.

> *Accessibility*   *What is the level of sophistication of the potential users of the server?*

Perhaps the key to defining accessibility lies in the number of applications to go on the server. Based on data from your corporation, you need to develop benchmarks on usage (light to heavy). A user in this sense excludes a member of the IS operational team. You need to resolve the number of essential applications and the requirements for growth on the server. How many users need to access data using a new accounting package, today and a year from now? If remote accessibility is required, you need to consider the level of communications hardware support, protocol requirements, and security requirements.

> *Compatibility*   *Does the customer want a closed system or an open system?*

There has to be a decision whether the server will be a standalone server with intranet support applications and protocols. Perhaps there is a reason to use e-mail to move data from one user to another; thus, there is this special requirement. Recognize that the e-mail system being referred to here is a closed one, for security reasons. In addition, an irrational concern over viruses may be an issue. There may also be the need (you may smile at this, in light of the prior statement) to include the group in the corporate e-mail system. The level of compatibility may also determine the size of the server.

> *Complexity*   *You need to determine what the terminal requirements are for this server, both local and remote.*

You need to know the number of users and their potential usage cycle. (Is this a five-day usage scenario or a seven-day scenario?) In addition, you need to know the complexity of any new applications and their graphic capabilities. Are there shared devices? Is the amount of memory or number of users more important? If there is to be remote access, then there are the requirements for protocols and support hardware, all requiring further sizing of the server.

Cost	*What is the amount of the approved funding for this project?*

If there is no approved funding, this project is not viable. You might go through a preproject proposal survey with the customer to establish costing estimates and then give the customer a range for potential costs. Do not give a single figure. More time will be spent negotiating over a single cost figure than a range of costs. Critical to costs is the growth potential. This should be one of the criteria for determining the range. For example, today you have X number of users, but a year from now you expect Z number of users. If you do the project for Z number of users, it may save you Y dollars rather than waiting a year to upgrade for these reasons.

Design	*What are the customer's measurable goals or expectations for the system?*

The essential word in the basic question is *measurable*. To develop scalability factors you need measurable objectives. The customer may state, "I want a server," but you need to get from the customer the major factors that could affect the server's size today and tomorrow. Are there any existing corporate guidelines for network design?

Environment	*What are the numbers for light, medium, and heavy load users?*

It is very important to know the type of usage as a factor in determining the server size. It is also important to know if number of users is more important than memory. Perhaps the number of potential accounting records may be important in the selection of a server, and any type of new accounting packages required. The benchmark for defining a user's usage level should be based on your historical IS data. What are the network topology requirements?

Functionality	*What are the expected software packages or applications to go on this server?*

Is it expected that the server will function as a Web server? If this is so, then scalability is a dominant factor in determining the server's characteristics. Are this server's functions to be integrated into the IS environment as a whole?

Integration   *Is the server a standalone or is it to be integrated into the IS as a whole?*

The level of integration might impact the scalability of the informational system as a whole. Though there may be new accounting packages, what might be the new traffic requirements? Are there any server functions that may cause system integration and, in particular, impact scalability beyond the need for more bandwidth?

Maintainability   *What maintenance packages are required to ensure that the server keeps an appropriate size?*

There may be a requirement for performance tools beyond the ones already available for IS. What are the data imaging requirements for the server?

Optimization   *What are the optimization requirements for any new accounting packages?*

There needs to be a technical discussion with any vendor or vendors involved with new software packages as to their special optimization requirements.

Platform dependency   *What are the platform requirements for new accounting software packages?*

Does this new software require larger workstations and laptops? Are there any other special hardware requirements that might affect the sizing for the project?

Purpose   *Does any measurable goal or expectation affect the sizing of the server, support equipment, or terminals?*

Redundancy   *See the note below for reliability.*

Reliability   *What are the expected reliability benchmarks of the customer?*

If there is an expected high level of reliability, does this mean there has to be some high level of redundancy in the server?

| *Security* | *What is the expected level of security?* |

Unless this server is to be standalone (highly unlikely), then you have to consider the requirements for either a proxy or firewall. Either of these options potentially affects the IS network and certainly impacts this server project.

| *Sophistication* | ***What are the user-friendly expectations of the customer?*** |

The more sophisticated any GUI is, the greater the impact on the project. Beyond just questions on the new server, you need to identify hidden requirements for usage of the IS network. Perhaps a part of the issue for a new server is the lack of capability to use the IS network as it is.

| *Speed* | *Any response to above-average transaction speed leads to more bandwidth.* |
| *Stability* | *When a customer says he has talked to a vendor and the vendor says its server never goes down, you need to talk to the vendor and determine technically how this is so.* |

You have to consider what the requirements are for a server never to crash. The secret may be redundancy, and this function may not exist on the basic server. You need to make the customer aware of the impact on a server's size to have a "no downtime" capability.

| *Time* | *You need to identify with the customer expectations for processing of data and transaction requirements.* |

More sophisticated requirements for handling data increase the size of the server for cache memory. You need to consider certain time-related issues that are technical such as CPU bottlenecks (memory and CPU processing time) and processing queue time (length is the visual indicator to the customer).

| *User friendliness* | *One level for determining user friendliness is the speed at which the customer can access and process the data.* |

Many of the answers for other abstract infrastructure components are really manifestations of the customer's expectations about the user friendliness. User friendliness is determined by how transparent system functions are, and evolving user friendliness is based on the system scalability (among other things).

[E]   Interoperability Interaction

A basic definition for interoperability is to what degree the various network components work with one another successfully. With this definition, how can interoperability be used in relationship with other abstract infrastructure components to assist you in managing and controlling an IS project?

Before looking at questions that might resolve interoperability issues with a customer, you must be clear in your mind what is and what is not possible with regard to interoperability. First, 100 percent interoperability is a theoretical notion. Second, the services that you might consider for interoperability include the following:

- Application deployment
- Data transactions
- File management
- Messaging
- Network management
- Security

Third, interoperability is a buzzword that many have heard (and used) and few understand. One might confuse other abstract infrastructure components such as compatibility with interoperability.

Fourth, when a customer says she believes that interoperability is a "good thing," you need to ask what is meant by a "good thing"? You recognize that interoperability is a moving target because of the dynamics of technology involved.

As with scalability, let us continue the discussion with the customer and the need for a server:

Accessibility   *Does the customer confuse accessibility with interoperability?*

Accessibility can easily be confused with interoperability. Perhaps the service with accessibility and interoperability requirements might be file management. The question is, "Can I use an alternate method to achieve the expected accessibility rather than having to include interoperability in the project mix?"

Compatibility   *When does product compatibility mean interoperability?*

Compatibility is probably the abstract infrastructure component most likely to be confused with interoperability. Are Microsoft's Office products compatible or interoperable? The products interact successfully with one another, so they must be compatible. But how did they achieve compatibility? The answer might be interoperability. This may be the essential distinction between these two infrastructure components: Compatibility is what the *users* see; interoperability is what the *applications* see.

Complexity	*What level of interoperability is realistic with the level of complexity of the expected system?*

One needs to consider how dynamic the applicable technology is. This might be as simple as the accounting package the customer wants is about to have a new major release. You then find out there is a new GUI.

Cost	*How does one minimize the cost and still reach an acceptable level of interoperability?*

When considering interoperability, keep in mind the 80–20 rule. The last 20 percent in attempting to achieve 100 percent interoperability is the cause for 80 percent of the costs. Costs should always be considered in the context of the level of interoperability required. The following might be a formula for beginning your estimates (scientifically unproved):

Interoperability costs = (number of sites involved) ×

(number of products involved − 1) × (installation costs)

Design	*What are the design requirements that generate the need for interoperability?*

Are the design requirements for interoperability horizontal, vertical, or both? You must recognize that many vendors trying to develop interoperability for their products think vertically. Interoperability design is a very high level of connectivity. It is the capability to link platforms of different operating systems and applications from multiple vendors as one system. Perhaps a core requisite for interoperability design is the need for a standard. This necessity leads to the following questions:

- Who writes the standard?
- Why should there be a standard?
- When should a standard be used?
- Where should the standard apply?
- How should a standard be used?

Environment	*What network conditions or circumstances cause an interoperability requirement?*

You need to consider traffic requirements when discussing interoperability. How does bandwidth requirement affect interoperability requirements? Is interoperability a practical effort on one server in an IS network?

Functionality	*What server functions have to be interoperable?*

The essential functions (services) that might require interoperability include file management, messaging, data transactions, and application deployment. A method that might be considered in designing and developing system interoperability is to use a switching (telephony) model.

Integration	*When the customer speaks about interoperability, is the customer talking about integration?*

Integration to the customer may mean user friendliness. What the customer sees is more important than what you see. Integration may mean to the customer that all the required applications are available from one point: their workstations. Notice the phrase "one location" is not used. While a customer may think there is a prerequisite for one server dedicated to the group's needs, that conception might be technically incorrect.

Maintainability	*What grade of maintenance is required to ensure user requirements for interoperability?*

You need to identify measurable factors for interoperability, so the cost factors might be established. It might be very important to know future costs in relation to present cost estimates. In the short term, the costs for maintenance for a server might be more than the original installation costs because of interoperability.

Optimization	*What performance tools are required to optimize a system with a certain level of interoperability?*

Optimization is important to you as an IS manager and it is important to the user through visual clues such as length of queues. Because interoperability is involved in many dynamic or changing technologies, you need to be advised by vendors how they can resolve optimization issues when interoperability is a part of the project mix.

Platform dependency	*Does the customer require a multiple platform environment and how does this impact interoperability requirements?*

The more platforms you have, the less likely you are going to have a high level of interoperability. The major factor in the validity of this statement is the level of technologies that can affect the success of interoperability. What you may achieve is compatibility among platforms rather than interoperability.

Purpose	*What are the purposes of having interoperability as defined by the users?*

Any reason for justification for any level of interoperability should have a technical basis, not because of a buzzword mentality. In addition, besides cost factors, one should consider the benefits in developing a justification list.

Redundancy	*What level of redundancy is required for interoperability?*

Does redundancy improve interoperability or hinder it? Do you need redundancy? Are there any redundancy costs? It can only be offset by benefits such as no downtime.

Reliability	*How does the need for interoperability affect server reliability?*

Are the requirements unique for the accounting group? If yes, how do these requirements affect the reliability for your informational system as a whole? If no, how do you use your present interoperability capabilities to satisfy the project goals?

Security	*How does interoperability affect security?*

While you as well as other IS managers may consider that interoperability is important to security, it might be just the opposite. It has been demonstrated that with highly compatible products from one company, it is easier for hackers to attack using a nasty tool of their trade, the virus. Can this scenario also be true for a system with high-level interoperability?

Sophistication	*What level of interoperability is required on the server?*

The basic question is, "How does interoperability improve the user's view of network friendliness?" You need concrete positive answers to this question before any interoperability system design or development is started.

Speed	*Does interoperability improve the server's speed?*

The user's view of user friendliness as to speed is usually either queue length or data processing time. Will interoperability be of benefit in either of these scenarios?

Stability   *How does interoperability affect the server's stability?*

Interoperability in the long term may make your system more stable. In the short term, there may be an issue. While one vendor may state that its product has interoperability with other products, one must recognize that no vendor has the capability to verify every possible interaction caused by unique system configurations.

Time   *How does interoperability affect the timing of data processing on the server?*

Timing is not important to the user except in its "visual" manifestations such as lengthy queues or slow data processing. You need to validate potential timing benefits if interoperability is a project requirement.

User friendliness   *Does interoperability improve user friendliness for the users?*

Of all the abstract infrastructure components, this is the most important to the customer. In reality, all the other components are wrapped up in this one. The technical issues are not important to the user. The issue is that the widget works easily and the way the customer wants. The concern for interoperability ultimately boils down to how you answer the question, "Do the benefits for an interoperability effort improve network user friendliness?"

[F] Portability Interaction

A basic definition for portability is a characteristic of software; it is the degree to which the software can be transferred from one environment to another. Portability includes four types of environments:

1. Database
2. Hardware
3. Network
4. Operating system

With this definition, how can portability be used in relationship to other abstract infrastructure components to assist you in managing and controlling an IS project? As with scalability and interoperability, let us continue the discussion with the customer who needs a server. You would not ask or state all 60 points given here and above. You need to select those that are appropriate to the customer and fill in the pertinent values.

MANAGER'S TIP

This area is highly speculative. The discussion is a challenge to the ideas on portability, the buzzword. Portability should be a flexible IS infrastructure component rather than just a marketing or development opportunity for moving code from one operating system to another or from one computer (hardware) to another.

Accessibility   *How would a portability effort improve accessibility for the server?*

The essential point is that you have multiple types of servers and the server of the project does not have the type of accessibility found on an existing server.

Compatibility   *Does any portability activity impact the system's compatibility level?*

When you port two applications to a new server OS type, are they still compatible with each other? Just because two applications are compatible in one environment does not automatically mean they will be compatible in the new environment.

Complexity   *Are the results of the project too complex for a high-level effort for portability?*

For a server such as the one under discussion, the above question would not be asked except in passing. This question is critical to any portability effort. While portability may ease a development effort, one must consider the consequences of porting software. In a very complex software program, even if developed in-house, portability can lead to crashes in the system because of unintentional configuration issues.

Cost   *What are the costs to reach a certain grade of portability?*

The cost for portability is measured against redevelopment cost. One hundred percent portability is theoretical, so you always have to consider the level, grade, or percent of portability.

Design   *What are the design requirements that might affect the use of portability for this project?*

There are a number of reasons for considering portability in a project. They include the following:

- Reduced development costs
- Potential reduction in future maintenance costs
- Improved performance, compatibility, functionality, and so forth
- Minimized use of resources
- Potentially identified capabilities of the software

> **Environment**   *Does the portability effort improve or change the network's conditions or circumstances?*

If the code that is ported includes the options for changing the system's configuration or has values that impact the system's configuration, you need to seriously evaluate the porting. Many environmental elements may be impacted by portability:

- Documentation (code and user)
- Hardware
- Operating system
- Other software
- Programmers
- Users

> **Functionality**   *Do you lose any functionality in porting the software?*

As will be said again under user friendliness: "If the ported software will not act exactly in the same manner as in the original environment, the user must be told up front before development. This means the programmers need to comprehend the effects of porting *before* development, not *after* completion of development." If your product (software) already has an established level of credibility, then you must have an equal, if not better, level in the ported software.

> **Integration**   *At what level will the portability effort be handled?*

A portability effort can be anywhere within the range of simple to complex. The more complex the effort, the more important it is to identify integration issues because complexity may increase instability. While the variables are the same, they may take on a new color. The range of complexity includes the following four stages:

1. Component
2. Program
3. Subsystem
4. System

Maintainability	*Does the portability effort reduce the mainte-nance effort?*

Porting a complete system doubles the maintenance effort because what is done on one must be done on the other. There is also the scenario where there is a software link to the larger environment and thus maintenance is not doubled. The question is, "Is this portability?"

Optimization	*What types of impacts can portability have on system optimization?*

Portability is usually handled through interfaces. These interfaces can provide the bases for creating software models. These models require standards. Optimization is based on standards and benchmarks. How do the standards from portability efforts relate to optimization standards? The answer can be stated at the local level.

Platform dependency	*Is it clear to the user that platform in the context of portability generally refers only to an operating system and hardware?*

Should platform dependency have any meaning beyond operating system and hardware?

Purpose	*How does a portability effort enhance the goal of the network as defined by the users?*

The priority in the use of portability may be a lessening in development time; however, the effort should be related to a measurable project goal.

Redundancy	*If you port software from one server to another, does that create unnecessary redundancy in a system?*

The basic question is asked because portability is done between pieces of hardware. The question is, "When you port software between system servers, do you have a portability effort or have you created unnecessary redundant code in your system?"

Reliability	*How does the portability effort impact the system's reliability?*

One of the essential phases of porting is adaptation. The act of adapting in itself opens questions of reliability. Having the duplicate code, the original and the adapted, in a system might cause a reliability issue. Notice the phrase "will cause" was not used in the previous sentence. You must consider the implications of two "versions" of the same code in the same system.

Security	*How does a portability effort improve security?*

The security issues for ported code stays the same. You can never justify a portability effort and say it improved security per se.

Sophistication	*How can a portability effort, from a user's view, simplify or enhance user friendliness in the network?*

This is not a trick question. If porting software from one operating system to another could improve productivity in that operating system environment, then perhaps you need to consider the portability effort. An example would be the porting of Microsoft Office products to a Linux operating system environment. What this example really states is that in your IS network, if you have an application that is highly user productive and you have multiple platforms, then you have to consider portability.

Speed	*Does the ported code have the same level of speed as in the original software?*

A change in speed can have two impacts. A slower speed can impact the user's view of the system. Second, a difference in speed might affect the system's internal clocks.

Stability	*Does the ported code have the same level of stability as in the original software?*

Porting might impact the system's stability.

Time	*Does the portability effort impact the timing of any operation?*

Internal timing is not important here, but does the user see longer queues and processing time because of portability?

User friendliness	*Can you achieve equal or better user friendliness than what exists in the original software with the ported software?*

The rule is simple. What the user expects is what the user has seen. If the ported software will not act exactly in the same manner as in the original environment, the user must be told up front before development. This means the programmers need to comprehend the effects of porting *before* development, not *after* completion of development. This statement may be a tough one to swallow.

§ 20.02   MANAGEMENT INVOLVEMENT

[A]   Overview

This is one area that is the responsibility of the IS tactical manager and IS operational managers.

[B]   Strategic Manager

The strategic manager should be aware that there is a high degree of abstraction that is critical to the comprehension of the IS environment.

[C]   Tactical Manager

The tactical manager is responsible for making the abstract infrastructure concrete for the customer when issues arise that might impact the infrastructure because of the project.

[D]   Operational Managers

IS operational managers should support the tactical manager with data so IS issues can be stated in a concrete manner to the customer. The training and documentation managers need to be aware of the implications of the IS abstract infrastructure for the design and development of user training and documentation.

On the CD-ROM

On the CD-ROM are:

1.   Chapter 20 Scalability Overview.ppt—Analysis for Scalability

2.   Chapter 20 Interoperability Overview.ppt—Analysis for Interoperability

3.   Chapter 20 Portability Overview.ppt—Analysis for Portability

---

Section Four

People Management

This section addresses two important people management concerns for any IS project: the team and customer involvement. This section looks at how to manage two teams from a Return on Investment (ROI) viewpoint. While the team may act as a dysfunctional individual, a project manager must consider the types of resistance each individual may put forth. Usually the customer is only considered the payee, but is it more logical to consider a customer as an active team member?

Chapter 21

Team Management

§ 21.01   OVERVIEW

[A]   Objectives

At the end of this chapter, you will be able to:

- List five makers of a successful team.
- List five breakers of a successful team.
- Identify three structures of a project management team.
- Identify six components of a ROI team management style.

437

- List 10 guidelines for managing and controlling resistance.
- Identify seven ROI approaches to managing technological resistance.
- Identify three ROI approaches to managing highly valued data opinions.
- Identify two ROI approaches to managing lack of trust position.
- Identify four ROI approaches to managing an ownership conviction.
- Identify five ROI approaches to managing a "project activity is too difficult" feeling.
- Identify three ROI approaches to managing "my method is best" belief.
- List five characteristics of a successful project team.
- Identify how the three managing levels may be involved resolving scalability, interoperability, and portability issues for your project.

[B]   Makers and Breakers of a Team

Beyond the issues discussed in this chapter, there are some essential makers and breakers of a team, but they also relate to being a manager, not just a project manager. Here are five makers:

1. Potential professional growth
2. Work is stimulating
3. Qualified team members
4. Defined goals
5. A recognition process

   Here are five breakers:

1. Undefined goals
2. Limited professional growth
3. Decisions based on power struggles
4. Minimum availability of resources
5. Uninvolved upper management

[C]   Three Structures of a Project Management Team

The structure of the project management team plays an essential role in how the team perceives itself. Whether the project manager is seen as the centerpiece (coordinated structure), the top of the hierarchy of the visual organizational chart (hierarchical structure), or as a connection between team members (interconnectivity structure), the team members will act accordingly. It is difficult for people to break the bounds of the structure within which they are placed.

Beyond the organizational structure (that has its own influence) is the view of the role of the project manager. There is one role the project manager cannot play and that is business manager. Over the years, various authors on management have given labels to different types of managers. Some of the positive labels include:

- Mentor
- Shaman
- Indian chief
- Coordinator
- Coach

Some of the negative labels include:

- Boss
- Tyrant
- Dictator
- Despot
- Autocrat

This chapter discusses the use of the label "benefactor." It takes a stance that there are benefits for everyone on the team and they come from a return on their own investments.

Coordinated Structure

The first model puts the program manager as the centerpiece or hub of the team. The handicap of this model is the project manager can easily lose control because in reality decisions are reached by the team members on the circle's rim. The project manager may or may not learn about critical decisions. The project manager may manage, but not control. Exhibit 21-1 is an example of a coordinated project team structure.

Hierarchical Structure

The second model puts the program manager at the top of the team. The handicap of this model is that the project manager is the decision maker and the source of all information. This makes the decision-making process one that is declarative rather than one based on negotiation. Exhibit 21-2 is an example of a hierarchical project team structure.

Exhibit 21-1: Coordinated Project Team Structure

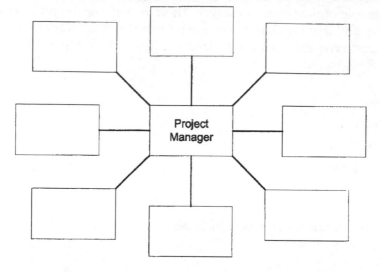

Interconnectivity Structure

The third model puts the program manager at the top of the team; however, there are connections among all the team members. There now is a place for decision making to be a negotiating process, but the project manager still represents a source of authority. Exhibit 21-3 is an example of an interconnectivity project team structure.

[D]   Return on Investment Team Management Style

Return on Investment (ROI) is usually thought of in terms of direct financial benefits. However, there are many indirect benefits that might be considered ROI and can be used by you to manage and control the project management

Exhibit 21-2: Hierarchical Project Team Structure

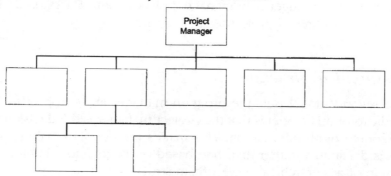

Exhibit 21-3: Interconnectivity Project Team Structure

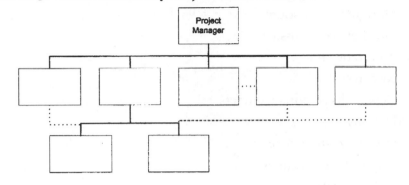

process as it relates to team management. The following is a list of areas where you might find benefits generated by a project. Focusing on these six areas can have a positive effect on the project's ROI. There are six broad areas with some subdivisions that you can use as starting points to resolve issues that cause team problems. In the sections to follow, these starting points will be used in discussing six types of issues that can impact the managing of a team.

1. Common environment
    — Applications with version control
    — Core training environment
    — Common tools
    — Ease of use
    — One browser
    — Remote access
    — Streamlined processes
2. Decentralized working environment (offices)
3. Enhanced productivity
4. Information efficiencies
    — Easier access
    — Faster access
    — Increase in accuracy
    — Increase in availability
    — Increase in communication
    — Increase in resources
    — Increase in timeliness
    — Just-in-time

— More marketing data

— More technical sources

— Quicker data transfer

5. Opportunities for

— New roles

— New skills or enhancements

6. Reductions in

— Documentation costs

— Duplicative resources

— Mailing costs

— Ordering time

— Printing costs

— Search effort time

— Software distribution

— Support costs

— Telephone support costs

[E]   Managing and Controlling Resistance Guidelines

There are many ways to manage and control a project team, but there is a common set of ideas for any positive method of leadership whether it is mentor, Indian chief, shaman, or just plain, old concerned manager. Remember that each team member represents not only himself or herself but also other people. The effect of what you say in a room to the project team is similar to what happens when you throw a stone in a pond and see the ripples. The following are 10 guidelines for managing and controlling resistance as it shows its ugly head either in group meetings or a one-on-one session:

1. Respect your most valuable assets: the people.
2. Keep the users goal oriented.
3. Keep a smile when you least want to have one.
4. Encourage partnership.
5. Develop initial support and keep building on it daily.
6. Have a plan and communicate the details.
7. Set realistic and achievable goals.
8. Control any technology; do not let it control you.
9. Sustain the moment.
10. Have a plan and follow it in an orderly manner.

[F]   Managing and Controlling Technological Resistance

People are fearful of or very uncomfortable with technology and its impact on their job status. This is the place to emphasize ease of use and access, commonality, availability of training, and the opportunities for more informational resources. The following is a list of benefits from new technology you might want to pay special attention to in resolving technological resistance:

- Common environment
    - Common tools
    - Ease of use
    - Remote access
    - Streamlined processes
- Decentralized working environment (offices)
- Enhanced productivity
- Information efficiencies
    - Easier access
    - Faster access
    - Increase in accuracy
    - Increase in availability
    - Increase in communication
    - Increase in resources
    - Increase in timeliness
    - Just-in-time
    - More marketing data
    - More technical sources
    - Quicker data transfer
- Reductions in
    - Documentation costs
    - Printing costs
    - Search effort time
    - Telephone support costs

[G]   Managing and Controlling Data Hoarding

Some people think their jobs are protected because of the information that they hold and do not share. You should emphasize their importance in the improved and enhanced information processes that come with the new system. Here is a list of benefits you might use to resolve issues such as the team member who does not believe that information should be shared with others in the corporation:

- Common environment
  — Applications with version control
  — Common tools
  — One browser
  — Streamlined processes
- Information efficiencies
  — Increase in accuracy
  — Increase in communication
  — Increase in resources
- Reductions in
  — Documentation costs
  — Duplicative resources
  — Printing costs
  — Search effort time
  — Support costs

[H] Managing and Controlling Lack of Trust Position

When a person says that "the other person cannot be trusted," honesty may not be the issue this person has in mind, so emphasize controls and the common environment. In addition, speak about a more efficient environment for communication. Here is a list of some of the starting points you might use to resolve questions of trust:

- Common environment
  — Applications with version control
  — Core training environment
  — Common tools
  — Streamlined processes
- Information efficiencies
  — Increase in accuracy
  — Increase in availability
  — Increase in communication
  — Increase in resources
  — Increase in timeliness

— Just-in-time

— More marketing data

— More technical sources

[I]   Managing and Controlling Ownership Conviction

There are occasions when you do not have enough of a resource for every-one, and those team members left out of the resource distribution may be a bit disgruntled. You have to emphasize the resources that are available to users: applications, tools, and utilities. Show that this person has an opportunity for a new awareness in information and in productivity. Here is a list of some of the starting points you might use to resolve wayward conviction:

- Common environment
  - Applications with version control
  - Common tools
  - Ease of use
  - One browser
  - Remote access
  - Streamlined processes
- Decentralized working environment (offices)
- Information efficiencies
  - Easier access
  - Faster access
  - Increase in accuracy
  - Increase in availability
  - Increase in communication
  - Increase in resources
  - Increase in timeliness
  - Just-in-time
  - More marketing data
  - More technical sources
  - Quicker data transfer
- Opportunities for
  - New roles
  - New skills or enhancements

[J] Managing and Controlling "Project Activity Is Too Difficult" Feeling

The words are *easy, easier,* and *training.* You need to emphasize the common environment. Here is a list of some of the starting points you might use to resolve fears of failure:

- Common environment
  - Core training environment
  - Common tools
  - Ease of use
  - One browser
  - Remote access
  - Streamlined processes
- Decentralized working environment (offices)
- Information efficiencies
  - Easier access
  - Faster access
  - Increase in accuracy
  - Increase in availability
  - Increase in communication
  - Increase in resources
  - Increase in timeliness
  - Just-in-time
  - More marketing data
  - More technical sources
  - Quicker data transfer
- Opportunities for
  - New roles
  - New skills or enhancements
- Reductions in search effort time

[K] Managing and Controlling a "My Method Is Best" Belief

Even after the team has agreed to a process, procedure, or standard, you may have a team member who feels his or her way is better. You need to ask this person to be a part of that process. Since this person knows the best path, he or she can give the advice as a part of a concerned team for a better company. Here is a list of some of the starting points you might use to resolve such a bias or prejudice:

- Common environment
  — Applications with version control
  — Core training environment
  — Common tools
  — One browser
  — Remote access
  — Streamlined processes
- Decentralized working environment (offices)
- Information efficiencies
  — Easier access
  — Faster access
  — Increase in accuracy
  — Increase in availability
  — Increase in communication
  — Increase in resources
  — Increase in timeliness

[L]   Characteristics of a Successful Team

There are many ways to judge a successful team. Here are five common characteristics of a successful team:

1. Meets the performance goals
2. Under or on schedule
3. Under or on budget
4. Flexible in responses to customer change requirements
5. Able to stretch beyond the expected

§ 21.02   MANAGEMENT INVOLVEMENT

[A]   Overview

The strategic manager is a benevolent observer of team activities, while the other members must play their roles on the team as equals.

[B] Strategic Manager and Teams

When there is a team management issue, the strategic manager must let the project manager resolve it. The strategic manager must be considered a benevolent observer and supporter of the project team.

[C] Tactical Manager and Teams

You need to adhere to these five golden principles of team management:

1. You lead, the team succeeds.
2. Communicate, communicate, communicate.
3. Praise in public, condemn in private.
4. Software does not rule, it is only your guide.
5. You have your own bias.

[D] Operational Managers and Their Teams

Each operational manager has his or her team and should follow the same golden rules of team management, as the project manager should. It is important to recognize that no one operational group is more important than another group.

On the CD-ROM

On the CD-ROM is:

1. Chapter 21 Overview.ppt—Chapter Overview, Team Management

Chapter 22

Customer Involvement

§ 22.01   OVERVIEW

[A]   Objectives

At the end of this chapter, you will be able to:

- State seven golden rules of initial negotiating.

- Ask 10 questions from the customer's view about the potential project manager and the project process.

- Give three reasons why the customer should always come first in any project considerations.

- Identify the basic reason for treating the customer as a stakeholder.

- State a definition for project management with the notion of customer included.

- List five examples of customer expectations caused by the project manager's actions.

449

- State the reason why customer acceptance should be considered a process, not an event.
- State 10 ways a quality product can produce customer satisfaction.
- List five types of project risks the customer can cause.
- State the essential principle in preparing customer presentations.
- List 10 areas of a project that a customer views as important.
- Identify how the three managing levels may be involved with customers.

[B]   Seven Golden Rules of the Initial Negotiation

The initial negotiation between you and the customer sets the tone for future project relations. This is the place where the foundations for the relationship are established, such as:

1. Integrity
2. Trust
3. Honor
4. Confidence
5. Assurance

The following seven golden rules assist in establishing the above five positive emotional views:

1. Know your customer.
2. Listen to the customer.
3. Talk on neutral ground.
4. Be clear on your capabilities.
5. Neither force nor be forced.
6. Respond to issues in a timely manner.
7. Establish the criteria of excellence.

The customer appreciates if you have taken time prior to entering the meeting to try to comprehend the customer's position. For example, in the accounting group's server scenario, you would analyze your historical data on the usage of this group on the IS network. If there are no data, you should at least look at an organizational chart of the group.

You should listen to what the customer has to say; perhaps the real issue is not the perceived need. The accounting group may want the server because the group does not get from the present IS network what is expected. Do not get into a confrontational mode.

The meeting should take place in a location that belongs to neither you nor the customer. People seem threatened when negotiating on anything while in the domain of the other party.

You need to be able to state your capabilities in the meeting to the extent the customer puts forth the data. You need to express to the customer your project management process. The customer then knows there is purpose and direction in handling the desired situation. An important part of this discussion deals with the question, "Is this project viable?" You need to know if the customer is only dreaming or ready to do a project. You need to know the amount of approved funding that exists. If there is none, then you need to make it clear to the customer that this is only a fact-finding meeting.

In addition, it is important to state the basic characteristics of a project as you view it without going into details. At least state that you think a project, as distinct from day-to-day work, includes the following:

- Specific start and end dates
- Specific allocation of resources (skills, equipment, and materials)
- Measurable goals
- Organized process to meet the customer's defined goals
- Specific team involvement

Success is achieved through compromise, not through force. Each party has expectations. Each party should walk away with a set of measurable goals and with a sense of a win–win condition.

When you state that you will follow up by a given date, do so. The customer may have an alternate plan. If you do delay, that reflects that you might not be able to meet project milestones. In addition, trust flies out the window. If you cannot meet your commitments in the small things, will you meet your commitments in the large things?

Finally, you need to demonstrate what your criteria are for excellence. The first step in this activity is to discuss your formalized project management process. When appropriate, you could summarize your technical position based on independent standards and benchmarks.

[C]   Ten Customer-Selection Criteria

In a negotiation, there are two sides of the table. You have to consider that you have to present yourself as not only technically competent but also managerially competent. Remember, even an internal customer may have the capability to go to an outside source to do the project. Always consider yourself in a competitive position. Be able to present yourself favorably in these 10 areas as seen through the customer's eyes:

1. Does the project manager have the resource capabilities to complete work on time and on budget?

2. Does the project manager have the technical capabilities to complete the project satisfactorily?

3. Does the project manager have an organized project process that represents a standard of excellence?

4. What kinds of relationships have been established with other customers by this project manager?

5. Does the project process fit with my expenditure capabilities?

6. Are there other offers that can achieve my goals better?

7. What advantages do I have from using this project manager?

8. How do the results of this project enhance my marketing position?

9. Does the pricing strategy meet my financial goals for this project?

10. Does the project manager's management give its support for this project?

The Customer Comes First

You always have to place the customer first. You need to comprehend the customer's expectations, perspectives, and positions. The customer is doing the funding. Have you and the project team given the customer the "bang" for the "buck"? Project success usually results in customer satisfaction and perhaps future opportunities. This endeavor does not mean that the customer always gets any change that is requested. You should have a change order process for resolving this type of situation.

Part of the confusion in working with the premise mentioned above is there are at least three types of customer relationships. Yes, you might vary a presentation according to customer type, but never forget your standards and benchmarks of excellence. The customer types are not good, bad, or worse, but the following:

- Financial investor
- End user
- Partner (alliance or joint venture)

It is always difficult to get the team to comprehend the differences among these three customer types. In fact, different team members may have different relationships so that all three types are your customers at the same time.

Customer as Stakeholder

A stakeholder is anyone with a personal stake in the project results. If the customer is the financial contributor or is going to pay for the product created from the project, then the customer has the primary investment in the project. Other stakeholders are, of course, you, the team, the strategic manager, consultants, and vendors. If the prior listed stakeholders are involved in the project, then it is logical that the customer should be considered more than an observer of the project process and be treated as a participant.

Customer and a Project Management Definition

One might simply state that project management is an organized process to achieve measurable goals within a specified duration, with allocated resources, and with a defined team. This is a valid definition but perhaps a better one would include the notion of the customer in the definition. For example, project management is a process that focuses on the customer's requirements and priorities to give the customer a quality product on time with a minimum utilization of resources. This process is based on a position that the process uses measurable goals for design, development, and testing, with the project team accountable for the results.

[D]   Types of Customer Expectations Caused by the Project Manager

Beyond the initial negotiations, the customer develops expectations because of your actions. There is one rule: No matter what else you do, be consistent. Here are five types of customer expectations you can generate intentionally or unintentionally:

1. Produce timely status reports.
2. Do small changes without costs.
3. Have an 8-to-5 work environment.
4. Be visible to the customer.
5. Be willing to consider the customer's perception of project issues.

Customer Acceptance

A big mistake for a project manager is to think that the customer will accept the final product without questions. Customer acceptance should have its own activity sequence. Customer acceptance is a selling process. Customer involvement is an evolving comprehension of the project's results, not one final "here-it-is" event.

[E]   Customer Satisfaction and Quality Control

An important goal of any project is to achieve customer satisfaction. Customer satisfaction might be defined in many ways, but it is exemplified by more business. There are at least nine qualifications of a quality product that reflect customer satisfaction:

1. Quality demonstrates an awareness of customer needs.
2. Quality equates to control.
3. Quality is commitment.
4. Quality is measurable.
5. Quality is support for the effort even when there are disagreements.
6. Quality means avoidance of costs for things unnecessary.
7. Quality means having the right skill at the right place at the right time.
8. Quality means there is some form of communication between you and the customer. Communications can establish a bond of confidence.
9. Quality requires metrics so analysis can be done to determine the degree of success.

Customer Involvement and Risks

Risks are not necessarily caused by the project team; the customer can generate risks also. Below are at least five types of customer-generated risks:

1. Financial support becomes unavailable
2. No participation in agreed-upon reviews
3. Response time to questions is not timely
4. Seems to have new interpretations of goals
5. Skill resources' availability degrades

Customer Presentations

There are many ways to present information visually. Chapters 12 and 13 discuss the use of Gantt charts and PERT network activity diagrams. Chapter 17 discusses the use of Microsoft products for project management. The essential principle in developing customer presentations is to state performance as to cost, time, and the project goals. Do not get into the technical details. If you have half an hour to present, limit the slides so you talk for no more than 20 minutes—that means about a dozen slides. You do not talk for the whole half-hour and then take questions. This type of action reflects on your ability to do time management well.

Customer's View of the Project

There may be many things the customer will look at, but only a few are important. Here is where the gold is:

- Measurable objectives
- Organized process
- Excellent line of communication
- Comfort with the technology
- Commitment to schedule
- Cost equalling performance
- The right people in the right place at the right time
- Upper management supporting the project
- Flexibility, when required
- Consistency

§ 22.02 MANAGEMENT INVOLVEMENT

[A] Overview

Each of the manager types has a clear responsibility in customer involvement. The strategic manager is the corporation spokesperson, the tactical manager is the project spokesperson, and the operational managers should adhere to the project goals until they receive an official change order.

[B] Strategic Manager and Customers

The strategic manager is the spokesperson for the corporation. The strategic manager should not make decisions about the project with a customer without prior discussion with the project manager. The project manager should be present when the decision is made and presented to the customer. When the strategic manager appoints an inexperienced person as project manager based on the customer's request, then the strategic manager has to ensure there is a strong support team.

[C] Tactical Manager and Customers

The tactical manager is the spokesperson for the project. The project manager is the interface with the customer for the company on project issues and the spokesperson for the project team.

[D] Operational Managers and Customers

The operational managers are not spokespersons to the customers; that is the tactical manager's responsibility. Operational managers are not to make project changes that are based on personal conversations with the customer. The responsibility of the operational managers is to adhere to the customer's measurable defined goals unless there is an official change order. The rule is that the customer should not be involved in the operational processes of the project. However, the customer should be involved in the status meetings or reports generated by the results.

While there must be as much openness with customers as possible, certain guidelines should be followed. When no project management representative is present when an operational manager has a discussion with a customer, the manager should send an e-mail to the project manager describing pertinent details. The operational managers must recognize that only the project manager can make commitments to resources and time for the project.

On the CD-ROM

On the CD-ROM is:

1. Chapter 22 Overview.ppt—Chapter Overview, Customer Involvement

---

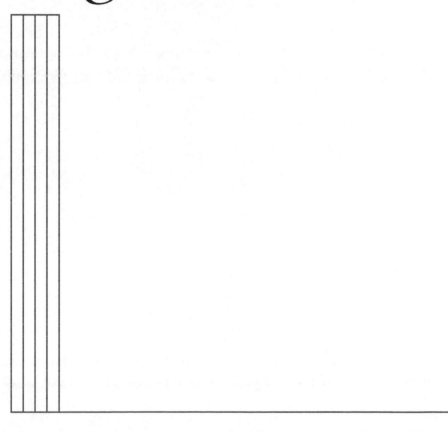

Section
Five

Putting It All
Together

This section compiles the responsibilities of the three management levels and describes four scenarios that use the information given in this book. These scenarios are a good overview of the topics discussed throughout the book.

Chapter 23

Management's Role in Project Management

§ 23.01   OVERVIEW

[A]   Objectives

At the end of this chapter, you will be able to:

- Determine whether a project is small or large based on local scenario.
- Identify the basic project process for writing the manuscript for this book.
- Develop a strategic manager's profile for project management.
- Develop a tactical manager's profile for project management.
- Develop an operational manager's profile for project management.
- Identify how the three managing levels should be involved in any project.

[B]   Small–Large Project Determination

One of the first roles of management is to determine the size and makeup of the project team. This is directly related to the size of the project, which is relative for each organization; each will have a different definition of what

461

is a large project. A man who weighs 200 pounds on a Sumo wrestling team is small. The same man as a coach for a little league team is large. The environment makes the determination of size in this case, and the same is true for calling a project small or large. To Boeing, a project of less than two years might be considered small, while to a startup company that amount of time would be impossible. Perhaps what is more important is the level of criticality of the project results on the corporation's strategic goals.

Each company has to decide the importance of an IS project. Here are five criteria that need to be considered:

1. Commitment of time
2. Percentage of allocated resources in comparison to those available to the whole company
3. Potential risks
4. Funding capabilities
5. Dynamics of applicable technology

[C] Writing a Manuscript as a Project Example

Whether the project consists of one person or a thousand, a project management process should be used. For one person, the process enforces a type of self-discipline. For a team of one thousand, it enforces consistency.

The next three chapters look at three scenarios for doing IS project management. Briefly, here is how the author used the same process for writing this book.

PHASE ONE

1. Literary agent identifies a publisher interested in a book on project management.
2. Out of the discussion with an acquisition editor, very specific requirements are given for writing a proposal through e-mail.
3. A 27-page proposal (single-spaced) is written. The proposal includes the specific objectives for each chapter.
4. The proposal is given a detailed review by an outside consultant.
5. The review is returned to the author.
6. A contract is agreed upon that includes two end dates, a bonus date and a required completion date, length of manuscript, and financial information.
7. Specific requirements are given as to the general document structure such as in Microsoft Word, a 10- or 11-point font, and a standard typestyle.

PHASE TWO

1. Based on historical data (time sheets) from book projects, I estimate the time in hours it would take to write a manuscript of 600 pages.

2. Page estimates are created for section overviews, the introduction, index, and glossary. The total is subtracted from 600 and the proposed number of chapters for the book is divided into this amount to get the average number of pages per chapter. This average is never considered by me as written in concrete but a goal to know I could have more pages in some chapters and fewer pages in others.

3. A Microsoft Excel worksheet is created so it includes the following information:

   - Calendar (days in column, months in row)
   - Sum totals based on minutes, then turned into hours
   - The next section of the worksheet includes
     — a column with all the major sections (introduction, section overviews, chapters, glossary, and index)
     — a row with the headers for number of words, number of pages, Flesch-Kincaid Grade level score, and variance from number of pages predicted for each book component. All totaled or averaged by book section and with a grand book total.
   - The next section of the worksheet is created after two thirds of the pages are completed. It includes calendar dates with three columns: 20 pages a day schedule, 10 pages a day schedule, and the actual status.

QUALITY CONTROL PHASE

1. The spelling and grammar check on Word is used first.

2. The book component is printed and manually edited.

3. The book component is set aside for a period and then manually edited for the second time.

4. The publisher also edits the manuscript for errors and consistency.

CLOSING PHASE

1. Manuscript is sent to publisher.

2. A report is sent to acquisition editor on small variances from the original, especially how ideas from the original proposal have been incorporated in the book.

3. Revisions are made in accordance with publisher's request.

4. All electronic documentation is put on a CD-ROM. CD-ROM is boxed with notes and a printed manuscript.

What does the above say? I project-managed the writing of this book by:

- Having measurable goals
- Planning my schedule
- Defining my resources
- Designing my product
- Developing my product
- Testing my product against a spell checker and against the original and review proposal
- Using a Microsoft Excel worksheet to assist me in managing and controlling my project

---

MANAGER'S TIP

There is a whole phase beyond my control that is important to this project. This is the publisher's phase, which included originally a marketing plan. The publisher has an editing process, printing procedures, and a distribution method.

---

§ 23.02 MANAGEMENT INVOLVEMENT

[A] Overview

Each of the three management types plays an important role in ensuring the success of the project. The following is a summary of each responsibilities of the strategic, tactical and operational managers.

[B] Strategic Manager's Profile for Project Management

A strategic manager may not do everything discussed in this section, but the strategic manager should consider everything discussed. A strategic manager would not expect to use PERT/CPM for any project except those of a complex nature with large numbers of resources involved; however, some type of Gantt chart would be expected. The following are actions that a strategic manager must consider during the IS project management process.

Scope Planning and Defining

The strategic manager should attend the first meeting and state at a minimum the following:

- The project supports certain corporate goals.
- The tactical manager has full authority to manage this project to its conclusion.
- A summary of the conclusions of the evaluation for the starting project based on the 20 questions given in § 1.04[D].

Activity Planning and Sequencing

The strategic manager should chair the project strategic reviews so a degree of objectivity can be achieved. The presence of this manager changes the character of the project team. These reviews should be held at a minimum at the end of each phase.

Resource Planning

The strategic manager should review the resource requirements. It is usually corporate policy for the strategic manager to review capital spending. This manager might be able to add justifications for the resources in the context of corporate goals. The strategic manager should support any procurement effort in a timely fashion.

Time Estimating

The strategic manager should ensure the availability of knowledgeable people, including outside consultants, to evaluate the time estimates. The manager should ensure that the project's time-estimating process is consistent with other time-estimating processes in the company. The manager should also assist the tactical manager in resolving any divisional issues on time estimates for the project.

Schedule Developing

The strategic manager should recognize that the project schedule is a plan, not a commitment, on the part of the project manager. The manager should ensure that the project's scheduling process is consistent with other scheduling processes in the company. The manager should also assist the tactical manager in resolving any divisional issues on the schedule for the project.

Cost Estimating

The strategic manager should ensure the availability of knowledgeable people, including outside consultants, to evaluate the cost estimates. The manager should ensure that the project's cost-estimating process is consistent with other cost-estimating processes in the company. The manager should also assist the tactical manager in resolving any divisional issues on cost estimates for the project.

Budget Developing

The strategic manager should not consider a project budget a commitment but instead a plan.

This manager should try to get from higher management an acceptance that the project budget is a separate management tool and should not be treated the same as the operational budgets are during quarterly reviews. If this acceptance cannot be achieved, then the strategic manager needs to work with the project manager and other business managers to ensure a consistent process for funding the budget.

Controlling Quality

The strategic manager has to ensure that there is an effective quality assurance and control effort for the project. The project quality mechanism should also be consistent with the corporate quality program. How important are ISO 9000-9004 certifications to your company?

The strategic manager needs to establish an appropriate battlefield for excellence. The four cornerstones of excellence are quality, a realistic schedule, a viable budget, and solid risk management.

Managing Risks and Opportunities

The strategic manager should emphasize the effort to minimize errors, not fight fires. This manager needs to support the project manager in cross-divisional areas to ensure a complete and comprehensive risk management program.

Project Modeling

The strategic manager should ensure that the tactical manager has adequate historical data and skilled people available to do sophisticated modeling, if required.

Network Optimization

The strategic manager has the obligation to support a viable network optimization policy. While the technical configuration issues are the responsibility of the IS manager, most optimization issues usually cross over organizational divisions. The strategic manager should work with the IS project manager to resolve any network optimization issues. The strategic manager should also ensure that the addition of new requirements for any IS management and performance tools is consistent with corporate goals.

Gantt Charts and Schedules

The strategic manager should make it clear to the project manager, especially a new one, that there is a need for a standardized executive summary. This manager should state the expectations and the potential uses of the Gantt chart.

PERT/CPM Techniques

Because PERT is labor and time intensive, the strategic manager needs to make a commitment that, when PERT is used, its chart will be a living and enforceable document. The manager also needs to make a commitment for training support for personnel within the IS group. The manager also needs to require a briefing to formulate types of executive summaries needed. Finally, the strategic manager must support the project manager in resolving potential risks that are identified using the scenario function of PERT.

Risk Analysis

The strategic manager must acknowledge risk analysis as a proper project management and control tool or technique. This manager should also expect to be kept regularly informed on the status of potential and identified risks. The strategic manager should support the acquisition and use of risk-analysis tools, including PERT/CPM.

Learning Curve Analysis

The strategic manager should support the project manager's efforts in using learning curve analysis to develop a foundation for long-term benefits. Perhaps techniques can be tested to improve repetitive tasks so costs might be lower. Since learning curve analysis requires the involvement of groups outside of IS, the strategic manager should give demonstrated support for any effort in this area.

Documentation

The strategic manager and other interested upper-level managers should use the executive project summaries to monitor results. The strategic manager should give directions as required to ensure that corporate policies are followed—for example, that the project quality plan is consistent with the corporate one. This manager should resolve cross-divisional issues for documentation. This manager should state clearly the requirements to ensure adequate monitoring.

Microsoft Office Products

The strategic manager should work with the tactical manager in defining the executive summary expectations. The strategic manager should make the tactical manager aware of any standards or templates available for output from Microsoft Office applications.

Legacy Software and Hardware

The strategic manager needs to know the impact of a project when it affects the capital budget. Are there funding sources for capital? This question has to be raised during the project viability preproject survey.

Profitability Analysis

The strategic manager needs to work with the IS tactical manager to develop a profitability analysis that can be presented to higher-level management, if necessary. This manager should assist in identifying potential sources within the corporation that may have done profitability analysis. Perhaps, most importantly, the strategic manager should state the expectations for the profitability analysis when the subject is first discussed.

Analysis for Scalability, Interoperability, and Portability

The strategic manager should be aware that there is a high degree of abstraction that is critical to the comprehension of the IS environment.

Team Management

When there is a team management issue, the strategic manager must let the project manager resolve it. The strategic manager must be considered a benevolent observer and supporter of the project team.

Customer Involvement

The strategic manager is the spokesperson for the corporation. The strategic manager should not make decisions about the project to a customer without prior discussion with the project manager. The project manager should be present when the decision is given to the customer. When the strategic manager appoints an inexperienced person as project manager based on the customer's request, then the strategic manager has to ensure that there is a strong support team.

[C]   Tactical Manager's Profile for Project Management

You would not do everything discussed below, but you would need to consider all the actions. You probably would do all the actions of general management; it is just a question of degree. For a very small project, you could state your measured objectives, schedule, and resource utilization in a few pages. In a large complex project, you could expect to have hundreds or even thousands of pages of project administrative documentation. The following are actions that the tactical manager must consider during any IS project management process.

Scope Planning and Defining

The tactical manager's primary responsibility is to ensure that there are measurable defined goals in the scope plan and definition:

- Do not rush.
- Do not be pressured in planning.
- Use historical data.
- The only silly question is the unasked question.
- Focus on the customer's needs rather than on the technical needs.
- Recognize that everything has equal value.
- Remember that the most important word in any project process is *client,* or *customer.*

There is one guiding principle for the tactical manager over all others: Never seek understanding. How do you measure understanding? Understanding is a very vague concept. You need to seek written agreement and as tight a set of measurable scope definitions as possible. Understanding is similar to building your castle on sand.

You need to manage the scope plan and its definitions as a contract. In a contract you have to identify constraints, the baseline, the terms, valid considerations, schedule, budget, required reports, monitoring procedures (all the various control mechanisms), and the closet procedures (historical and financial).

Activity Planning and Sequencing

The tactical manager has a number of actions to consider at this point; however, if the following things are not done, the others will be less than secure. All team members need to attend all of the meetings on activity planning and sequencing. There can be no substitutes.

Here are 16 actions the project manager should accomplish during the activity planning and sequencing phase:

1. Be prepared to run the meetings.

2. Assign resource (skills, equipment, and materials) dependencies.

3. Construct a sequence of activities and their associated times, the basis for the schedule.

4. Define procurement requirements, that is, the need for outside resources.

5. Define project activity parameters and constraints based on the project goals.

6. Determine skill levels required for critical activities and groups of activities.

7. Develop cost estimates against an activity or a group of related activities.

8. Ensure that the operational managers bring to the table support activity data.

9. Establish a project organization structure that includes links between an activity and a person.

10. Establish benchmarks for handling project administrative paperwork, training, and documentation.

11. Have a comprehensive quality control policy with specific activities and a defined sequence of activities that requires the performance of this function throughout the project process.

12. Identify potential risks and opportunities.

13. Identify standards that may affect the project activities.

14. Link budget items with defined activities with customer needs.

15. Remember that customer needs come before technical desires.

16. Write the activity plan using fully confirmed project activities.

Resource Planning

The fundamental tactical actions of the project manager include the following:

- Assist the operational managers in preparing documentation for procuring resources.

- Assist the operational managers in identifying resource links.

- Consider customer needs in acquiring resources.

- Consider if there are alternatives.
- Develop a formula for the availability of people.
- Emphasize the need for skills rather than headcount.
- Ensure that there are budget allocations to support resource requirements.
- Ensure that there are criteria that establish resource needs.
- Identify skills first by labor classification, such as programmer, then by name.
- Know why and how a resource is going to be utilized in the project.
- Resolve capital spending issues.
- Resolve issues of the availability of resources to meet the schedule.
- Validate the need for any resource through a detailed analysis.
- Work with operational managers to ensure a balancing of resources.
- Work with the strategic manager to identify available resources.
- Write the resource plan.

Two guiding principles for a project manager are never to make the following assumptions:

- A skill will be available when needed and for the time required.
- Equipment will be delivered on time as required.
- Resource requirements will stay stable throughout the project.

and that the project manager needs to work within these three resource constraints:

1. Vendor resources will be available on a restricted basis.
2. Computer resources may be limited even for an IS project.
3. Skill resources are usually available on a part-time basis.

Time Estimating

The basic tactical actions of the project manager include the following:

- Ensure that there are criteria for defining time estimates.
- Define the estimates against the project goals.
- Define estimates to average capabilities.
- Do not factor in overtime or possible part-time efforts.
- Time estimates should be done, if possible, by the person who is going to do the activity.

- Define the time measurements (hours, eight-hour days, or 20-day work months).

- Collect all the estimates before doing a total overview.

- Use technical support of vendors to define any installation or configuration time estimates.

- Establish a process in which time estimating becomes more a science than an art.

- Resolve a too-large total of time estimates for the project, beginning with the smallest and working to the largest.

- Set daily project priorities to manage time-estimate issues.

- Analyze time estimates to see possible impacts on the skills, resources, and materials needed for the project.

- Determine with the operational managers what risks might develop with changes to the time estimates.

- Resolve time issues such as getting a required resource well in advance of required date.

- Use project management software to assist in evaluating time estimates.

- Determine how time estimates impact costs (each operational area probably has its own cost per labor-hour).

- Determine how the budget cycle might impact the time estimates, especially those in the fourth quarter.

- Include time estimates for quality control and assurance.

- Determine how time estimates may impact acquisition of outside resources.

- Document issues and discuss them at meetings.

- Look for "forgotten" activities that need time estimates such as meetings, training, and documenting.

- Factor procurement requirements into appropriate time estimates.

- Finish the time-estimating process before attempting to do the scheduling process.

Schedule Developing

The essential tactical actions of the project manager include the following:

- Align the schedule to the customer's expectations.

- Analyze the schedule to see possible impacts on the skills, resources, and materials needed for the project.

- Communicate with vendors, if applicable, on the status of the schedule.

- Create the schedule against the project goals.
- Define estimates to average capabilities.
- Define the lag–lead time relationships.
- Define the start–end time dependencies.
- Determine how the schedule is impacted if you vary cost potentials.
- Determine how the acquisition of outside resources affects the schedule.
- Determine how the budget cycle might impact the schedule, especially in the fourth quarter.
- Determine with the operational managers what risks might develop with the defined schedule.
- Discuss with the procurement group project requirements.
- Do resource and time leveling.
- Document assumptions and constraints for developing the schedule.
- Document issues and discuss them at meetings.
- Ensure resource availability in accordance with the schedule.
- Ensure that the schedule reflects realistically the training and documentation requirements.
- Ensure that the quality control and assurance schedule is appropriate.
- Look for "forgotten" activities that need to be in the schedule.
- Set daily project priorities to manage the schedule.
- Smooth the schedule through a balancing of activities, time, and resources.
- Use project management software to assist in evaluating the status of the schedule.
- Use project management software to validate various potential scheduling scenarios.
- Use the activities to determine the schedule, not the other way around.
- Validate the schedule by getting everyone's concurrence.

Cost Estimating

The essential tactical actions of the project manager include the following:

- Ensure that there are criteria for defining costs estimates.
- Define the estimates against the project goals.
- Define estimates to average capabilities.
- Do not factor in potential changes in costs.

- Cost estimates should be done, if possible, by the person who is going to do the activity.

- Define the cost measurements (hours, eight-hour days, or 20-day work months).

- Analyze cost estimates to see possible impacts on the skills, resources, and materials required for the project.

- Collect all the estimates before doing a total.

- Determine how cost estimates impact time estimates (each operational area probably has its own cost per hour).

- Determine how cost estimates may impact acquisition of outside resources.

- Determine how the budget cycle might impact the cost estimates, especially those in the fourth quarter.

- Determine with the operational managers what risks might develop with changes to the cost estimates.

- Document issues and discuss them at meetings.

- Establish a process whereby cost estimating becomes more of a science than an art.

- Factor procurement requirements into appropriate cost estimates.

- Finish the cost-estimating process before attempting to do the budgeting process.

- Include cost estimates for quality control and assurance.

- Look for "forgotten" activities that need cost estimates such as training or documentation.

- Resolve a too-large total of cost estimates for the project beginning with the least amounts and working to the largest amounts.

- Resolve costs issues well in advance of the "spending" date.

- Set daily project priorities to manage cost-estimating issues.

- Use project management software to assist in evaluating cost estimates.

- Use technical support of vendors to define any installation or configuration cost estimates.

Budget Developing

There is one occasion when the project manager must act as a business manager. This occasion is not an activity of project management. The occasion is the negotiation of who pays for the activities. The timing of payments affect the budget's schedule and its spending by month.

The essential tactical actions of the project manager include the following:

- Be aware of events that affect monthly budget reports (especially validate time-sheet inputs).
- Be aware of the impact of each vendor's invoicing cycle (for example, you spend in the second quarter, the vendor's invoice appears in the fourth quarter).
- Ensure that cost estimates are correctly entered by category or subcategory. (Refine the cost estimates into as many budget items as possible.)
- Ensure that operational managers do monthly budget status reports.
- Ensure reliable cost estimates.
- Ensure reliable resource estimates.
- Ensure reliable time estimates.
- Ensure that predicted spending is reliably given by month.
- Ensure that you have a budget to manage project administration.
- Hold a periodic (usually monthly) meeting on budgetary issues.
- Identify funding for contingencies such as emergency travel.
- Identify capital costs.
- Seek the lowest staff charges.
- Seek to reduce extraordinary costs such as travel.
- Use project management software to evaluate spending prior to any monthly budget report. (Assist in identifying possible input errors, omitted spending, or late invoices.)

Controlling Quality

The essential tactical actions of the project manager include the following:

- Place quality planning at the top of the project agenda.
- Ensure that there are significant time and cost estimates for:
  — monitoring activities
  — testing deliverables
  — evaluating performance
  — measuring performance
  — correcting performance deviations, errors
- Guarantee that there are time estimates for peer reviews.
- Have a configuration control mechanism.

- Create an appropriate reporting system on quality issues.
- Assure that quality issues stay at the deliverable level rather being considered personal.
- Have separate lines in the budget for quality assurance and control
- Have a location where all standard and quality-related documentation is available to all.

Managing Risks and Opportunities

The essential actions of the project management include the following:

- Discuss risk potentials at all scheduled meetings, as a fixed agenda item.
- Identify people to correct and do quick technical analyses of risks.
- Identify people who can do evaluations of issues.
- Ensure that risk management has the time in the schedule to do a proper job.
- Ensure that there is funding in the budget for risk management, distinctive from the quality assurance and control functions.
- Ensure that there are skilled personnel to handle risk evaluations.
- Ensure that there is a contingency fund to handle significant risk issues.
- Ensure that there are criteria developed during the planning phase for identifying risks.
- Be responsible for risk management.
- Have a risk-management program that involves external resources.
- Identify any special equipment that may be required to do analyses of potential risks as determined during the analysis and evaluation of the project goals.

Project Modeling

The tactical manager has to answer the essential question about modeling: "Will the model assist in managing the project?" Even when doing simple extrapolations, the tactical manager must ensure that there are adequate historical data and experiences available to reach realistic decisions. The IS tactical or project manager must identify descriptive data that can be used in making project management decisions such as a cabling inventory. Any financial modeling should be consistent with any corporate model.

Network Optimization

While the tactical project manager should not necessarily involve a customer in the technical minutia of network optimization, there is the need to raise questions that may lead to the requirement for additional management and performance tools. Network optimization issues during a project are directed more toward vendors and the customer.

Gantt Charts and Schedules

The tactical manger should expect contractors and in some cases consultants to present Gantt charts as a part of their proposals. This action should give you a visual list of proposed activities and the expected amount of time per activity according to each contractor. You might use the chart to evaluate the presented price for work from the contractor. These charts become a standard format or environment for contractors and consultants to report their status.

As the project manager, you should use the Gantt chart method to assist in the following five actions:

1. Develop initial project plan
2. Refine the project plan
3. Track project status
4. Revise project activity requirements
5. Report project status

PERT/CPM Techniques

Like any powerful project management tool, a PERT/CPM application has a learning curve. It is suggested you have a person on your staff who uses this tool and is statistically oriented to assist you in the general control and management of the operational tasks or activities of the IS network. Since you are responsible for a complex system with many interdependent components, many attributes, and a multitude of functional and physical links, the use of a PERT application is logical.

Remember that software only speeds up the opportunity to do scenarios. It does not manage the project; you do. In addition, remember to remind higher-level managers and customers that you have to input the data before you can use the software effectively. The secret of success will always be experience.

The following 16 specific actions are required by you if you use PERT/CPM, even if your customer is not the federal government:

1. Define the work elements.
2. Identify the project organization structure.
3. Integrate the company's processes with one another.
4. Establish cost and schedule performance measurements.

5. Sequence work based on interdependencies.

6. Identify all indicators such as milestones and performance goals.

7. Establish and maintain a time-phased budget baseline.

8. Identify budget items by significant cost elements (labor, materials, so forth).

9. Identify the activities in discrete work packages.

10. Identify when an activity is not measurable as a level of effort.

11. Establish overhead budgets for each significant organizational indirect cost.

12. Reconcile cost estimates with actual costs.

13. Record direct costs in accordance with standard budgetary practices.

14. Identify all indirect costs that will be allocated to the project's budget.

15. Develop monthly reports, especially for budget status.

16. Prevent revisions to the project budget except for authorized changes.

Risk Analysis

You have to control the risks; you cannot let the risks control you. A risk may be beyond your direct control in any of a hundred project closets, but once it is out, you are the person that has to solve the risk.

As project manager, you can do at least two things to minimize potential risks:

1. Establish measurable objectives, benchmarks, and performance standards.

2. Prepare for potential risks by using a risk analysis tool.

You need to handle risk analysis in a positive manner. You should ask, "How can we resolve this risk if it happens?" You should not ask, "What can go wrong?" The word "wrong" does imply a moral decision. One should use the word "incorrectly" since that implies a potential measurable standard or benchmark.

You must regularly evaluate identified potential risks and define new ones with the use of risk-analysis tools and techniques. You control and manage risks through the following:

- Team meetings

- Informational conferences with the strategic manager and customers

- Project status reports

- Use of risk-analysis tools to develop solutions to potential risks

You need to overcome the attitudes in the corporate environment that risks are not discussed until they happen and that doing risk analysis is an alarmist activity. Overcome these attitudes by the following:

- Documenting all risks
- Keeping management informed
- Presenting measurable recommendations
- Making sure management comprehends the consequences
- Keeping a neutral position by never saying, "I told you so."

Learning Curve Analysis

You need to frame solutions to learning curve issues in terms of whether comprehension and training are improved a certain percentage. If so, then it is expected there will a potential percentage (range) of improvement in production efficiency for this activity. It is important to give a range rather than a fixed percentage because you should not make a commitment to an absolute figure to the strategic manager and other upper-level managers.

You may need someone who has knowledge of statistics to manipulate the learning curve data for the project. Nonetheless, it still is your responsibility to comprehend the output and then present it to the team and to the strategic manager.

Documentation

The tactical manager has the responsibility to develop executive summaries, a decoding of the technical jargon, so the strategic manager is comfortable with the project's status. You should use the documentation as a tool to control the project but not to suppress initiative. You should keep the strategic manager informed the minute that project documentation might slip. The difficult issue is to manage documentation requirements and standards across different divisions. Many of the writers of the project documentation may be new to the project environment versus the business environment and, if also interested in project results, may be overly enthusiastic and cloud issues with details. Of course, you might have the reverse and not be able to find the details because of high-level highlights. You must distinguish between the support and the administrative types of documents. You must recognize when one document should be closed and another one continue.

Microsoft Office Products

There is one error that will do you in quicker than anything else: It is not a too-small font, or too-crowded slides. It is not a presentation without graphics. It is not a presentation with either too few or many slides. It is a misspelled word. Set aside any document to be presented to management and review it again later before presenting it.

There are 10 questions you need to consider when using office-type applications to do project management:

1. Is an application available for all to use?
2. How effective can I be with different applications to get the most for the least amount of effort?
3. Are there standards available on output of the applications?
4. What are the criteria for an executive summary presentation?
5. What are the criteria for a customer status report presentation?
6. Do I have available someone skilled in one or more of the office-type applications?
7. What standards are required so operational inputs can be easily merged together to develop project reports?
8. What templates are required to create presentations?
9. How can I use a newsletter effectively?
10. How can I use a Web page for project management?

Legacy Software and Hardware

The tactical manager needs to comprehend the implications on the legacy software and hardware of the IS network created by any project.

Profitability Analysis

When doing a project profitability analysis you have to act with your business manager hat on, but when you do the project, you use the analysis as a standard for achieving project goals. You are the person responsible for constructing the analysis. You need to ensure that you have reliable data from the operational managers. Finally, you need to write an effective report or create an effective presentation.

Analysis for Scalability, Interoperability, and Portability

The tactical manager is responsible for making the abstract infrastructure concrete for the customer when issues arise during the project that might impact the infrastructure.

Team Management

You need to adhere to these five golden principles of team management:

1. You lead, the team succeeds.
2. Communicate, communicate, communicate.
3. Praise in public, condemn in private.
4. Software does not rule the project, you guide it.
5. You have your own bias.

Customer Involvement

The tactical manager is the spokesperson for the project. The project manager is the interface with the customer for the company on project issues and the spokesperson for the project team.

[D]   Operational Manager's Profile for Project Management

As the tactical manager, an operational manager would consider to what degree any of the following actions would be done to achieve success while minimizing risk. All the general project management actions need to be at least considered for any project. Any operational manager, whether technical or not, must consider the following actions during the IS project management process.

Scope Planning and Defining

The operational managers should assist the tactical manager in fulfilling that manager's primary responsibility by acquiring the support data to have realistic measurable goals.

- Recognize that creating the scope plan and definition is a team effort.
- Remember that the purpose of the project is customer satisfaction.
- Remember that you are accountable for some part of the project process on a day-to-day basis and you need to set forth a realistic set of measurable responsibilities to the tactical manager and to the team.
- Identify how you and your team can be most efficient and effective in achieving the defined project goals for the scope plan and definition in a timely and cost-effective manner.
- Do not let your specialized concern, whether it is technical, training, documenting, or marketing, override listening to what the customer has to say.

Activity Planning and Sequencing

Probably the operational managers need to acknowledge—more than the tactical manager does—this dictum: The customer comes first, the technical considerations second. No operational area is more important than the defined goals of the project. No operational area is more important than another operational area. It takes the whole to achieve success.

The operational managers need to accomplish the following:

- Identify technical issues or risks that may impact the activity plan.
- Come to meetings with support data for activities from their area.
- Attend all the meetings, do not send an alternate.
- Inform personal team of the outcome of a meeting in a positive manner.
- Identify the implications of required skill levels.
- Identify training and documentation requirements.
- Identify standards and benchmarks that might impact project goals.
- Establish cost estimates.
- Prepare an operational sequence of activities.
- Identify the impact of parameters and constraints of project goals on operational efforts.

Resource Planning

It is the responsibility of the operational managers to give to the IS administrator, the tactical manager, realistic requirements and detailed justifications for any resource needs. The scope plan should be used as the starting point. The customer's needs should be the core for the utilization of any resource, not technical justification.

The following actions require an operational manager's attention in managing the resource plan:

- Balance project resources.
- Be able to justify the why and how a resource is going to be utilized.
- Consider customer needs in acquiring resources.
- Consider if there are alternatives.
- Develop a formula for the availability of people for your group.
- Emphasize the need for skills rather than headcount.
- Procure approved resources.
- Support the tactical manager with justifications for the resource plan.
- Work with the tactical manager to identify resource links.

- Work within the constraints and assumptions of the scope plan in identifying resource requirements.

Time Estimating

The basic functions of the operational managers include the following:

- Identify the people knowledgeable to do the time estimates.
- Notify the tactical manager if there is no one available to do certain time estimates.
- Use the criteria created by the project team for developing the time estimates.
- Limit padding; actually, you should do no padding.
- Review time estimates beginning with the smallest to the largest for signs of excess.
- Include time estimates for quality control and assurance.
- Look for "forgotten" activities that need time estimates such as meetings, training, and documenting.
- Review the inputs of the project management software used by the tactical manager for your operational area.

Schedule Developing

The essential functions of the operational managers include the following:

- Communicate to your team their part in the schedule and the significance of their actions.
- Ensure that the schedule includes quality control and assurance for your operational area.
- Look for "forgotten" activities that need to be included in the schedule.
- Notify the tactical manager when a known slippage is going to happen to the schedule.
- Review the inputs of the project management software used by the tactical manager for any errors in the schedule for your operational area.

Cost Estimating

The basic functions of the operational managers include the following:

- Identify the people knowledgeable to do the cost estimates.
- Include cost estimates for quality control and assurance.

- Limit padding; actually, you should do no padding—use a contingency fund.
- Look for "forgotten" activities that need cost estimates such as training or documenting.
- Notify the tactical manager if there is no one available to do certain cost estimates.
- Review cost estimates, beginning with the least amount to the largest, for signs of excess.
- Review the inputs of the project management software used by the tactical manager for your area to check for any corrections.
- Use the criteria from the project team for developing the cost estimates.

Budget Developing

The basic functions of the operational managers include the following:

- Be aware of the monthly budget constraints that affect your project efforts.
- Ensure reliable cost estimates.
- Ensure reliable resource estimates.
- Ensure reliable time estimates.
- Ensure that if your employees do time sheets, they need to reflect only the effort directed toward the project.
- Inform the tactical manager as soon as possible of any budgetary issue.
- Review with the tactical manager the results from the project management software.
- When you have a budget that includes project spending, then you need to treat those items as a project manager, not as a business manager.

Controlling Quality

The essential actions of the operational managers include the following:

- Support the tactical manager to ensure that there is an appropriate quality program for the project.
- Ensure that the best technicians attend the peer reviews.
- Manage deliverables so they adhere to the configuration control mechanism.
- Report promptly on quality issues and resolutions.

- Support quality assurance and control in its function so that it will not be obtrusive on the day-to-day project operations.

Managing Risks and Opportunities

The tasks of an operational manager for risk management include the following:

- Identify policies, procedures, benchmarks, and standards that assist in minimizing performance errors during the planning, design, development, and implementation phases for your component of the project.
- Support the project manager's efforts in risk management.
- Document risk issues in your area.
- Identify personnel in your area that can assist in minimizing performance errors.
- Assist the quality group in the analysis and evaluation of any identified risk in your operational area.

Project Modeling

An operational manager should reflect that any operational model has to be integrated into a system or project model. An operational model is a less-than-perfect reflection of reality. An operation manager needs to comprehend the importance of extrapolated modeling using historical data and the experiences of the team.

Network Optimization

A system operational manager's prime responsibility to the tactical manager is to identify requirements for management and performance optimization tools. Most project operational managers are not involved with this specific IS issue.

Gantt Charts and Schedules

Operational managers should work with the project manager to develop a standard method and symbols for the project's Gantt charts so there can be an easy integration of data. Operational managers should do Gantt charts for their areas for basic project planning; that is, their project activities of responsibility. An operational manager must consider how the information in a Gantt chart can be presented as an executive summary.

PERT/CPM Techniques

Any operational manager needs to be involved in the seven-step process for developing a PERT chart. The manager needs to verify that all tasks for the operational area are noted and that all activity durations are correct. All managers need to work with the tactical manager to ensure that the project PERT chart is a living, viable document.

Risk Analysis

Each operational manager must recognize that when the tactical manager does risk analysis it is not a threatening act. It is the responsibility of the operational managers to minimize the risks and support the tactical manager in managing the risk's solutions.

Any insight into identifying a potential risk should be seen as a positive, not a negative.

Learning Curve Analysis

Two important operational managers that see significant results from learning curve analyses are those in training and documentation. In addition, any manager who is involved with repetitive tasks should be concerned about this technique. While a programming manager may not first think coding is repetitive, there should be second thoughts in this area. How often and in what manner do programmers apply the rules of the programming (coding) language used?

Documentation

An operational manager has to recognize the need to compromise between documentation for a business goal and for a project goal. Any operational manager needs to consider project documentation as a project team member rather than as an individual business manager. One should recognize the parallel dynamics of a project versus the usually hierarchical dynamics of a business. Any operational manager should lend her or his experiences to ensure that the documentation reflects the measurable goals of the project. Also, when a milestone is achieved, ensure that the documentation reflects the accomplishments of the project to that milestone.

Microsoft Office Products

Operational managers should first consider how they might use the output generated from the office-type applications for their teams. Second, they should be involved in the development of standards since they will be the basic source for information that is used in presentations, checklists, forms, databases, and so forth.

Legacy Software and Hardware

When it comes to the nuts-and-bolts level, the IS operational managers need to analyze the project's goals to detail the impacts of those goals on any IS legacy software and hardware. Most of the non-IS operational managers do have to be concerned with this, except those in documentation and training.

Profitability Analysis

The operational managers have two responsibilities in the constructing of a profitability analysis. First, they need to ensure that the input is reliable. Second, they should review the report for accuracy for their areas and for impacts on their areas.

Analysis for Scalability, Interoperability, and Portability

IS operational managers should support the tactical manager with data so IS issues can be stated in a concrete manner to the customer. The training and documentation managers need to be aware of the implications of the IS abstract infrastructure for the design and development of user training and documentation.

Team Management

Each operational manager has her or his team. Each should follow the same golden rules of team management as the project manager. Managers need to recognize that no one operational group is more important than another group.

Customer Involvement

The operational managers are not spokespersons to the customers; that is the tactical manager's responsibility. Operational managers are not to make project changes that are based on personal conversations with the customer. The responsibility of the operational managers is to adhere to the customer's measurable defined goals unless there is an official change order.

While there must be as much openness with customers as possible, certain guidelines should be followed. If no representative is present when an operational manager has a discussion with a customer, the manager should send an e-mail to the project manager of pertinent details. The operational managers must recognize that only the project manager can make commitments to resources and time for the project.

On the CD-ROM

On the CD-ROM are:

1. Chapter 23 Strategic Manager.ppt—Strategic Manager's Responsibilities

2. Chapter 23 Tactical Manager.ppt—Tactical Manager's Responsibilities

3. Chapter 23 Operational Manager.ppt—Operational Manager's Responsibilities

---

Chapter 24

Project Management in a Microsoft Environment

§ 24.01   OVERVIEW

[A]   Objectives

At the end of this chapter, you will be able to:

- Identify a basic scenario for a streaming media server project.

- Brainstorm a preproposal survey based on the question, "Is this project viable?" in a Microsoft products environment for a discussion with upper-level managers on a streaming media server project.

- Use an example 13-slide initial project proposal for upper-level management for a streaming media server project.

- Identify 13 areas that a project manager needs to consider for managing and controlling a streaming media server project.

- Do preliminary activity planning brainstorming for the installation of a streaming media server.

- Do preliminary resource planning brainstorming for the installation of a streaming media server.

[B]   Project Scenario

Some of your corporation's groups have come to you, the IS manager, about having streaming media functions in the IS network. The essential feature of streaming media is that a downloading audio or video file begins to play while being transmitted to the player.

You think this may be an appropriate IS project and you decide to prepare a proposal for your manager. This means you need to prepare for a preproposal survey (Chapter 1). A part of the survey is to identify the funding sources for the project. The proposal phase begins when there is allocated money in one or more budgets for the project. One possibility is that all the concerned groups will fund a budget line for the project in the IS operational budget.

This scenario is based on the premise of a one-product network backbone. Chapter 23 discussed the use of the project management process by an individual. Chapters 25 and 26 look at the use of the project management process in the contexts of two network architecture paradigms: client/server and objected-oriented. The major difficulty in discussing a one-product environment is that it is more theoretical than real. You need to consider that there are at least six basic Microsoft Windows operating systems in the user world and the implications of this point are not discussed in this scenario. The operating systems are:

- Windows 98
- Windows NT Server 4.0
- Windows CE
- Windows 2000
- Windows ME
- Windows XP

[C]   Preproposal Survey Brainstorming

The preproposal survey is given here along with the types of brainstorming notes you might make to yourself. This is in preparation for a discussion on the viability of this project with a strategic manager, the upper-level manager who will be responsible for the strategic results of the project.

1. ARE POTENTIAL MATERIALS AND EQUIPMENT AVAILABLE TO ACHIEVE PROJECT RESULTS?   Is it possible that the Windows 2000 server can be used? What is the potential streaming media traffic? Will there be capital money available if a new server is required? There are a number of Windows Media Tools required:

- Windows Media Encoder
- Windows Media Author
- Windows Media Indexer

- Plug-in for Adobe Premiere
- VidToASF
- Publish to ASF
- PowerPoint Internet Assistant

According to Microsoft Technical Specifications, the following are recommended requirements. Rather than including minimum requirements, the recommendation requirements are used because of scalability for the IS network. In addition, the customer has expectations, and those expectations may not be completely fulfilled using the minimums.

Windows Media Server Components and Administrative Tools

Component	Recommendation
Processor	Intel Pentium II 266 MHz or better
Memory	128 MB or more
Network Interface Card	Ethernet card, TCP/IP
Available Hard Disk Space	21 MB
Software	Microsoft Internet Explorer 5.0 or later; Microsoft Windows NT version 4.0 with Service Pack 4 (SP4) or later

Windows Media Tools

Component	Recommendation
Processor	Intel Pentium II 266 MHz or better
Memory (RAM)	64 MB
Software	Microsoft Windows 98 or Microsoft Windows NT Server version 4.0 with Service Pack 5 (real-time and scaleable encoding of audio and video up to 320 × 240 × 15 frames per second).
Audio card	Any sound card compatible with Creative Labs Sound Blaster 16
Video capture card	A video capture card that supports Video for Windows.

You will need to determine the user environment as to workstation capabilities, Internet connection, and browser, including version level.

MANAGER'S TIP

One might expect in a large corporation to have software standards for the user environment; however, the IS group perhaps has not had the opportunity or funds to upgrade all the workstations.

---

2. ARE POTENTIAL RESOURCES AVAILABLE TO ACHIEVE THE PROJECT RESULTS? You need to determine the impact of streaming on IS network bandwidth, and to determine time estimates for creating streaming media files, designing and developing the server, and implementation. Are the necessary skill types available for working with Advanced Streaming File format (ASF), CODECs (Compression/ Decompression), and media encoding? What kinds of documentation and training are required? Are potential costs for resources (server software and hardware, workstation software and hardware, especially high-speed modems) going to be too high to achieve project results? You need to get everyone to recognize that with any new technology, it probably will take twice as long to complete the project as expected. ActiveX controls are needed for embedding the Windows Media Player at the Web site. You need to consider a standalone Windows Media Player. What are the daily maintenance requirements? What are the performance monitoring requirements?

3. ARE PROJECT COSTS GOING TO BE TOO HIGH TO ACHIEVE PROJECT RESULTS? You need to get project budget allocations and potential allocations from concerned parties and compare to estimates from Microsoft representative for tools, services, and player plus internal costs. Consider the need for a new server. What are the costs per workstation? What are upgrade workstation costs?

4. ARE THERE APPROPRIATE PROJECT JUSTIFICATIONS TO ACHIEVE PROJECT RESULTS? Are there sufficient audio and video files available to use the server immediately? What kinds of revenues can be generated for the IS group and the corporation? Are there sufficient reductions in labor-hours for justifying the server? Are there alternatives to using the server that are efficient and effective? How does this project enhance the existing Web effort? How can this project be integrated into the present Web effort? Can this project be done in phases? Can there be a set of priorities established as to when a certain group starts using streaming media? A set of measurable objectives is needed to justify the project. Organize the notes from the various groups to see if there is a consensus of goals (ensure that each group gives a set of measurable goals). Who are the audiences?

5. ARE THERE APPROPRIATE SKILLS AVAILABLE TO ACHIEVE PROJECT RESULTS? Skilled people are needed who comprehend Windows Media Technologies. They should be able to create, deliver, and implement streaming media files in the Advanced Streaming Media (ASF). They also should be capable of authoring interactive streaming media files and rich multimedia presentations (individual customer group responsibilities). Are outside consultants required? Are there internal consultants available?

6. ARE THERE BUDGETARY MONIES AVAILABLE TO ACHIEVE THE PROJECT RESULTS? What is the level of commitment of each group as to budget allocations and making available appropriate skill types? Can budget allocations be made incremental such as planning, design, and developing with implementation?

7. **ARE THERE PROJECT TOOLS AVAILABLE TO ENSURE CONTROL TO ACHIEVE PROJECT RESULTS?** What new tools are required for this effort? What legacy tools can be used in this project? The seven Windows Media Tools are needed. The use of available performance tools for this project needs to be determined.

8. **DO THE PROJECT RESULTS MEET THE STRATEGIC GOALS OF THE COMPANY?** Identify corporate strategic goals to deliver in a timely manner information to the customers and internal IS network users. Impact on IS goals and future commitments needs to be determined.

9. **DO THE PROJECT RESULTS REFLECT EFFICIENCY AND INNOVATION?** How will a streaming media server improve the present efforts for distributing multimedia to corporate customers and internal users? Can radical innovation activities be done in such areas as documentation, training, and IS customer service using streaming media?

10. **HOW MAY THE PROJECT RESULTS IMPACT ANY PRODUCT PRICING?** Talk is needed with training and documentation about pay-for-view opportunities. Can the use of interactive guidelines reduce costs in the IS customer service group?

11. **HOW MAY PROJECT RESULTS MEET CUSTOMER NEEDS?** Potential applications from adding a streaming media server for internal and external uses include news, e-commerce data, large customer document transfers, marketing product graphics and corporate training. What are the efforts in these areas today and planned for the future?

12. **HOW STABLE IS THE IS ORGANIZATION FOR ACHIEVING THE PROJECT RESULTS?** Identify any major changes in the organization that could potentially impact the project. What people are leaving? What people are about to be promoted?

13. **HOW STABLE IS THE TECHNOLOGY REQUIRED TO ACHIEVE PROJECT RESULTS?** What are the potential impacts on choosing a certain version of Windows Media Technologies and is there going to be a new release soon? Review documentation on Microsoft's Web site for the latest marketing and technical information. Are there any alternatives to this particular technology?

14. **HOW WILL THE RESULTS IMPACT THE RETURN ON INVESTMENT (ROI)?** Can the IS group or the corporation generate revenues based on this project? Can the corporation charge for streaming either customer documentation or training through the Web? Are there any indirect-cost savings such as reduction in cost of present multimedia distributions to customers?

15. **IS THE DEADLINE REALISTIC TO ACHIEVE PROJECT RESULTS?** Time estimates are needed on design, development, and installation from a Microsoft representative. Does any potential customer have a specific end-date requirement, and if so, what is the reason?

16. WHAT ARE THE EVENTS THAT CAN CAUSE THE PROJECT TO FAIL? Will we try to do too much too quickly? The customer's expectation of high quality and continuous viewing may not be met. The user's experience must be straightforward. The user may not have the level of modem required to achieve satisfactory results. There is always the potential for software bugs with any new technology.

17. WHAT ARE THE EVENTS THAT CAN MAKE THE PROJECT SUCCESSFUL? What types of documentation are available on installed streaming media servers from Microsoft and technical journals? There is probably a large amount of information on the Web on streaming media technology. You can always go to a news group and ask a question. Potential consultants can assist with the project. Microsoft tends to put together one-stop packages that usually work at a satisfactory level to many users.

18. WHAT ARE THE POSSIBLE IMPACTS OF THE END RESULTS ON THE INFORMATION SYSTEM? How will streaming media impact the bandwidth? What will be the new requirements on IS customer service? Will new personnel be required to maintain this effort? Potential issues include bandwidth, compression, compatibility, media standards, transfer protocols, and security (firewall). For streaming media there appear to be three basic categories of issues: creating, delivering, and viewing of files. A stated benchmark is that when the application is optimized, it should support more than 1,200 28.8-Kbps clients on a single-processor Pentium II server. Is there any degradation in service as you get closer to the upper limit of 1,200?

19. WHAT ARE THE POSSIBLE RESISTANT CONCERNS TO PROJECT RESULTS? Will some of the groups back out of their commitments if streaming media is done in phases? How strong are the budget commitments? Will some groups permit their people to support other groups in this effort?

20. WHAT IS THE LEVEL OF FORMAL AUTHORITY OF THE IS PROJECT MANAGER TO ACHIEVE THE PROJECT RESULTS? Upper-level management needs to give a written commitment that you can resolve project issues across divisions.

[D]   Initial Proposal Presentation

Below is the outline for an example presentation to the strategic manager using Microsoft PowerPoint. On the CD-ROM, see "Chapter 24 Initial Proposal Presentation.ppt."

This presentation is limited to 13 slides for a half-hour presentation with questions. This presentation is to give the strategic manager a "feel" for the project. The technical details are in the preproposal activity.

Slide 1

Streaming Media Server Project

Slide 2

Potential Applications

- News
- Corporate training
- Marketing presentations
- Customer documentation
- IS customer service guides

Slide 3

Key Function

Begins playing the video or audio clip when the download starts

Slide 4

Importance

- On-demand requests
- Live presentations
- Video presentations in association with a marketing effort
- Enhanced Web presence

Slide 5

Potential Revenues

- Pay-for-view (Training)
- Marketing presentations

Slide 6

Components

- Windows NT Server
- Windows Media Tools
- Windows Media Services
- Windows Media Player

Slide 7

Participating Groups

- Product Project Management
- Training

- Customer Documentation
- IS Customer Service

Slide 8

Budget Allocations

- Product Project Management
- IS Customer Service

Slide 9

Potential Budget Allocations

- Training
- Customer Documentation

Slide 10

Advantages

- Quicker distribution of multimedia files internally and externally
- Enhanced changes in the informational distribution processes for marketing, documentation, and training
- Improved IS customer service

Slide 11

Special Requirements

- New tools for IS and multimedia
- Additional personnel to support interactive media development and IS maintenance
- Training in Windows Media Technologies

Slide 12

Impacts

- Enhanced textual presentations
- Sound (music, narration, special effects)
- Video
- Interactive presentations

Slide 13

Conclusion

You can have real-time messaging that is visual and with sound

§ 24.02 MAJOR PROJECT MANAGEMENT AREAS

[A] Overview

This section is a minimum set of major project management areas you need to consider in managing and controlling this project. These areas are discussed in detail in Section One, Chapters 1 to 10. Why is the word *areas* used rather than *activities?* For example, the quality control area includes these five activities:

1. Writing Quality Control and Assurance Plan
2. Identifying personnel
3. Establishing cost and time estimates
4. Gathering benchmarks and standards
5. Developing quality control milestones

The essential project management areas (feel free to add to the list) are:

- Preproposal survey
- Kickoff meeting
- Measurable project objectives defined
- Activities planned and sequenced with associated cost, time, and resource estimates
- Resources determined as to when, who is going to use, length of use, and costs (capital costs)
- Time estimates established for activities (labor-hours), which includes duration (activity from beginning to end in calendar time)
- Schedule developed that includes associated people and resources using techniques such as Gantt charts and PERT network activity diagrams
- Cost estimates developed that are related to activities, resources, and budget lines
- Project budget created based on corporate accounting requirements. If possible, there should be a separate project budget instead of having project expenditures and revenues merged into one or more budgets
- Quality control and assurance system developed
- Initial risk analysis done (beyond the one done in preproposal)
- Project management documentation process defined
- Communication program defined

Notice that there is no comment on the technical areas. These areas are the responsibilities of the operational managers. Remember, the basic responsibilities of the project manager are to manage and control the project administrative activities, not manage and control the day-to-day technical activities.

[B]   Activity Planning Brainstorming

This section gives examples of ideas that might be put forth during the initial meeting on developing the activity plan. The ideas are given as a brainstorming session based on the information given earlier. You still have to establish sequence, time, cost, and resource estimates with each activity, as discussed in Chapter 3.

This list is not complete, but a major start:

1. Create ASF files.
2. Develop streaming media server.
3. Develop implementation plan.
4. Get identified skills.
5. Ensure that all goals are measurable.
6. Get standards and benchmarks.
7. Identify workstation requirements and the level of compliance.
8. Get a presentation from a Microsoft representative.
9. Develop a quality control system.
10. Do activity sequencing.
11. Give resource estimates (cost, where, when, availability).
12. Give time estimates, including duration.
13. Give cost estimates (budgeted or not budgeted).
14. Perform risk analysis.
15. Plan schedule.
16. Develop budget.
17. Develop communication plan.
18. Make incentive plan.
19. Do training.
20. Provide documentation.

[C]   Resource Planning Brainstorming

This section gives examples of ideas that might be put forth during the initial meeting on developing the resource plan. The ideas are given as a brainstorming session based on the information given earlier. You still have to establish activity relationships, when required and for how long, cost and resource estimates with each activity as discussed in Chapter 4. You also need to identify skill levels for people and benchmarks for hardware. The list below is not complete, but a major start:

1. MCSE Windows 2000 Server skill
2. Multimedia (encoding a plus) skill
3. A consultant that has done this type of project several times
4. Microsoft Windows 2000 server
5. Windows Media Tools package
6. Recommended hardware and memory requirements in accordance with Microsoft technical specifications
7. Data on user workstations
8. Time estimates and duration for use of skills
9. When hardware is required
10. ASF skill
11. Data on available files for streaming media
12. Maintenance skill
13. Present Web features
14. Available IS resources (skills, hardware, and software)
15. Support people requirements
16. Chart on how resources are linked to goals and activities
17. Impact statement (resource unavailable)
18. Procurement requirements
19. Capital requirements
20. Training requirements

On the CD-ROM

On the CD-ROM are:

1. Chapter 24 Overview.ppt—Chapter Overview, Project Management in a Microsoft Environment
2. Chapter 24 Initial Proposal Presentation.ppt—Example Proposal Presentation to Strategic Manager

Chapter 25

Project Management and the Client/Server Paradigm

§ 25.01   Overview
  [A]   Objectives
  [B]   Project Scenario
  [C]   Preproposal Survey Brainstorming
  [D]   Initial Proposal Presentation
  [E]   Major Project Management Areas
  [F]   Activity Planning Brainstorming
  [G]   Resource Planning Brainstorming

§ 25.01   OVERVIEW

[A]   Objectives

At the end of this chapter, you will be able to:

- Identify a basic scenario for a firewall project using the client/server paradigm.
- Brainstorm a preproposal survey based on the question "Is this project viable?" for a firewall using the client/server paradigm project.
- Use an example 13-slide initial firewall project proposal for upper-level management using the client/server paradigm.
- Identify 13 areas that a project manager needs to consider for managing and controlling a firewall project in a client/server paradigm.
- Do preliminary activity planning brainstorming for the installation of a firewall using the client/server paradigm.
- Do preliminary resource planning brainstorming for the installation of a firewall using the client/server paradigm.

[B]   Project Scenario

The accounting group has discussed with you, the IS manager, their requirement for a firewall to protect their data. The accounting group also uses data from the human resource group. The new firewall has to protect this data. The accounting group and the procurement group use common databases that need mutual security of the firewall. They think their data is being hacked. Since there is a firewall for the Internet, it must be an internal situation.

You think this may be an appropriate IS project to improve intranet security and you decide to prepare a proposal for your manager. You do question whether there has been any hacking. This means you need to prepare for a preproposal survey (Chapter 1). A part of the survey is to identify the funding sources for the project. The proposal phase begins when there is allocated money in one or more budgets for the project. One possibility is that the accounting and procurement groups will fund a budget line for the project in the IS operational budget.

This scenario is based on using the language of the client/server paradigm to project manage the installation of a new firewall. Chapter 23 discussed the use of the project management process by an individual. Chapter 24 looked at adding a streaming media server in a Microsoft environment (one product). Chapter 26 looks at the use of the project management process for installing a CORBA Web server using the object-oriented paradigm.

[C]   Preproposal Survey Brainstorming

The preproposal survey is given here with the types of brainstorming notes you might make to yourself. This effort is in preparation for a discussion on the viability of this project with a strategic manager, the upper-level manager who will be responsible for the strategic results of the project.

1. ARE POTENTIAL MATERIALS AND EQUIPMENT AVAILABLE TO ACHIEVE PROJECT RESULTS? Will there be capital money available if a new firewall is required? There may be an alternative control system. What legacy software and hardware may be applicable to this project?

2. ARE POTENTIAL RESOURCES AVAILABLE TO ACHIEVE THE PROJECT RESULTS? Can you afford for my IS personnel to be taken off their operational duties and be placed on this project? Is it cost effective to outsource this project? Since you got this far, you guess you can support the project if it is extended to a more comprehensive security system.

3. ARE PROJECT COSTS GOING TO BE TOO HIGH TO ACHIEVE PROJECT RESULTS? Is the accounting group willing to spend the money for a firewall with the features and functions they expect? The range can be from $500 to $4,500 or more for the firewall software. There might need to be a new file server plus the firewall because of a potential large number of clients (accounting, procurement, and human resources). Is accounting willing to change its data transfer procedures? Probably a more important issue than the dollars: How many

clients have to be on this server? The basic rule is never run any services on a computer that is used as a firewall.

4. ARE THERE APPROPRIATE PROJECT JUSTIFICATIONS TO ACHIEVE PROJECT RESULTS? The "measurable" justification is that the accounting manager thinks there has been at least one unauthorized attempt per week to get into the accounting database. How does the account manager know this? Since there is a firewall on the IS network, there is either a network security failure (at least one internal hacker) or the accounting manager is mistaken. No red flags from IS reports.

5. ARE THERE APPROPRIATE SKILLS AVAILABLE TO ACHIEVE PROJECT RESULTS? There are people in the IS group who have installed a firewall before. A further definition is needed of expectations of the accounting group as to level of security. What about a departmental security policy? Could this be a modification of the IS Security Policy?

6. ARE THERE BUDGETARY MONIES AVAILABLE TO ACHIEVE THE PROJECT RESULTS? What is the level of commitment of the accounting group and perhaps the procurement group as to budget allocations? Might budget allocations be made incremental, such as planning, design, and developing with implementation? This perhaps needs to be a one-package effort.

7. ARE THERE PROJECT TOOLS AVAILABLE TO ENSURE CONTROL TO ACHIEVE PROJECT RESULTS? What new tools are required for this effort? What legacy tools can be used in this project? Which available performance tools to use for this project needs to be determined. Does the accounting manager really need any reports or should this be an operational controlled server to protect accounting's data?

8. DO THE PROJECT RESULTS MEET THE STRATEGIC GOALS OF THE COMPANY? The firewall needs to:

- Adhere to the procedures or standards outlined in the corporate security policy.
- Use a security standard such as the Digital Encryption Standard (DES).
- Use a server interface from RSA Data Security.

9. DO THE PROJECT RESULTS REFLECT EFFICIENCY AND INNOVATION? What are the consequences if someone breaks into accounting's databases? Destroys data? Changes data? Reads data?

10. HOW MAY PROJECT RESULTS IMPACT ANY PRODUCT PRICING? What are the indirect savings to the corporation because of this firewall? See the response to question 9.

11. HOW MAY PROJECT RESULTS MEET CUSTOMER NEEDS? Protection is an obvious answer. What will be the resistance to tighter data transfer controls and a password system? Measurable security goals are needed other than "no hacker at anytime."

12. HOW STABLE IS THE IS ORGANIZATION FOR ACHIEVING THE PROJECT RESULTS? Identify any major changes in the organization that could potentially impact the project. What people are leaving? What people are about to be promoted? How are things in the financial group? Network stability is okay as long as we go with a vendor that has a compatible and interoperable product to the present IS security system.

13. HOW STABLE IS THE TECHNOLOGY REQUIRED TO ACHIEVE PROJECT RESULTS? What is the realistic level of security expected? Are there any alternatives to adding a firewall?

14. HOW WILL THE RESULTS IMPACT THE RETURN ON INVESTMENT (ROI)? What are potential indirect-cost savings because of the new security? See the response to question 9.

15. IS THE DEADLINE REALISTIC TO ACHIEVE PROJECT RESULTS? Does accounting have a specific end-date requirement and, if so, what is the reason? How realistic is this hacking issue?

16. WHAT ARE THE EVENTS THAT CAN CAUSE THE PROJECT TO FAIL? The customer's expectation of high-quality security might not be met. The user's experience with an additional password system must be straightforward. Accounting wants something significantly different from the present IS security system.

17. WHAT ARE THE EVENTS THAT CAN MAKE THE PROJECT SUCCESSFUL? There is a large amount of information on the Web on using a firewall. The IS group has installed its own IS network firewall.

18. WHAT ARE THE POSSIBLE IMPACTS OF THE END RESULTS ON THE INFORMATION SYSTEM? What will be the new requirements on IS customer service? Will new personnel be required to maintain this effort? How does the issue raised impact the security of the present security system? What in the Security Policy has to be changed?

19. WHAT ARE THE POSSIBLE RESISTANT CONCERNS TO PROJECT RESULTS? The process in using the firewall may appear to be too restrictive to some of the users.

Upper-level management may see this matter as one for IS because of present security safeguards.

20. What is the level of formal authority of the IS project manager to achieve the project results? Upper-level management needs to give a written commitment that can be used to resolve project issues across groups.

MANAGER'S TIP

After reading the responses to the survey, do you get an idea that the IS manager has a hidden agenda? Watch for hidden agendas in project management. A person might have a hidden agenda, and the most dangerous person to have one is the potential project manager. There are two projects here: They are installing a firewall, and creating a virtual (logical) accounting group network.

Are you confused over the survey? You are thinking that a firewall is usually the only computer of the intranet that is attached to the outside world (Internet). It is a proxy for each intranet client. The issue raised here is the need for an internal firewall. If the IS manager is getting no red flags of possible hackers, either there is a problem with the IS firewall's security protocols or there is at least one disgruntled employee who is playing the role of hacker. While this is not the way to approach a problem, the IS manager appears to want to have a set of virtual local area networks (LANs) behind firewalls as the IS network design for the wide area network (WAN).

In response 2, the IS manager is perhaps more fully considering the concept of the client/server paradigm. The paradigm considers a distributed system divided among one or more servers handling client tasks to resolve requests for a particular set of protocols, and in this case it is the ones for a firewall. The IS manager may be envisioning a set of distributed firewalls in contrast to the single Internet firewall. This model considers the network security as protection against disgruntled employees who are potential hackers. This scenario may be more common today than the "Internet hacker" scenario. This network permits clients and servers to be distributed (located) on a variety of nodes.

[D]   Initial Proposal Presentation

Below is the outline for an example presentation to the strategic manager using Microsoft PowerPoint. On the CD-ROM, see "Chapter 25 Accounting Firewall Project Proposal.ppt."

This presentation is limited to thirteen slides for a half-hour presentation with questions. This presentation is to give the strategic manager a "feel" for the project. The technical details are in the preproposal activity.

Slide 1

Accounting Firewall Project

Slide 2

Basic Goals

- Reduces internal security risks
- Furthers the development of the IS distributed security client/server model
- Protects the corporation's reputation

Slide 3

Key Function

An internal firewall to protect against disgruntled employee threats toward accounting databases

Slide 4

Types of Attacks

- Denial of service
- Destruction of data
- Intrusion
- Theft of data

Slide 5

Types of Attackers

- Crackers
- Hackers
- Joyriders
- Spies

Slide 6

What Is a Firewall?

- Controlled entry point
- Control barrier
- Controlled exit point

Slide 7

Participating Groups

- Accounting
- Procurement
- Human Resources
- IS Group

Slide 8

Budget Allocations

- Financial Group
- IS Group

Slide 9

Potential Budget Allocations

- Human Resources

Slide 10

Advantages

Reduces internal security threats to the financial group where data can be

- Read
- Changed
- Destroyed

Slide 11

Special Requirements

- Server
- Firewall server and software
- New security tools for IS
- Additional two employees (potential)

Slide 12

Impacts

- Changes to accounting data transfer procedures
- Changes to the IS network design

- Better internal security controls
- Security model for other groups within the corporation

Slide 13

Conclusion

New firewall limits internal security exposures, improves internal security effectiveness, and protects the corporation's reputation

[E] Major Project Management Areas

This section is a minimum set of major project management areas you need to consider in managing and controlling this project. These areas are discussed in detail in Section One, Chapters 1–10. Why is the word "areas" used rather than "activities"? For example, the Quality Control area includes these five activities:

1. Writing Quality Control and Assurance Plan
2. Identifying personnel
3. Establishing cost and time estimates
4. Gathering benchmarks and standards
5. Developing quality control milestones

The essential project management areas (feel free to add to the list) are:

- Pre-proposal survey
- Kickoff meeting
- Measurable project objectives defined
- Activities planned and sequenced with associated cost, time, and resource estimates
- Resources determined as to when, who is going to use, length of use, and costs (capital costs)
- Time estimates established for activities (labor-hours) and this includes duration (activity from beginning to end in calendar time)
- Schedule is developed that includes associated people and resources using techniques such as Gantt charts and PERT network activity diagrams
- Cost estimates are developed that are related to activities, resources, and budget lines
- Project budget is created based on corporate accounting requirements;

if possible, there should be a separate project budget instead of having the project expenditures and revenues merged into one or more budgets

- Quality Control and Assurance system developed
- Initial risk analysis done (beyond the one done in preproposal)
- Project management documentation process defined
- Communication program defined

Notice there is no comment on the technical areas. These areas are the responsibilities of the operational managers. Remember, the basic responsibilities of the project manager are to manage and control the project administrative activities, not manage and control the day-to-day technical activities.

[F]   Activity Planning Brainstorming

This section gives examples of ideas that might be put forth during the initial meeting on developing the activity plan. The ideas are presented as a brainstorming session based on the information given earlier. You still have to establish sequence, time, cost, and resource estimates with each activity as discussed in Chapter 3. This list is not complete, but a major start:

1. Survey existing conditions
2. Establish measurable requirements
3. Choose a firewall that meets existing conditions and requirements
4. Develop a security strategy
5. Implement the server
6. Plan the virtual (logical) network for the accounting group
   - Client load estimate
   - Network map
   - Data link definitions
   - Security protocols
7. Get identified skills
   - Firewall
   - Security
   - Server
   - SQL, maybe
8. Design an accounting client/server security model
9. Create rules base
10. Get standards and benchmarks
11. Identify workstation requirements and the level of password compliance

12. Develop an objects manager GUI

13. Get a presentation from server vendor representative

14. Quality control system

15. Define a security services manager

16. Activity sequencing

17. Resource estimates (cost, where, when, availability)

18. Time estimates including duration

19. Cost estimates (budgeted or not budgeted)

20. Risk analysis

21. Schedule

22. Budget

23. Communication plan

24. Incentive plan

25. Training

26. Maintenance requirements

27. Documentation

28. Create a response strategy

29. Check Internet news groups for information
    - alt.security
    - alt.security.announce
    - comp.security.firewall

30. Check for firewall mailing list

[G] Resource Planning Brainstorming

This section gives examples of ideas that might be put forth during the initial meeting on developing the activity plan. The ideas are given as a brainstorming session based on the information given earlier. You still have to establish activity relationships, when required and for how long, and cost and resource estimates with each activity as discussed in Chapter 4. You also need to identify skill levels for people and benchmarks for hardware. The following list is not complete, but a major start:

1. Firewall skill

2. Security system skill

3. A consultant from firewall vendor

4. Firewall server

5. Firewall tools package

- Authentication
- Analysis
- Filtering
- Proxy
- Utilities

6. Time estimates and duration for use of skills
7. When is the hardware required?
8. Maintenance skill
9. Available IS resources (skills, hardware, and software)
10. Support people requirements
11. Chart on how resources are linked to goals and activities
12. Impact statement (resource unavailable)
13. Procurement requirements
14. Capital requirements
15. Training requirements

On the CD-ROM

On the CD-ROM are:

1. Chapter 25 Overview.ppt—Chapter Overview, Project Management and the Client/Server Paradigm

2. Chapter 25 Accounting Firewall Project Proposal.ppt—Example Proposal Presentation to Strategic Manager

Chapter 26

Project Management and the CORBA Paradigm

§ 26.01   Overview
> [A]   Objectives
> [B]   Project Scenario
> [C]   Preproposal Survey Brainstorming
> [D]   Initial Proposal Presentation
> [E]   Major Project Management Areas
> [F]   Activity Planning Brainstorming
> [G]   Resource Planning Brainstorming
> [H]   Analysis of the Scenario

§ 26.01   OVERVIEW

[A]   Objectives

At the end of this chapter, you will be able to:

- Identify a basic scenario for a CORBA Web server project.
- Brainstorm a preproposal survey based on the question "Is this project viable?" for a CORBA Web server project.
- Use an example 13-slide initial CORBA Web server project proposal for upper-level management using the object-oriented paradigm.
- Identify thirteen areas that a project manager needs to consider for managing and controlling CORBA Web server project.
- Do preliminary activity planning brainstorming for the installation of a CORBA Web server.
- Do preliminary resource planning brainstorming for the installation of a CORBA Web server.

[B]   Project Scenario

You found that some of the applications in the IS network make distributed requests, but there is no wait time for responses. They require notifications when there are available responses. Because CORBA communication uses a synchronous request and response, an application can issue a request and poll for the response. Using this concept, you might be able to develop a more complex application architecture than with the client/server paradigm.

Perhaps server communication might be improved by developing a CORBA Web server. CORBA IDL defines this type of server as an Interface, which then implements a particular interface. This implementation is a distributed object. A client communicates through an object reference. Network communications happen when an operation is performed on the object reference.

There are two important acronyms used in this chapter. CORBA stands for Common Object Request Broker Architecture. IDL stands for Interface Definition Language. In addition, CORBA architecture refers to client and server; these concepts are not exactly the same as in the client/server architecture. The roles of these two components or objects can be reversed during a remote method invocation. There are other subtleties, but this chapter is not on CORBA; it's a project management scenario in a CORBA paradigm.

There is the position that CORBA can be used to create distributed, cross-platform applications that include reusable modules. Because your network is expanding very rapidly and there is the possibility of a merger, you need to consider any technology that might assist in your management of your IS network.

The basic buzzwords about Java are also pertinent to thinking about CORBA. They are scalability, interoperability, and portability. In addition, there are three important network issues that you have to resolve:

- Need a cross-platform environment
- Open standards is an important issue
- IS network is expanding rapidly

Because you think you need to move to a new technology, albeit still unstable, you prepare for a preproposal survey (Chapter 1). A part of the survey is to identify the funding sources for the project. You need upper-level management to buy into this project and to give you special project funding outside of your operational budget.

This scenario is based on using the language of the object-oriented paradigm as implemented through the CORBA specifications to project manage the installation of a new CORBA Web server. Chapter 23 discussed the use of the project management process by an individual. Chapter 24 looked at adding a streaming media server in a Microsoft environment (one product). Chapter 25 looked at the use of the project management process for installing an intranet firewall within a client/server architecture.

This chapter takes a very broad sweep at a very complex technology, as both client/server architecture and streaming media are. It is essential to comprehend the project management style differences among Chapters 23–26. A very simplistic notion is used in this chapter to parallel Chapter 25: Where you had a client/server paradigm, you have in this chapter an object/interface.

[C]   Preproposal Survey Brainstorming

The preproposal survey is discussed here with the types of brainstorming notes you might make to yourself. This is in preparation for a discussion on the viability of this project with a strategic manager, the upper-level manager who will be responsible for the strategic results of the project. You are selling your own ideas rather than a potential customer's ideas.

1. ARE POTENTIAL MATERIALS AND EQUIPMENT AVAILABLE TO ACHIEVE PROJECT RESULTS?   You need budget approval for a server. You need to check with vendor about additional hardware requirements.

2. ARE POTENTIAL RESOURCES AVAILABLE TO ACHIEVE THE PROJECT RESULTS?   Do you need to create a special team to do coding (Java and IDL) or do you outsource? What is the impact on the legacy infrastructure?

3. ARE PROJECT COSTS GOING TO BE TOO HIGH TO ACHIEVE PROJECT RESULTS?   Do you need to acquire cost specification for at least three vendors because of procurement policy?

4. ARE THERE APPROPRIATE PROJECT JUSTIFICATIONS TO ACHIEVE PROJECT RESULTS?   The potential merger, rapid growth, and special workstation requirements should be ample justification. You need to show how this server might save labor-hours.

5. ARE THERE APPROPRIATE SKILLS AVAILABLE TO ACHIEVE PROJECT RESULTS?   While Java and server skills are available, how do these skills relate to CORBA requirements? You probably will need skill sets for CORBA architecture and IDL. Discuss with several vendors and then develop skills criteria.

6. ARE THERE BUDGETARY MONIES AVAILABLE TO ACHIEVE THE PROJECT RESULTS?   You need to get the boss to approve the project money separate from the operational budget.

7. ARE THERE PROJECT TOOLS AVAILABLE TO ENSURE CONTROL TO ACHIEVE PROJECT RESULTS?   What new tools are required for this effort? Can legacy tools be used in this project? You need to determine the use of available performance tools for this project.

8. DO THE PROJECT RESULTS MEET THE STRATEGIC GOALS OF THE COMPANY? The CORBA Web server might assist in the new plans for the company's Web effort.

9. DO THE PROJECT RESULTS REFLECT EFFICIENCY AND INNOVATION? This project is certainly innovative. It seems in every magazine one reads, there is an article on CORBA. It is on the cutting edge of a new technology that is still trying to find its direction.

10. HOW MAY PROJECT RESULTS IMPACT ANY PRODUCT PRICING? What are the indirect savings to the corporation because of this server?

11. HOW MAY PROJECT RESULTS MEET CUSTOMER NEEDS? Can you show how this server will be better than the present Web server?

12. HOW STABLE IS THE IS ORGANIZATION FOR ACHIEVING THE PROJECT RESULTS? Identify any major changes in the organization that could potentially impact the project. What people are leaving? What people are about to be promoted?

13. HOW STABLE IS THE TECHNOLOGY REQUIRED TO ACHIEVE PROJECT RESULTS? CORBA 1.0 came out in 1991. The CORBA 3.0 specification was released in late 1999. Most of the market is still working with CORBA 2.2. There is also the issue that the Object Management Group (OMG) is more vendor driven than standard driven.

14. HOW WILL THE RESULTS IMPACT THE RETURN ON INVESTMENT (ROI)? What are potential indirect cost savings because of the new server? Can there be additional server capabilities that assist in generating revenues?

15. IS THE DEADLINE REALISTIC TO ACHIEVE PROJECT RESULTS? What is a reasonable date to get this server implemented? You need to talk to the vendors about data.

16. WHAT ARE THE EVENTS THAT CAN CAUSE THE PROJECT TO FAIL? Examples include the boss does not approve a budget; you do not get the skills required; the technology is too unstable; the project requires too many changes to your present network.

17. WHAT ARE THE EVENTS THAT CAN MAKE THE PROJECT SUCCESSFUL? The boss is willing to let you experiment in this area. The selected vendor has experience and is reliable. There are no major impacts on the rest of the network. Costs can be kept down.

18. WHAT ARE THE POSSIBLE IMPACTS OF THE END RESULTS ON THE INFORMATION SYSTEM? What will be the new requirements on IS customer service? Will new personnel be required to maintain this effort? How does this issue impact the security of the present security system? What in the security policy has to be changed?

19. WHAT ARE THE POSSIBLE RESISTANT CONCERNS TO PROJECT RESULTS? Too many of the IS personnel may want to stay with a technology in which they have a comfort zone. People may ask, why change a Web server that works?

20. WHAT IS THE LEVEL OF FORMAL AUTHORITY OF THE IS PROJECT MANAGER TO ACHIEVE THE PROJECT RESULTS? Upper-level management needs to give you a written commitment that you can resolve project issues across groups, in particular with those that have an interest in the present Web site.

Based on the above responses, the IS manager does not seem ready to proceed with the preproposal phase. For the sake of discussion, let us assume that the IS manager got a bit more information, actually more than a bit, and goes ahead. Unfortunately a few IS managers might try to do the preproposal presentation without all the information. This approach involves selling the idea and then praying one can deliver. In such a situation, project management really is required.

[D]   Initial Proposal Presentation

Below is the outline for an example presentation to the strategic manager using Microsoft PowerPoint. On the CD-ROM, see "Chapter 26 CORBA Web Server Project Proposal.ppt."

This presentation is limited to 13 slides for a half-hour presentation with questions. This presentation is to give the strategic manager a "feel" for the project. The technical details are in the preproposal activity.

Slide 1

CORBA Web Server Project

Slide 2

Basic Goals

- Cross-platform environment
- Open standards
- Assist in rapid network growth

Slide 3

Key Function

Improve the speed of applications and enhance Web site capabilities

Slide 4

Importance

- Have different types of computers for potential merger (portability)
- Enhanced Web presence
- Portability a key network design concept for the next century

Slide 5

Potential Revenues

- Potential labor-hours saved
- Enhanced Web site
- More dynamic network architecture design

Slide 6

Components

- CORBA Web Server
- Tools
- Security software

Slide 7

Participating Groups

- IS development group
- Potential—all groups using the present Web site

Slide 8

Budget Allocations

Special seed development money required

Slide 9

Potential Budget Allocations

- Web site users

Slide 10

Advantages

- Quicker distribution of applications
- Enhanced changes in the informational distribution processes
- Improved Web site capabilities

Slide 11

Special Requirements

- Server
- Tools
- Security software
- Vendor support

Slide 12

Impacts

- Enhanced Web site
- Enhanced application distribution
- Better network control of potential merger computers

Slide 13

Conclusion

Prepare the corporation to compete more effectively and efficiently with new network technologies in the next century.

[E] Major Project Management Areas

This section is a minimum set of major project management areas you need to consider in managing and controlling this project. These areas are discussed in detail in Section One, Chapters 1–10. Why is the word *areas* used rather than *activities?* For example, the quality control area includes these five activities:

1. Writing Quality Control and Assurance Plan
2. Identifying personnel
3. Establishing cost and time estimates
4. Gathering benchmarks and standards
5. Developing quality control milestones

The essential project management areas (feel free to add to the list) are:

- Preproposal survey is developed.
- Kickoff meeting is held.
- Measurable project objectives are defined.
- Activities are planned and sequenced with associated cost, time, and resource estimates.
- Resources are determined as to when, who is going to use, length of use, and costs (capital costs).
- Time estimates are established for activities (labor-hours), which includes duration (activity from beginning to end in calendar time).
- Schedule is developed that includes associated people and resources using techniques such as Gantt charts and PERT network activity diagrams.
- Cost estimates are developed that are related to activities, resources, and budget lines.
- Project budget is created based on corporate accounting requirements. But, if possible, there should be a separate project budget rather than the project expenditures and revenues being merged into one or more budgets.
- Quality control and assurance system is developed.
- Initial risk analysis is done (beyond the one done in preproposal).
- Project management documentation process is defined.
- Communication program is defined.

Notice there is no comment on the technical areas. These areas are the responsibilities of the operational managers. Remember, the basic responsibilities of the project manager are to manage and control the project administrative activities, not manage and control the day-to-day technical activities.

[F] Activity Planning Brainstorming

This section gives examples of ideas that might be put forth during the initial meeting on developing the activity plan. The ideas are given as a brainstorming session based on the information given earlier. You still have to establish sequence, time, cost, and resource estimates with each activity, as discussed in Chapter 3. The list below is not complete, but a major start:

1. Survey existing conditions.
2. Establish measurable requirements.
3. Determine the implementation activation policy:

- Shared server
- Unshared server
- Persistent server
- Server per method

4. Generate and link the server skeletons.

5. Write the server application code:
   - Server application initialization
   - Service request handler
   - Server application shut down

6. Build the client side.

7. Implement the server.

8. Get identified skills:
   - CORBA
   - Java
   - Server
   - Security

9. Get standards and benchmarks.

10. Determine service interfaces.

11. Get presentations from server vendor representatives.

12. Devleop a quality control system.

13. Do activity sequencing.

14. Estimate resources (cost, where, when, availability).

15. Estimate time, including duration.

16. Estimate costs (budgeted or not budgeted).

17. Perform risk analysis.

18. Make up a schedule.

19. Do a budget.

20. Develop a communication plan.

21. Develop an incentive plan.

22. Perform training.

23. Determine maintenance requirements.

24. Get documentation.

[G]   Resource Planning Brainstorming

This section gives examples of ideas that might be put forth during the initial meeting on developing the activity plan. The ideas are presented as a brainstorming session based on the information given earlier. You still have to establish activity relationships, when required and for how long, and cost and resource estimates with each activity as discussed in Chapter 4. You also need to identify skill levels for people and benchmarks for hardware. The list below is not complete, but a major start:

- CORBA skill
- CORBA IDL skill
- Java expert skill (team leader)
- A consultant from CORBA server vendor
- Java intermediate skill (four or more)
- Time estimates and duration for use of skills
- Determination as to when hardware is required
- Maintenance skill
- Available IS resources (skills, hardware, and software)
- Support people requirements
- Chart on how resources are linked to goals and activities
- Impact statement (resource unavailable)
- Procurement requirements
- Capital requirements
- Training requirements
- Documentation requirements

[H]   Analysis of the Scenario

In this scenario it appears that the IS manager is selling an idea rather than a project. It is an idea rather than a solution to a measurable issue. In the other three scenarios, there were measurable issues: a book to be written, an improvement to do multimedia distribution, and a firewall to protect databases that possibly were under attack by hackers or disgruntled employees. This type of scenario might happen when an IS manager views what is actually a global change in the network and only sees it as a local change.

Before this scenario can be a project, two things have to happen: First, clear measurable definitions of the functionality and technical capabilities of the server need to be established. Second, the network impacts of the server on the network's infrastructure need to be defined. The first requires further research with various vendors. The second requires a scalability, interoperability, and portability analysis against the selected server functionality and capabilities, as discussed in Chapter 18. From this analysis, using the 60 questions or points, one can develop a new scenario, a fundamental change to the network's architecture rather than a simple addition of a network component or object.

On the CD-ROM

On the CD-ROM are:

1. Chapter 26 Overview.ppt—Chapter Overview, Project Management and the CORBA Paradigm

2. Chapter 26 CORBA Web Server Project Proposal.ppt—Example Proposal Presentation to Strategic Manager

Glossary

Accountability is the act of accepting the responsibility of the results of an act whether it is success or failure. The usual form is "I accept responsibility for the failure," or "The team accepts responsibility for the success."

An **action plan** is the description of what is required to be completed and when it is to be completed.

An **activity** is the effort required to achieve a measurable result that uses time and resources.

Activity codes are used to identify each unique activity category in a project. Activities can then be assigned activity codes for grouping purposes.

An **activity id** is a unique identifier for each activity.

An **activity plan** is a set of definitions. A definition includes the activity's constraints from the scope plan.

Activity planning is documenting a plan that establishes constraints and assumptions for any action taken during the project process.

Activity sequencing is the determination of a logical order of activities that are used in developing a realistic and achievable schedule.

Activity-on-Arrow (AOA) represents in a network diagram a sequence where the arrow is the symbol for the activity, while a circle symbolizes the event.

Activity-on-Node (AON) represents in a network diagram a sequence where the arrow is the symbol for work precedence, while a circle or box symbolizes the activity.

The **actual dates** for an activity are the dates recorded for when an activity actually started and finished.

AMA stands for the American Management Association, a professional organization that does important studies on the state of project management in the United States.

An **architectural model** is descriptive, an inventory of reality. A common IS architectural model is a cabling blueprint.

An **assumption** is a prediction that something will be true, either an action or an event that ensures project success such as "there will be identified potential risks, but somehow they will be overcome."

An **audit** is a formal study of the project as a whole, or a project's component, as to status (progress and results), costs, and procedures.

Authority is the investment to manage and control a series of activities such as a project. For example, the critical statement the strategic manager has to make is "the project manager has the authority to make all decisions required to achieve a successful project."

A **barchart** is a graphical representation of a schedule of activites using bars.

A **baseline plan** is the initial approved point from which any deviations will be determined using standards and benchmarks.

A **benchmark** is a specific technical level of excellence.

A **budget** is a plan in which costs are organized into debits and credits (expenses and revenues). It is a formal plan that uses a chart of accounts to give structure to estimates for expenses and revenues.

Budgeting is taking cost estimates and entering them into a formal financial structure.

A **burst point** is a point in a PERT network diagram where an activity interrelates with two or more other activities. See also *sink point*.

The **Business Affiliate Plan** provides information when the project or a part of the project is to be the responsibility of a third-party developer.

The **Business Justification** is the general rationale for making the financial investment.

The **Business Justification Update** document assures the current view of the implementation of any project goals that have performance criteria meet previous commitments and management expectations.

A **checklist** is an organized list, possibly a standard of action that usually has to be followed in sequence to accomplish a specified goal. However, a checklist can be as simple as a set of options for answering the question, "Have I considered the following items for this activity?"

The **Commercial Specification** is an evolution of the Business Justification. It identifies the market need and gives adequate requirement and limitation data for the design and development group(s).

Communication is an oral or written transfer of date or information among individuals.

Communications is the process of getting the correct data to the correct person at the correct time in a cost-effective mode.

A **confidence level** is the acceptance level of risk usually determined statistically by a percentage of time or cost.

A **conflict** is an out-of-balance among available skills, priorities, or resources.

A **constraint** is a parameter, limitation, or a boundary for the project plan such as the budget or the schedule.

A **consultant** is a person not from the normal resource pool with experience on solving a specific project issue. The consultant usually works from a biased position.

The **Content Agreement** is the written "contract" between the development group and the marketing group as to the content and functions of the project.

Contingency is the rational preparation for change.

A **contingency plan** is the preparation for a pessimistic scenario to become reality.

Control is the monitoring of progress and the checking for variances in the plan.

Corporate values are a common set of beliefs held by the corporate stakeholders about their business environment.

A **cost-benefit analysis** is the development of a ratio to determine if a project is financially viable.

Cost codes are used to identify and assign costs to activities.

Cost estimating is the process of establishing or defining the amount to be budgeted for an activity based on constraints and assumptions from the project goals for the duration of the activity, the average skills required to complete the activity, and the resources required to complete the activity.

A **critical activity** is one which, if not completed, results in project failure.

Criticality is a position on the team where the individual in this situation has specific skills, usually technical, that if not available to the project, puts the entire project at risk.

A **critical path** is when there is no available time for the slippage of the activity (no slack time).

The **Critical Path Method (CPM)**, in its simplest form, is selecting the "must" activities or tasks and doing them in the shortest possible amount of time and within the shortest duration. It is a network diagramming technique. CPM can be used to estimate the project's earliest completion by establishing time estimates for the longest series of activities.

A **cross-functional team** is the most common type of team for a corporate IS project and includes many technical and support groups with a multiple set of skills, ideas, goals, attitudes, and so forth.

The **Customer Documentation Strategy** provides how timely, high-quality project documentation becomes available. There really is a triad in quality: control, documentation, and training.

The **data date** is used as a starting point for calculating the schedule. When the schedule is updated, this value is changed to the current date.

A **deliverable** is a clearly defined project result, product, or service. It is an outcome.

Dependency means that a task has to be completed before a succeeding task can be completed. For example, coding has to be completed before code testing can be completed.

The **Design and Development Plan** drives the project Integration Plan that captures all major design and development deliverables and milestones for management tracking and reporting.

The **discrete model** uses mathematical distributions (raw or massaged) in a systematic series of equations.

Duration is the total time involved of an activity including production time and wait time.

A **dynamic model** permits you to do "real-time" scenarios that can be used to manage a project.

Effectiveness is the attained measure of quality to complete the activity or event.

Efficiency is the measurement of output based on amount of input.

Emulation is a process to imitate the physical components and the infra-structure.

The **end–end dependency** means that an activity cannot end until another activity has also ended.

The **end–start dependency** means that an activity must end before another can start.

An **estimate** is a guess based on opinion or a forecast based on experience. Cost, time, and resource estimates are the foundations for project planning.

An **event** is a point in time such as the start or end of an activity.

Expectation is a stated project goal that can become a perceived undocumented result.

Extrapolation modeling is the theoretical process of extending historical data.

Feedback is an activity that should be held on a regular basis; it is where the status of the project being evaluated can be clearly stated based on measurable standards or benchmarks.

The **Field Introduction Requirements** document reflects the strategy and detailed plans to verify conformance to specification and functionality as defined in the Project Specification.

Float. See *slack time*.

A **Gantt chart** is a visual presentation, a horizontal bar chart, of activities against time. It is named after its developer, Henry Laurence Gantt.

A **gate** is another term for milestone or a major project event.

Headcount is a factor used by business managers in planning an annual budget, but it should not be used by project managers.

A **histogram** is the opposite of a Gantt chart because vertical bars are used to represent values.

Goal characteristics have to be measurable, specific, and potentially possible.

An **iconic model** is equivalent to a software demonstration, a scaled-down version of the project's results.

Information system project management is a documented parallel process within a set schedule, within a defined budget, with available resources and skills to achieve defined user expectations for a networking environment that has as its primary function the requirement to transmit data among human users.

The **Initial Budget Estimates** provides a view of the expected development costs. The estimate is usually based on the Preliminary Project Specification. This document is updated in the Project Cost Update.

The **Initial Funding Requirements** document is for monitoring and reporting project costs at each major phase of implementation. There should be comparisons to the original funding document used to establish financial targets and expected milestones and deliverables. This document can also be included in the Project Cost Update.

The **International Organization for Standardization (ISO)** is a consortium that tries to set standards in a variety of areas.

Interoperability is to what degree the various network components work with one another successfully.

ISO 9000 is a quality system standard for any product, service, or process.

ISO 9001 is a quality system standard for design, production, and installation of a product or service.

ISO 9002 is a quality system model for quality assurance in production and installation.

ISO 9003 is a quality system model for quality assurance in final inspection and testing.

ISO 9004 is a set of quality management guidelines for any organization to use to develop and implement a quality system.

Lag time is the time between two activities because of the nature of the activities.

Lead time is the overlapping time of two activities.

A **learning curve** is a graphical representation of repetitive tasks that, when done on a continuous basis, lead to a reduction in activity duration, resources, and costs.

Leveling is the technique to smooth out peaks and valleys for the use of resources.

Logistics is the process of getting the correct resource to the correct location at the correct time.

Management is the process of working with people, resources, equipment, and materials to achieve organizational goals.

A **management review** is a regularly scheduled performance review.

Management team is a supervisory team that coordinates broad issues that affect the corporation.

The **Market Analysis Report** documents and verifies market opportunities and justifies the features, services, and applications for the project goals.

A **milestone** is a clearly defined date of start or of 100 percent completion.

A **model** is a theoretical environment with as much data as possible to reflect reality adequately for decision making.

Negotiation is the art of compromise where both parties can walk away from the table feeling they each won.

A **network diagram** as exemplified by PERT or CPM is a series of tasks in linked sequences. The project network diagram is one sequence.

A **node** is a network event that is achieved or is not achieved. A milestone is a node type.

An **objective** is a set of measurable goals to achieve a defined target that, if not achieved, has critical results.

An **open end** activity has no predecessor, successor or both. Only the project start and completion activities should be open ended.

An **operational manager** is a person who handles the day-to-day operations or activities for a specific functional group or area that has been defined in the project plan.

An **opportunity** is a situation that will positively affect the project in time, money, resources or all three in a significant manner.

An **optimistic estimate** is an assumption that holds everything will go as planned.

An **organizational chart** is normally a visual representation of who reports to whom and shows hierarchical and perhaps functional relationships among organization groups. The Project Organizational Chart needs to include the core project responsibilities of each team member.

Organizational culture is a common set of assumptions, principles, processes, and structures held or used by members of a corporation, company, or even a project team.

Padding is an informal action (adding time or cost to an estimate) that should not take place. It should be formalized as a contingency plan.

A **path** is a sequence of lines within a network diagram with the most important being the one labeled critical.

A **predecessor** activity must occur before another activity.

Performance is the act or level of work demonstrated and judged based on identified skill level.

A **pessimistic estimate** is an assumption that if something can go wrong, it will.

A **phase** is a project segment such as planning, designing, and developing.

PMI stands for the **Project Management Institute,** a professional organization that studies and promotes project management.

A **political situation** is when at least two people get together to resolve an issue. This means you cannot forget that politics is the foundation for any project interactions.

Portability is a characteristic of software. It is the degree to which the software can be transferred from one environment to another.

A **precedence diagram** is another name for an activity-on-node diagram.

A **program** is a type of recurring project such as the annual budget, not to be confused with a set of programming code or a book you get at a sports event.

Program Evaluation and Review Technique (PERT) was developed for the United States Department of Defense in the late 1950s. Specifically it was developed by the consulting firm of Booz, Allen, and Hamilton for the U.S. Navy's Polaris submarine project, Polaris Weapon System. It combines statistics and network diagrams.

A **project** is an organized set of activities to reach a measurable outcome within a specified duration.

A **project budget** is the duration (work-time plus the wait-time) of the project cycle.

The **Project Cost Updates** document updates initial project cost estimates at each major phase of implementation with comparison to the Initial Budget Estimate.

A **project's duration** is the total number of calendar days involved from start to end, including the project manager's activities in closing the project.

Project management has many aliases, including program management, product management, and construction management. In all cases, it is the managing, controlling, and integrating of activities, resources, time, and costs to achieve a defined measurable outcome within a specified duration.

The **project manager** is the person with overall responsibility for managing and controlling the project activities (defined and undefined) to achieve a measurable outcome within a specified duration and budget.

The **Project Proposal** is a formal response to the Commercial Specification that describes the requirements for a project.

A **project schedule** is a formal response to the Commercial Specification that specifies the requirements for a project.

The **Project Specification** is a formal response to the Commercial Specification that specifies the requirements for a project.

The **Project Support Plan** ensures that the project is supportable in a market environment. This plan should include a process for customer support.

A **project team** is an organization that is put together to achieve a specific set of measurable goals within a specific time and with limited resources, equipment, and materials.

Quality assurance is based on performance. It is the establishing of performance standards, then measuring and evaluating project performance against these standards.

A **quality audit** is an independent evaluation or test of some component of the project by qualified personnel.

Quality control acts to meet the standards through the gathering of performance information, inspecting, monitoring, and testing.

Quality management uses control and assurance to prevent risks and, if a risk occurs, to minimize it.

The **Quality Plan** defines the role of quality control and assurance in all phases of the project process.

A **realistic estimate** is an assumption there will probably be a few difficulties, but with compromise, the difficulties will be overcome.

A **resource** is anything that supports the project. This includes in general terms money, skills, materials, time, facilities, and equipment.

Resource planning is establishing support requirements for a project as to costs, availability, start date and end date (length of time for use plus duration), and technical specifications.

Responsibility is the obligation or accountability given through assignment to complete a specific activity or event.

A **risk** is not a problem; its effect can have an adverse or disastrous consequence on the project's outcome. It is a performance error.

Risk analysis is a technique, tool, or method for assessing, either quantitatively or qualitatively, or both, the impacts of an identified risk or a potential risk identified through a scenario.

Risk management is resolving or managing both negative and positive opportunities.

Role is a skill set with a label that perhaps explains the reasons for the actions and behavior of the actor.

Scalability is to what degree a network can be enhanced without a major change in design.

A **scenario** is a set of possibilities that could happen to cause a risk.

The **schedule** is the duration of the project, including production time and wait time. It is also a production plan for the allocation of activities with deadlines.

Scheduling is the activity that formalizes the time estimates within a calendar structure. It is an integration of sequencing activities, resource planning, cost estimating, and time estimating.

Scope is the amount of work and resources (skills, materials, and requirement) required for project completion.

Scope defining is extending the measurable goals to become general procedures with measurable constraints and viable assumptions.

The **scope plan** is the strategic view of the constraints and assumptions of the project as developed by the project team.

Scope planning is defining the goals and performance expectations of your project goals in measurable terms and getting an agreement on them.

Simulation may be a process to imitate the physical components of your informational system. Simulation has a counterpart: emulation.

A **sink point** is a point in a PERT network diagram where two or more other activities interrelate with a single activity. See also *burst point*.

Skill level is a factor used by a project manager in planning a project's budget rather than using headcount.

Slack time is the difference between earliest and latest (start or finish) times for an activity or event.

Slippage (budget) is when a budget item is overspent.

Slippage (time) is expected when you know about a schedule problem before the due date; it is unexpected when you learn about the fact after the due date.

Specific goals are project goals that are measurable, unambiguous, and match exactly the customer's stated expectations.

The **sponsor** is the one who provides the resources and the working environment to make possible the achievement of project goals.

A **stakeholder** is any person or organization interested in the project. This includes the customer, your boss, you, the workers, and interested government regulators.

A **standard** is usually external and an industry-accepted document for achieving quality for one or more of the project-defined expected goals.

The **start–end dependency** means that an activity must begin before another activity can end.

The **start–start dependency** means that one activity must start before another.

The **state-change model** is concerned with conditions and events that can change the state of your enterprise network.

A **Statement of Work (SOW)** is an integrated set of descriptions as to project activities, goals, risks, and resources to complete a measurable outcome.

A **strategic manager** should be thought of as a Greek general, not a twentieth-century general who is more a bureaucrat than a player. This manager heads an area of a corporation that includes the IS project as a part of that person's performance goals.

A **successor** activity follows another activity.

A **symbolic model** is a representation of the product's properties and relationships.

A **system** is an interactive set of tasks or groups that forms a whole with dynamics that impact all the components.

System engineering is the attempt to integrate and to synthesize entire systems to act as one entity.

The **tactical manager** is the one responsible for the overall flow of the project process so that the strategic goals are met.

A **task** is a cohesive work unit that is meaningful for tracking. Writing a line of code is not a task, but writing a module that handles a specific function is a task.

A **team** is a group with a common purpose and with skills that complement one another.

The **Third-Party Market Agreement** provides the plans where the project or a part of the project is to be the responsibility of a third-party developer.

The **Third-Party Service Plan** provides how the project is to be serviced by a third-party developer.

Time estimating is concerned with the duration of an individual activity or groups of related activities.

A **trade-off** is an act of balancing project constraints.

The **Training Strategy** shows how training is to be designed, developed, implemented, and verified.

The **Trial (Beta) Strategy** identifies the software and hardware elements in the project that are a part of any trial. Also, the where, when, and by whom should be included in the strategy. This provides a clear identification of the testing requirements plus the extent of the resources and capabilities to test.

Variance is any deviation from the planned work, whether it is costs, time, or resources.

A **work breakdown structure (WBS)** uses numerical coding to provide a hierarchy of project components.

Index

References are to sections.